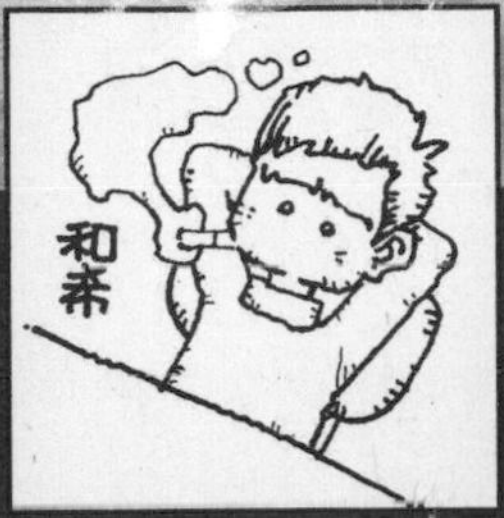
和希

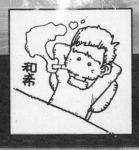

KAZUKI TAKAHASHI

Mr. Yoshida, the *ZEXAL* writer, has helped out on every *Yu-Gi-Oh!* anime series. He's more important to the current *Yu-Gi-Oh!* world than I am, and I created the original!

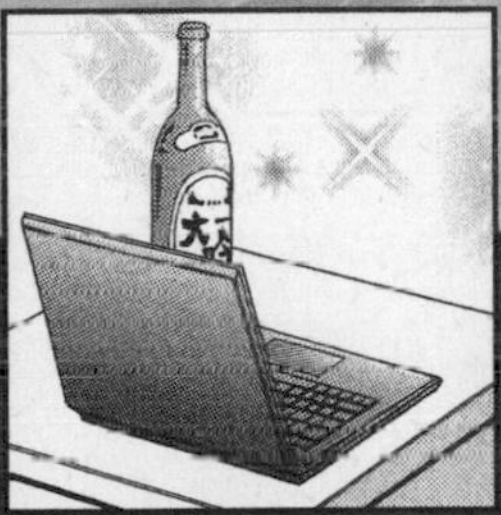

SHIN YOSHIDA

In this volume, you'll finally get to see Yuma take on the second and third assassins! Enjoy watching all these unique characters duel!

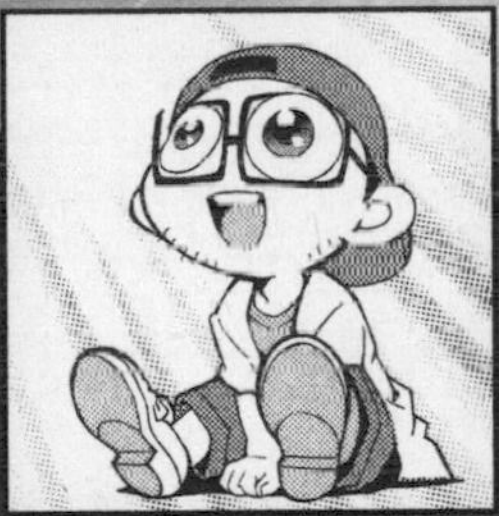

NAOHITO MIYOSHI

The manga's jetting into its own unique story! Things unfold a bit differently than they do in the anime, and at first working on this part made me nervous, but now I'm having fun again! Keep cheering us on!

Volume 3
SHONEN JUMP Manga Edition

Original Concept by **KAZUKI TAKAHASHI**
Production Support: STUDIO DICE
Story by **SHIN YOSHIDA**
Art by **NAOHITO MIYOSHI**

Translation & English Adaptation **TAYLOR ENGEL AND IAN REID, HC LANGUAGE SOLUTIONS**
Touch-up Art & Lettering **JOHN HUNT**
Designer **STACIE YAMAKI**
Editor **MIKE MONTESA**

YU-GI-OH! ZEXAL © 2010 by Kazuki Takahashi, Shin Yoshida, Naohito Miyoshi
All rights reserved.
First published in Japan in 2010 by SHUEISHA Inc., Tokyo.
English translation rights arranged by SHUEISHA Inc.

Based on Animation TV series YU-GI-OH! ZEXAL
© 1996 Kazuki Takahashi
© 2011 NAS · TV TOKYO

Printed in the U.S.A.

Published by VIZ Media, LLC
P.O. Box 77010
San Francisco, CA 94107

10 9 8 7 6 5 4 3 2 1
First printing, June 2013

www.viz.com

PARENTAL ADVISORY
YU-GI-OH! ZEXAL is rated T for Teen
and is recommended for ages 13 and up.
This volume contains fantasy violence.
ratings.viz.com

www.shonenjump.com

Yu-Gi-Oh! ZEXAL

VOLUME 3:
The Second Assassin!!

Original Concept by KAZUKI TAKAHASHI
Production Support: STUDIO DICE
Story by SHIN YOSHIDA
Art by NAOHITO MIYOSHI

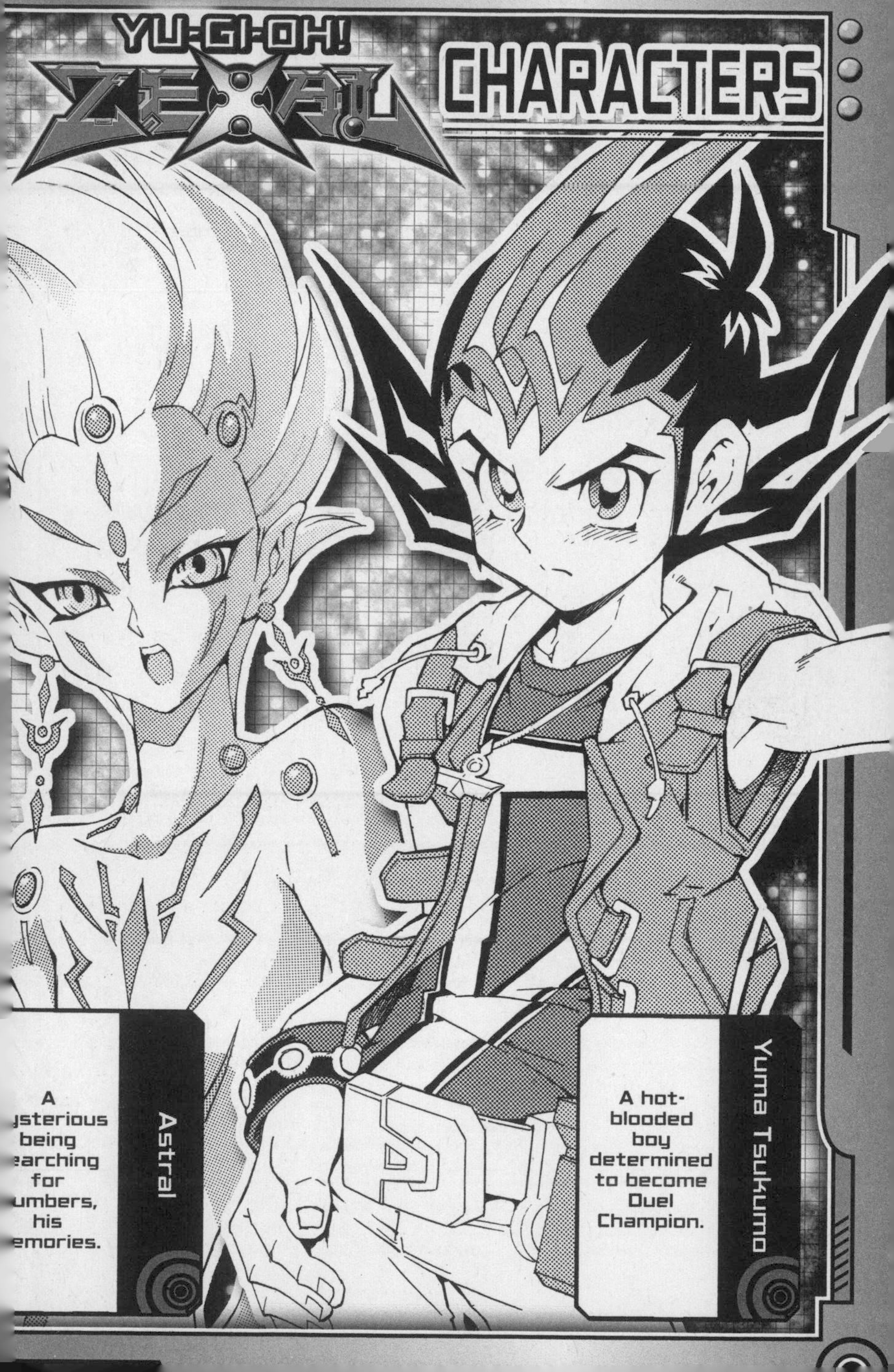
YU-GI-OH!
ZEXAL
CHARACTERS
Yuma Tsukumo
A hot-blooded boy determined to become Duel Champion.
Astral
A ysterious being earching for umbers, his emories.

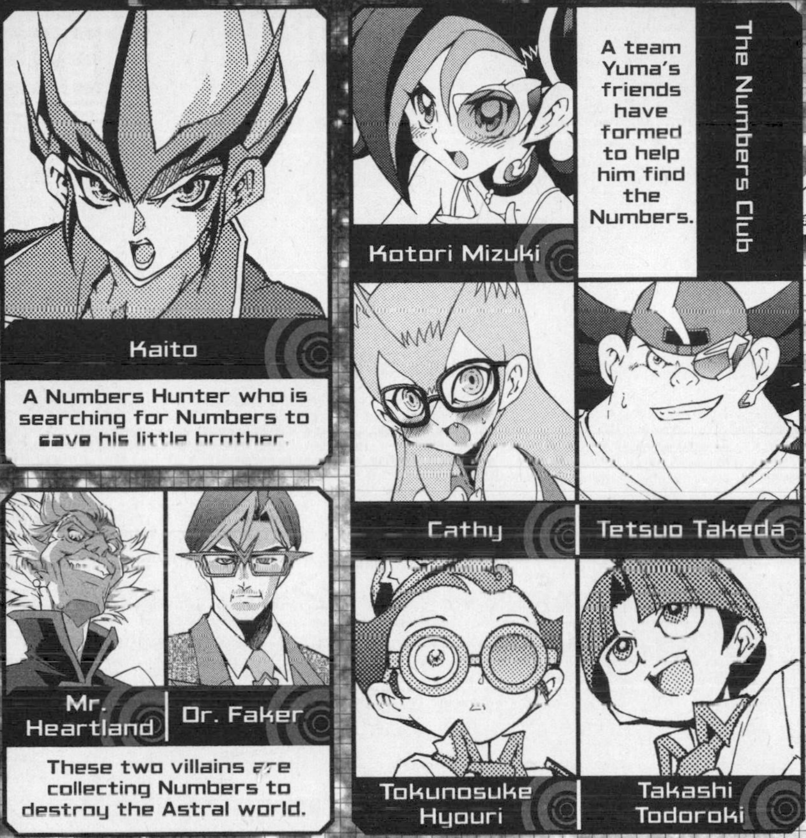

The Numbers Club
A team Yuma's friends have formed to help him find the Numbers.
Kotori Mizuki
Tetsuo Takeda
Cathy
Takashi Todoroki
Tokunosuke Hyouri
Kaito
A Numbers Hunter who is searching for Numbers to save his little brother.
Dr. Faker
Mr. Heartland
These two villains are collecting Numbers to destroy the Astral world.

Previously...

Yuma tackles every challenge that comes his way, and he doesn't give up. Although his skills are suspect, he's crazy about dueling!

One day, Yuma's rival Tetsuo has his deck stolen by Shark, the school's biggest delinquent and duelist, and Yuma ends up dueling Shark. During the duel, the charm Yuma's parents gave him opens a mysterious door, and a strange being called Astral appears!!

Astral is a genius duelist, but only Yuma can see him. Astral's lost memories have become special cards called "Numbers." That begins Yuma and Astral's strange career together.

Then a "Numbers Hunter" named Kaito appears to duel Yuma. Kaito is a tough duelist, and although the duel is canceled partway through, Yuma and Astral are losing badly...

In order to beat Kaito, Yuma and his friends decide to find all the Numbers cards. They infiltrate Heartland because they heard there were Numbers Hunters there, and manage to defeat the first assassin, Captain Corn. But then...

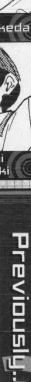

VOLUME 3
The Second Assassin!!

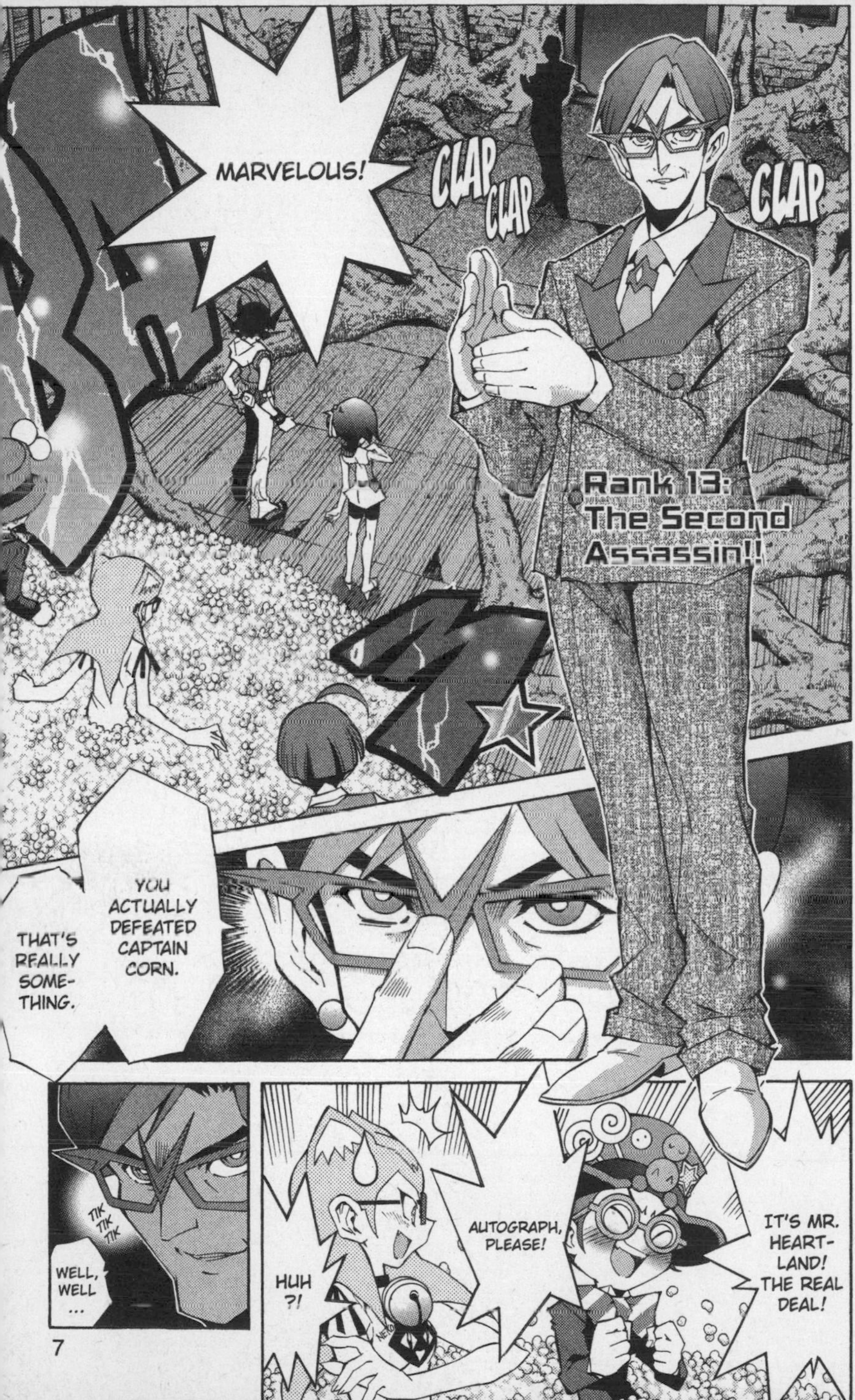
CLAP
CLAP
CLAP
MARVELOUS!
Rank 13: The Second Assassin!!
YOU ACTUALLY DEFEATED CAPTAIN CORN.
THAT'S REALLY SOME-THING.
IT'S MR. HEART-LAND! THE REAL DEAL!
AUTOGRAPH, PLEASE!
HUH ?!
TIK TIK TIK
WELL, WELL ...

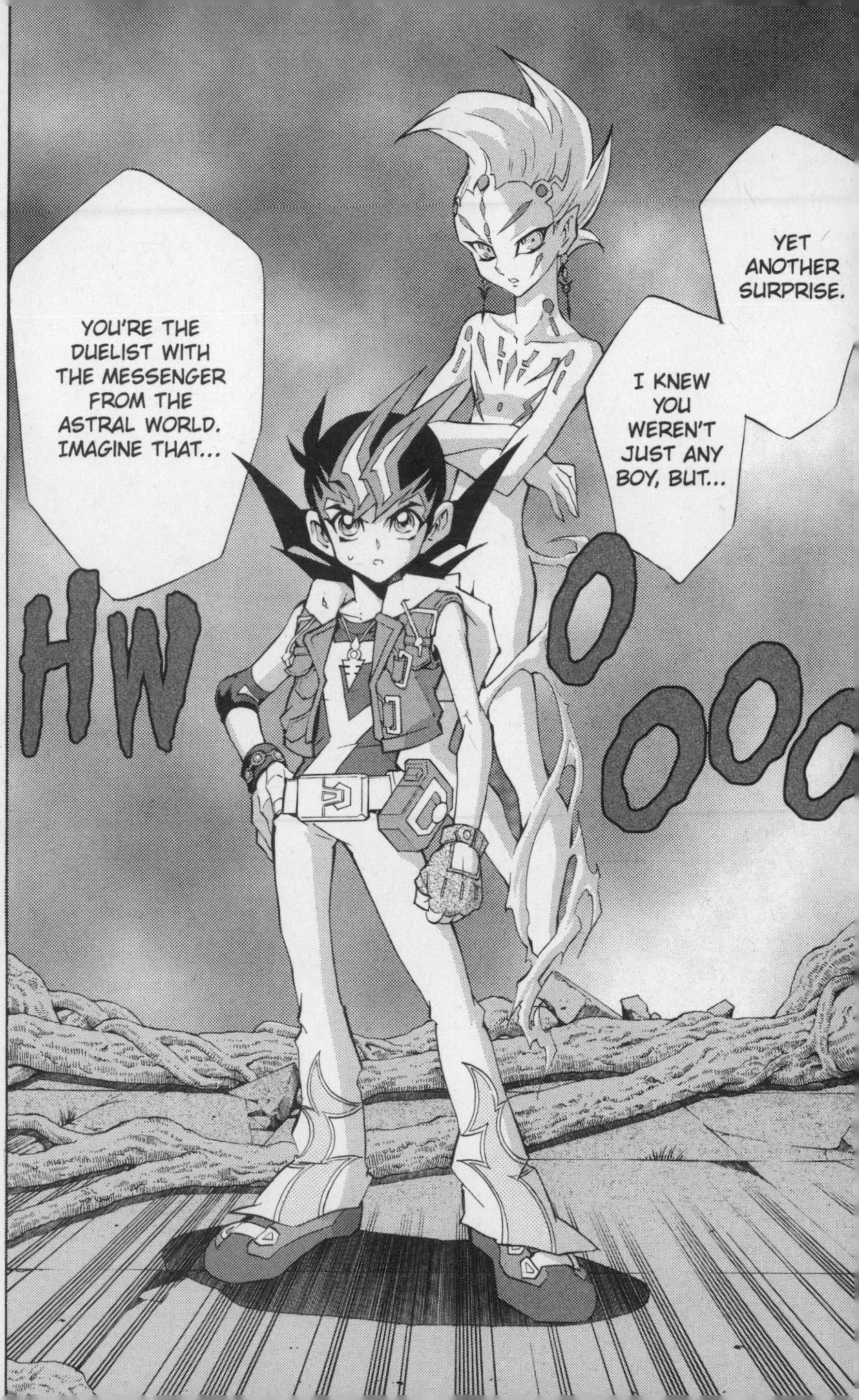
YET ANOTHER SURPRISE.
I KNEW YOU WEREN'T JUST ANY BOY, BUT...
YOU'RE THE DUELIST WITH THE MESSENGER FROM THE ASTRAL WORLD. IMAGINE THAT...
HWOOOO

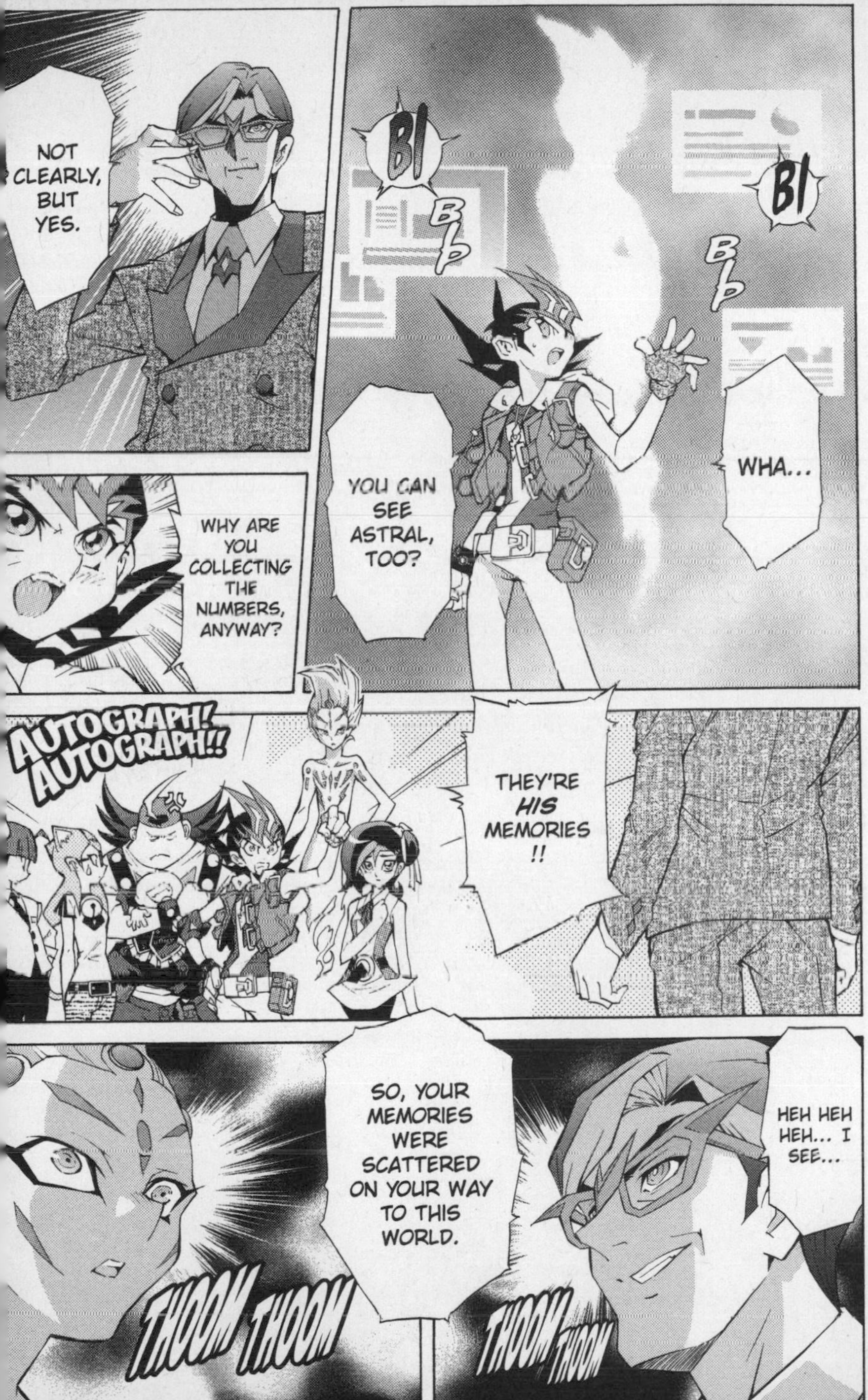
BI
Bb
BI
Bb
WHA...
YOU CAN SEE ASTRAL, TOO?
NOT CLEARLY, BUT YES.
WHY ARE YOU COLLECTING THE NUMBERS, ANYWAY?
THEY'RE *HIS* MEMORIES!!
AUTOGRAPH! AUTOGRAPH!!
HEH HEH HEH... I SEE...
SO, YOUR MEMORIES WERE SCATTERED ON YOUR WAY TO THIS WORLD.
THOOM THOOM
THOOM THOOM

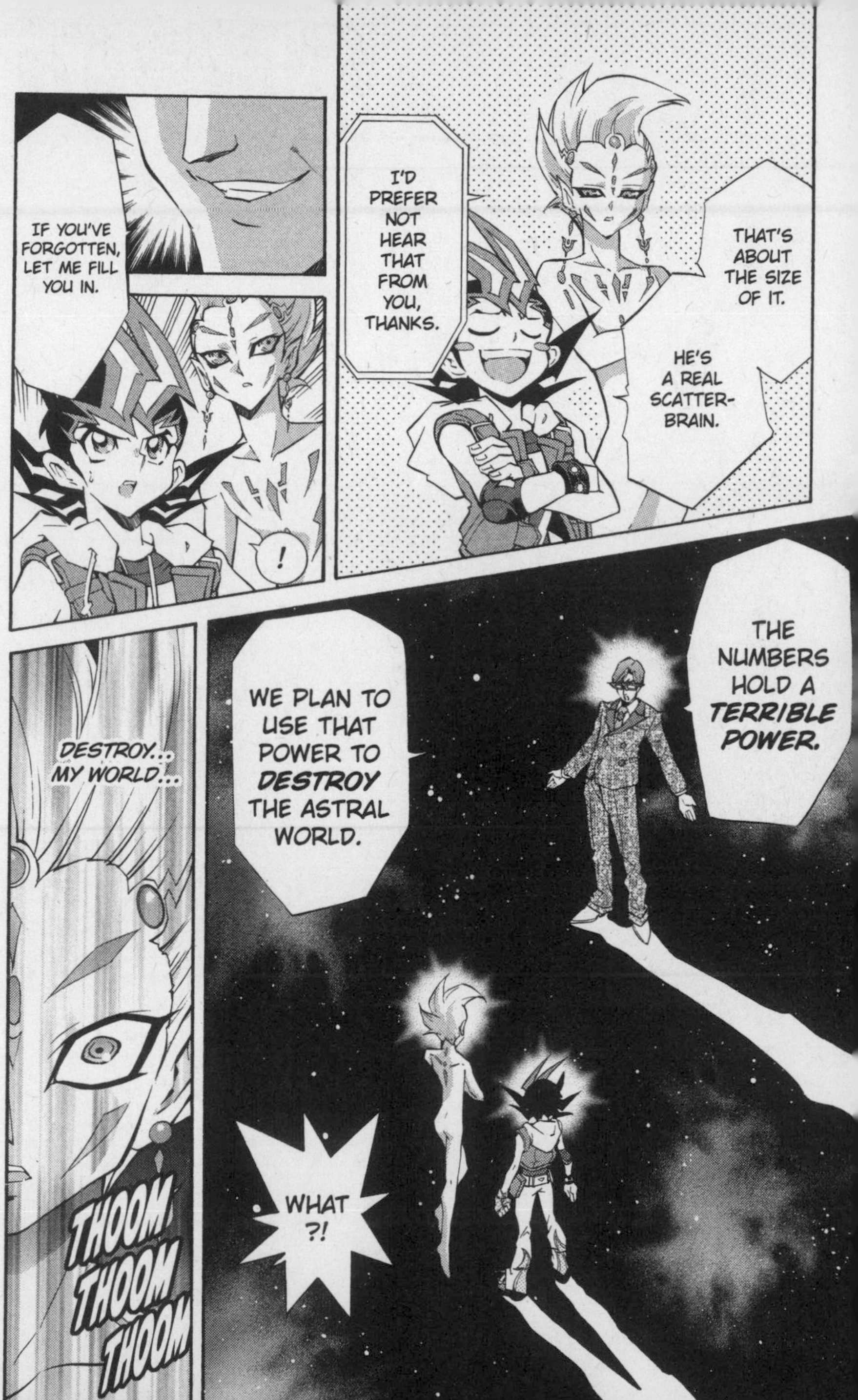
THAT'S ABOUT THE SIZE OF IT.
HE'S A REAL SCATTER-BRAIN.
I'D PREFER NOT HEAR THAT FROM YOU, THANKS.
IF YOU'VE FORGOTTEN, LET ME FILL YOU IN.
!
THE NUMBERS HOLD A TERRIBLE POWER.
WE PLAN TO USE THAT POWER TO DESTROY THE ASTRAL WORLD.
WHAT ?!
DESTROY... MY WORLD...
THOOM THOOM THOOM

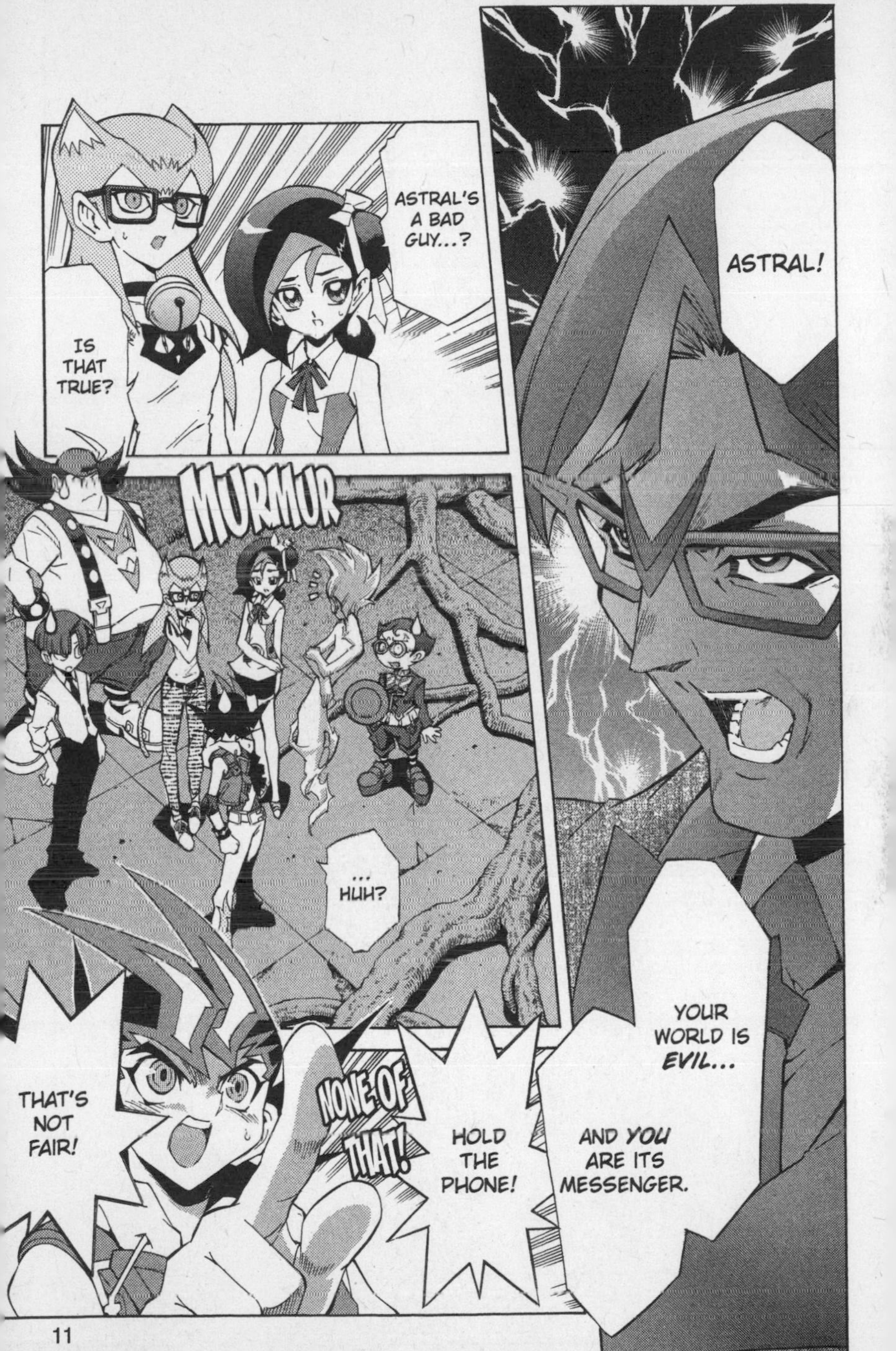
ASTRAL!
YOUR WORLD IS EVIL...
AND YOU ARE ITS MESSENGER.
ASTRAL'S A BAD GUY...?
IS THAT TRUE?
MURMUR
... HUH?
HOLD THE PHONE!
NONE OF THAT!
THAT'S NOT FAIR!

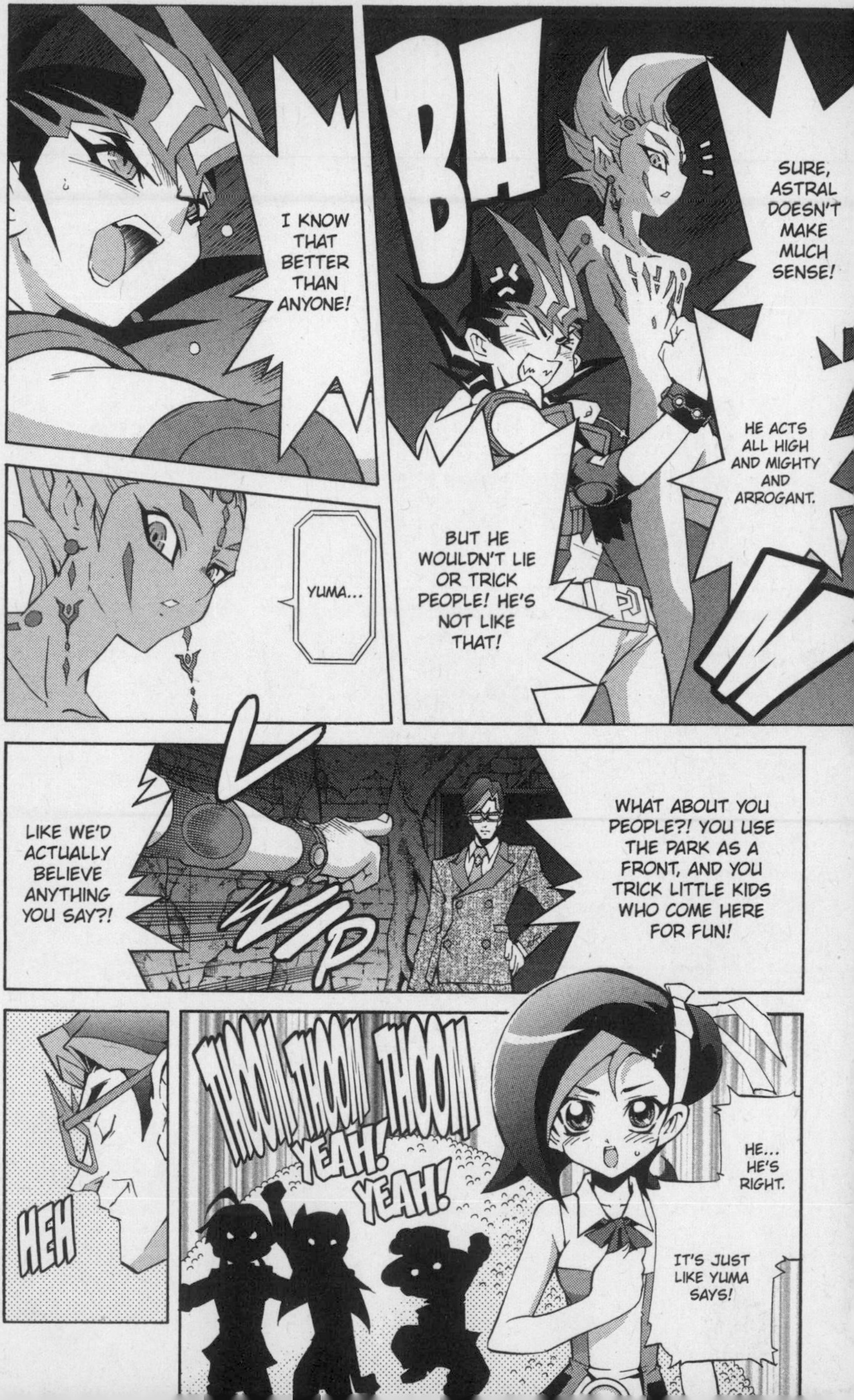
BA
M
SURE, ASTRAL DOESN'T MAKE MUCH SENSE!
HE ACTS ALL HIGH AND MIGHTY AND ARROGANT.
BUT HE WOULDN'T LIE OR TRICK PEOPLE! HE'S NOT LIKE THAT!
I KNOW THAT BETTER THAN ANYONE!
YUMA...
WHAT ABOUT YOU PEOPLE?! YOU USE THE PARK AS A FRONT, AND YOU TRICK LITTLE KIDS WHO COME HERE FOR FUN!
WIP
LIKE WE'D ACTUALLY BELIEVE ANYTHING YOU SAY?!
HE... HE'S RIGHT.
THOOM THOOM THOOM
YEAH! YEAH!
IT'S JUST LIKE YUMA SAYS!
HEH

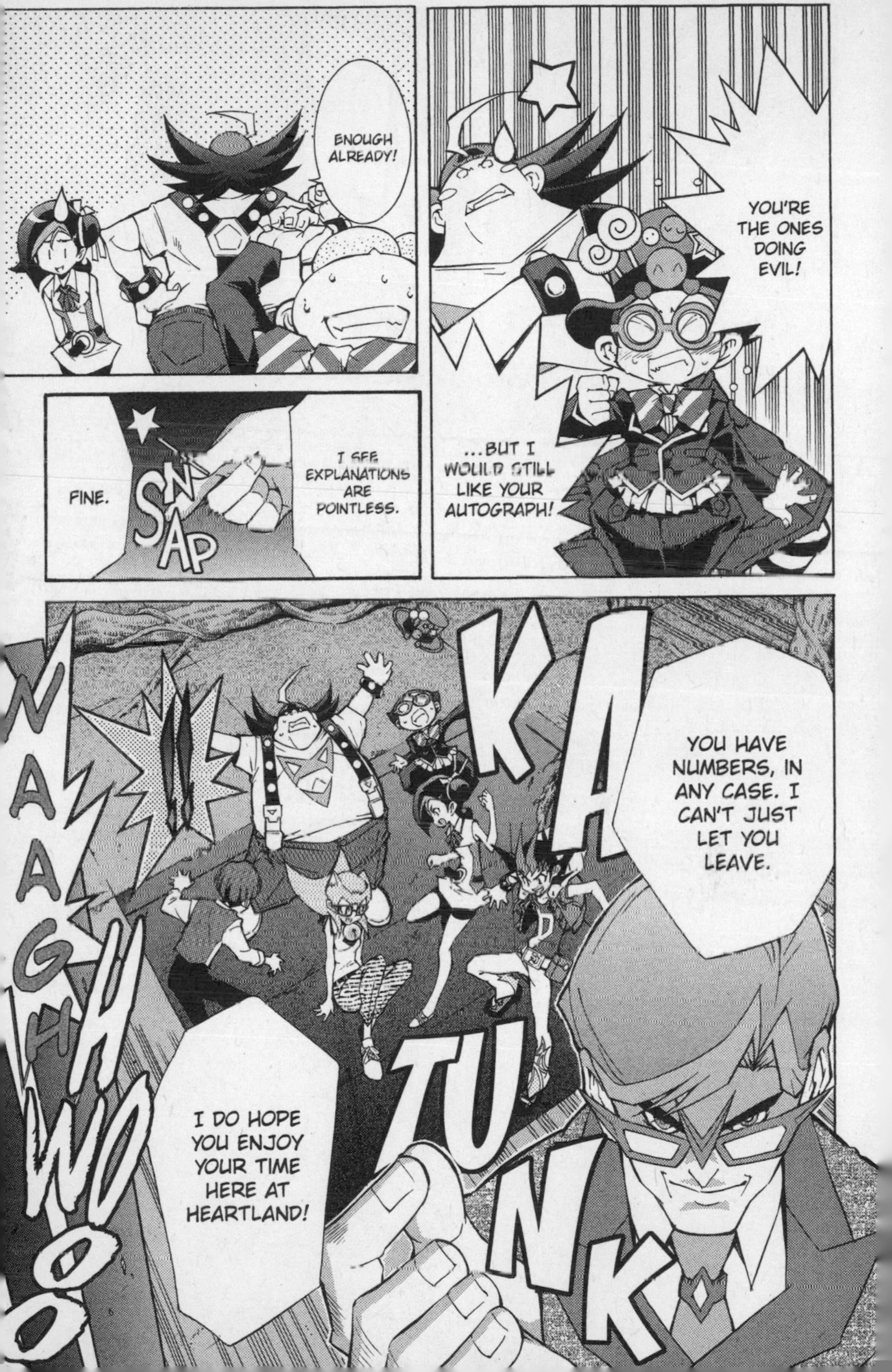
YOU'RE THE ONES DOING EVIL!
...BUT I WOULD STILL LIKE YOUR AUTOGRAPH!
ENOUGH ALREADY!
I SEE EXPLANATIONS ARE POINTLESS.
SNAP
FINE.
KA
YOU HAVE NUMBERS, IN ANY CASE. I CAN'T JUST LET YOU LEAVE.
TUNK
NAAGH
WHOOO
I DO HOPE YOU ENJOY YOUR TIME HERE AT HEARTLAND!

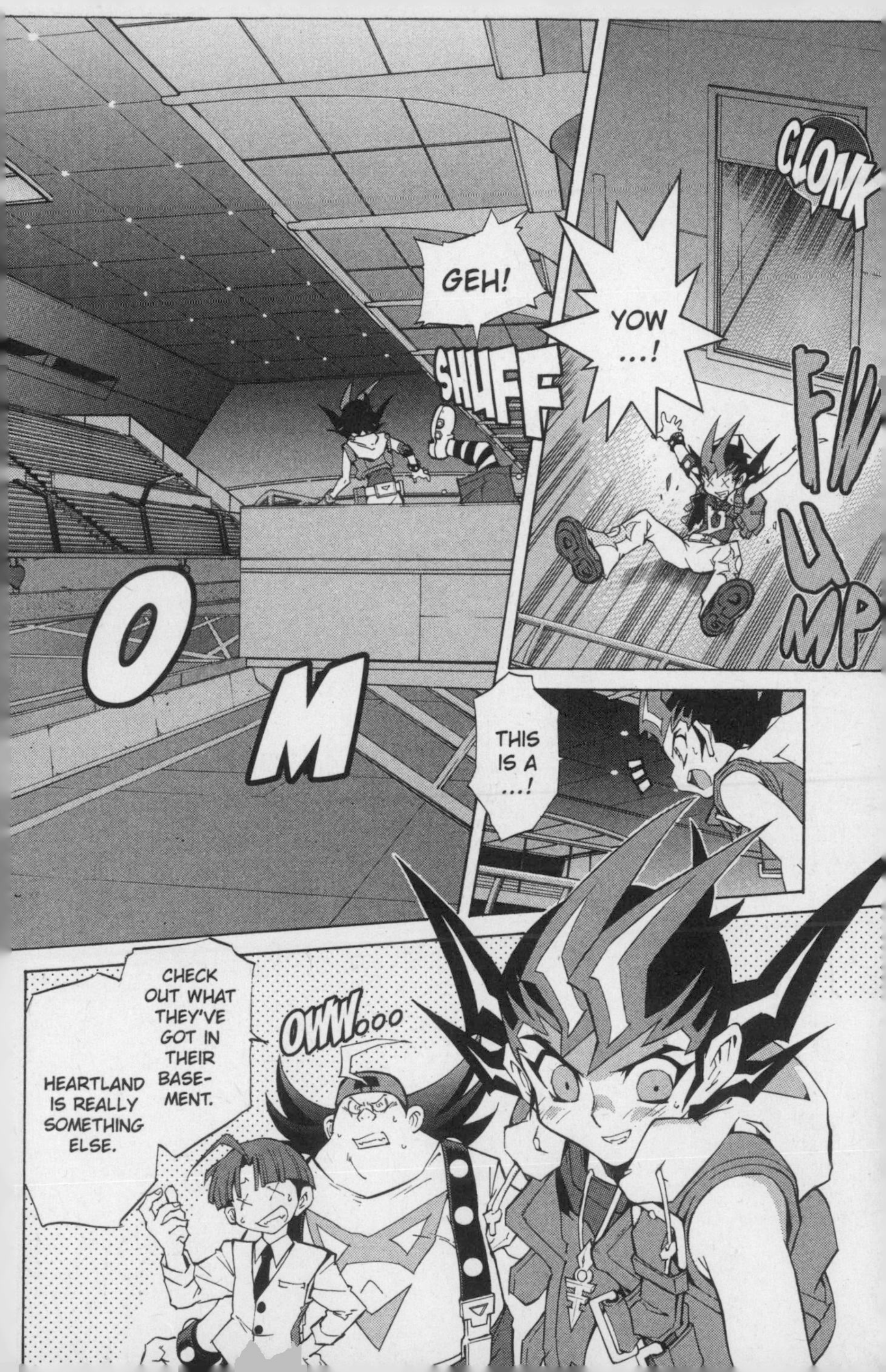
CLONK
YOW ...!
FWUMP
THIS IS A ...!
GEH!
SHUFF
O M
CHECK OUT WHAT THEY'VE GOT IN THEIR BASEMENT.
HEARTLAND IS REALLY SOMETHING ELSE.
OWWooo

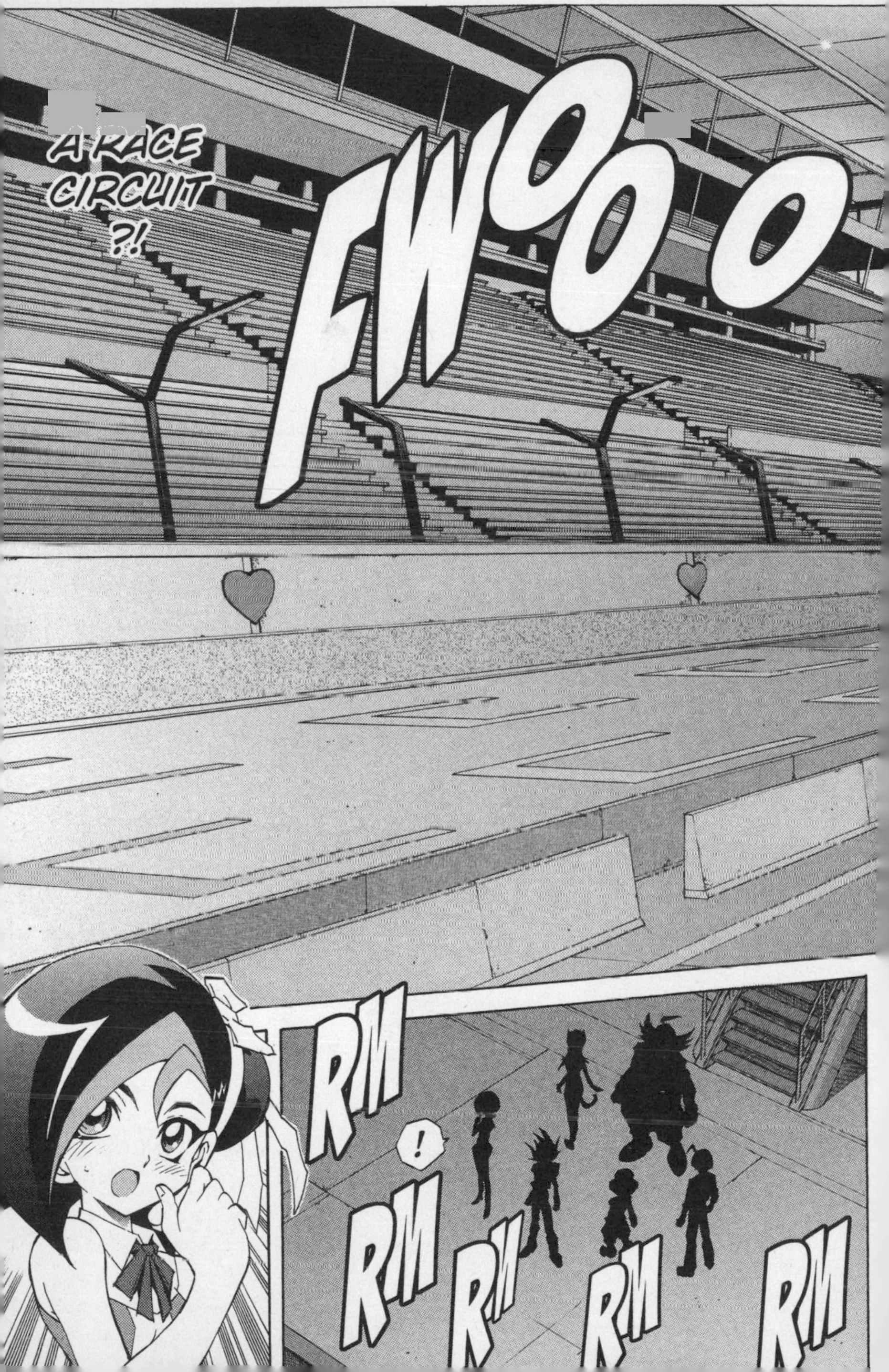
FWOOO
A RACE CIRCUIT ?!
RM
!
RM
RM
RM
RM
RM

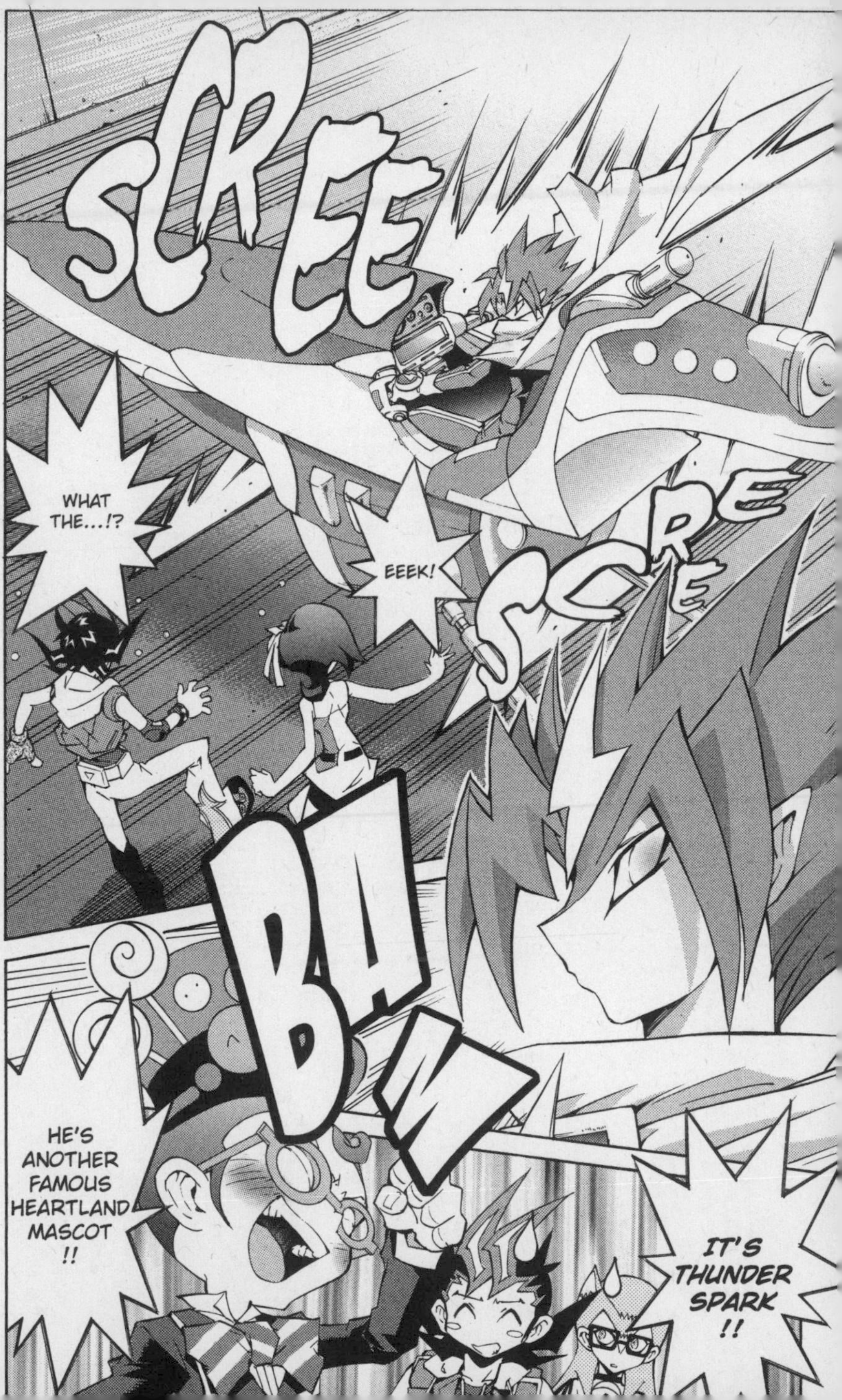
SCREE
SCREE
EEEK!
WHAT THE...!?
BAM
IT'S THUNDER SPARK!!
HE'S ANOTHER FAMOUS HEARTLAND MASCOT!!

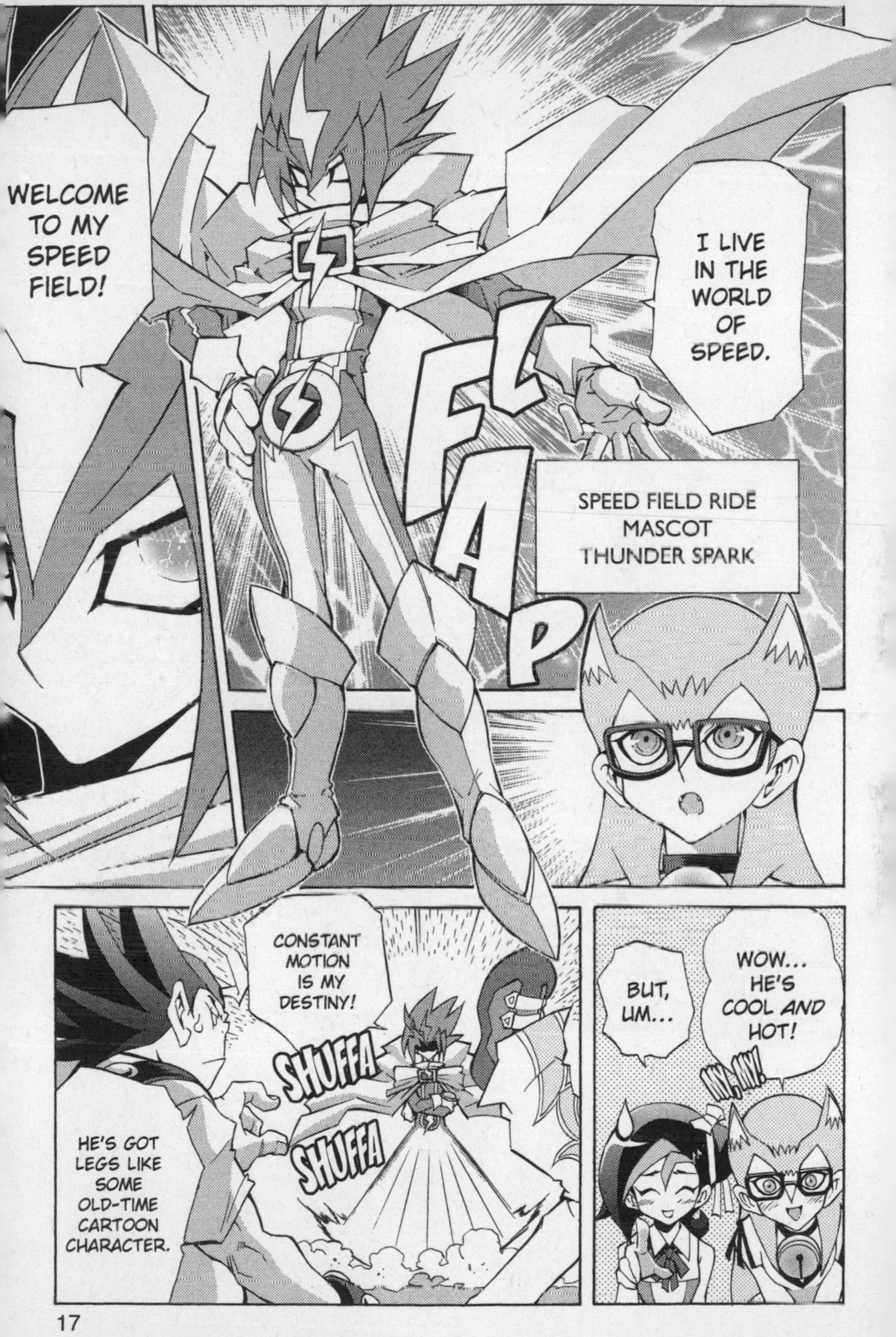
I LIVE IN THE WORLD OF SPEED.
WELCOME TO MY SPEED FIELD!
FLAP
SPEED FIELD RIDE MASCOT THUNDER SPARK
WOW... HE'S COOL AND HOT!
MY, MY!
BUT, UM...
CONSTANT MOTION IS MY DESTINY!
SHUFFA
SHUFFA
HE'S GOT LEGS LIKE SOME OLD-TIME CARTOON CHARACTER.

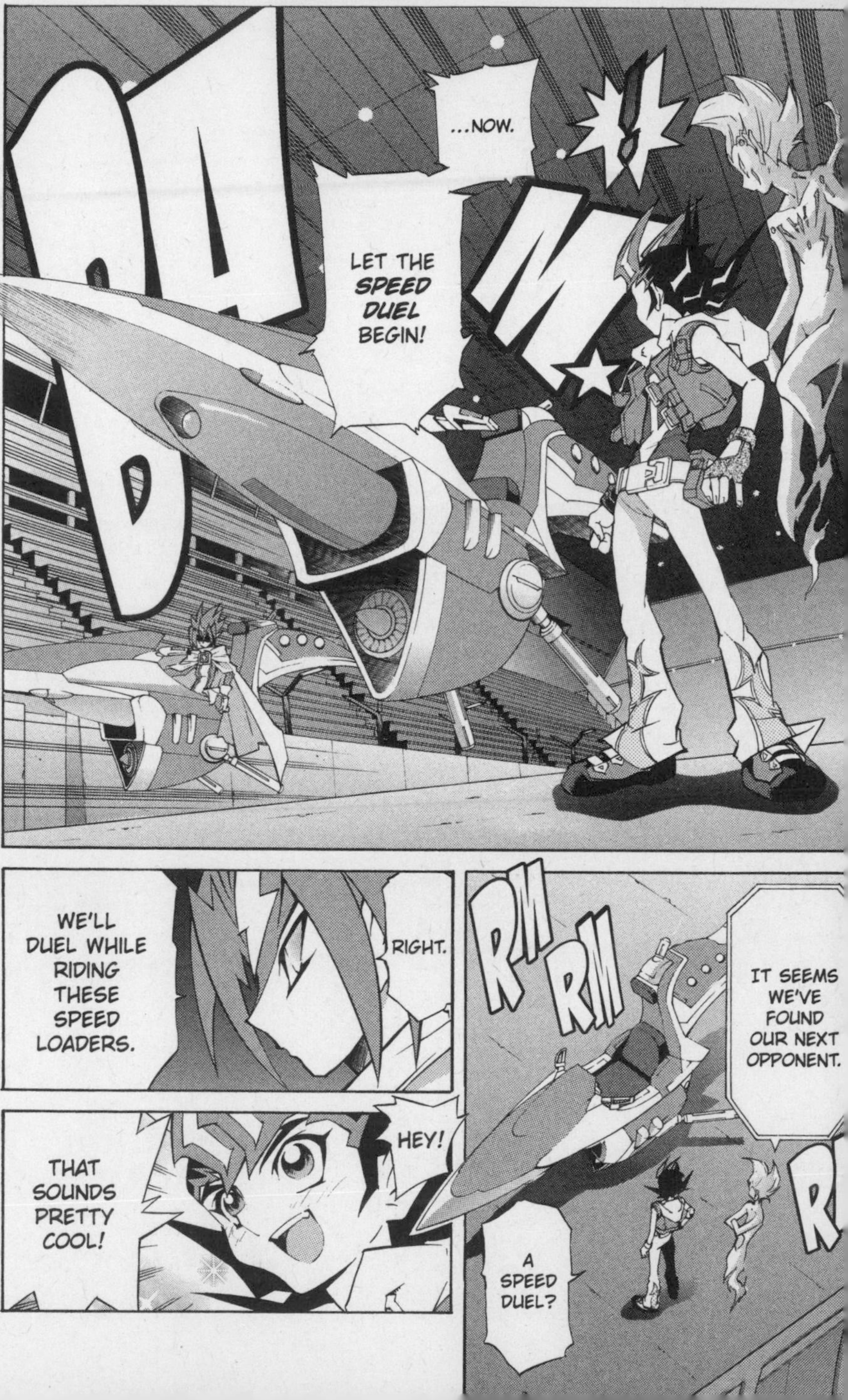
!
...NOW.
LET THE SPEED DUEL BEGIN!
RM RM
IT SEEMS WE'VE FOUND OUR NEXT OPPONENT.
A SPEED DUEL?
RIGHT.
WE'LL DUEL WHILE RIDING THESE SPEED LOADERS.
HEY!
THAT SOUNDS PRETTY COOL!

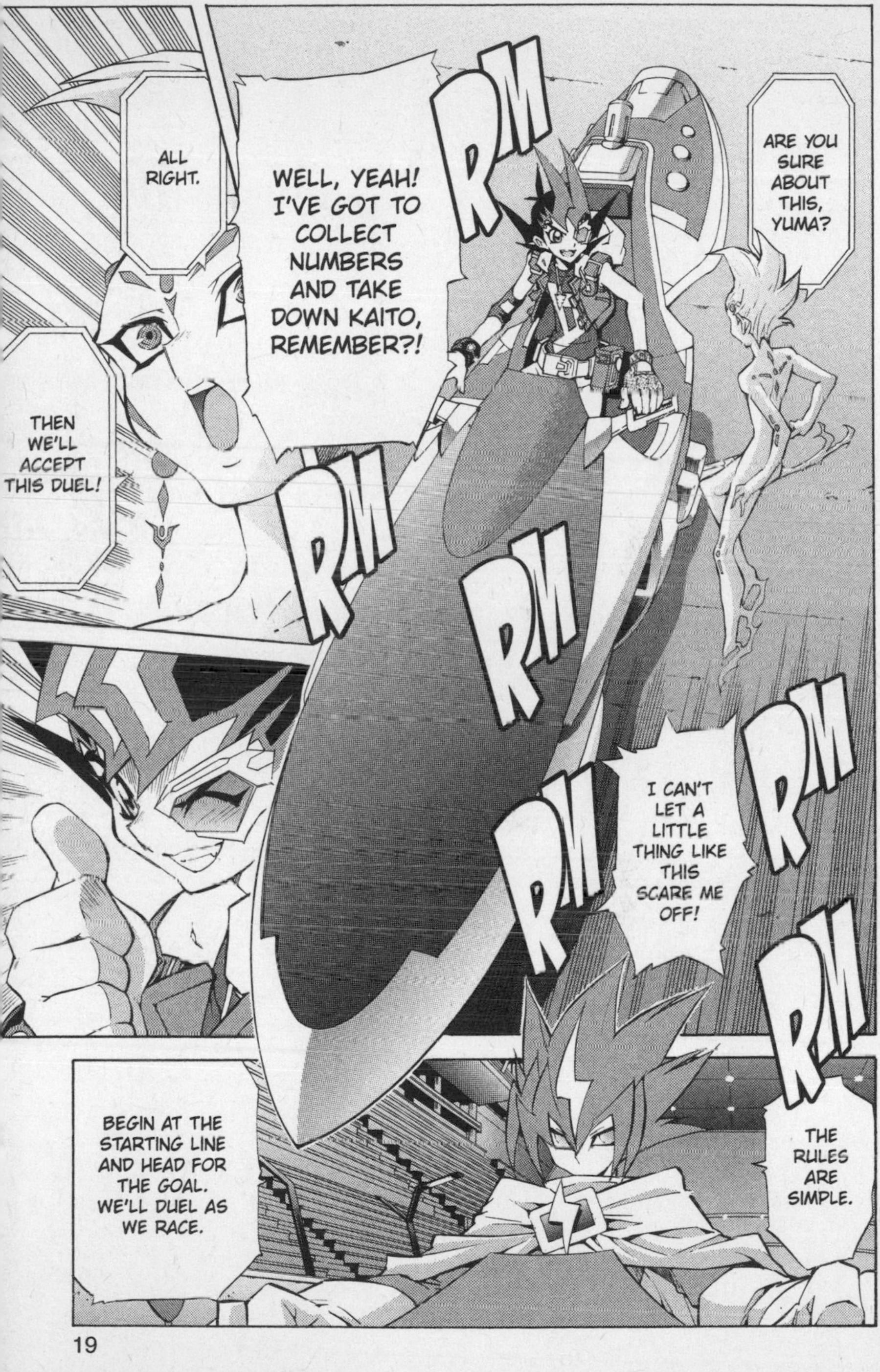
ARE YOU SURE ABOUT THIS, YUMA?
WELL, YEAH! I'VE GOT TO COLLECT NUMBERS AND TAKE DOWN KAITO, REMEMBER?!
RM
RM
RM
RM
RM
RM
I CAN'T LET A LITTLE THING LIKE THIS SCARE ME OFF!
ALL RIGHT.
THEN WE'LL ACCEPT THIS DUEL!
THE RULES ARE SIMPLE.
BEGIN AT THE STARTING LINE AND HEAD FOR THE GOAL. WE'LL DUEL AS WE RACE.

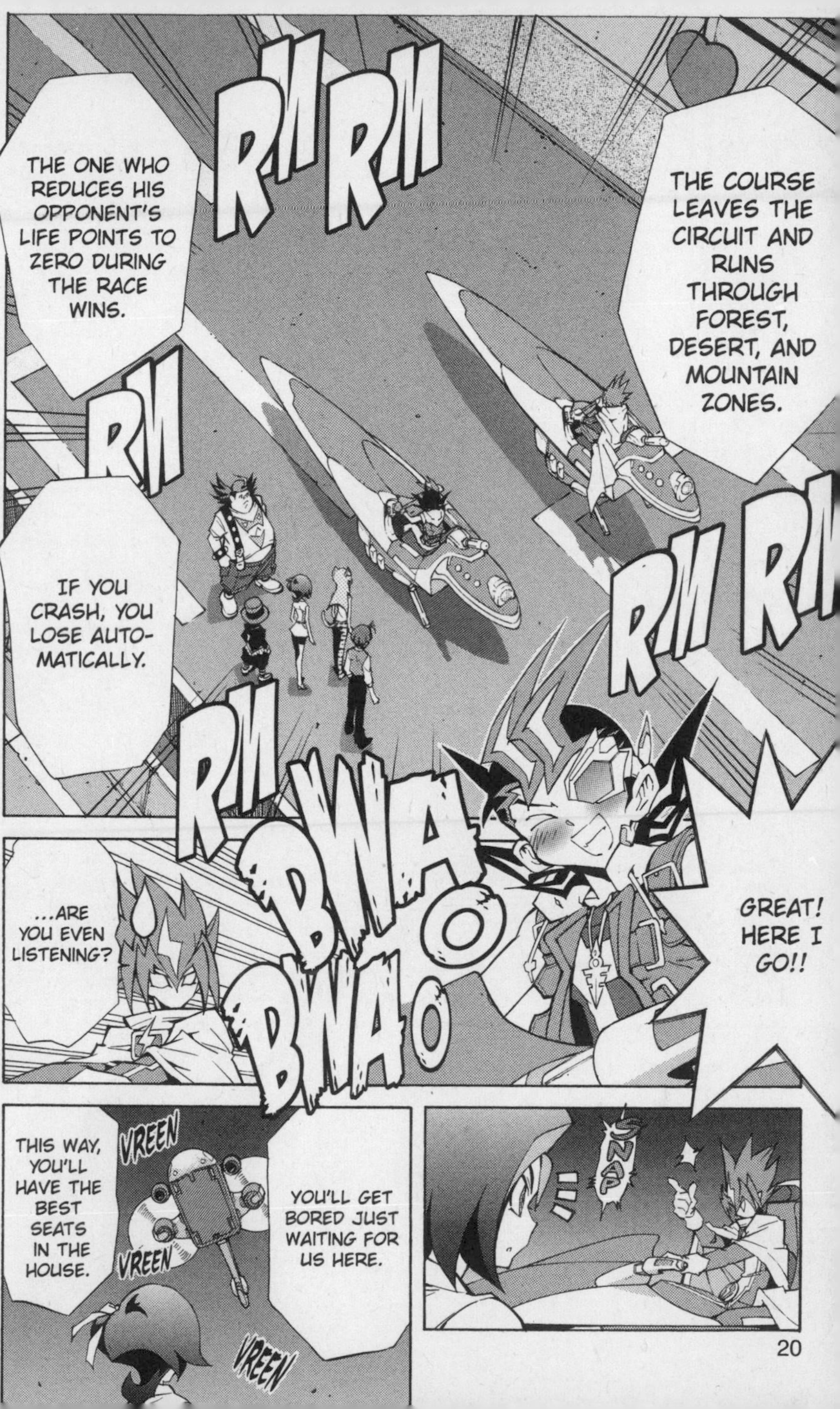
RMRM
THE COURSE LEAVES THE CIRCUIT AND RUNS THROUGH FOREST, DESERT, AND MOUNTAIN ZONES.
THE ONE WHO REDUCES HIS OPPONENT'S LIFE POINTS TO ZERO DURING THE RACE WINS.
RM
RMRM
IF YOU CRASH, YOU LOSE AUTO-MATICALLY.
RM
GREAT! HERE I GO!!
BWAO
BWAO
...ARE YOU EVEN LISTENING?
SNAP
YOU'LL GET BORED JUST WAITING FOR US HERE.
VREEN
THIS WAY, YOU'LL HAVE THE BEST SEATS IN THE HOUSE.
VREEN
VREEN

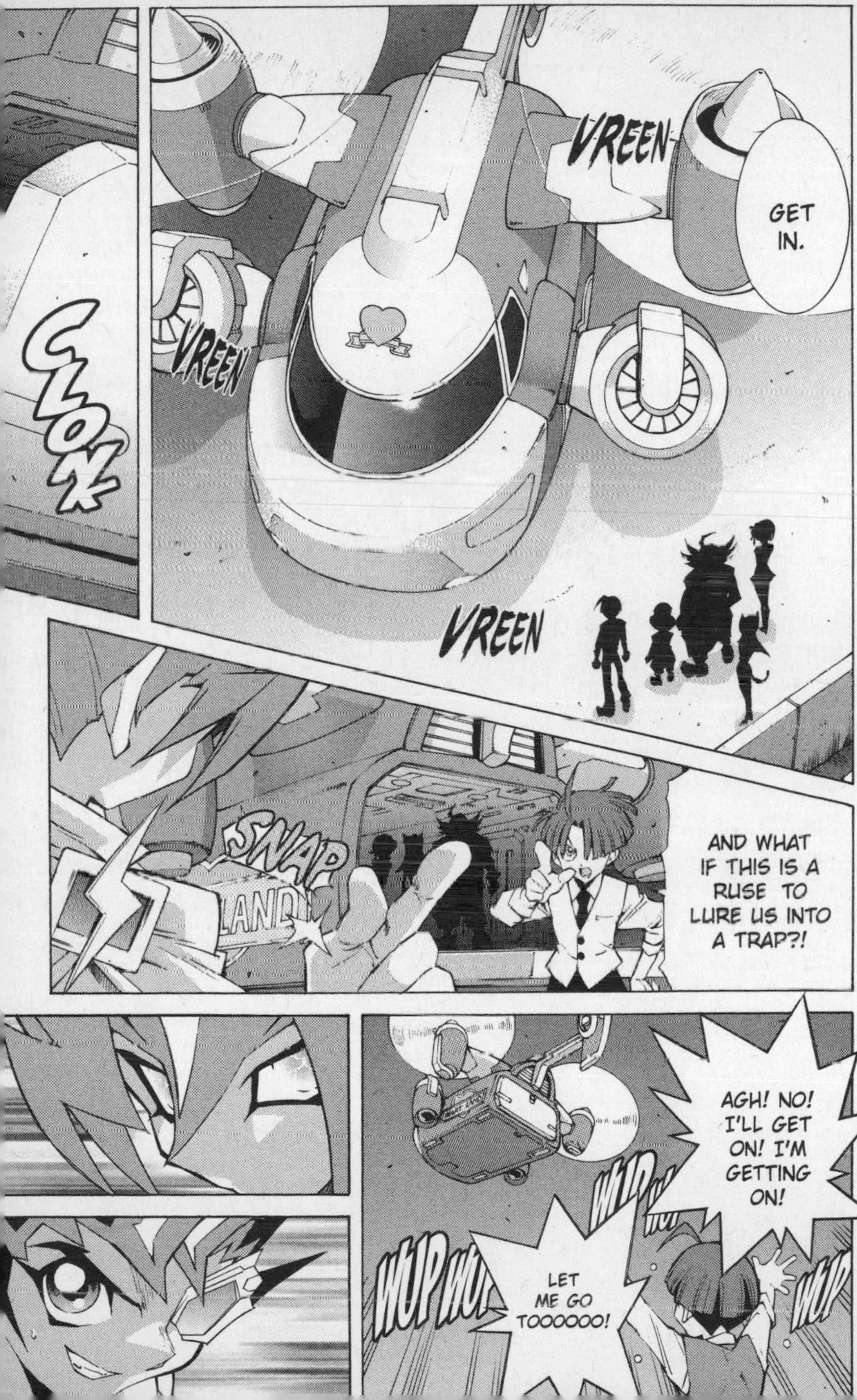
GET IN.
VREEN
VREEN
VREEN
CLONK
AND WHAT IF THIS IS A RUSE TO LURE US INTO A TRAP?!
SNAP
LAND
AGH! NO! I'LL GET ON! I'M GETTING ON!
LET ME GO TOOOOOOO!
WUP WUP

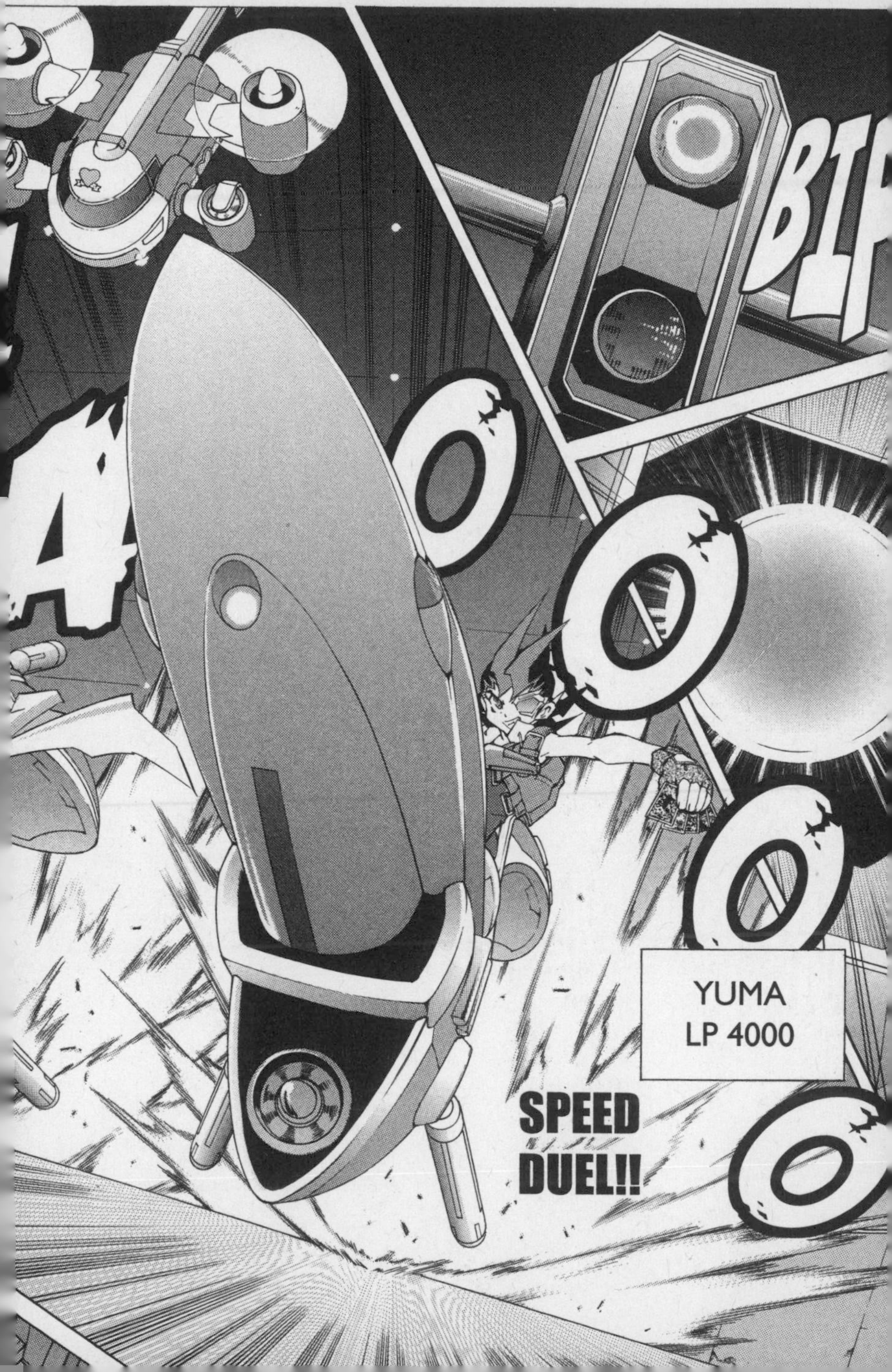
BIP
4
YUMA
LP 4000
SPEED
DUEL!!

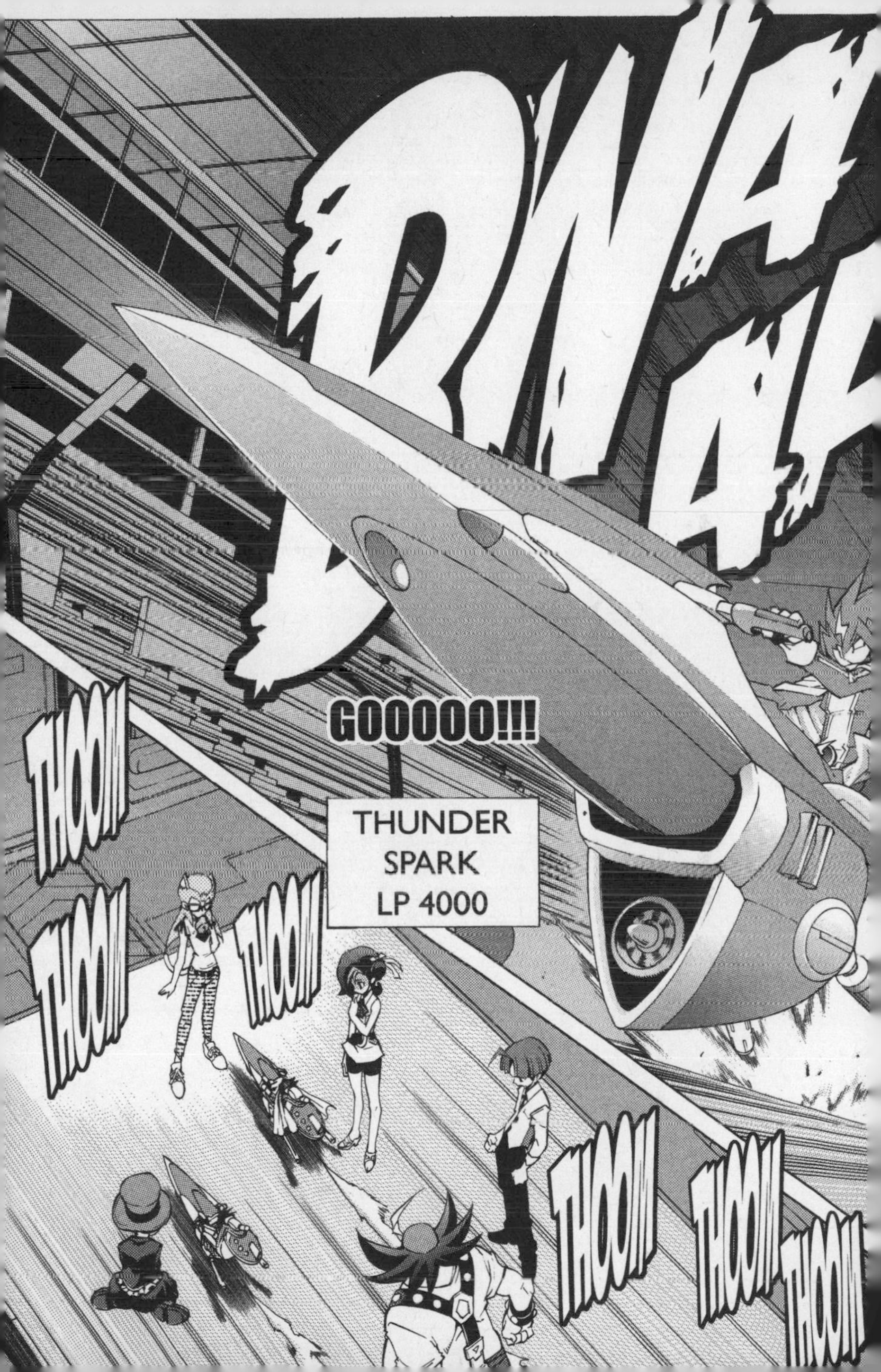
GOOOOOO!!!
THUNDER
SPARK
LP 4000
THOOM
THOOM
THOOM
THOOM
THOOM
THOOM

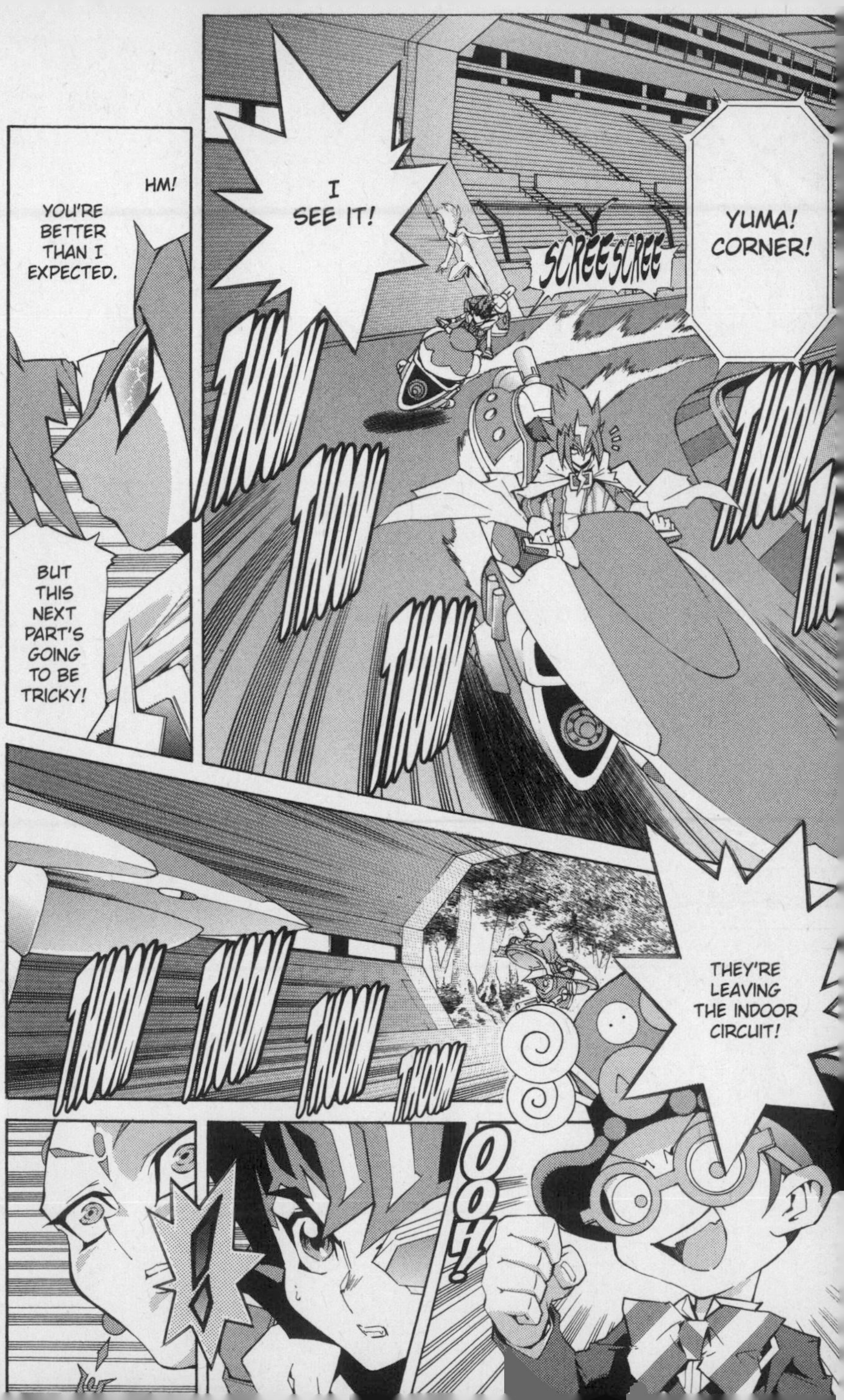
YUMA! CORNER!
I SEE IT!
SCREE SCREE
THOOM
THOOM
THOOM
THOOM
HM!
YOU'RE BETTER THAN I EXPECTED.
BUT THIS NEXT PART'S GOING TO BE TRICKY!
THEY'RE LEAVING THE INDOOR CIRCUIT!
THOOM THOOM THOOM THOOM
OOOH!

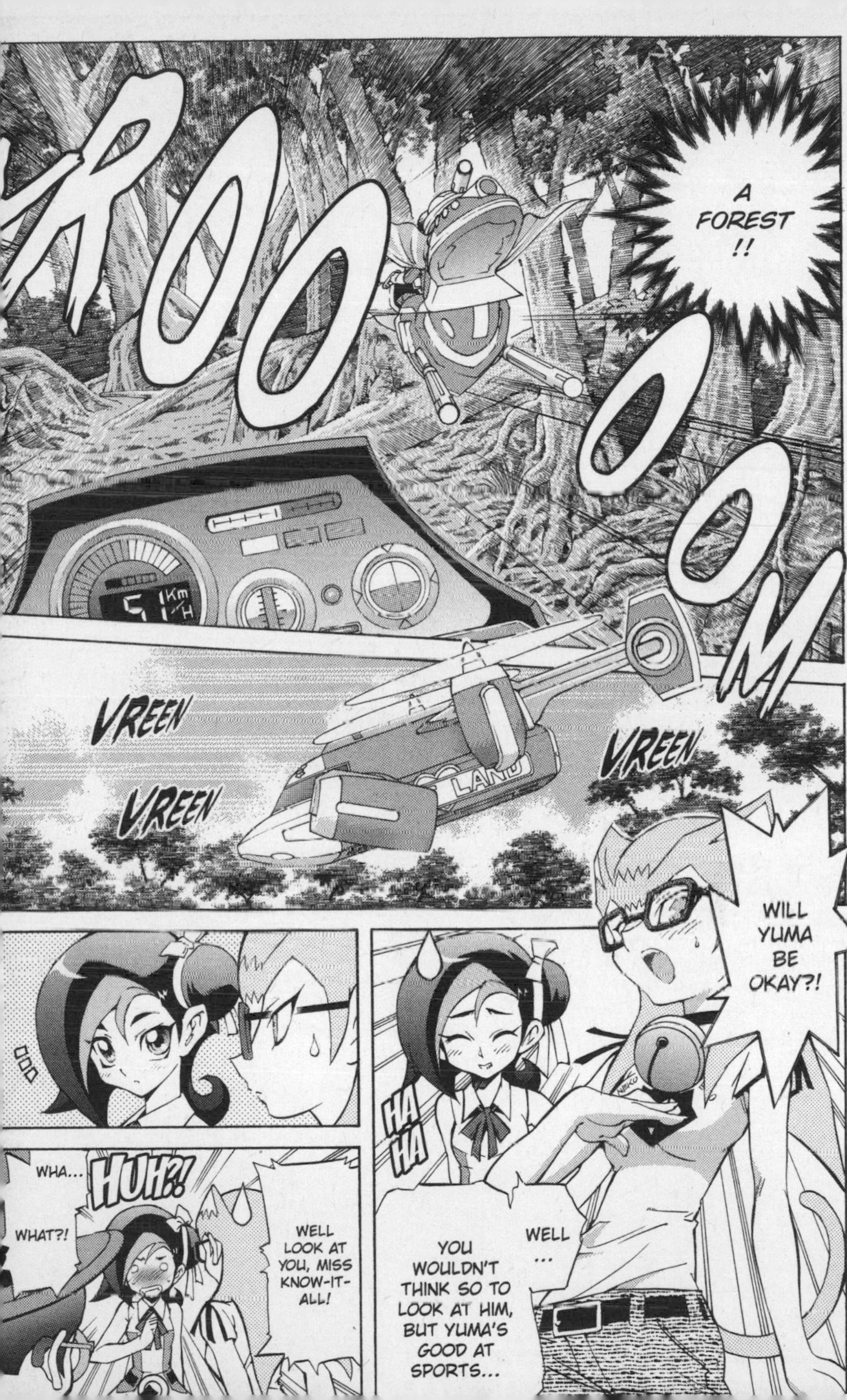
KROOOOOOM
A FOREST!!
VREEN
VREEN
VREEN
WILL YUMA BE OKAY?!
HA HA
WELL...
YOU WOULDN'T THINK SO TO LOOK AT HIM, BUT YUMA'S GOOD AT SPORTS...
HUH?!
WHA...
WHAT?!
WELL LOOK AT YOU, MISS KNOW-IT-ALL!

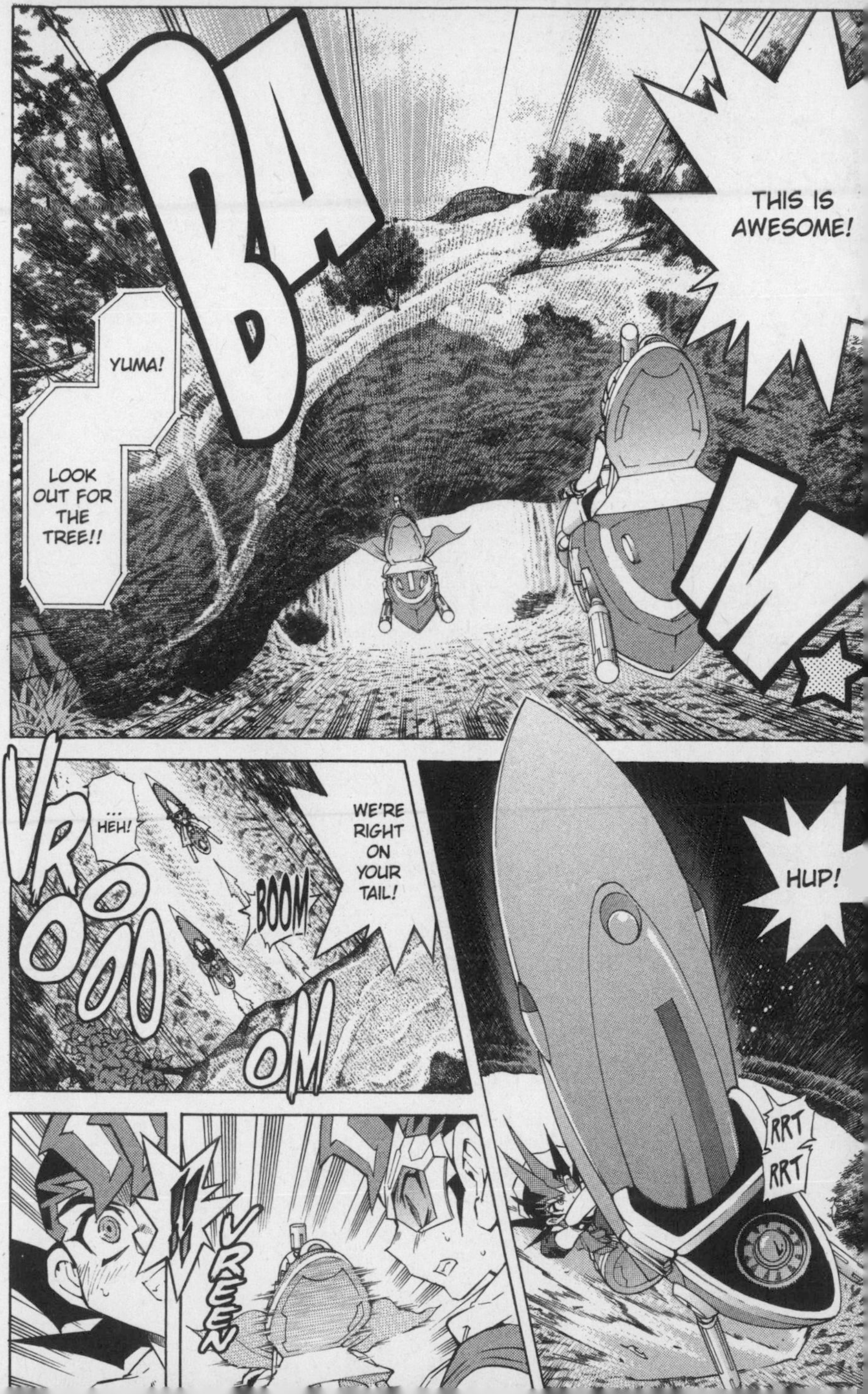

THIS IS AWESOME!
BAM
YUMA!
LOOK OUT FOR THE TREE!!
HUP!
RRT RRT
WE'RE RIGHT ON YOUR TAIL!
... HEH!
BOOM
VROOOOOOM
VREEN
!!

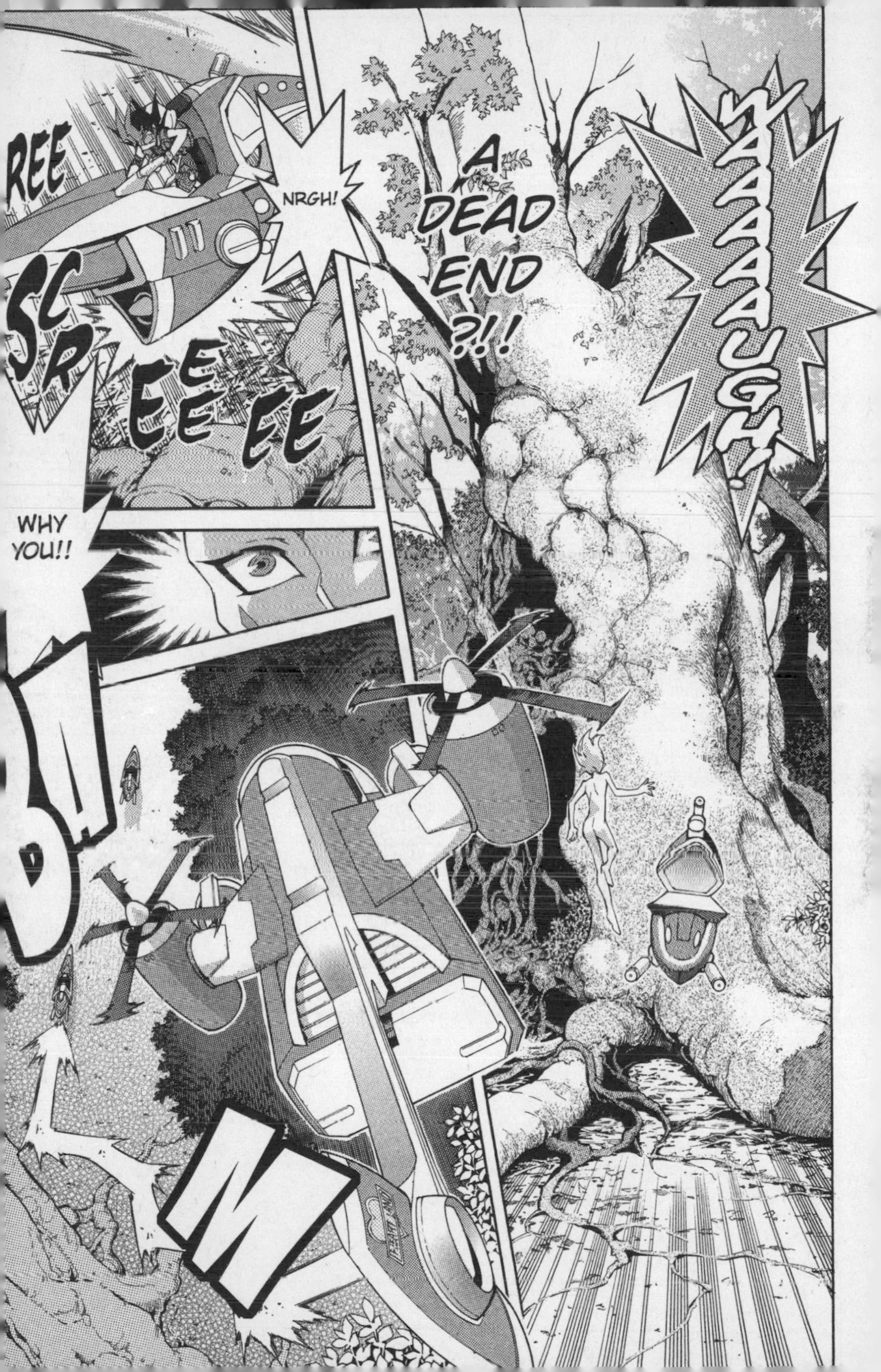
WAAAAAUGH!
A DEAD END ?!!
NRGH!
REE
WHY YOU!!

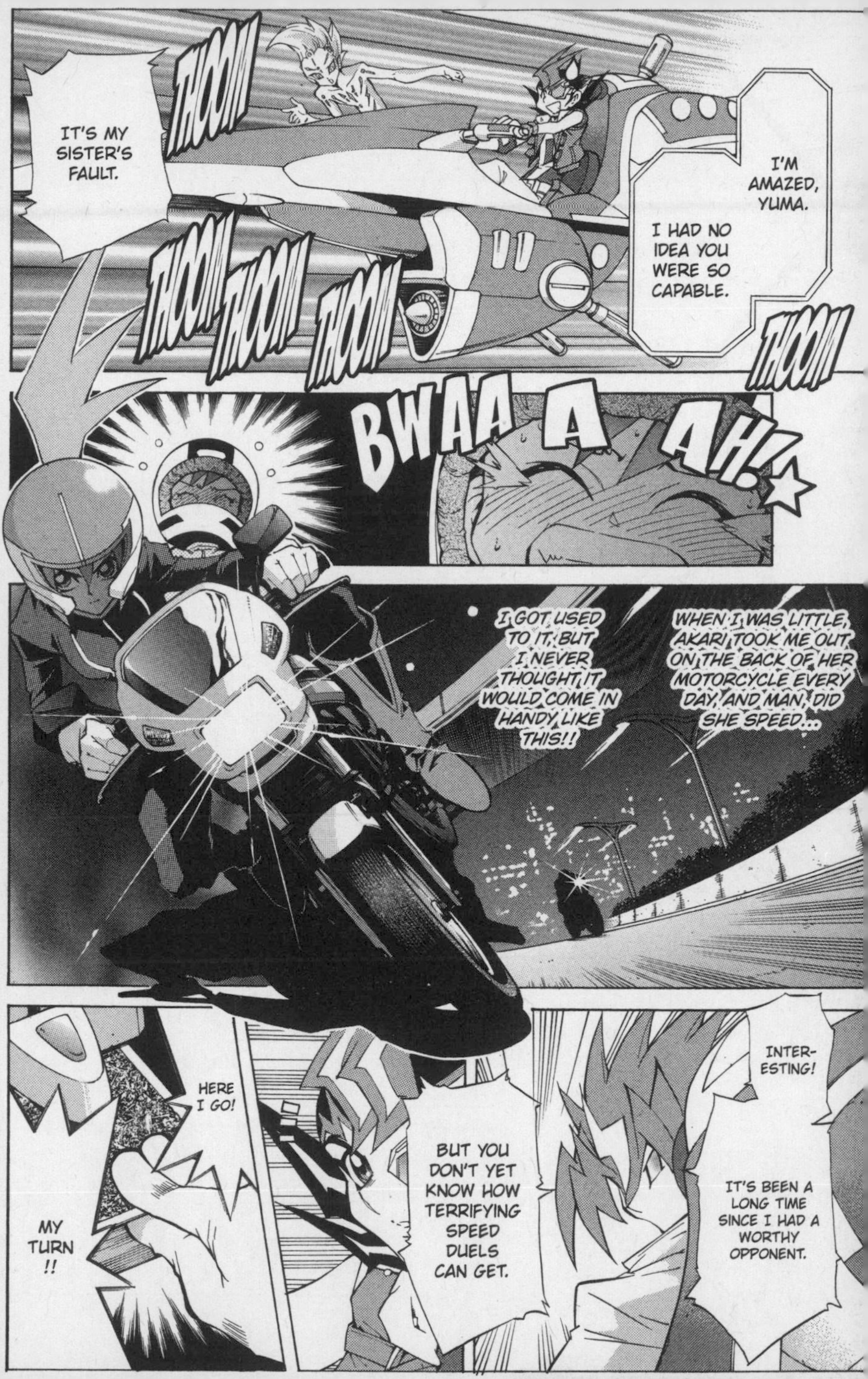
I'M AMAZED, YUMA.
I HAD NO IDEA YOU WERE SO CAPABLE.
THOOM
THOOM
THOOM
THOOM
IT'S MY SISTER'S FAULT.
THOOM
BWAAA A AH!!
WHEN I WAS LITTLE, AKARI TOOK ME OUT ON THE BACK OF HER MOTORCYCLE EVERY DAY, AND MAN, DID SHE SPEED...
I GOT USED TO IT, BUT I NEVER THOUGHT IT WOULD COME IN HANDY LIKE THIS!!
INTER-ESTING!
IT'S BEEN A LONG TIME SINCE I HAD A WORTHY OPPONENT.
BUT YOU DON'T YET KNOW HOW TERRIFYING SPEED DUELS CAN GET.
HERE I GO!
MY TURN!!

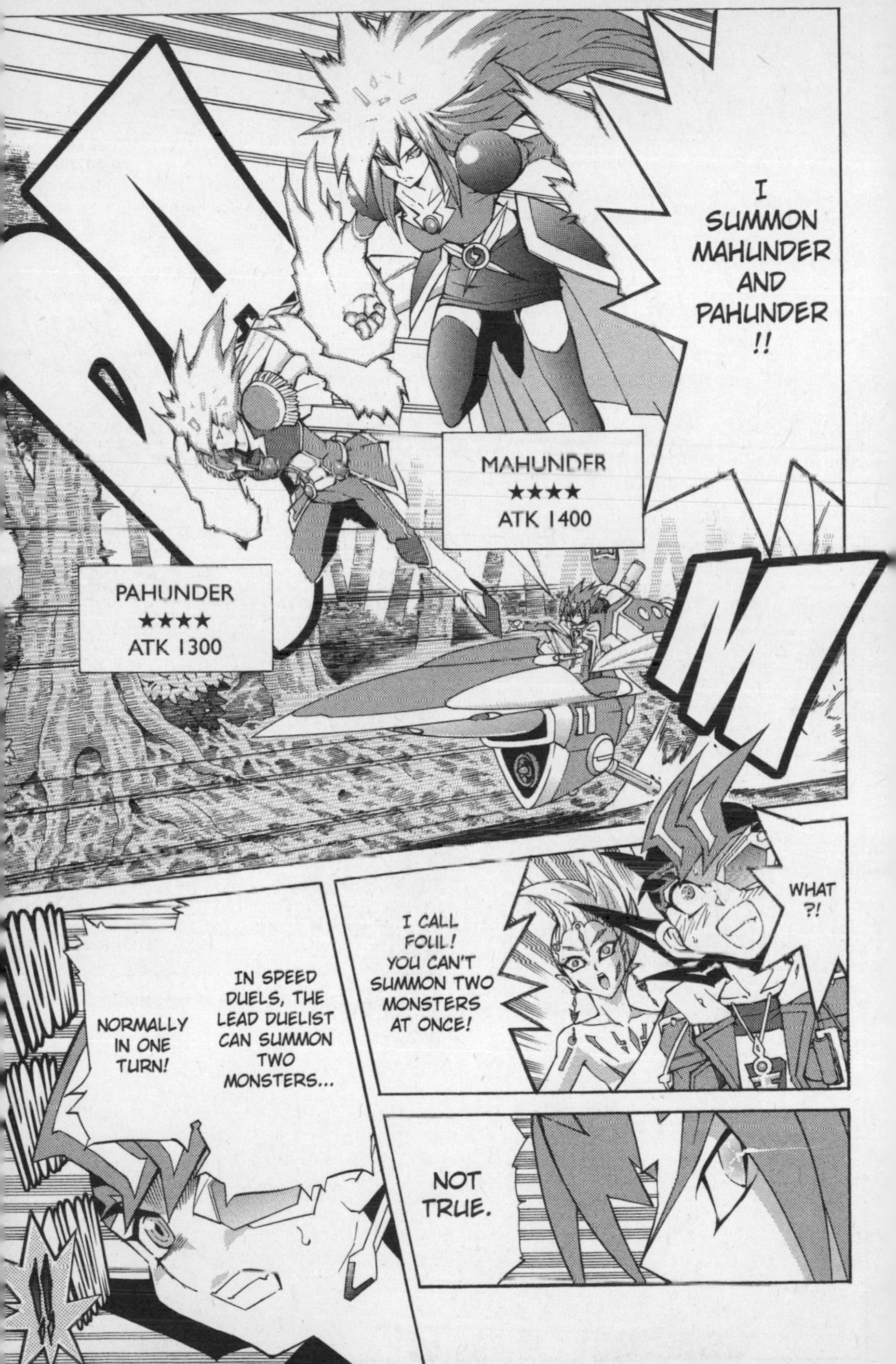
I SUMMON MAHUNDER AND PAHUNDER!!
MAHUNDER ★★★★ ATK 1400
PAHUNDER ★★★★ ATK 1300
WHAT?!
I CALL FOUL! YOU CAN'T SUMMON TWO MONSTERS AT ONCE!
NOT TRUE.
IN SPEED DUELS, THE LEAD DUELIST CAN SUMMON TWO MONSTERS...
NORMALLY IN ONE TURN!

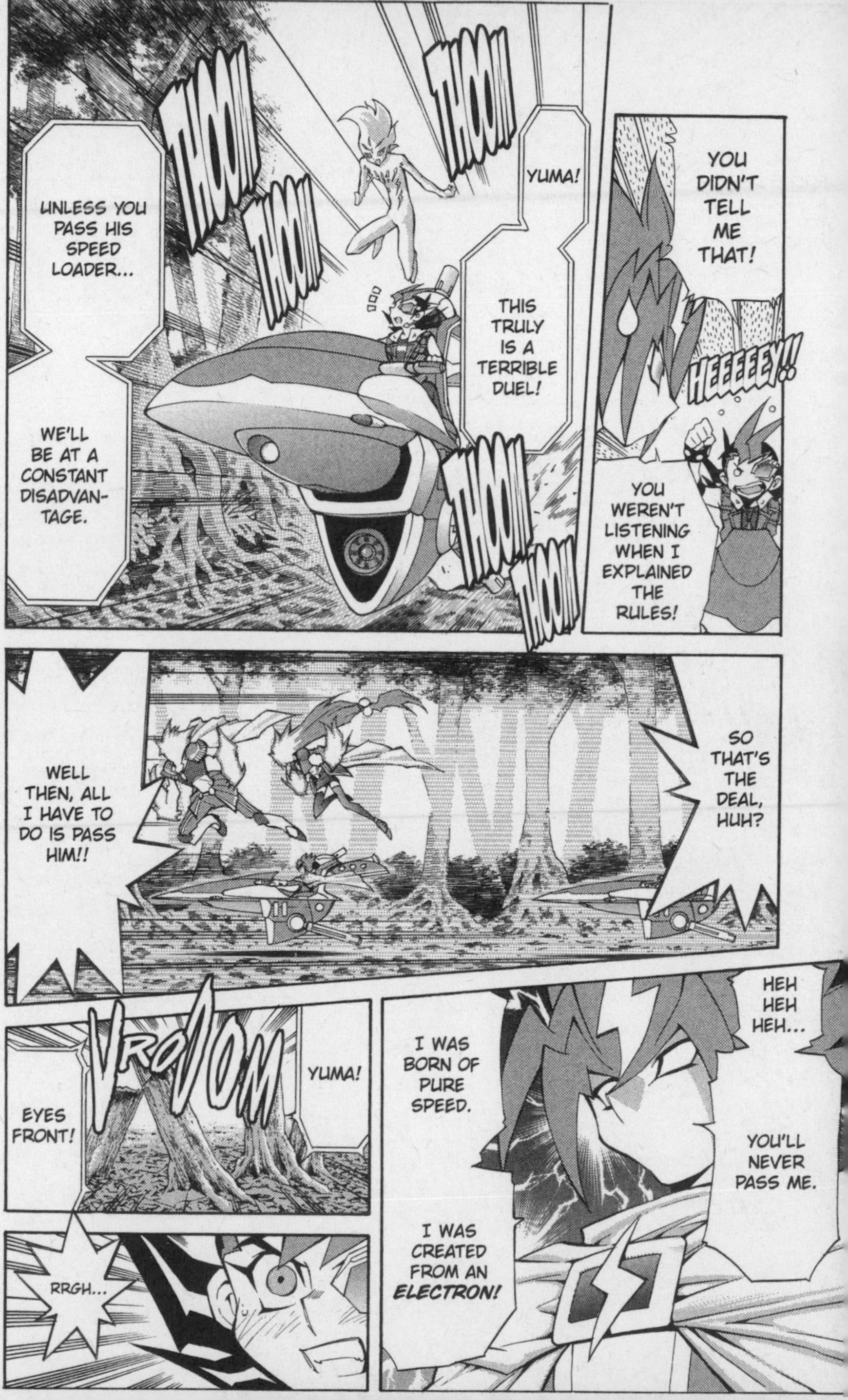
YOU DIDN'T TELL ME THAT!
HEEEEEY!!
YOU WEREN'T LISTENING WHEN I EXPLAINED THE RULES!
THOOM
YUMA!
THIS TRULY IS A TERRIBLE DUEL!
THOOM
THOOM
UNLESS YOU PASS HIS SPEED LOADER...
WE'LL BE AT A CONSTANT DISADVANTAGE.
THOOM
THOOM
SO THAT'S THE DEAL, HUH?
WELL THEN, ALL I HAVE TO DO IS PASS HIM!!
HEH HEH HEH...
I WAS BORN OF PURE SPEED.
YOU'LL NEVER PASS ME.
I WAS CREATED FROM AN *ELECTRON!*
VROOOM
YUMA!
EYES FRONT!
RRGH...

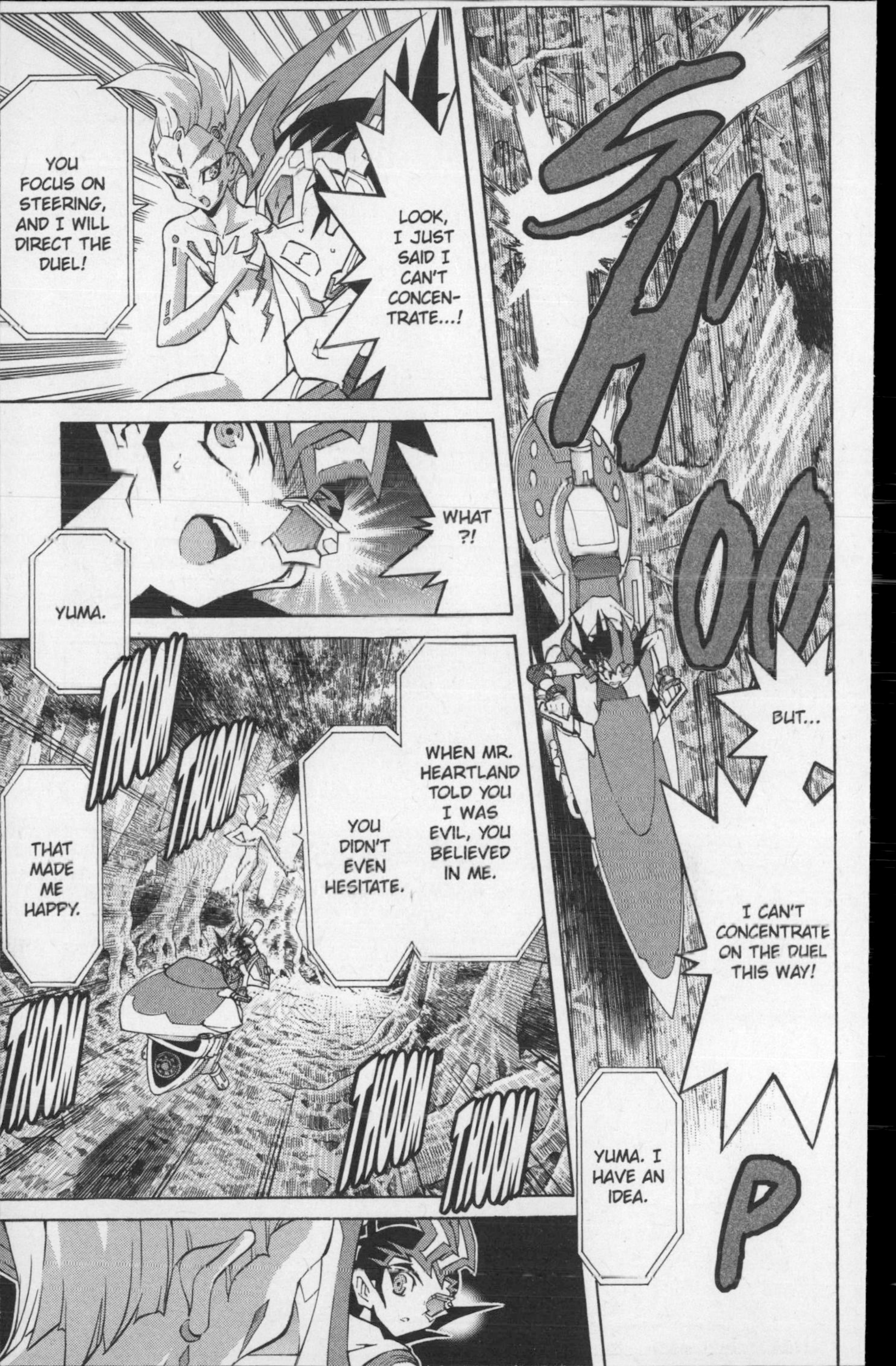
BUT...
I CAN'T CONCENTRATE ON THE DUEL THIS WAY!
YUMA. I HAVE AN IDEA.
YOU FOCUS ON STEERING, AND I WILL DIRECT THE DUEL!
LOOK, I JUST SAID I CAN'T CONCENTRATE...!
WHAT?!
YUMA.
WHEN MR. HEARTLAND TOLD YOU I WAS EVIL, YOU BELIEVED IN ME.
YOU DIDN'T EVEN HESITATE.
THAT MADE ME HAPPY.
THOOM
THOOM
THOOM
THOOM
THOOM

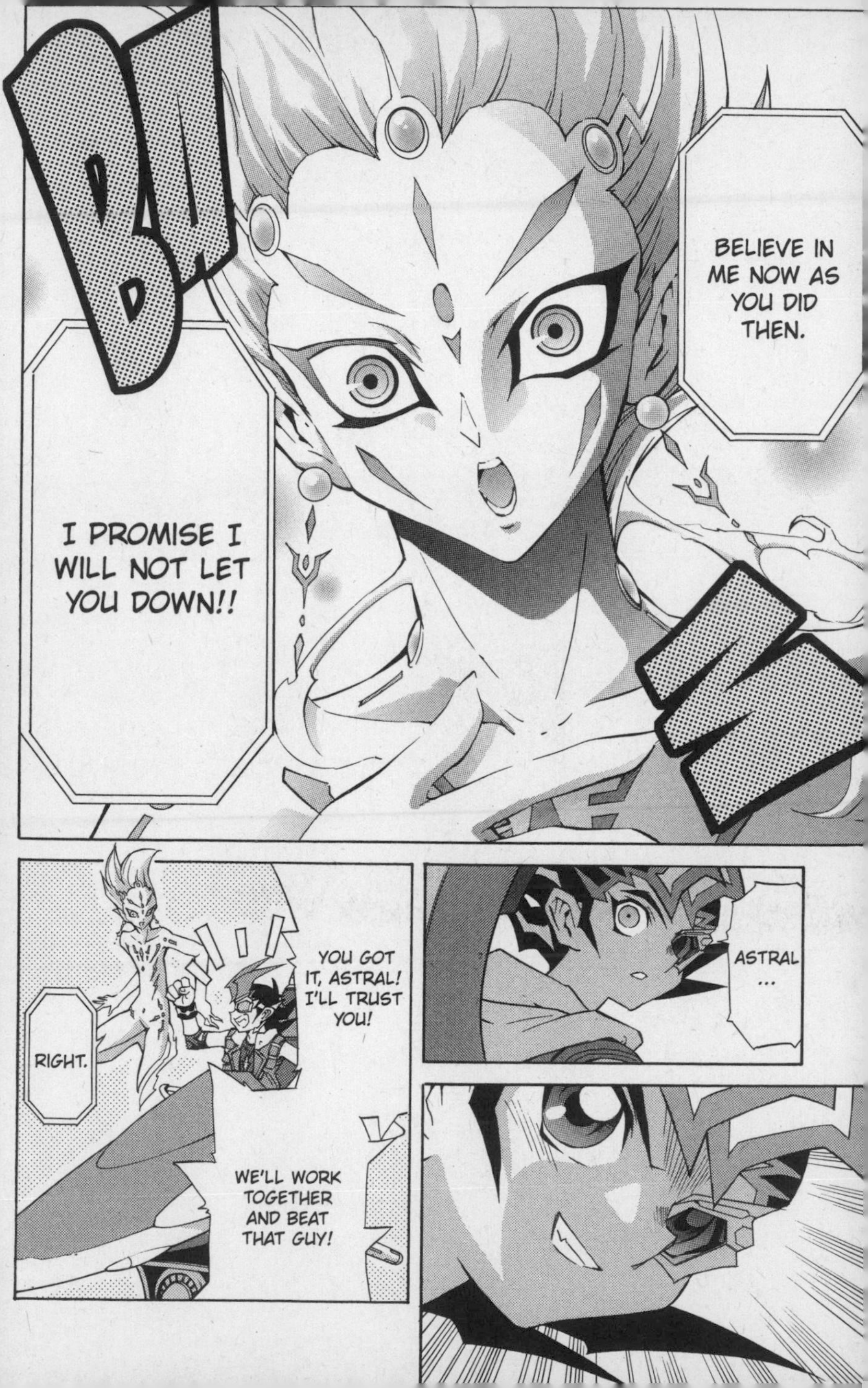
BELIEVE IN ME NOW AS YOU DID THEN.
I PROMISE I WILL NOT LET YOU DOWN!!
ASTRAL ...
YOU GOT IT, ASTRAL! I'LL TRUST YOU!
RIGHT.
WE'LL WORK TOGETHER AND BEAT THAT GUY!

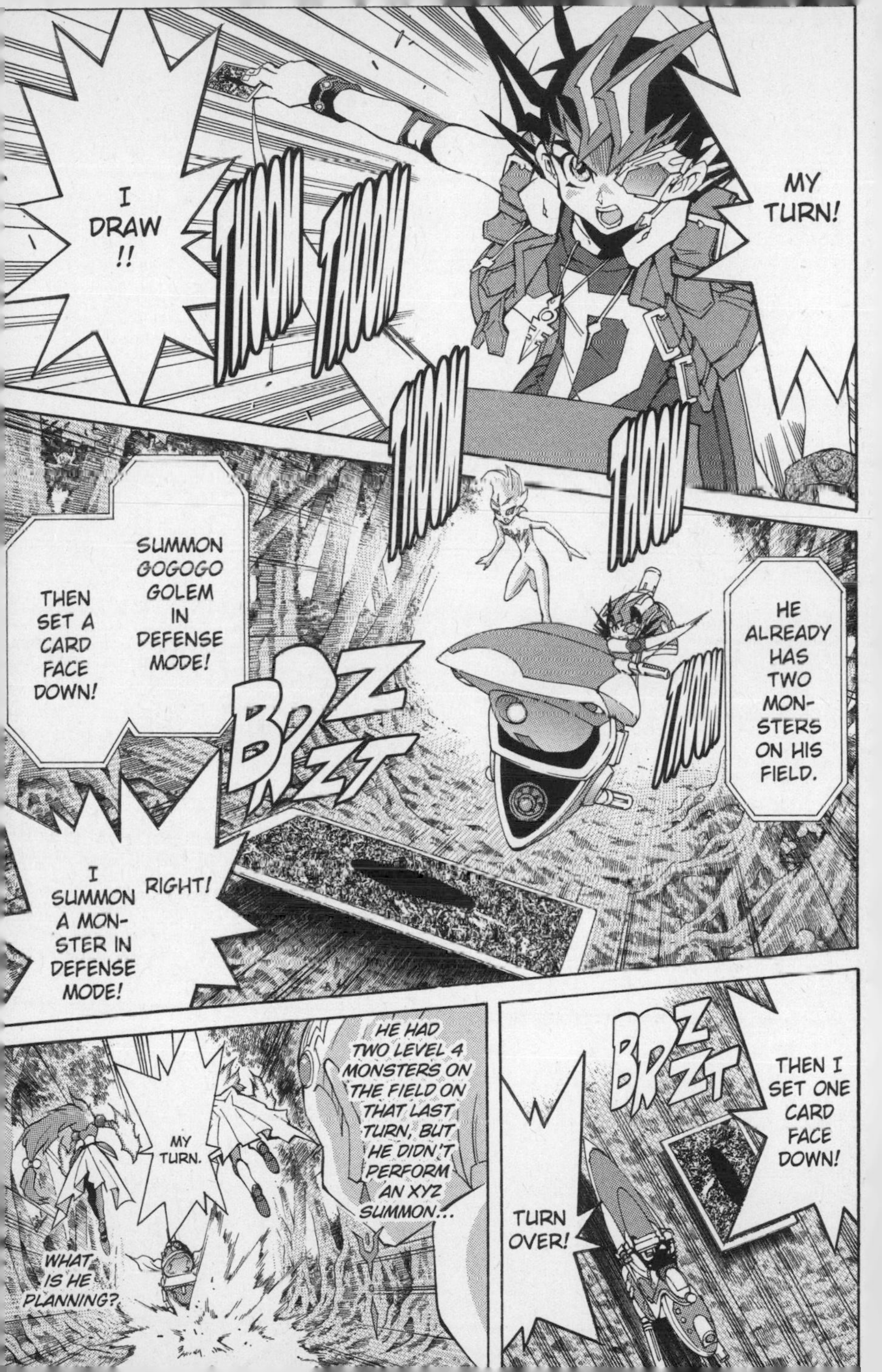
MY TURN!
I DRAW!!
THOOM THOOM
THOOM THOOM
HE ALREADY HAS TWO MONSTERS ON HIS FIELD.
THOOM
SUMMON GOGOGO GOLEM IN DEFENSE MODE!
THEN SET A CARD FACE DOWN!
BRZZT
RIGHT!
I SUMMON A MONSTER IN DEFENSE MODE!
BRZZT
THEN I SET ONE CARD FACE DOWN!
TURN OVER!
HE HAD TWO LEVEL 4 MONSTERS ON THE FIELD ON THAT LAST TURN, BUT HE DIDN'T PERFORM AN XYZ SUMMON...
MY TURN.
WHAT IS HE PLANNING?

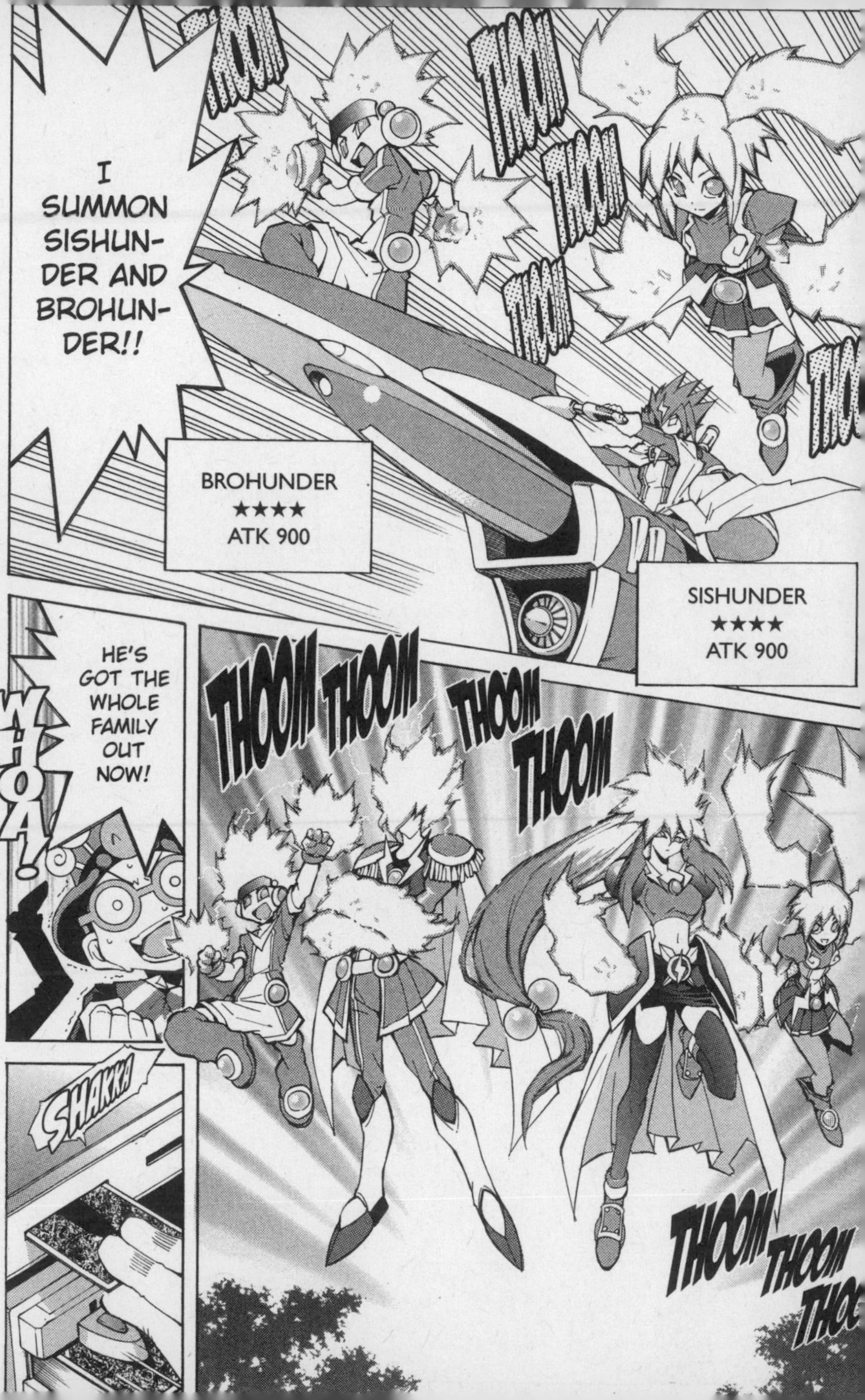
THOOM
THOOM THOOM THOOM
THOOM
I SUMMON SISHUNDER AND BROHUNDER!!
BROHUNDER
★★★★
ATK 900
SISHUNDER
★★★★
ATK 900
THOOM THOOM THOOM THOOM
THOOM THOOM THOO
HE'S GOT THE WHOLE FAMILY OUT NOW!
WHOA!
SHAKKA

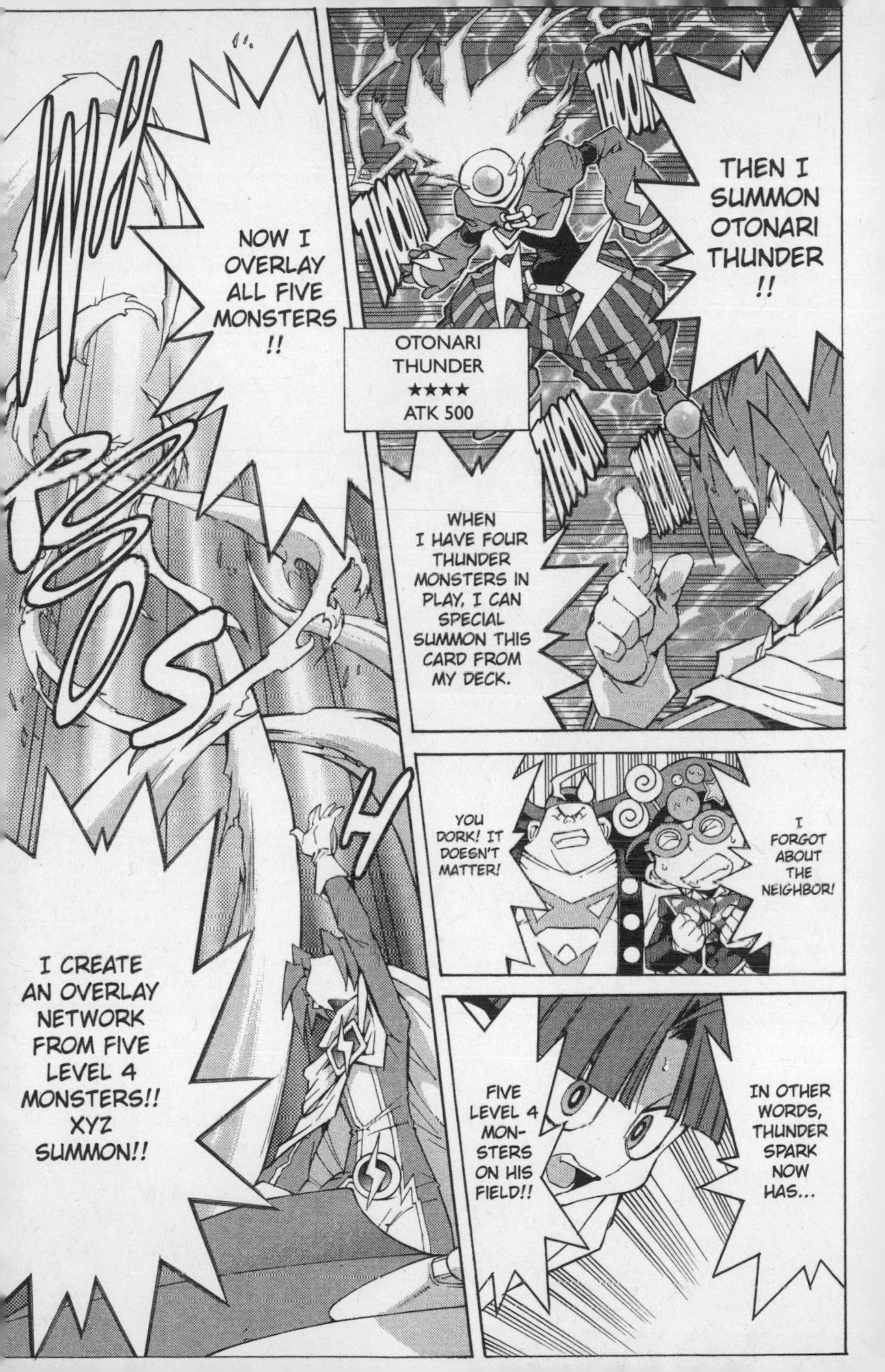
THOOM
THOOM
THEN I SUMMON OTONARI THUNDER!!
OTONARI THUNDER
★★★★
ATK 500
THOOM
THOOM
WHEN I HAVE FOUR THUNDER MONSTERS IN PLAY, I CAN SPECIAL SUMMON THIS CARD FROM MY DECK.
I FORGOT ABOUT THE NEIGHBOR!
YOU DORK! IT DOESN'T MATTER!
IN OTHER WORDS, THUNDER SPARK NOW HAS...
FIVE LEVEL 4 MON-STERS ON HIS FIELD!!
NOW I OVERLAY ALL FIVE MONSTERS!!
WHOOSH
I CREATE AN OVERLAY NETWORK FROM FIVE LEVEL 4 MONSTERS!! XYZ SUMMON!!

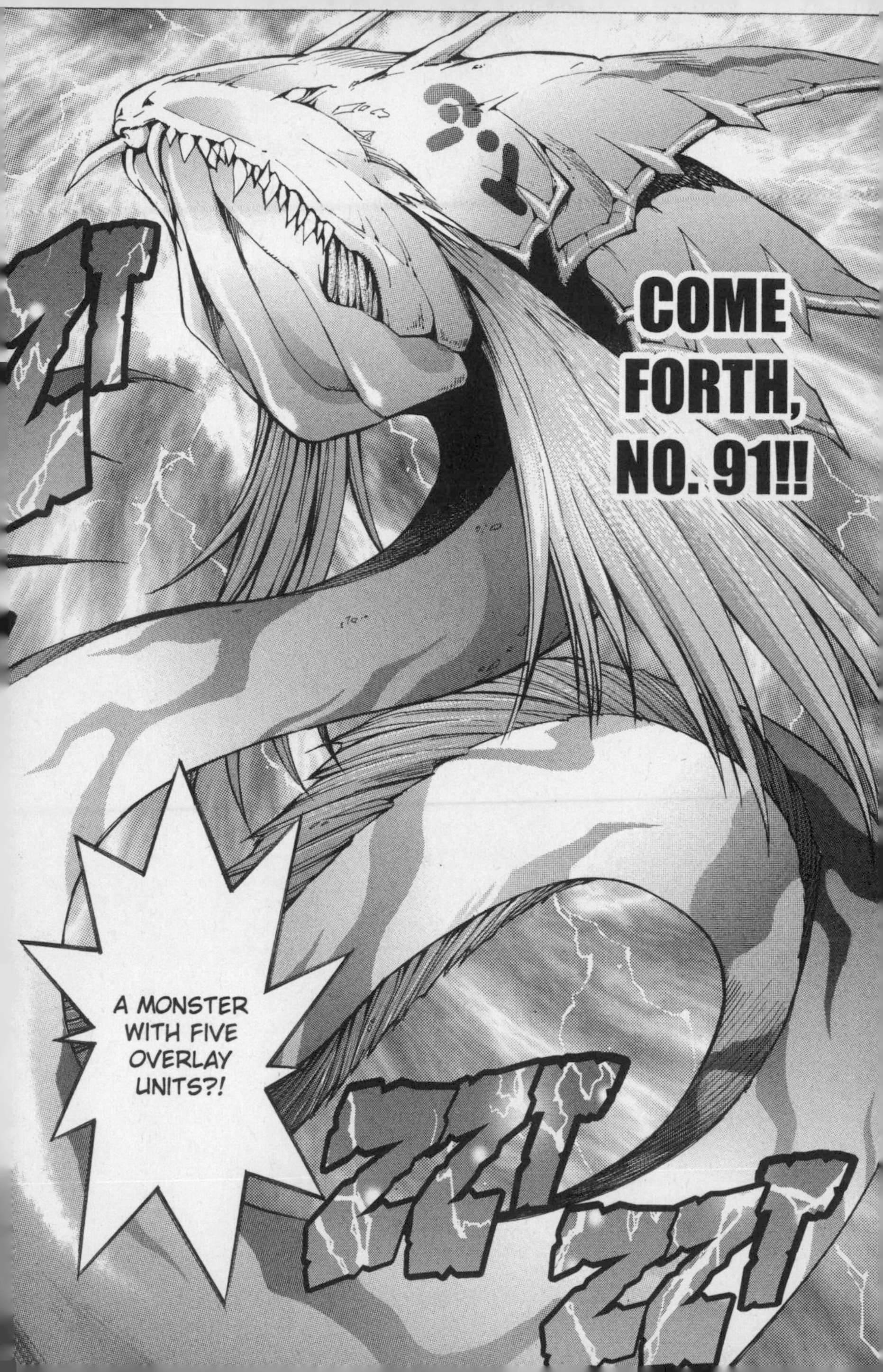
COME FORTH, NO. 91!!
A MONSTER WITH FIVE OVERLAY UNITS?!

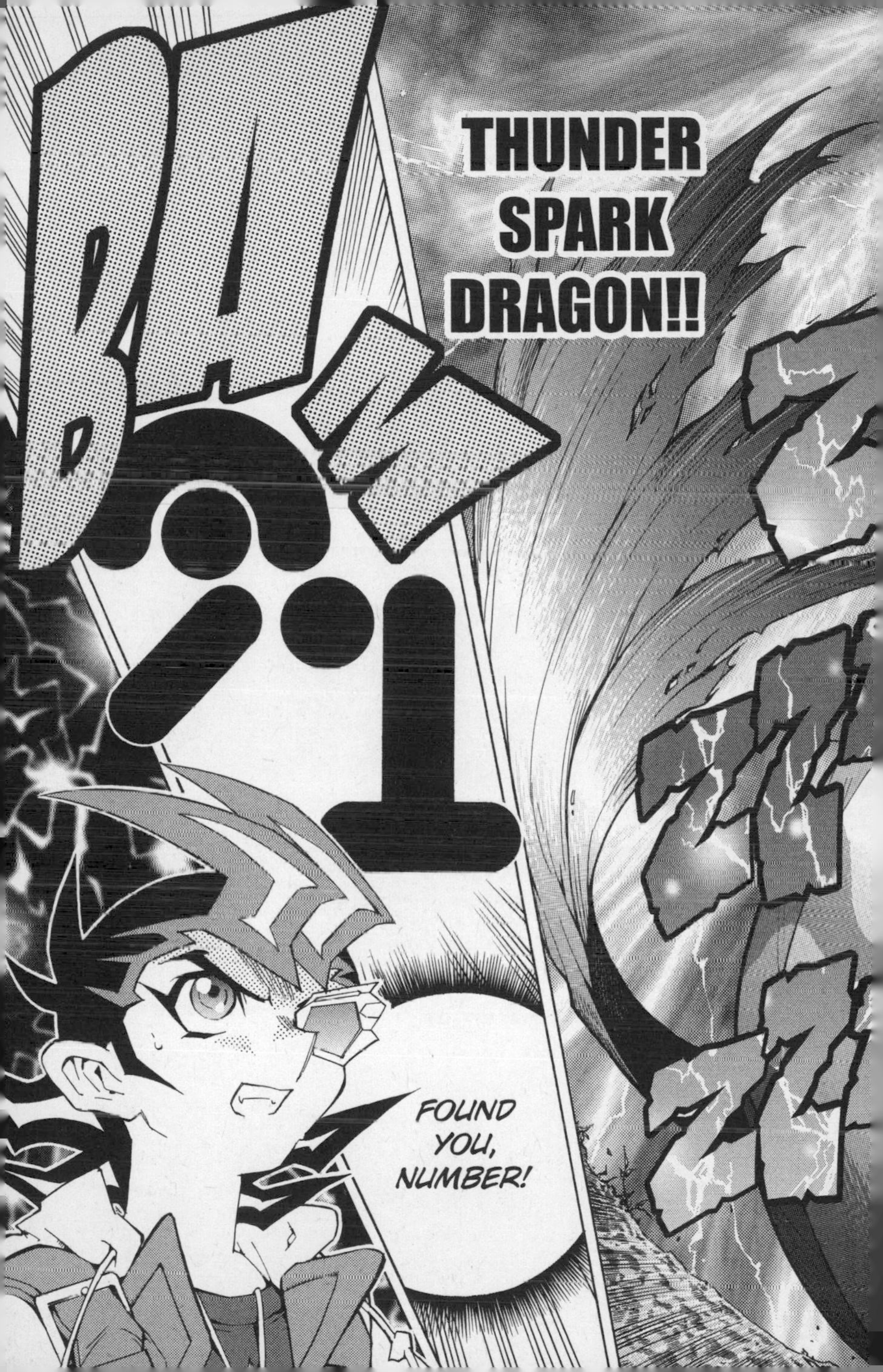
THUNDER SPARK DRAGON!!
FOUND YOU, NUMBER!

YU-GI-OH!
ZEXAL

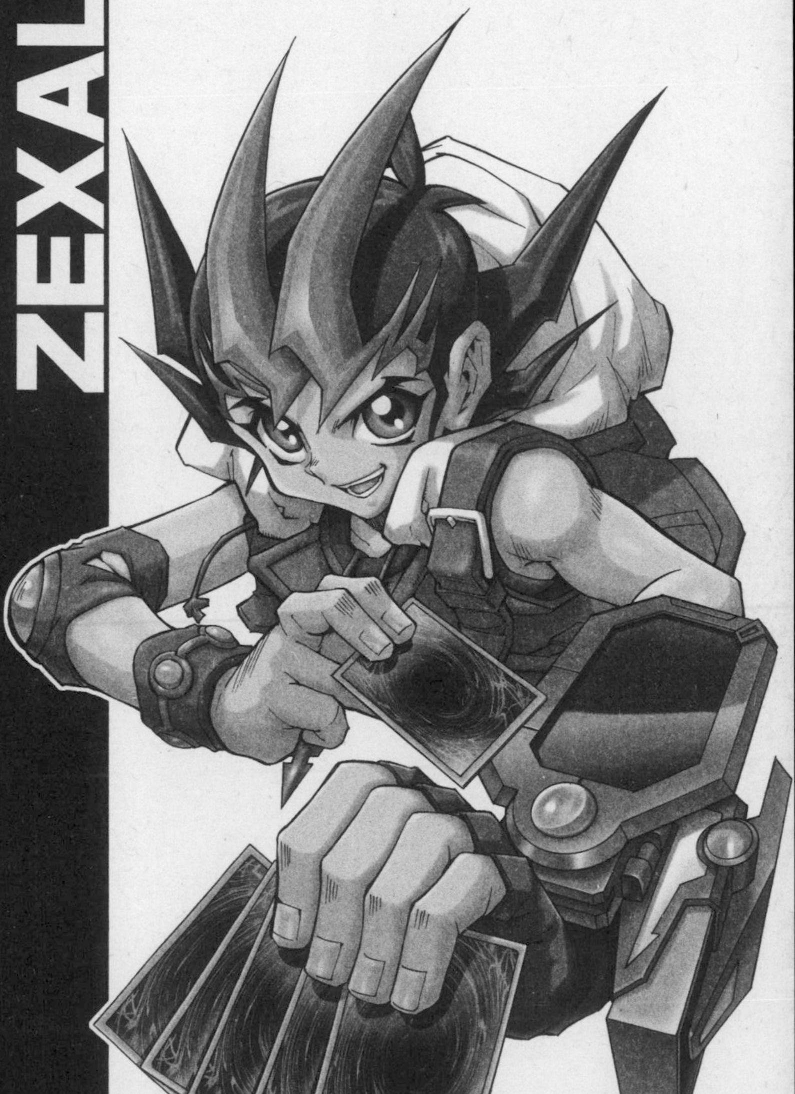

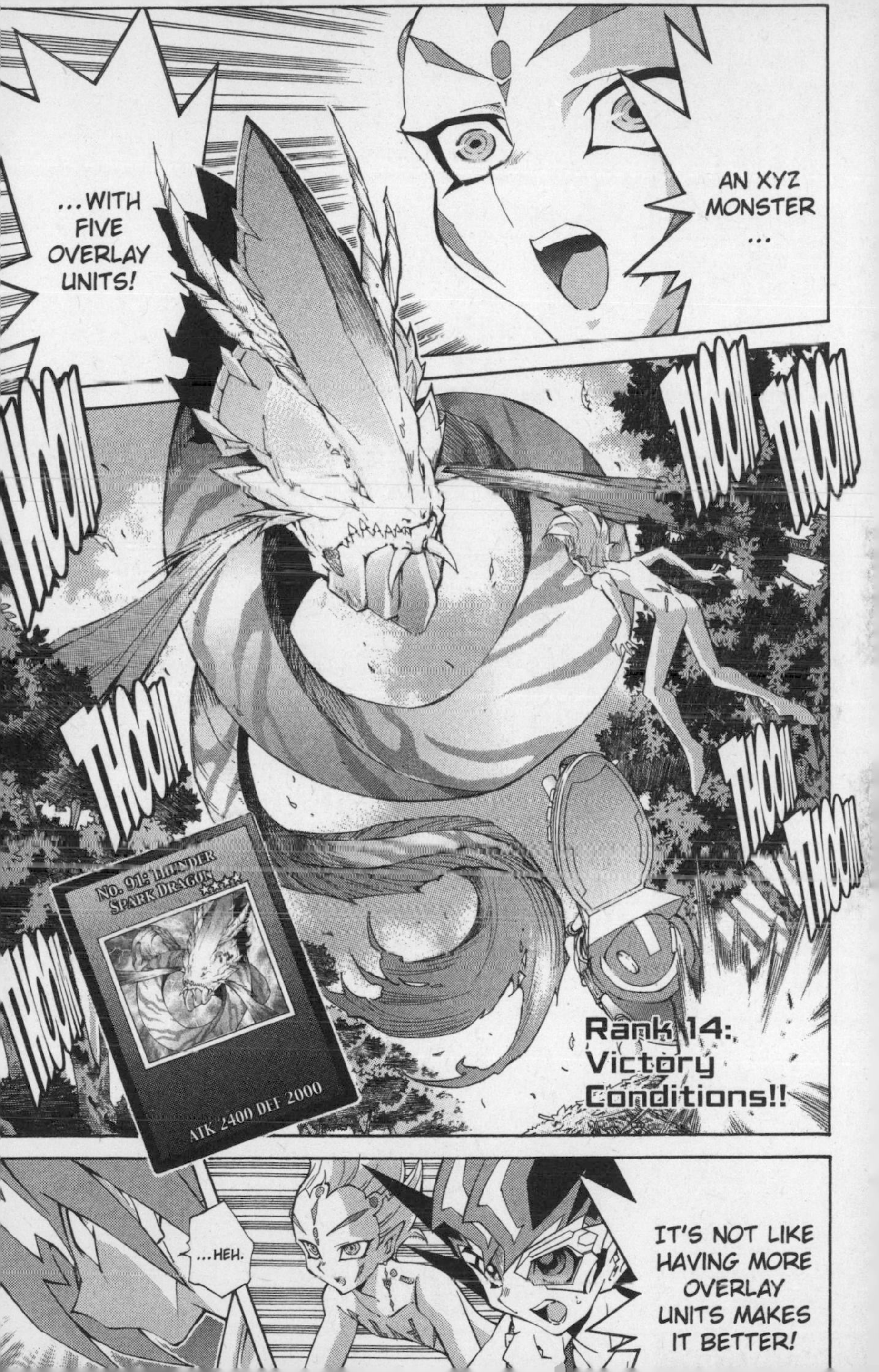
AN XYZ MONSTER...
...WITH FIVE OVERLAY UNITS!
THOOM
THOOM
THOOM
THOOM
THOOM
THOOM
THOOM
Rank 14: Victory Conditions!!
No. 91: Thunder Spark Dragon
ATK 2400 DEF 2000
IT'S NOT LIKE HAVING MORE OVERLAY UNITS MAKES IT BETTER!
...HEH.

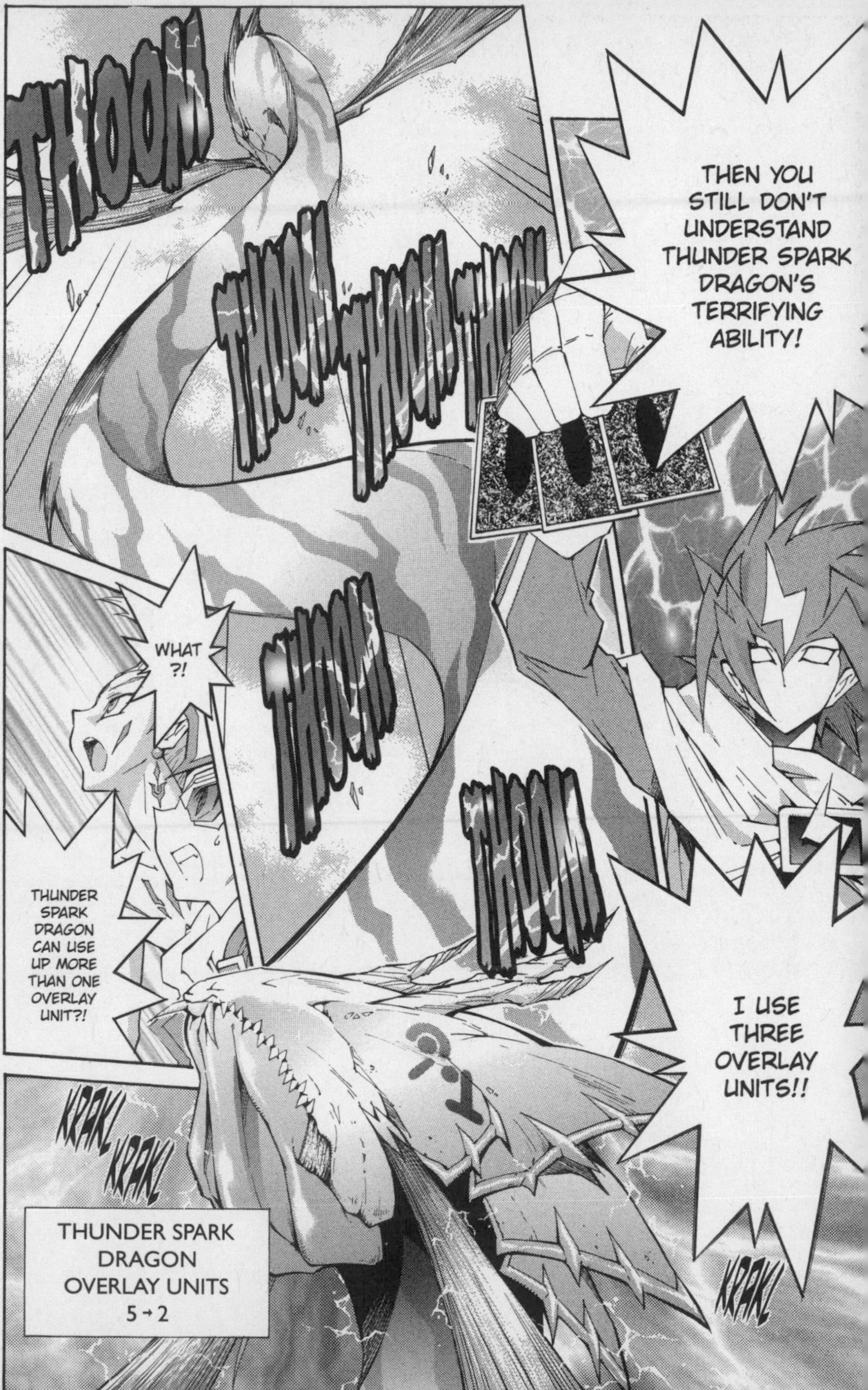
THEN YOU STILL DON'T UNDERSTAND THUNDER SPARK DRAGON'S TERRIFYING ABILITY!
THOOM
THOOM THOOM THOOM
THOOM
THOOM
I USE THREE OVERLAY UNITS!!
WHAT?!
THUNDER SPARK DRAGON CAN USE UP MORE THAN ONE OVERLAY UNIT?!
KRAK! KRAK!
KRAK!
THUNDER SPARK DRAGON OVERLAY UNITS 5→2

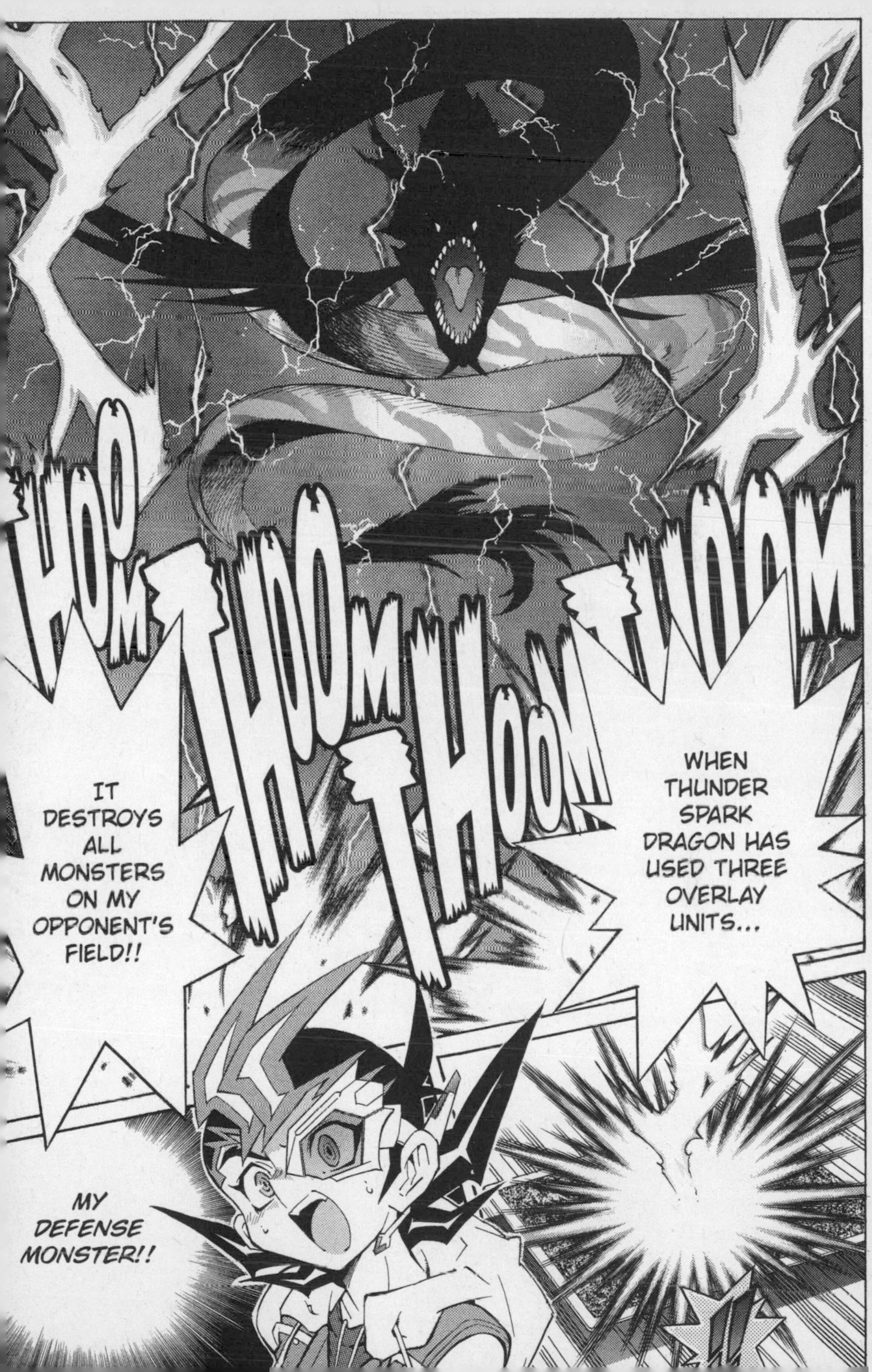
THOOM
THOOM
THOOM
HOOM
WHEN THUNDER SPARK DRAGON HAS USED THREE OVERLAY UNITS...
IT DESTROYS ALL MONSTERS ON MY OPPONENT'S FIELD!!
MY DEFENSE MONSTER!!

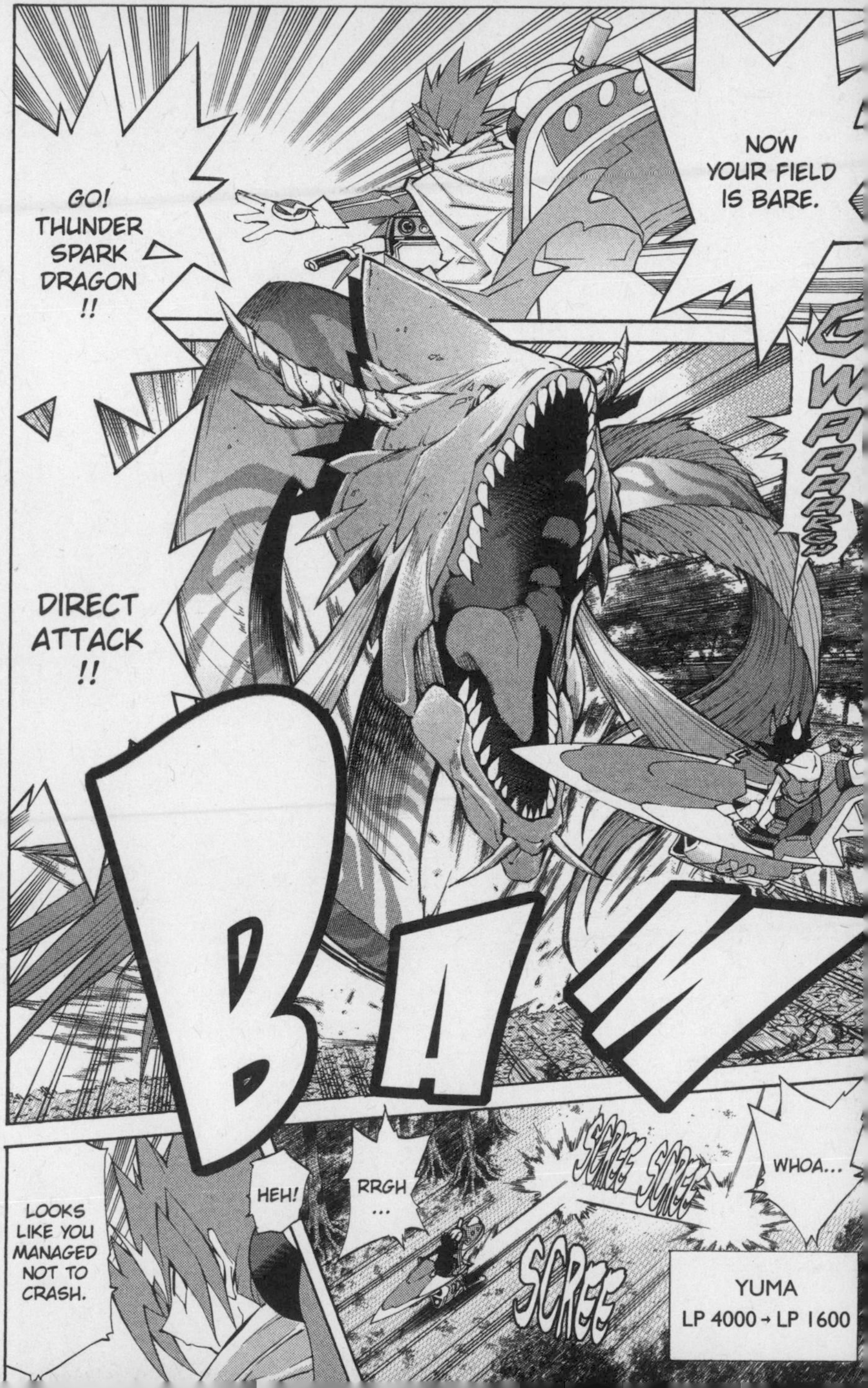
NOW YOUR FIELD IS BARE.
GO! THUNDER SPARK DRAGON !!
DIRECT ATTACK !!
BAM
WHOA...
SCREE SCREE
YUMA LP 4000 → LP 1600
SCREE
RRGH ...
HEH!
LOOKS LIKE YOU MANAGED NOT TO CRASH.

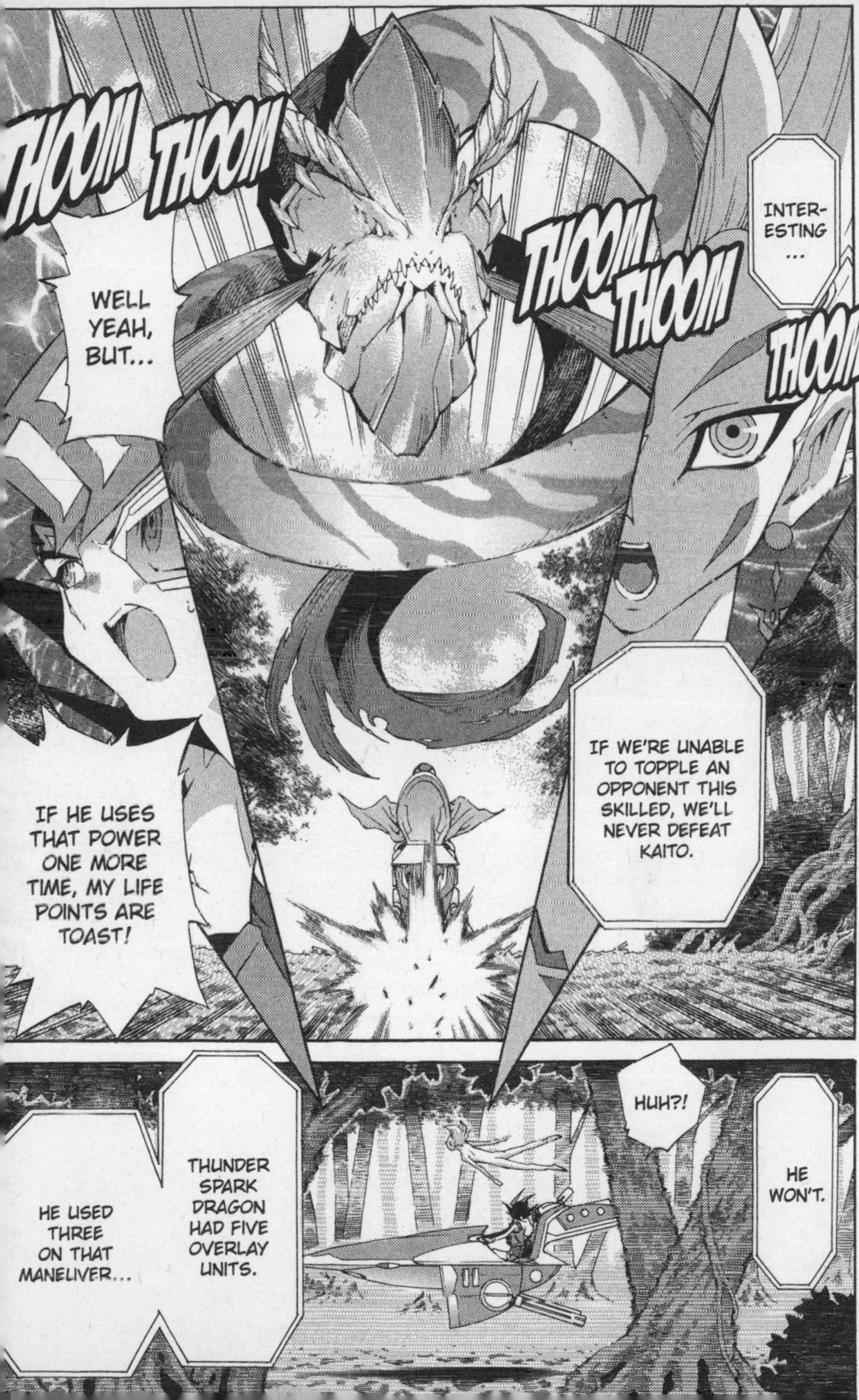
INTER-
ESTING
...
THOOM
THOOM THOOM
THOOM THOOM
WELL YEAH, BUT...
IF WE'RE UNABLE TO TOPPLE AN OPPONENT THIS SKILLED, WE'LL NEVER DEFEAT KAITO.
IF HE USES THAT POWER ONE MORE TIME, MY LIFE POINTS ARE TOAST!
HE WON'T.
HUH?!
THUNDER SPARK DRAGON HAD FIVE OVERLAY UNITS.
HE USED THREE ON THAT MANEUVER...

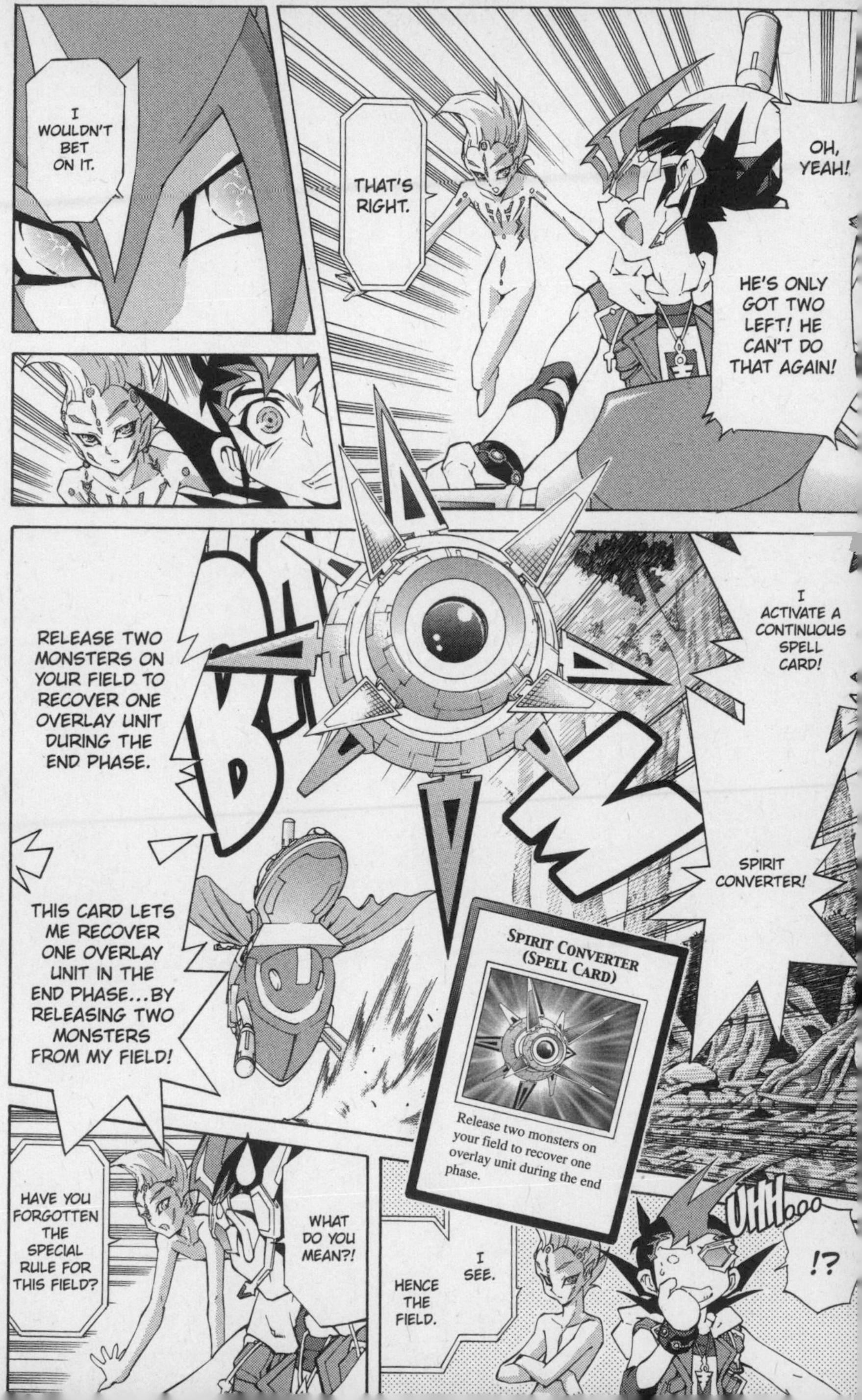
OH, YEAH!
HE'S ONLY GOT TWO LEFT! HE CAN'T DO THAT AGAIN!
THAT'S RIGHT.
I WOULDN'T BET ON IT.
I ACTIVATE A CONTINUOUS SPELL CARD!
SPIRIT CONVERTER!
SPIRIT CONVERTER (SPELL CARD)
Release two monsters on your field to recover one overlay unit during the end phase.
RELEASE TWO MONSTERS ON YOUR FIELD TO RECOVER ONE OVERLAY UNIT DURING THE END PHASE.
THIS CARD LETS ME RECOVER ONE OVERLAY UNIT IN THE END PHASE...BY RELEASING TWO MONSTERS FROM MY FIELD!
UHHooo
!?
I SEE.
HENCE THE FIELD.
WHAT DO YOU MEAN?!
HAVE YOU FORGOTTEN THE SPECIAL RULE FOR THIS FIELD?

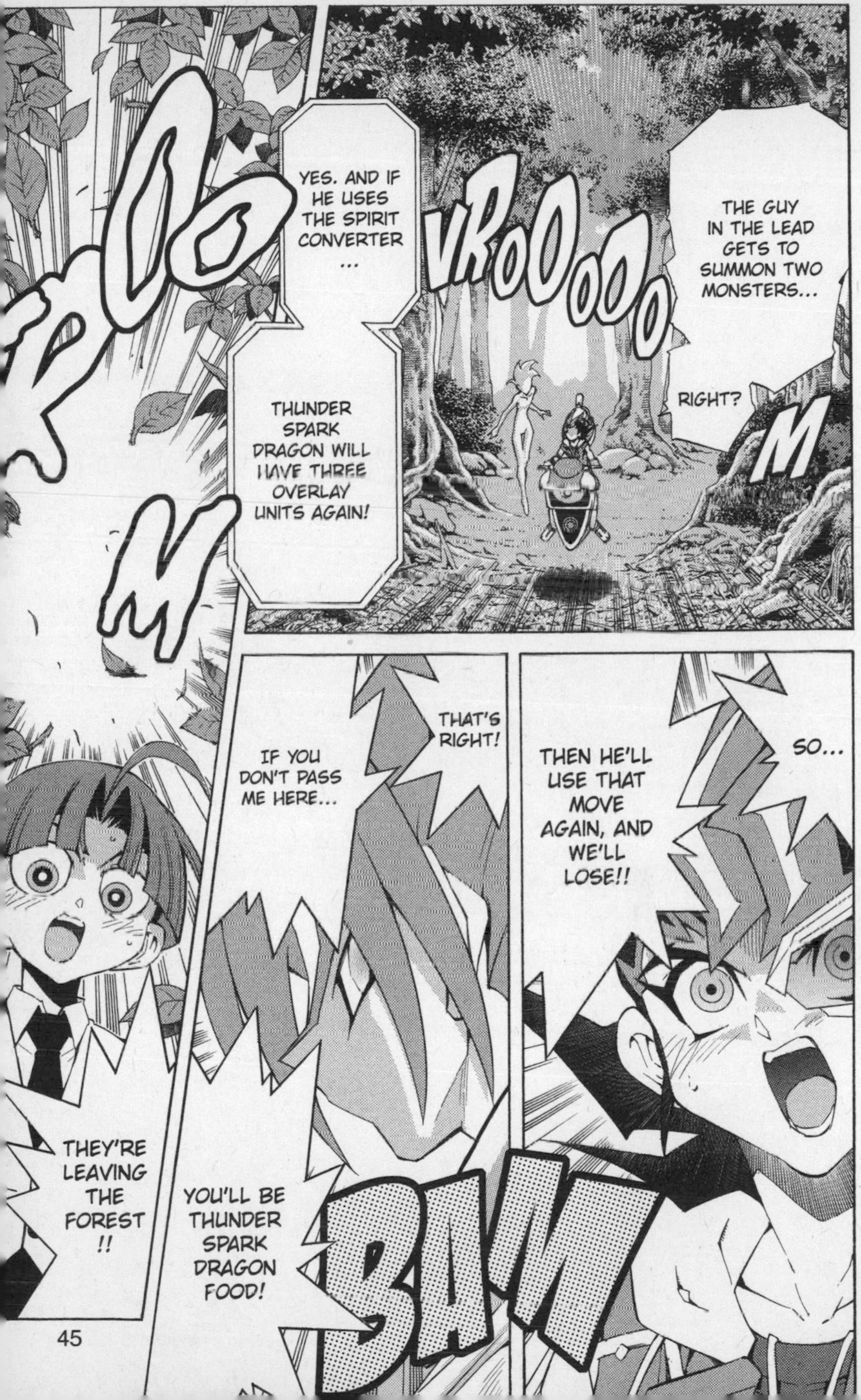
THE GUY IN THE LEAD GETS TO SUMMON TWO MONSTERS...
RIGHT?
YES. AND IF HE USES THE SPIRIT CONVERTER ...
THUNDER SPARK DRAGON WILL HAVE THREE OVERLAY UNITS AGAIN!
SO...
THEN HE'LL USE THAT MOVE AGAIN, AND WE'LL LOSE!!
BAM
THAT'S RIGHT!
IF YOU DON'T PASS ME HERE...
YOU'LL BE THUNDER SPARK DRAGON FOOD!
THEY'RE LEAVING THE FOREST !!

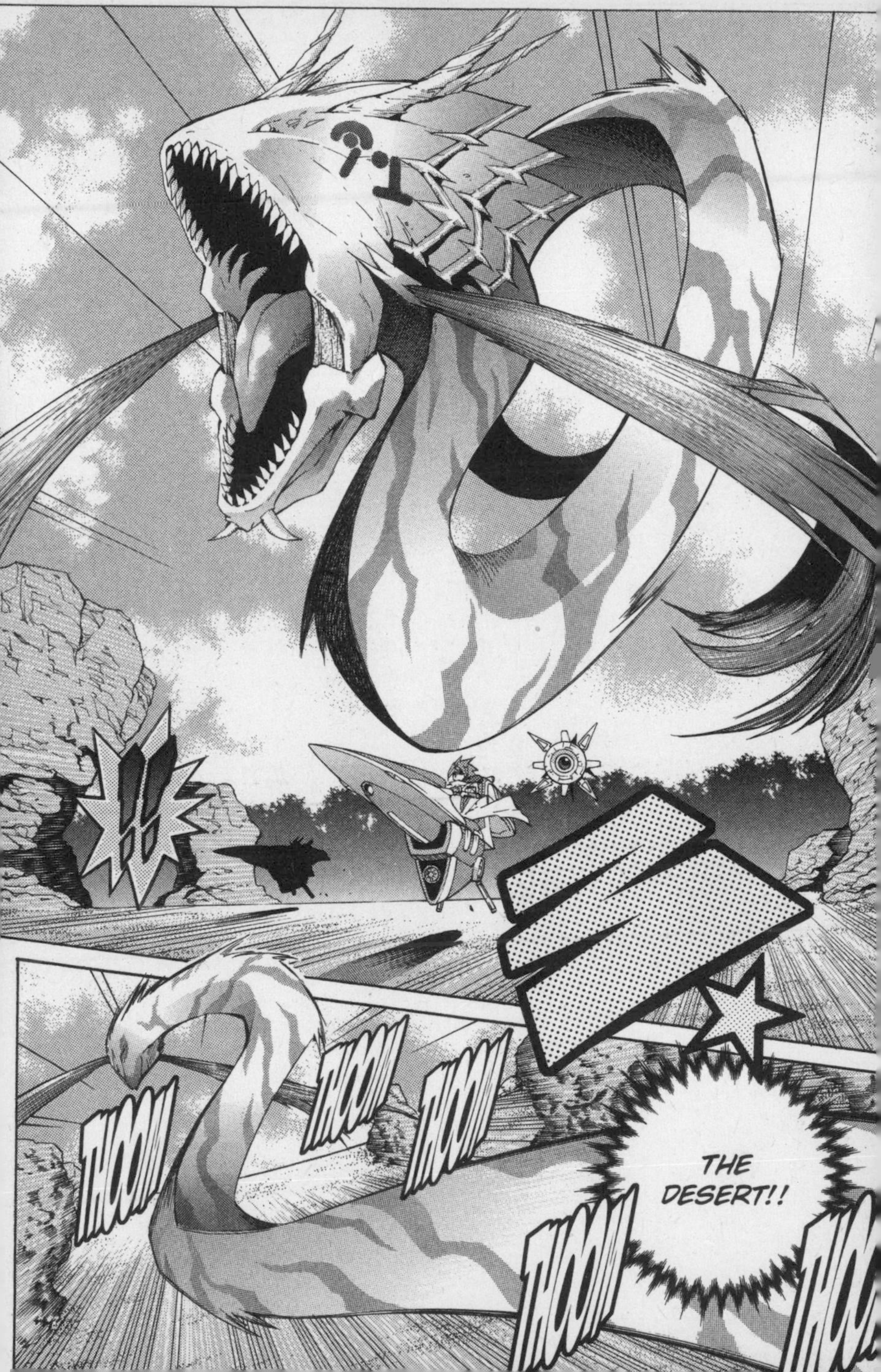
THE DESERT!!
THOOM
THOOM
THOOM
THOOM

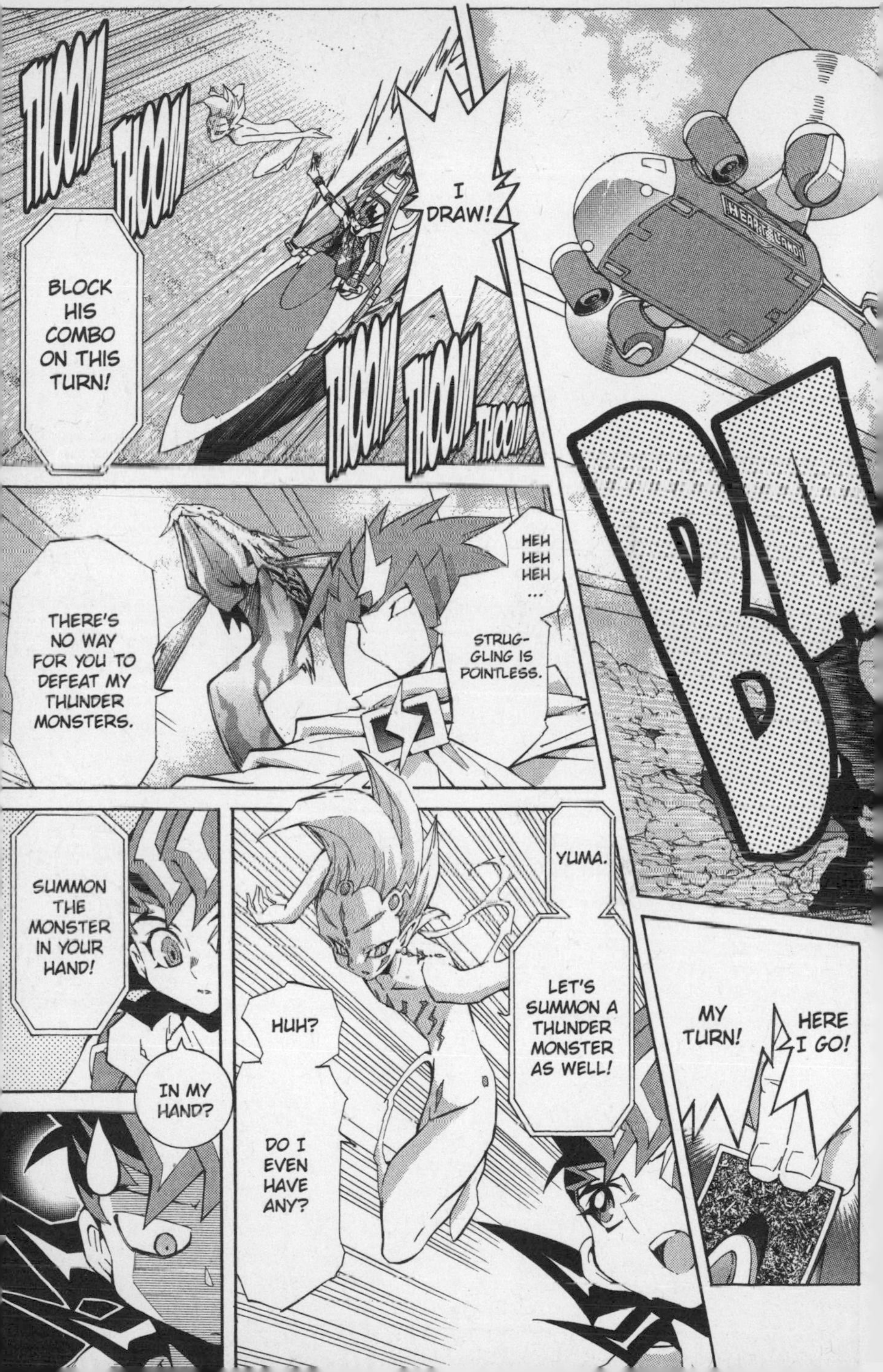
BA
I DRAW!
THOOM
THOOM
THOOM
THOOM
THOOM
BLOCK HIS COMBO ON THIS TURN!
HEH HEH HEH ...
STRUG-GLING IS POINTLESS.
THERE'S NO WAY FOR YOU TO DEFEAT MY THUNDER MONSTERS.
HERE I GO!
MY TURN!
YUMA.
LET'S SUMMON A THUNDER MONSTER AS WELL!
HUH?
DO I EVEN HAVE ANY?
SUMMON THE MONSTER IN YOUR HAND!
IN MY HAND?

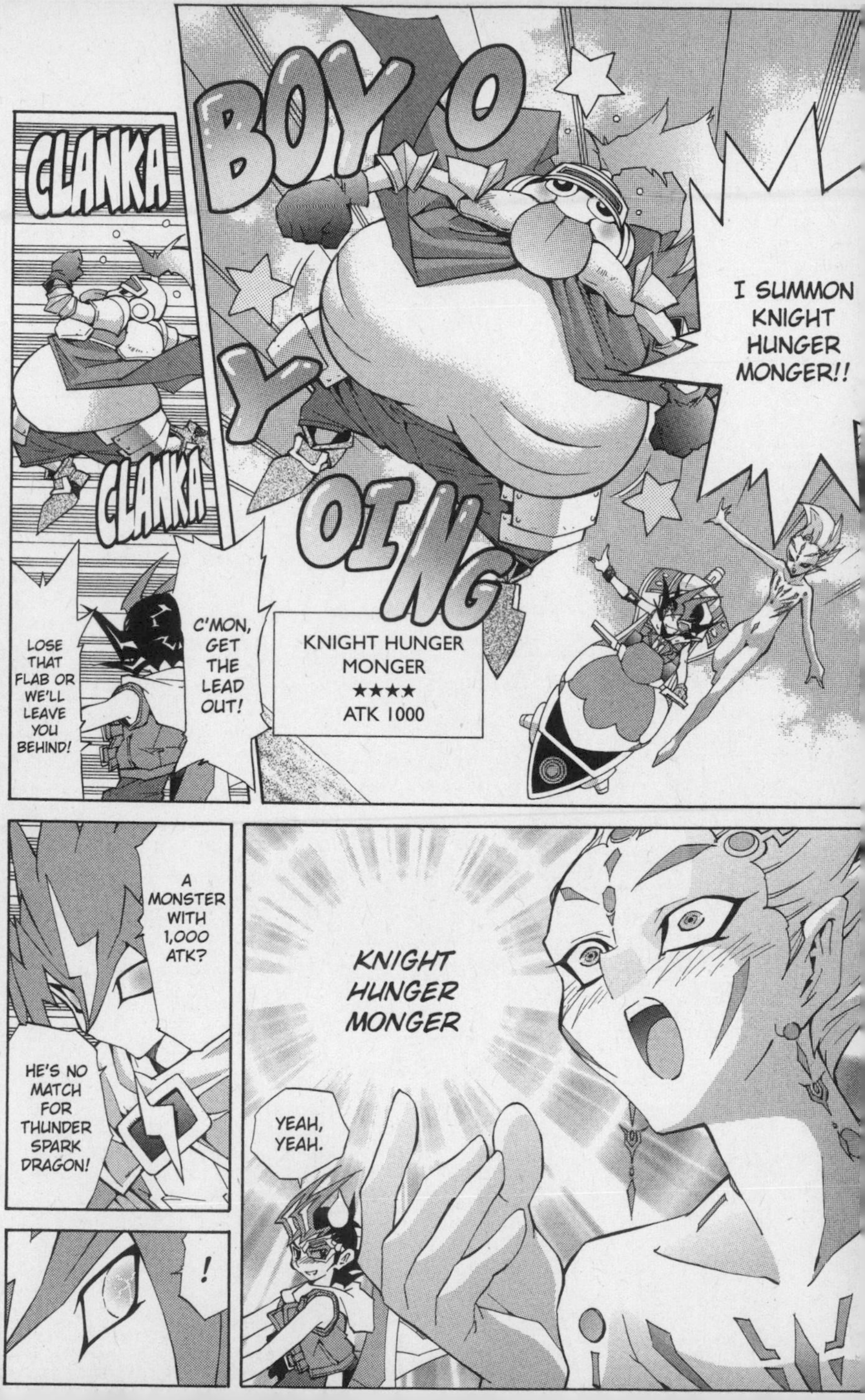
BOYOYOING
I SUMMON KNIGHT HUNGER MONGER!!
KNIGHT HUNGER MONGER ★★★★ ATK 1000
C'MON, GET THE LEAD OUT!
CLANKA
CLANKA
LOSE THAT FLAB OR WE'LL LEAVE YOU BEHIND!
KNIGHT HUNGER MONGER
YEAH, YEAH.
A MONSTER WITH 1,000 ATK?
HE'S NO MATCH FOR THUNDER SPARK DRAGON!
!

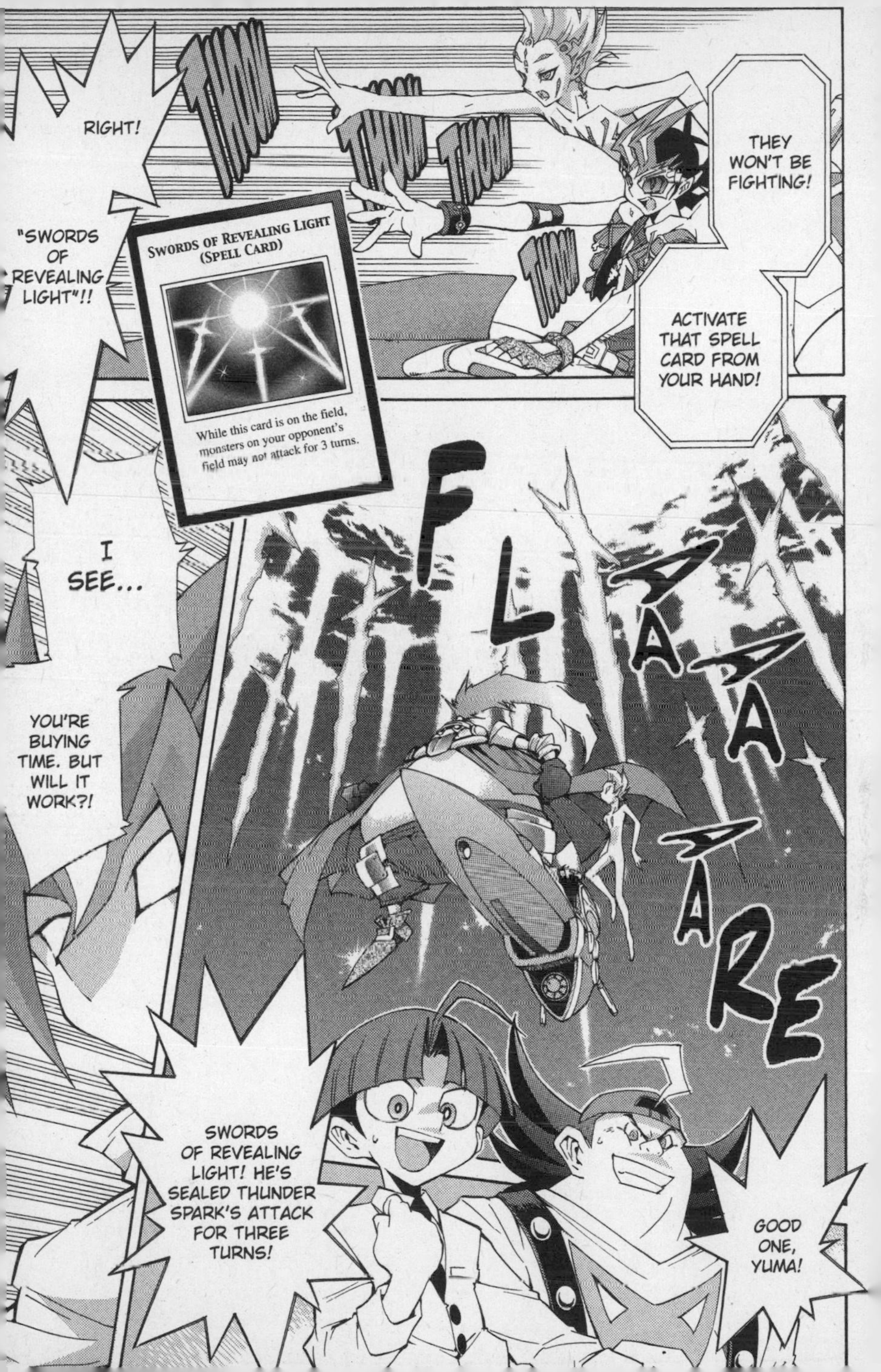
THEY WON'T BE FIGHTING!
ACTIVATE THAT SPELL CARD FROM YOUR HAND!
THOOM
THOOM
THOOM
THOOM
RIGHT!
"SWORDS OF REVEALING LIGHT"!!
Swords of Revealing Light (Spell Card)
While this card is on the field, monsters on your opponent's field may not attack for 3 turns.
FLAAAARE
SWORDS OF REVEALING LIGHT! HE'S SEALED THUNDER SPARK'S ATTACK FOR THREE TURNS!
GOOD ONE, YUMA!
I SEE...
YOU'RE BUYING TIME. BUT WILL IT WORK?!

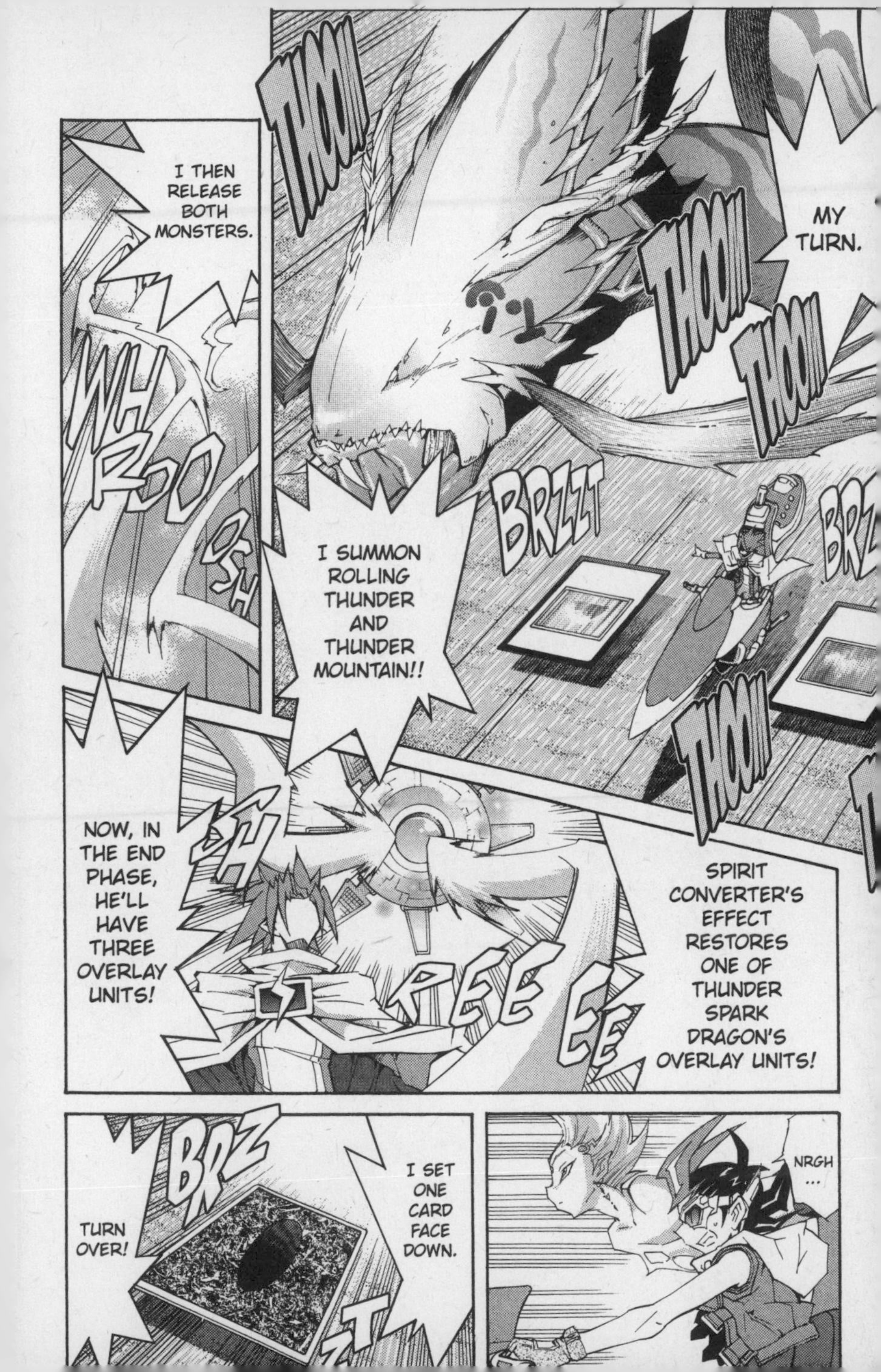
THOOM
MY TURN.
THOOM
THOOM
BRZZT
I SUMMON ROLLING THUNDER AND THUNDER MOUNTAIN!!
THOOM
I THEN RELEASE BOTH MONSTERS.
WHROOOSH
SPIRIT CONVERTER'S EFFECT RESTORES ONE OF THUNDER SPARK DRAGON'S OVERLAY UNITS!
PEEEEE
SHH
NOW, IN THE END PHASE, HE'LL HAVE THREE OVERLAY UNITS!
NRGH ...
I SET ONE CARD FACE DOWN.
BRZZT
TURN OVER!

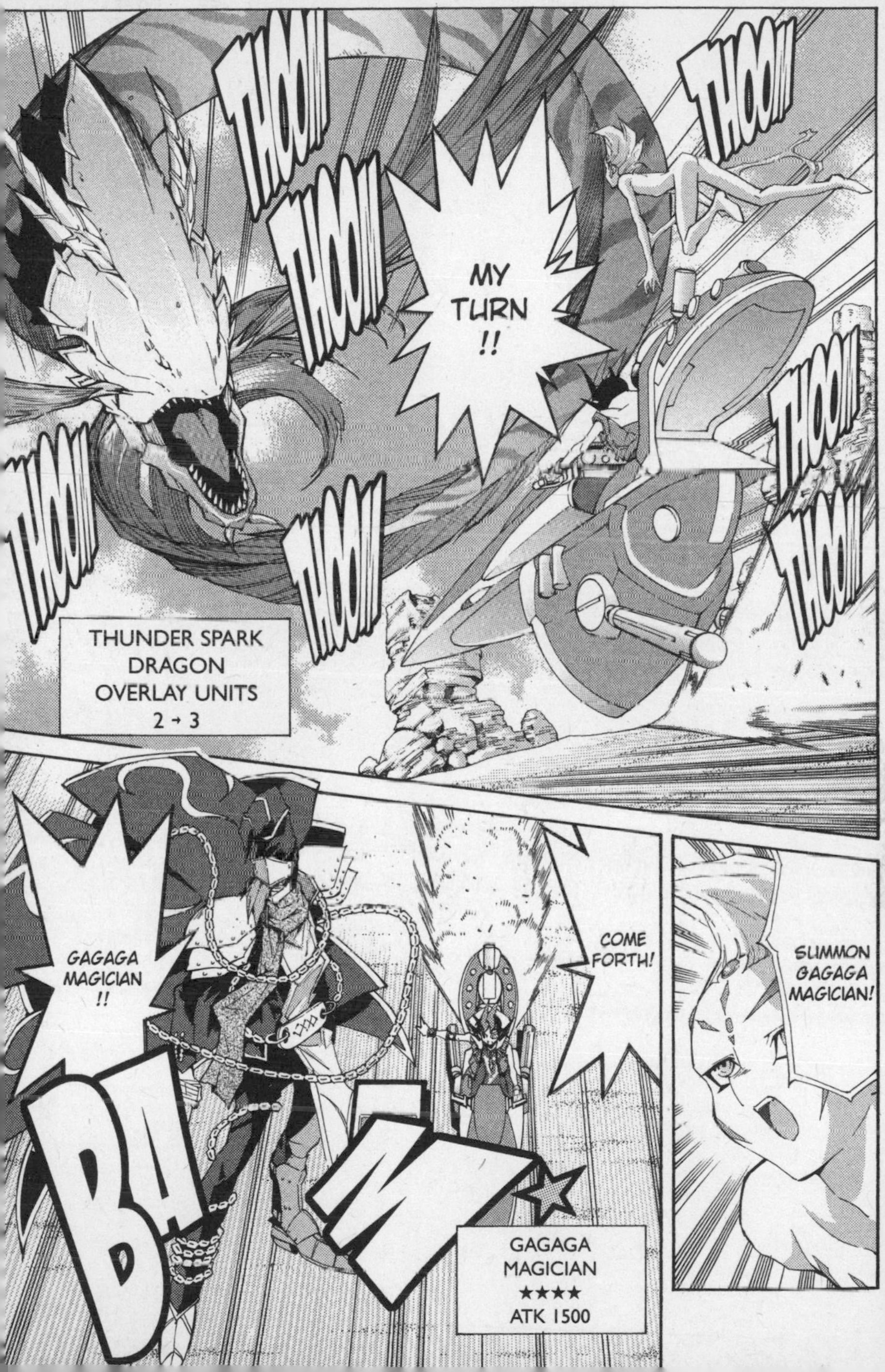
THOOM
THOOM
MY TURN !!
THOOM
THOOM
THOOM
THOOM
THOOM
THUNDER SPARK DRAGON OVERLAY UNITS 2 → 3
SUMMON GAGAGA MAGICIAN!
COME FORTH!
GAGAGA MAGICIAN !!
BAM
GAGAGA MAGICIAN ★★★★ ATK 1500

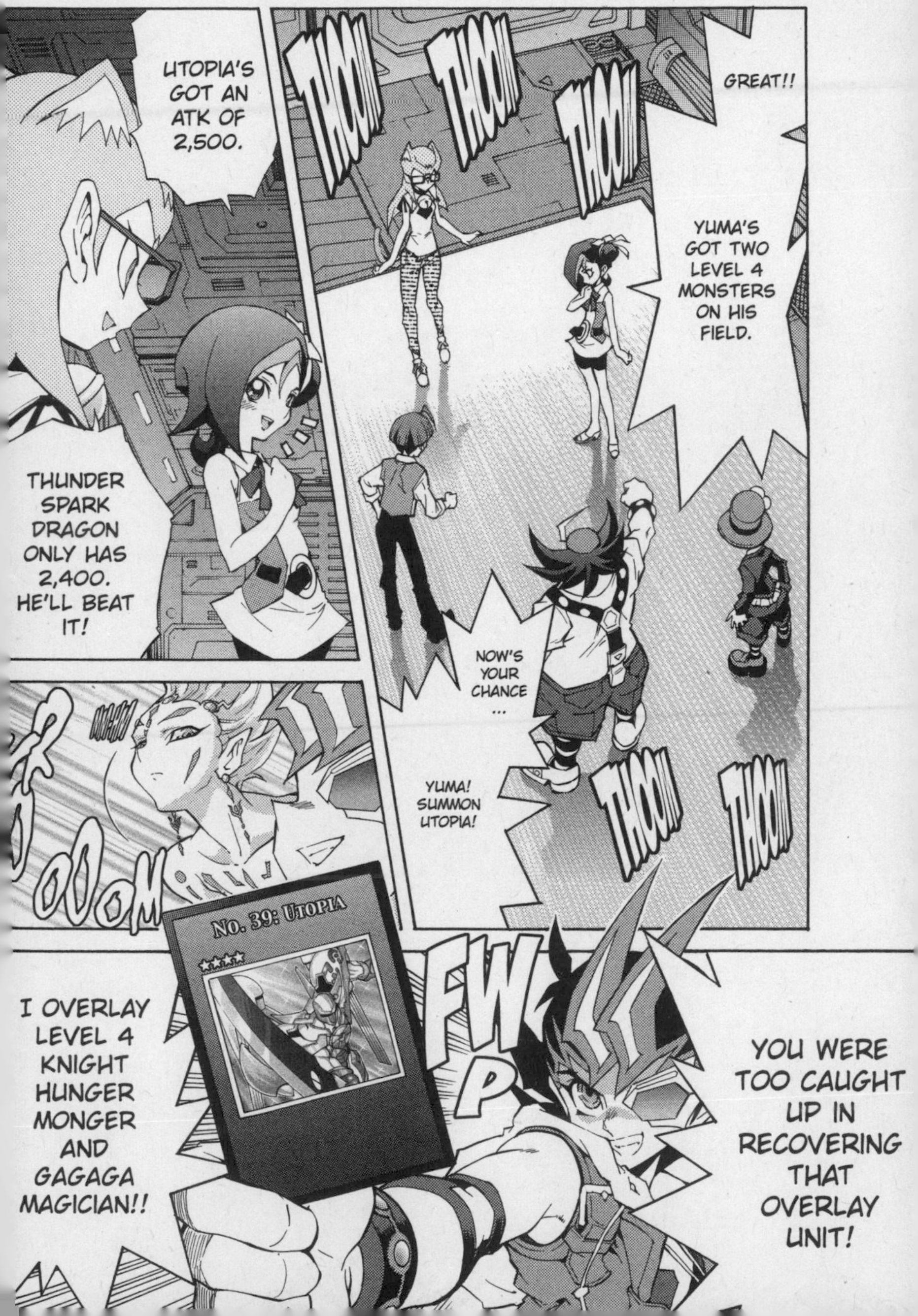
GREAT!!
THOOM
THOOM
THOOM
YUMA'S GOT TWO LEVEL 4 MONSTERS ON HIS FIELD.
NOW'S YOUR CHANCE ...
YUMA! SUMMON UTOPIA!
THOOM
THOOM
UTOPIA'S GOT AN ATK OF 2,500.
THUNDER SPARK DRAGON ONLY HAS 2,400. HE'LL BEAT IT!
VOOOM
YOU WERE TOO CAUGHT UP IN RECOVERING THAT OVERLAY UNIT!
FWP
No. 39: UTOPIA
I OVERLAY LEVEL 4 KNIGHT HUNGER MONGER AND GAGAGA MAGICIAN!!

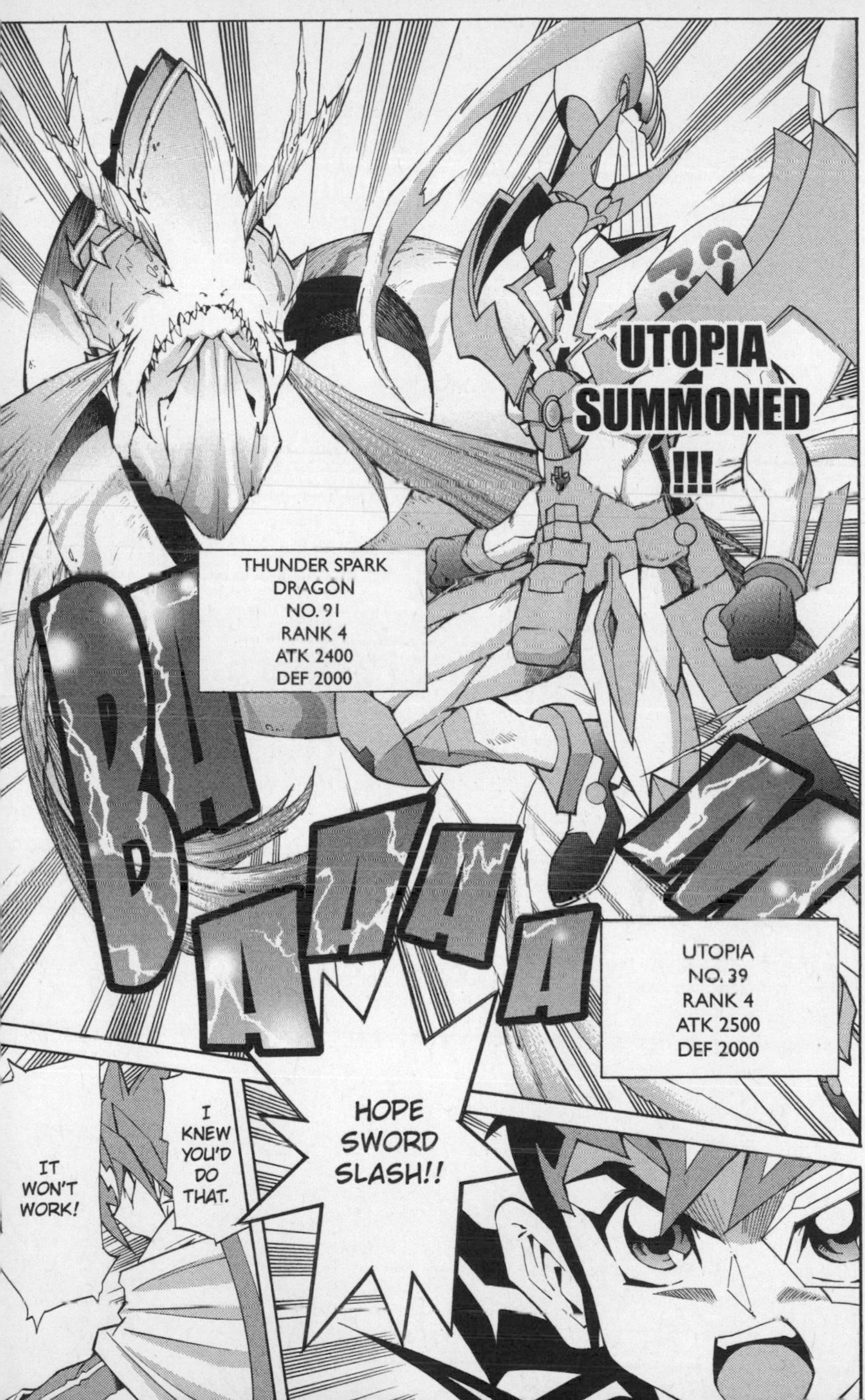
UTOPIA SUMMONED!!!
THUNDER SPARK DRAGON NO. 91 RANK 4 ATK 2400 DEF 2000
BAAAAAM
UTOPIA NO. 39 RANK 4 ATK 2500 DEF 2000
HOPE SWORD SLASH!!
I KNEW YOU'D DO THAT.
IT WON'T WORK!

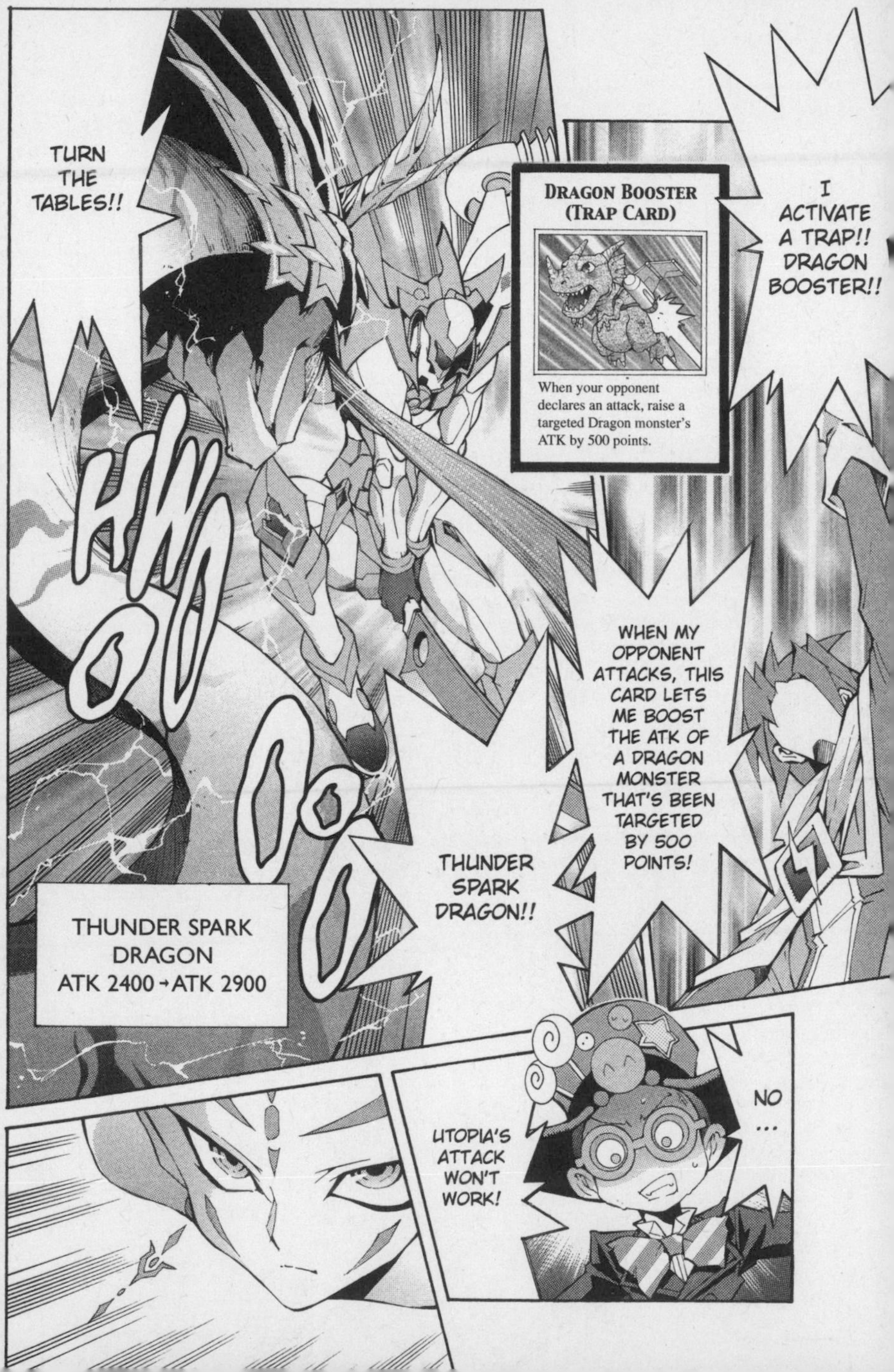
I ACTIVATE A TRAP!! DRAGON BOOSTER!!
DRAGON BOOSTER (TRAP CARD)
When your opponent declares an attack, raise a targeted Dragon monster's ATK by 500 points.
TURN THE TABLES!!
WHEN MY OPPONENT ATTACKS, THIS CARD LETS ME BOOST THE ATK OF A DRAGON MONSTER THAT'S BEEN TARGETED BY 500 POINTS!
THUNDER SPARK DRAGON!!
HWOOOO
THUNDER SPARK DRAGON ATK 2400→ATK 2900
NO ...
UTOPIA'S ATTACK WON'T WORK!

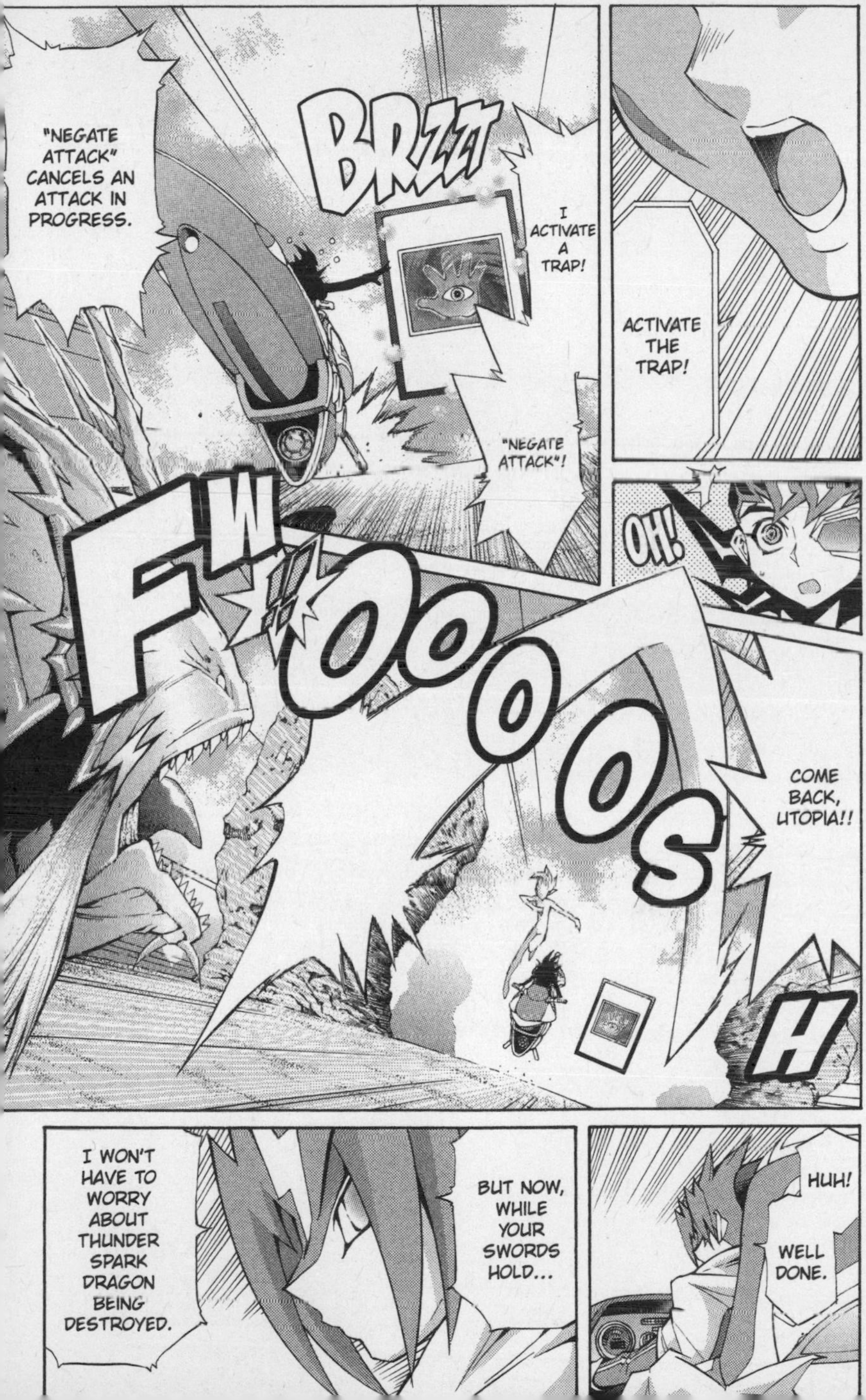
ACTIVATE THE TRAP!
BRZZT
I ACTIVATE A TRAP!
"NEGATE ATTACK"!
"NEGATE ATTACK" CANCELS AN ATTACK IN PROGRESS.
OH!
FWOOOOSH
COME BACK, UTOPIA!!
HUH!
WELL DONE.
BUT NOW, WHILE YOUR SWORDS HOLD...
I WON'T HAVE TO WORRY ABOUT THUNDER SPARK DRAGON BEING DESTROYED.

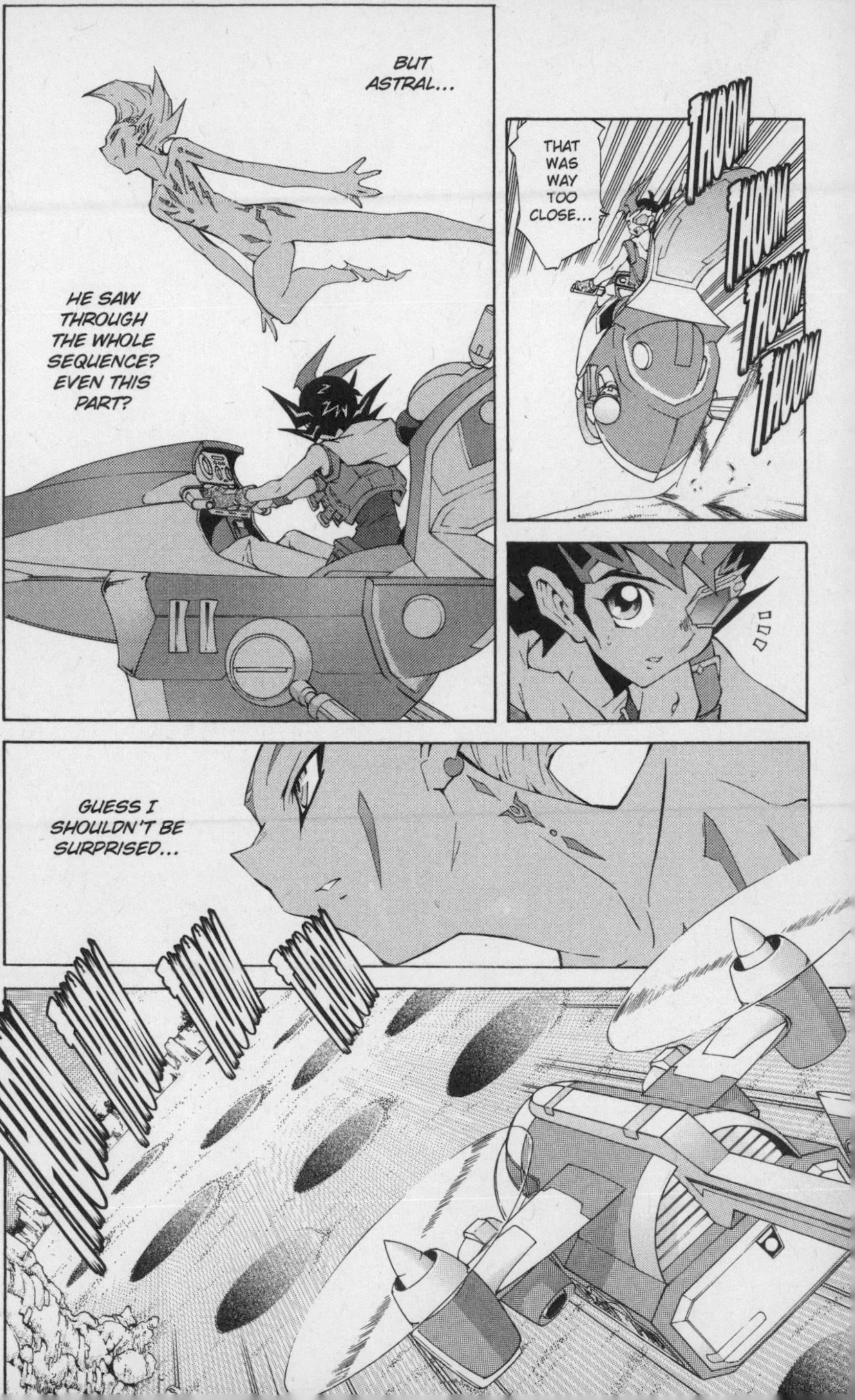
THAT WAS WAY TOO CLOSE...
THOOM THOOM THOOM THOOM
BUT ASTRAL...
HE SAW THROUGH THE WHOLE SEQUENCE? EVEN THIS PART?
GUESS I SHOULDN'T BE SURPRISED...

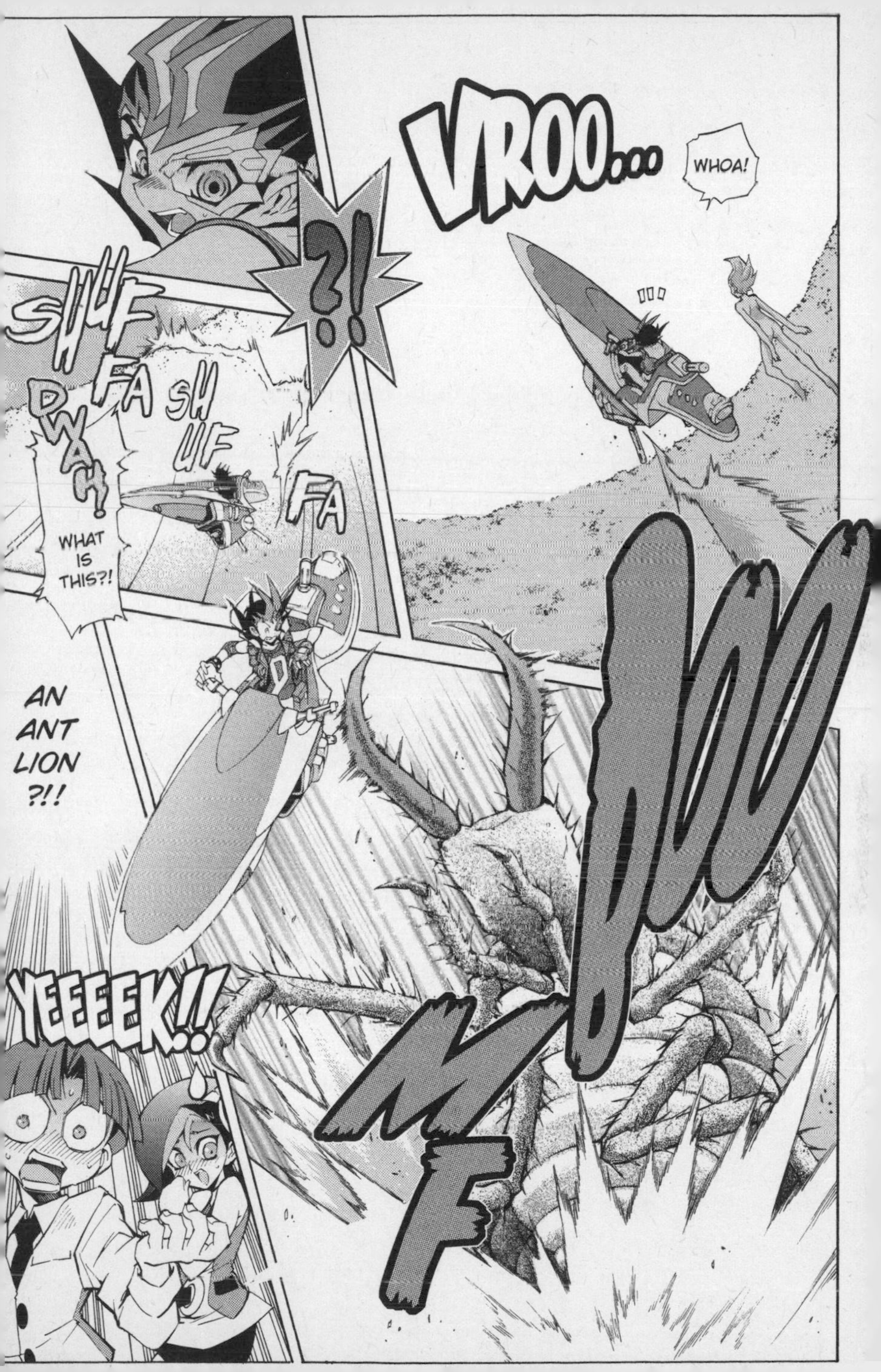
VROO...
WHOA!
...
?!
SHUF
FA
SHUF
FA
DWAH!
WHAT IS THIS?!
AN ANT LION ?!!
YEEEEK!!

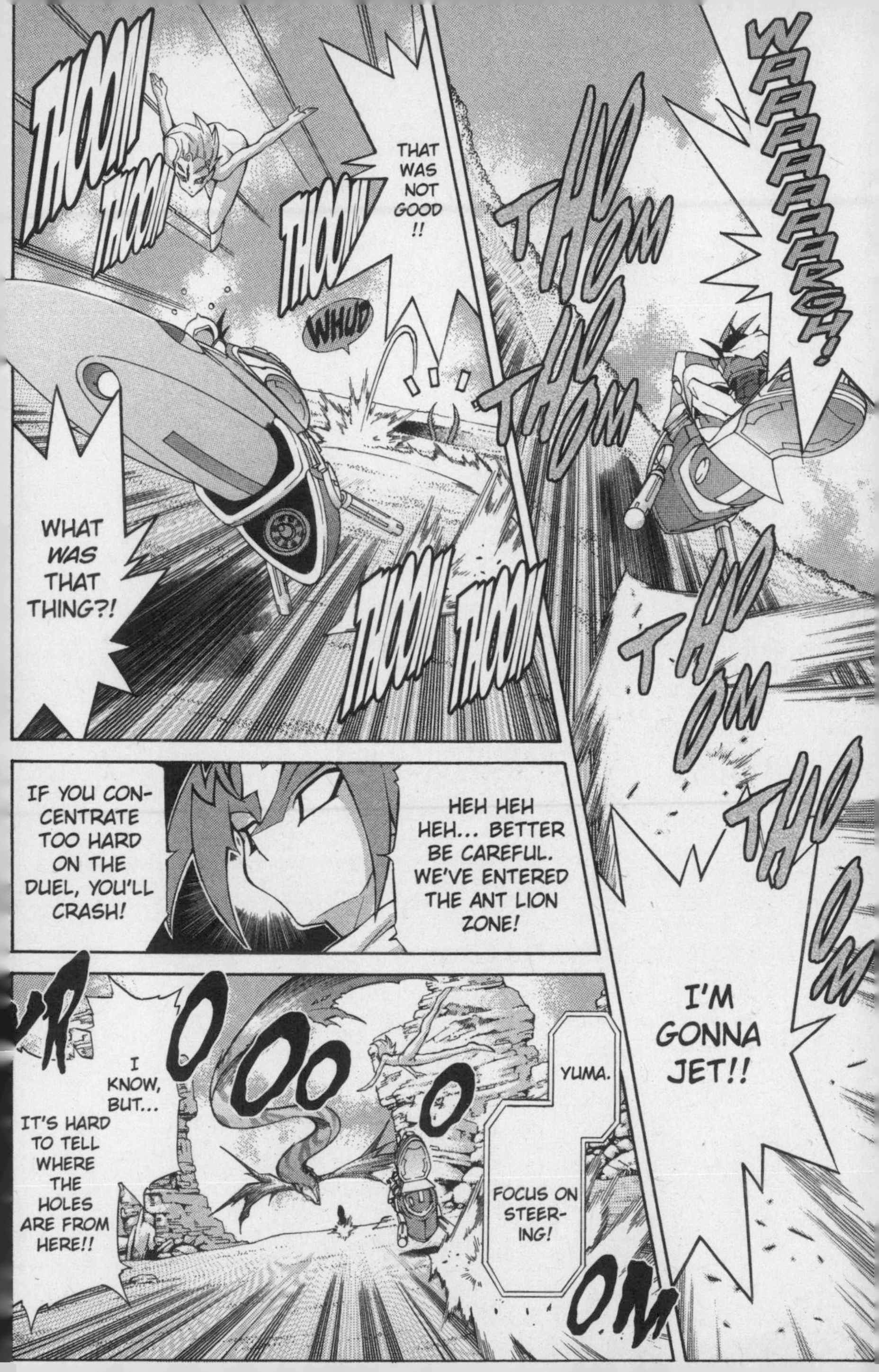
WAAAAAAAAGH!
THOOM
THOOM
THOOM
THOOOM
I'M GONNA JET!!
THOOM
THOOM
THOOM
THAT WAS NOT GOOD!!
WHUD
...
WHAT *WAS* THAT THING?!
THOOM
THOOM
HEH HEH HEH... BETTER BE CAREFUL. WE'VE ENTERED THE ANT LION ZONE!
IF YOU CON-CENTRATE TOO HARD ON THE DUEL, YOU'LL CRASH!
YUMA.
FOCUS ON STEER-ING!
VROOOOOOM
I KNOW, BUT...
IT'S HARD TO TELL WHERE THE HOLES ARE FROM HERE!!

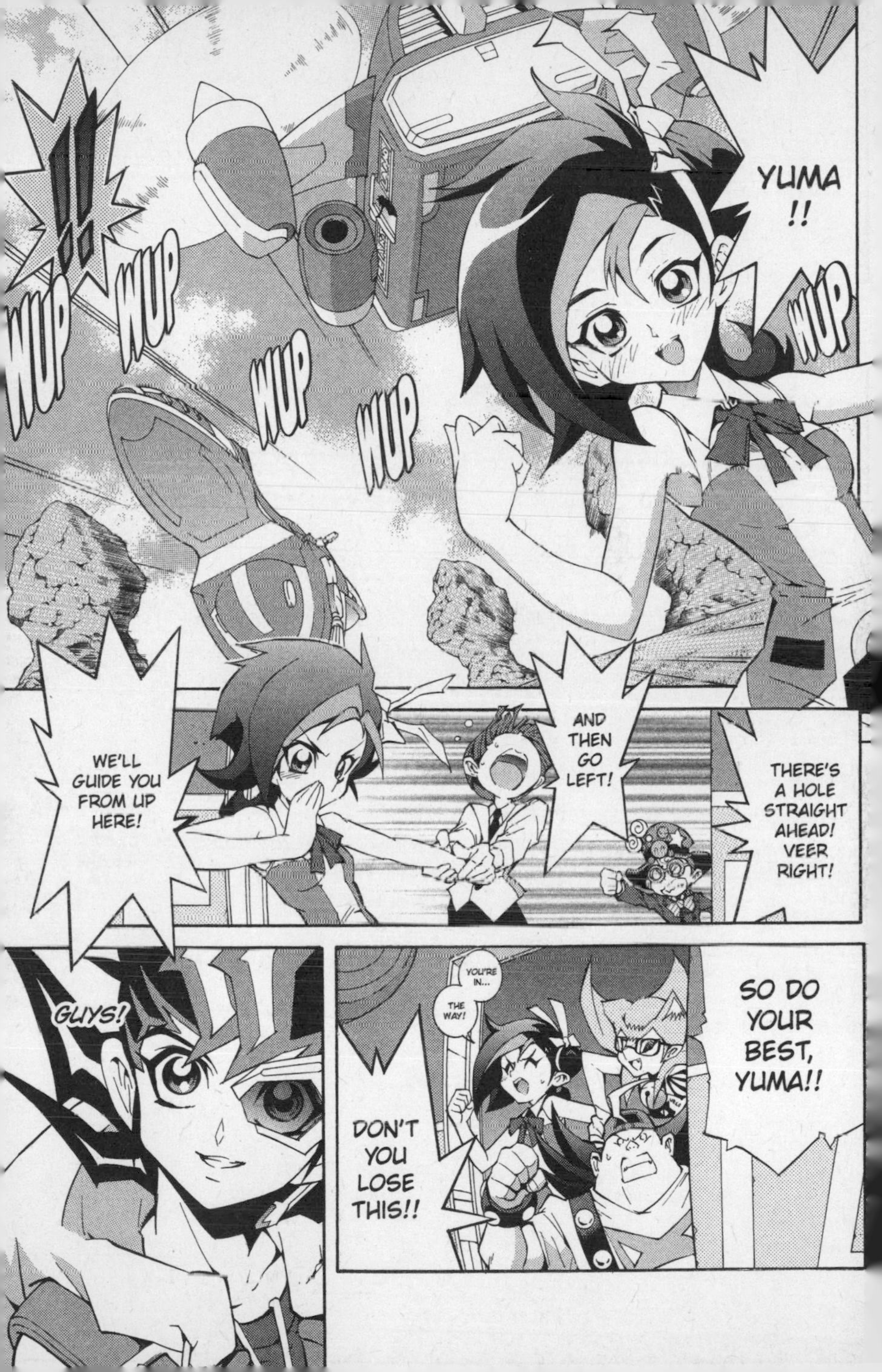
YUMA!!
WUP
WUP
WUP
WUP
WUP
!!
THERE'S A HOLE STRAIGHT AHEAD! VEER RIGHT!
AND THEN GO LEFT!
WE'LL GUIDE YOU FROM UP HERE!
SO DO YOUR BEST, YUMA!!
YOU'RE IN...
THE WAY!
DON'T YOU LOSE THIS!!
GUYS!

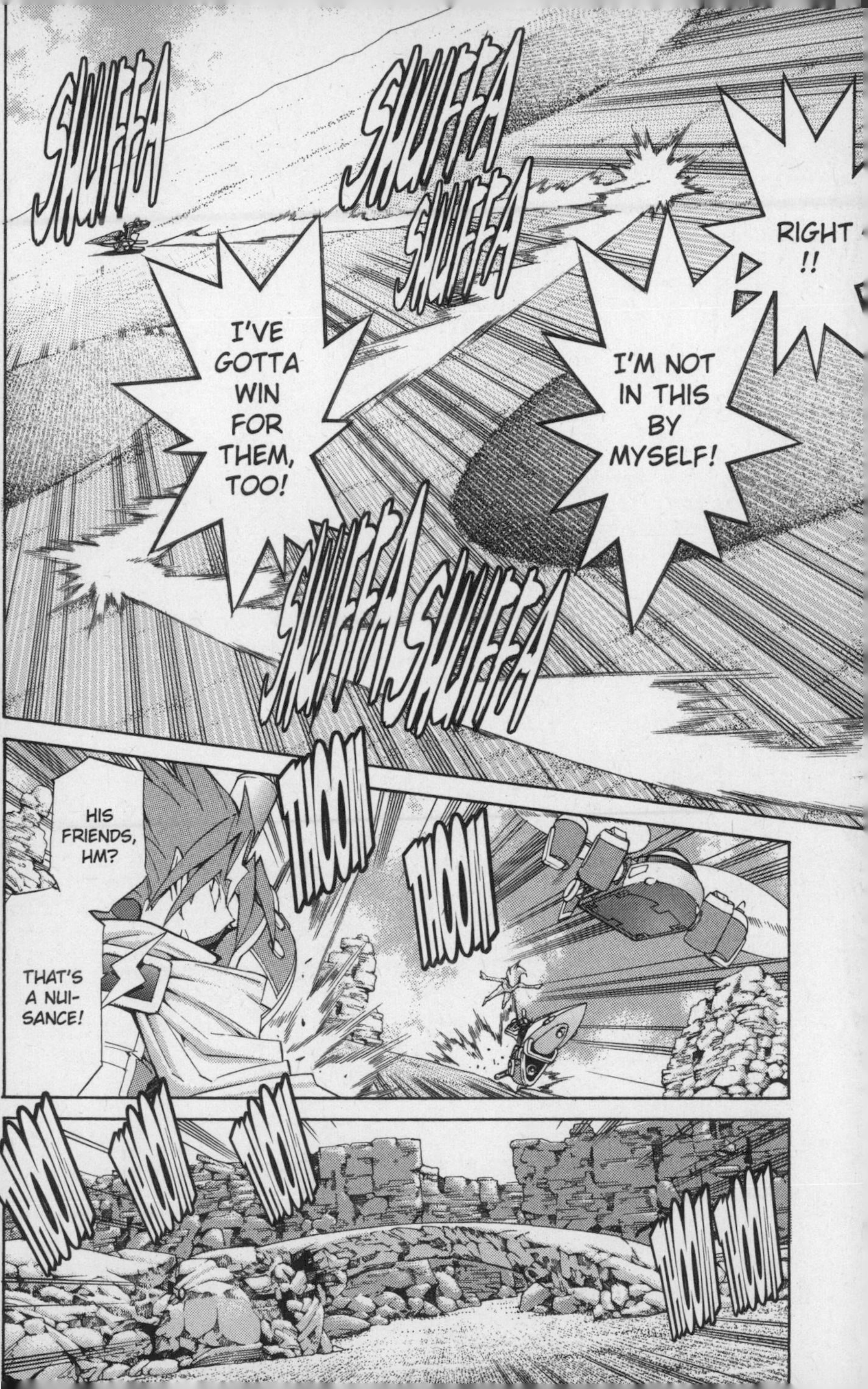
RIGHT!!
I'M NOT IN THIS BY MYSELF!
I'VE GOTTA WIN FOR THEM, TOO!
THOOM
THOOM
HIS FRIENDS, HM?
THAT'S A NUI-SANCE!
THOOM THOOM
THOOM THOOM THOOM

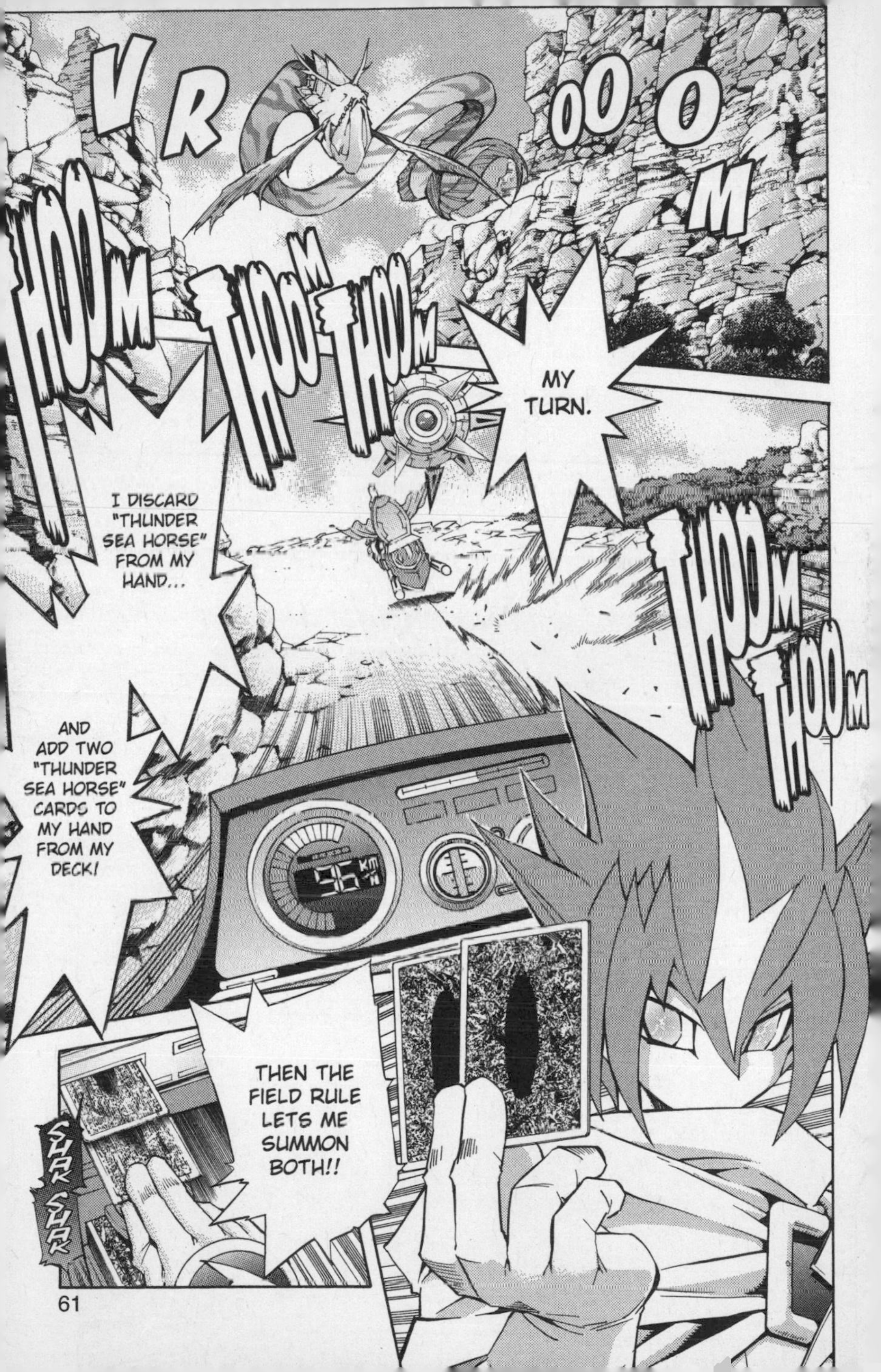
VROOOOM
THOOM THOOM THOOM
MY TURN.
THOOM THOOM
I DISCARD "THUNDER SEA HORSE" FROM MY HAND...
AND ADD TWO "THUNDER SEA HORSE" CARDS TO MY HAND FROM MY DECK!
96 km/h
THEN THE FIELD RULE LETS ME SUMMON BOTH!!
SHAK SHAK

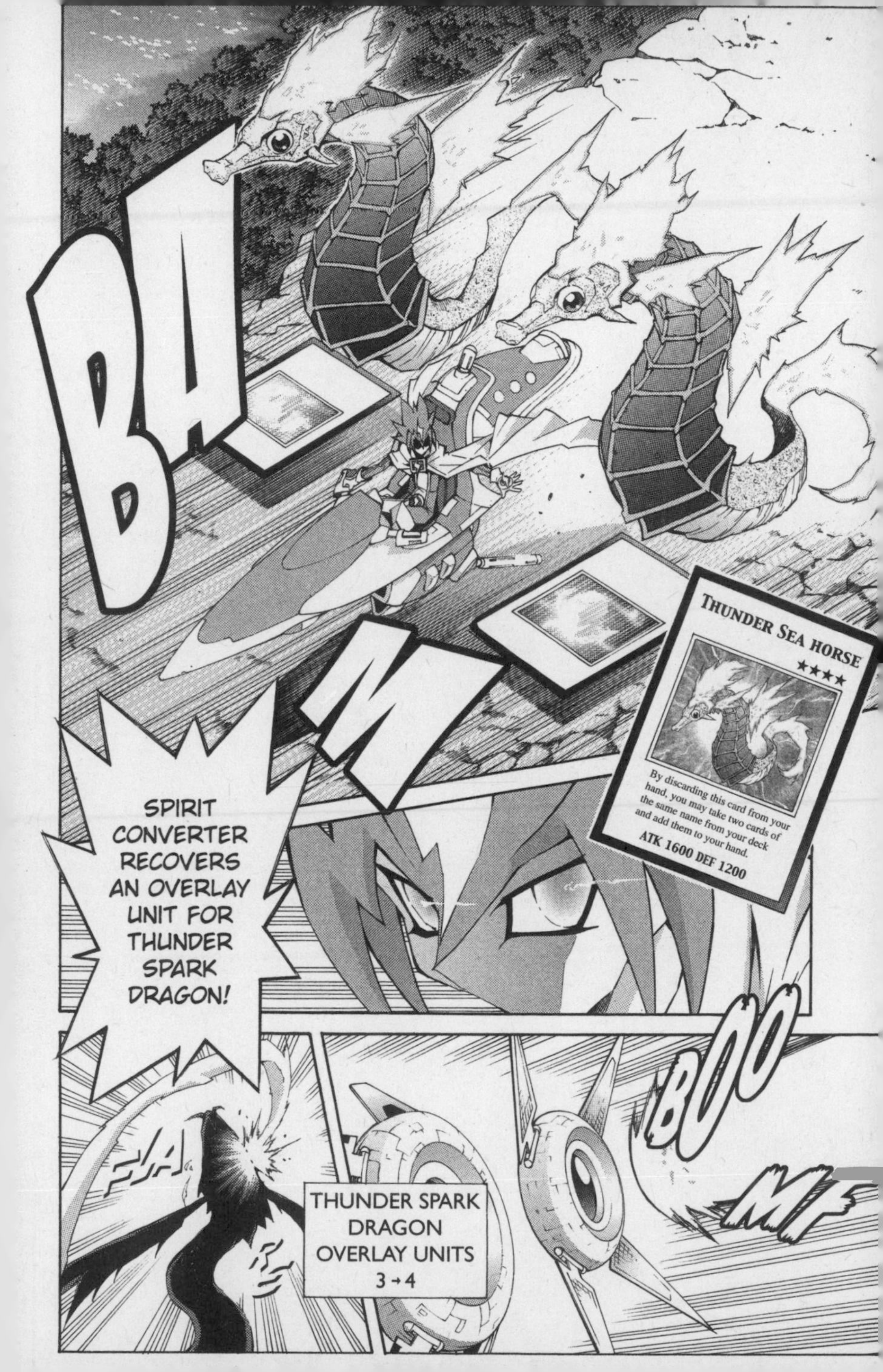
BAM
THUNDER SEA HORSE
★★★★
By discarding this card from your hand, you may take two cards of the same name from your deck and add them to your hand.
ATK 1600 DEF 1200
SPIRIT CONVERTER RECOVERS AN OVERLAY UNIT FOR THUNDER SPARK DRAGON!
BOOM
THUNDER SPARK DRAGON OVERLAY UNITS 3→4

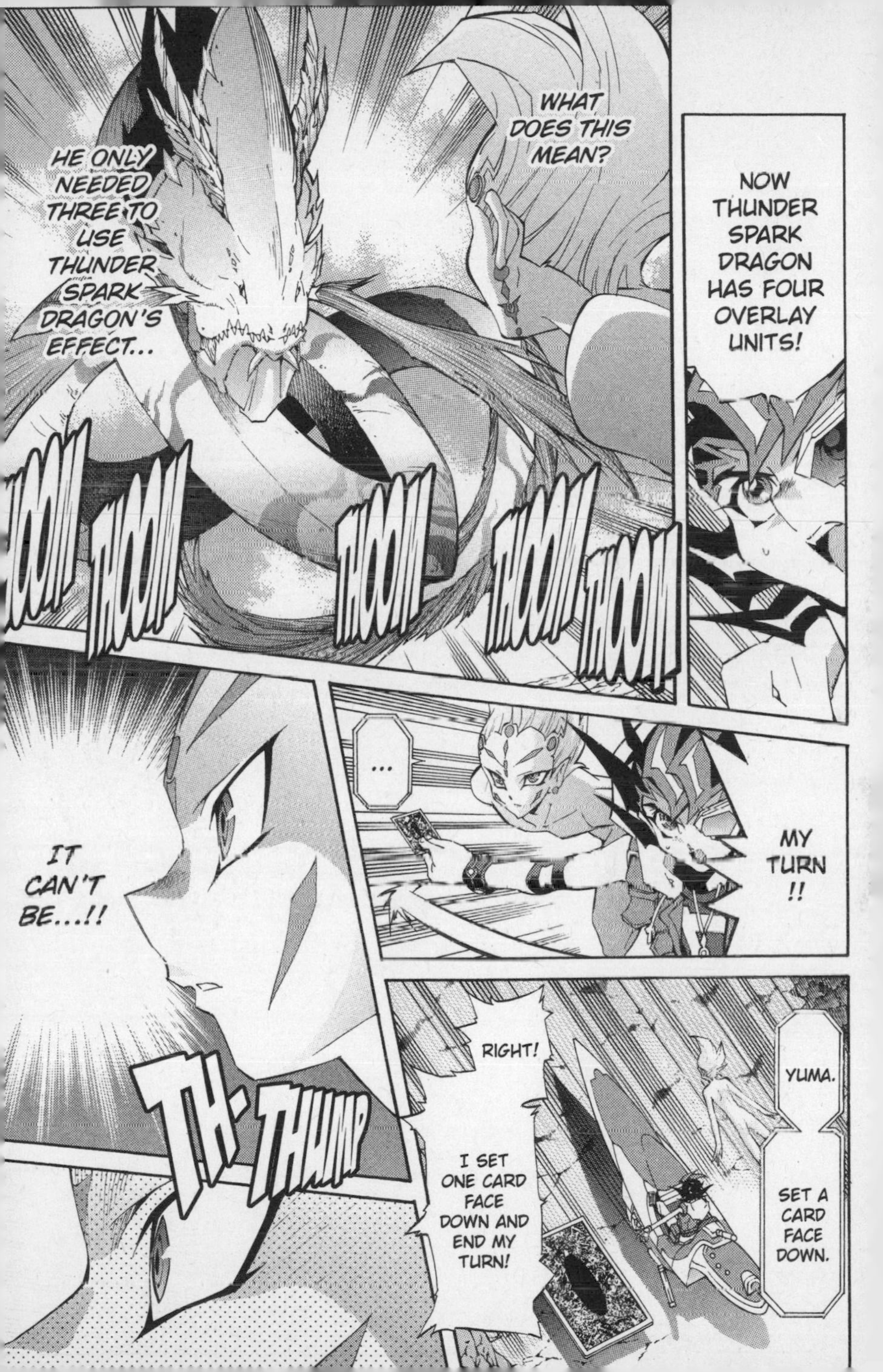
NOW THUNDER SPARK DRAGON HAS FOUR OVERLAY UNITS!
WHAT DOES THIS MEAN?
HE ONLY NEEDED THREE TO USE THUNDER SPARK DRAGON'S EFFECT...
THOOM
THOOM
THOOM
THOOM
THOOM
MY TURN!!
...
YUMA.
SET A CARD FACE DOWN.
RIGHT!
I SET ONE CARD FACE DOWN AND END MY TURN!
IT CAN'T BE...!!
TH-THUMP

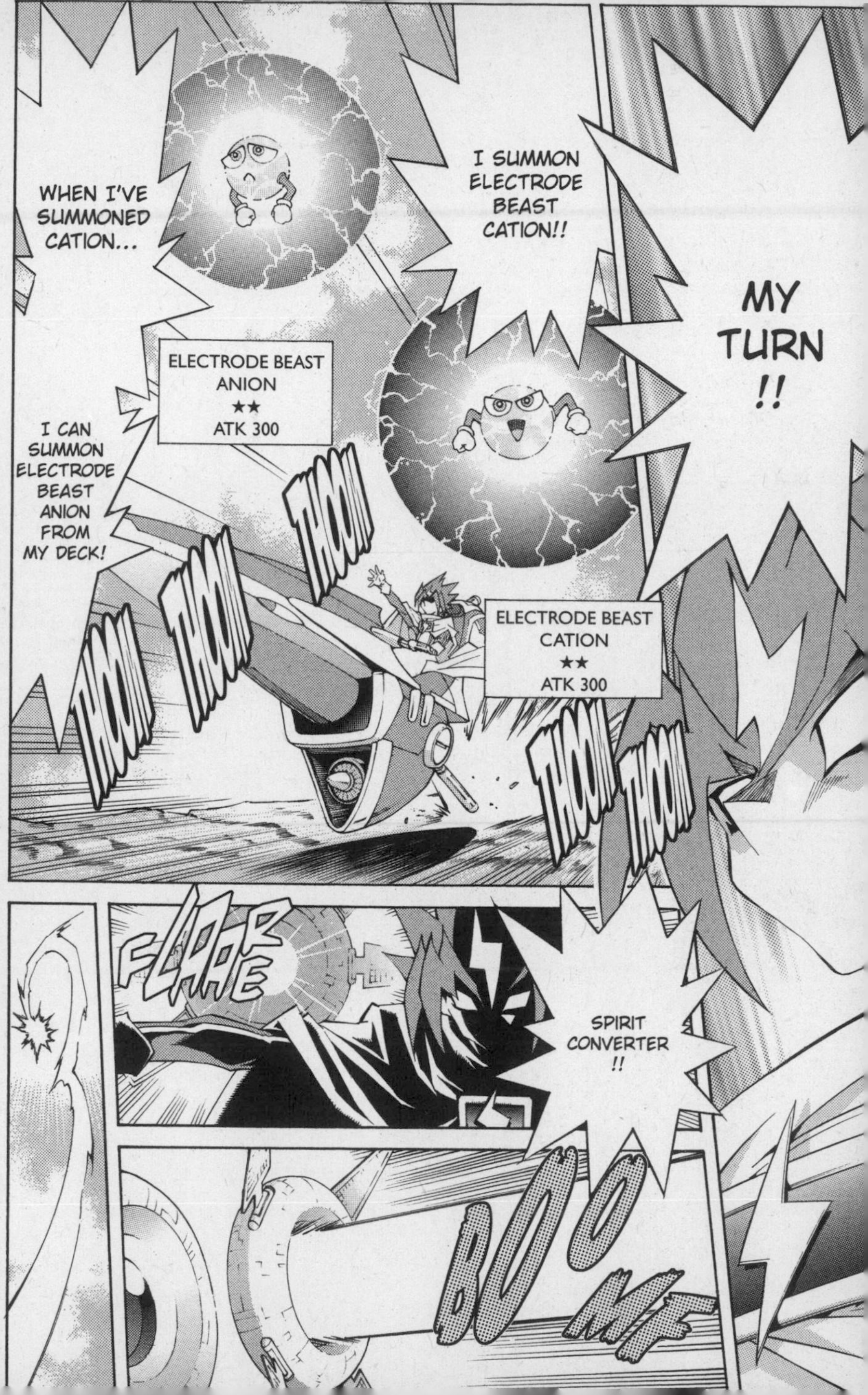
MY TURN!!
I SUMMON ELECTRODE BEAST CATION!!
ELECTRODE BEAST CATION ★★ ATK 300
THOOM
THOOM
WHEN I'VE SUMMONED CATION...
I CAN SUMMON ELECTRODE BEAST ANION FROM MY DECK!
ELECTRODE BEAST ANION ★★ ATK 300
THOOM
THOOM
THOOM
SPIRIT CONVERTER!!
FLARE
BOOOMF

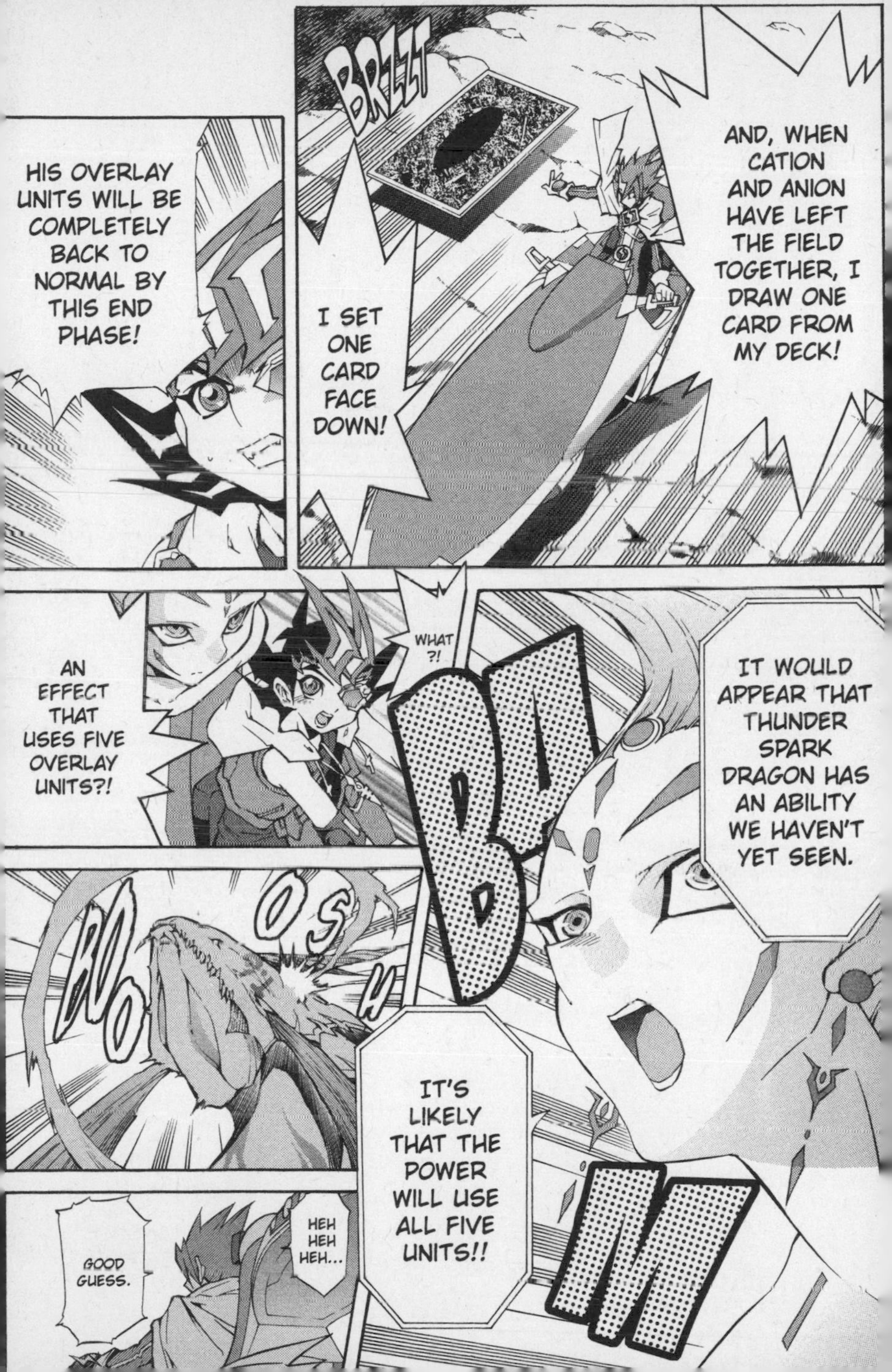
BREZZT
AND, WHEN CATION AND ANION HAVE LEFT THE FIELD TOGETHER, I DRAW ONE CARD FROM MY DECK!
I SET ONE CARD FACE DOWN!
HIS OVERLAY UNITS WILL BE COMPLETELY BACK TO NORMAL BY THIS END PHASE!
IT WOULD APPEAR THAT THUNDER SPARK DRAGON HAS AN ABILITY WE HAVEN'T YET SEEN.
BAM
IT'S LIKELY THAT THE POWER WILL USE ALL FIVE UNITS!!
WHAT ?!
AN EFFECT THAT USES FIVE OVERLAY UNITS?!
BOOOSH
HEH HEH HEH...
GOOD GUESS.

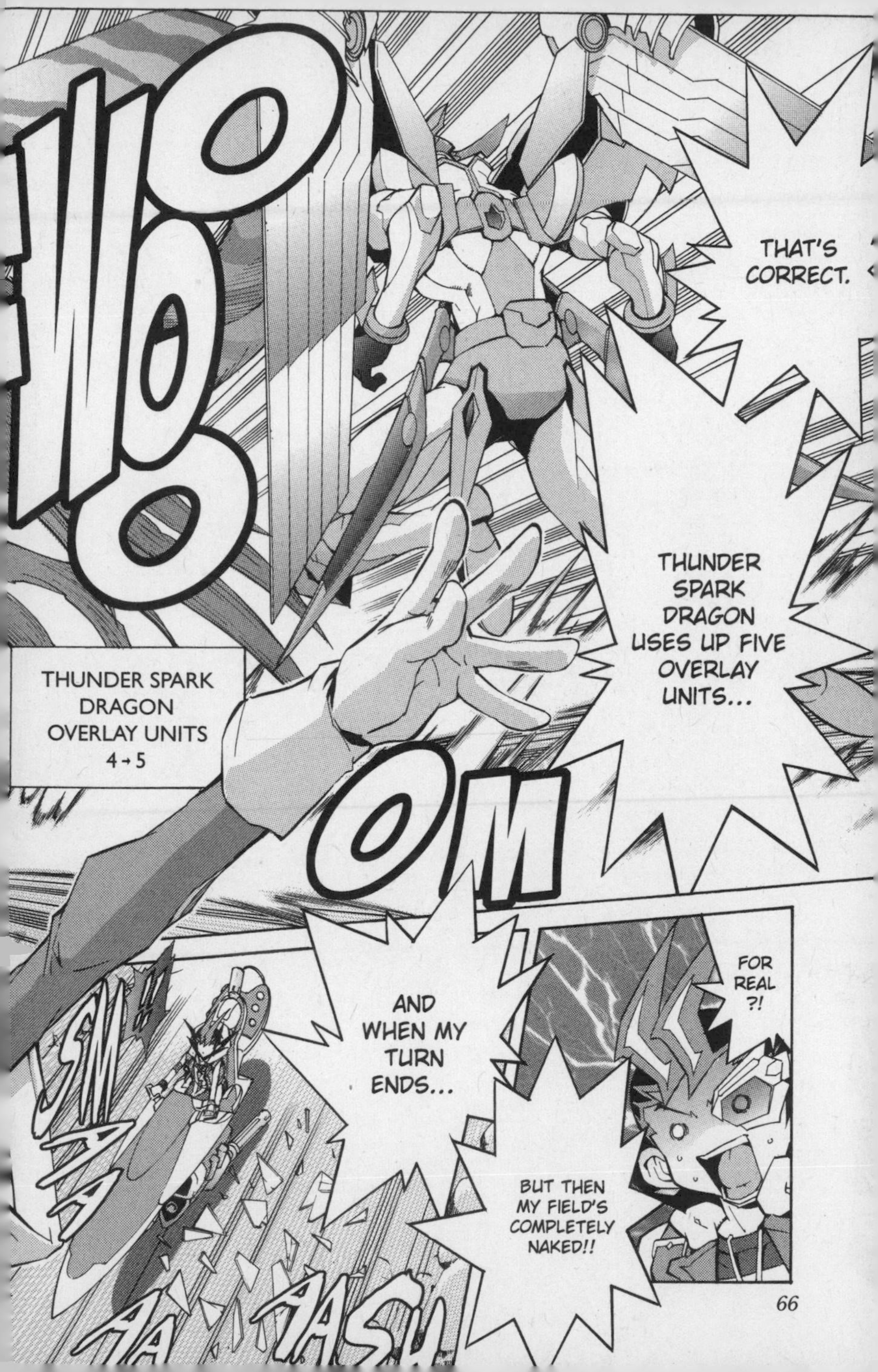
THAT'S CORRECT.
THUNDER SPARK DRAGON USES UP FIVE OVERLAY UNITS...
THUNDER SPARK DRAGON OVERLAY UNITS 4→5
AND WHEN MY TURN ENDS...
FOR REAL?!
BUT THEN MY FIELD'S COMPLETELY NAKED!!

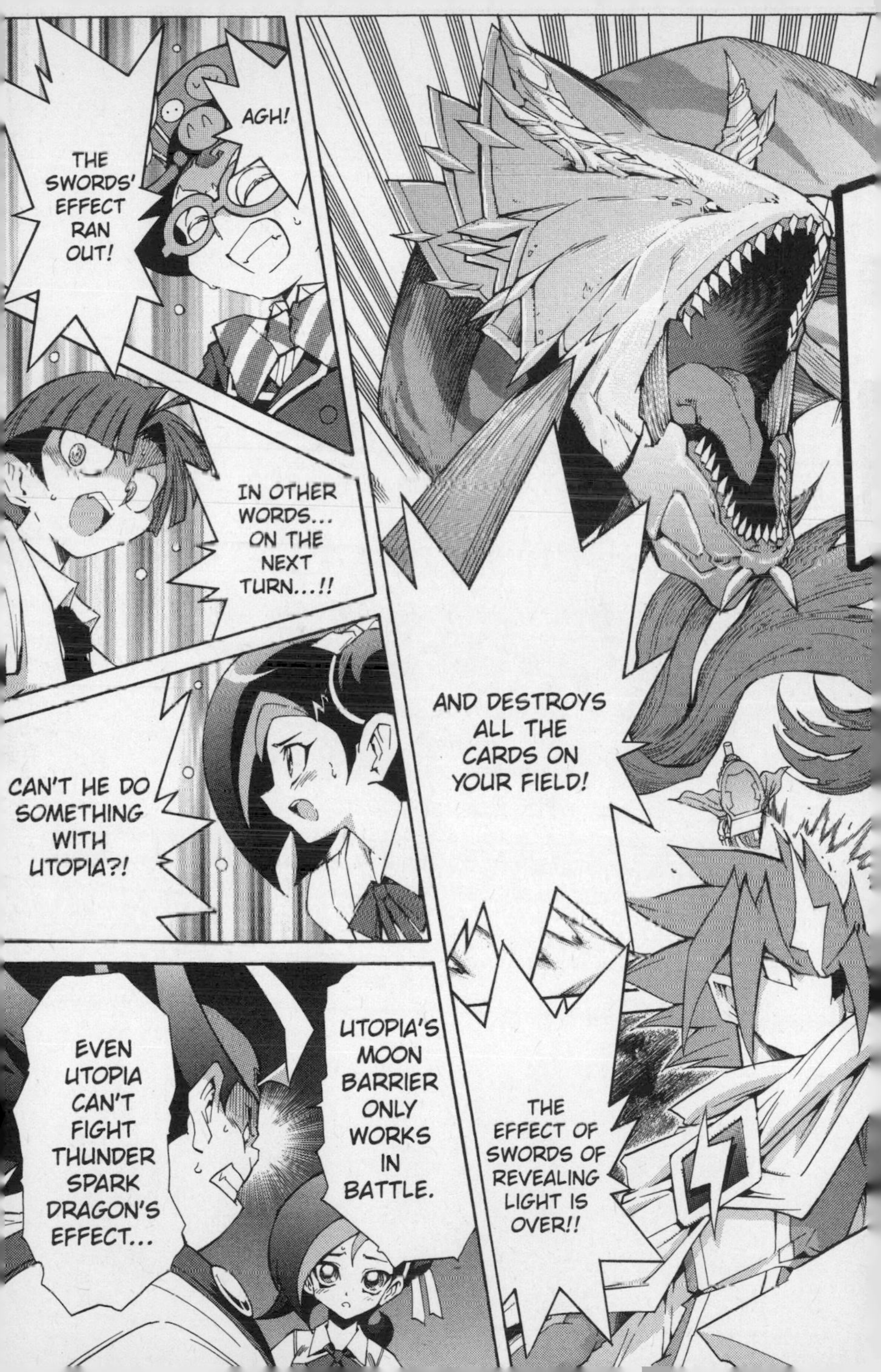

AND DESTROYS ALL THE CARDS ON YOUR FIELD!
THE EFFECT OF SWORDS OF REVEALING LIGHT IS OVER!!
AGH!
THE SWORDS' EFFECT RAN OUT!
IN OTHER WORDS... ON THE NEXT TURN...!!
CAN'T HE DO SOMETHING WITH UTOPIA?!
UTOPIA'S MOON BARRIER ONLY WORKS IN BATTLE.
EVEN UTOPIA CAN'T FIGHT THUNDER SPARK DRAGON'S EFFECT...

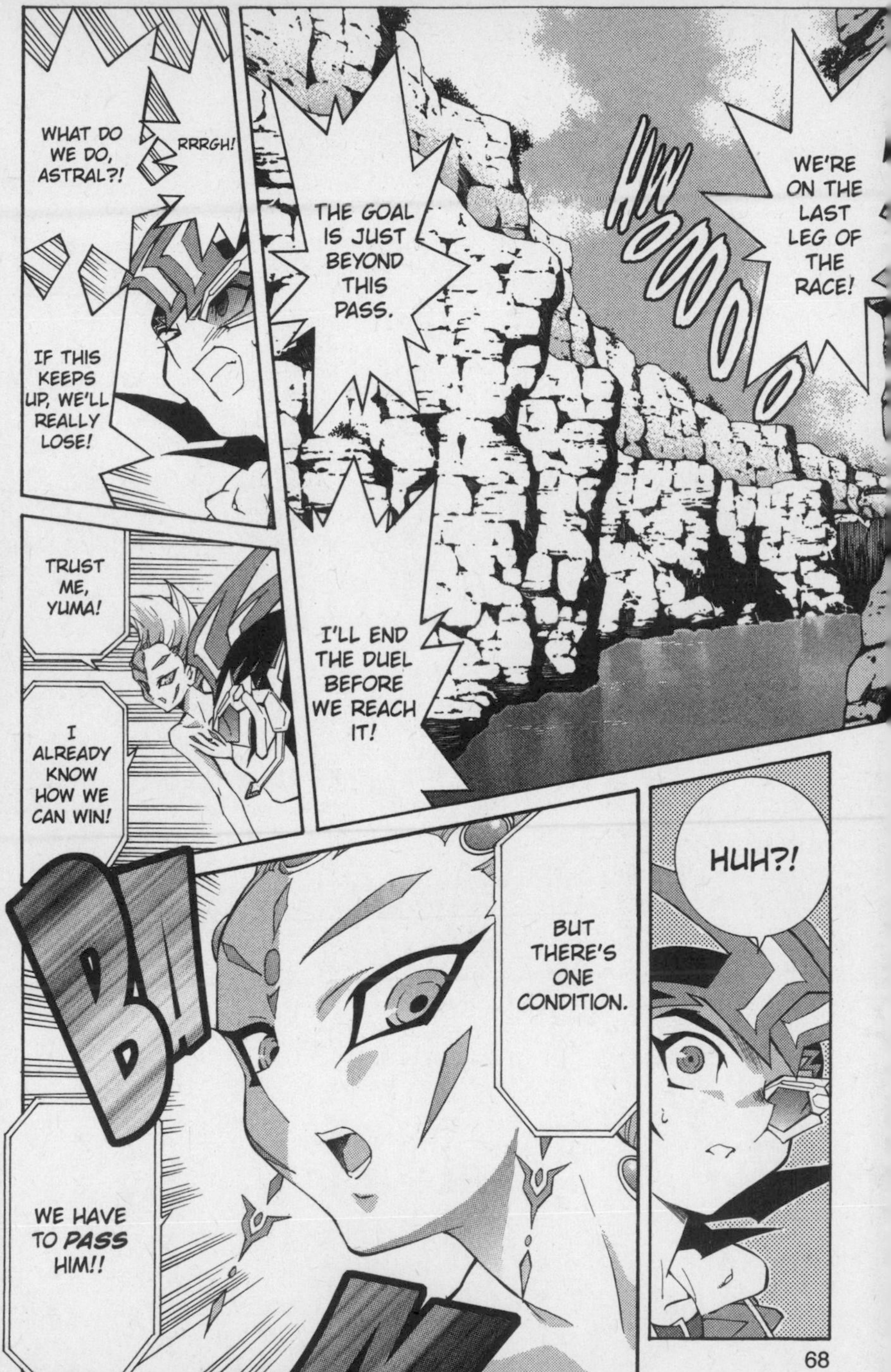
WE'RE ON THE LAST LEG OF THE RACE!
HWOOOOOO
THE GOAL IS JUST BEYOND THIS PASS.
WHAT DO WE DO, ASTRAL?!
RRRGH!
IF THIS KEEPS UP, WE'LL REALLY LOSE!
TRUST ME, YUMA!
I ALREADY KNOW HOW WE CAN WIN!
I'LL END THE DUEL BEFORE WE REACH IT!
HUH?!
BUT THERE'S ONE CONDITION.
BA
N
WE HAVE TO ***PASS*** HIM!!

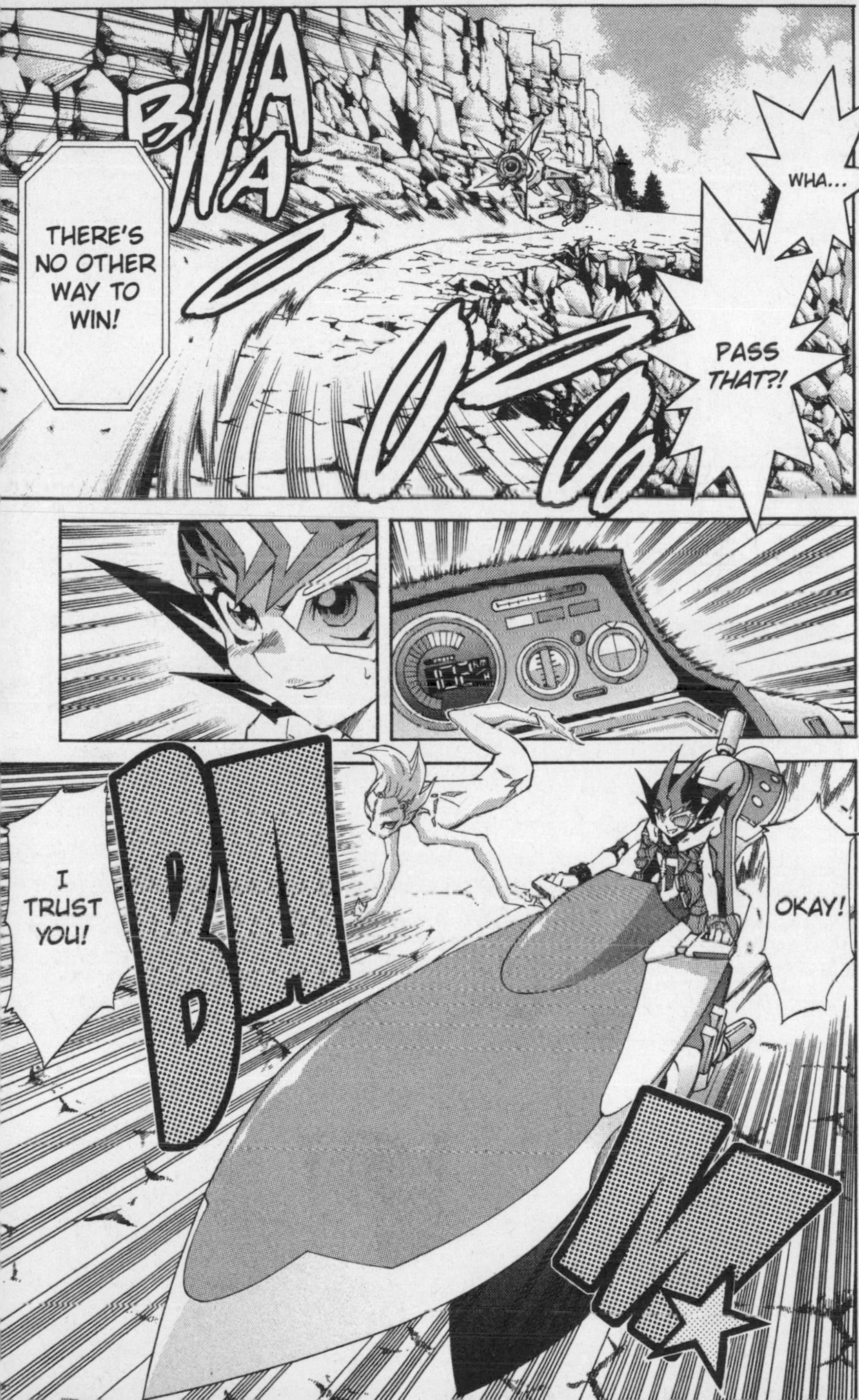
WHA...
PASS THAT?!
BWAA
THERE'S NO OTHER WAY TO WIN!
OKAY!
BAM!
I TRUST YOU!

YU-GI-OH!
ZEXAL

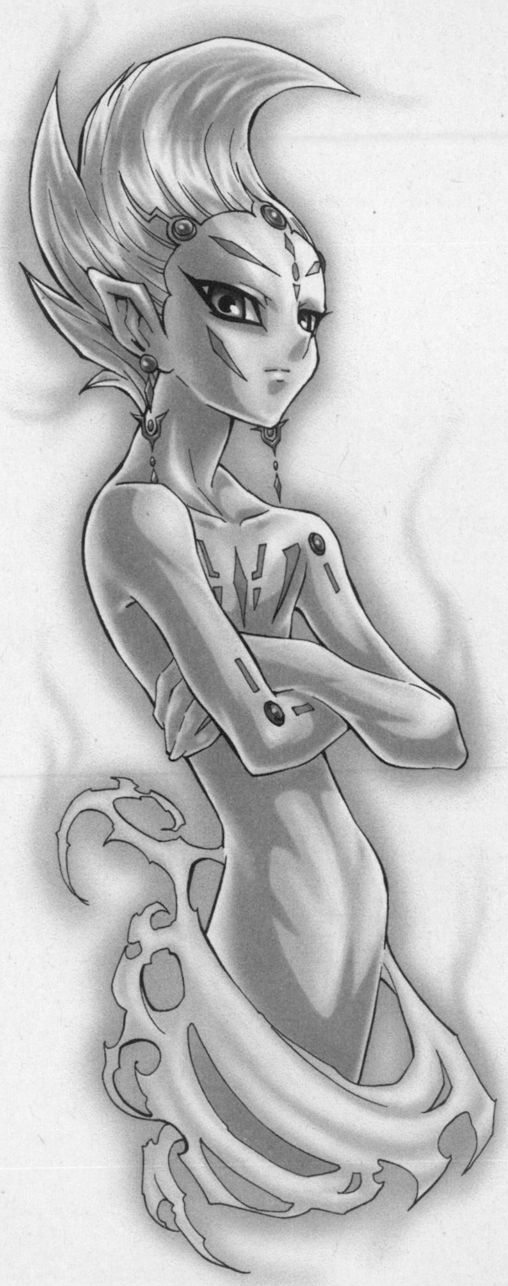

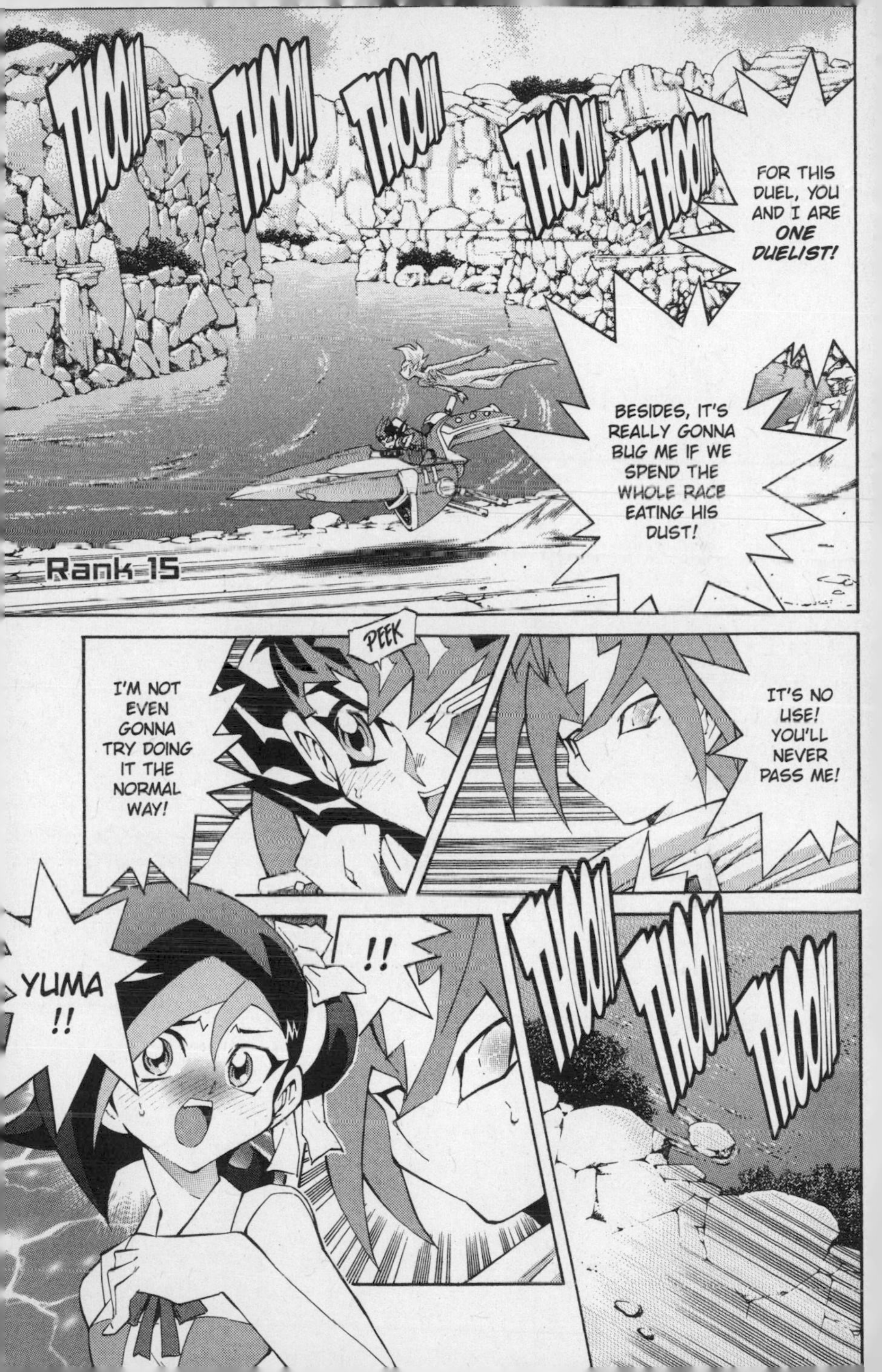
FOR THIS DUEL, YOU AND I ARE ONE DUELIST!
BESIDES, IT'S REALLY GONNA BUG ME IF WE SPEND THE WHOLE RACE EATING HIS DUST!
THOOM
THOOM
THOOM
THOOM
THOOM
Rank 15
IT'S NO USE! YOU'LL NEVER PASS ME!
PEEK
I'M NOT EVEN GONNA TRY DOING IT THE NORMAL WAY!
THOOM
THOOM
THOOM
!!
YUMA !!

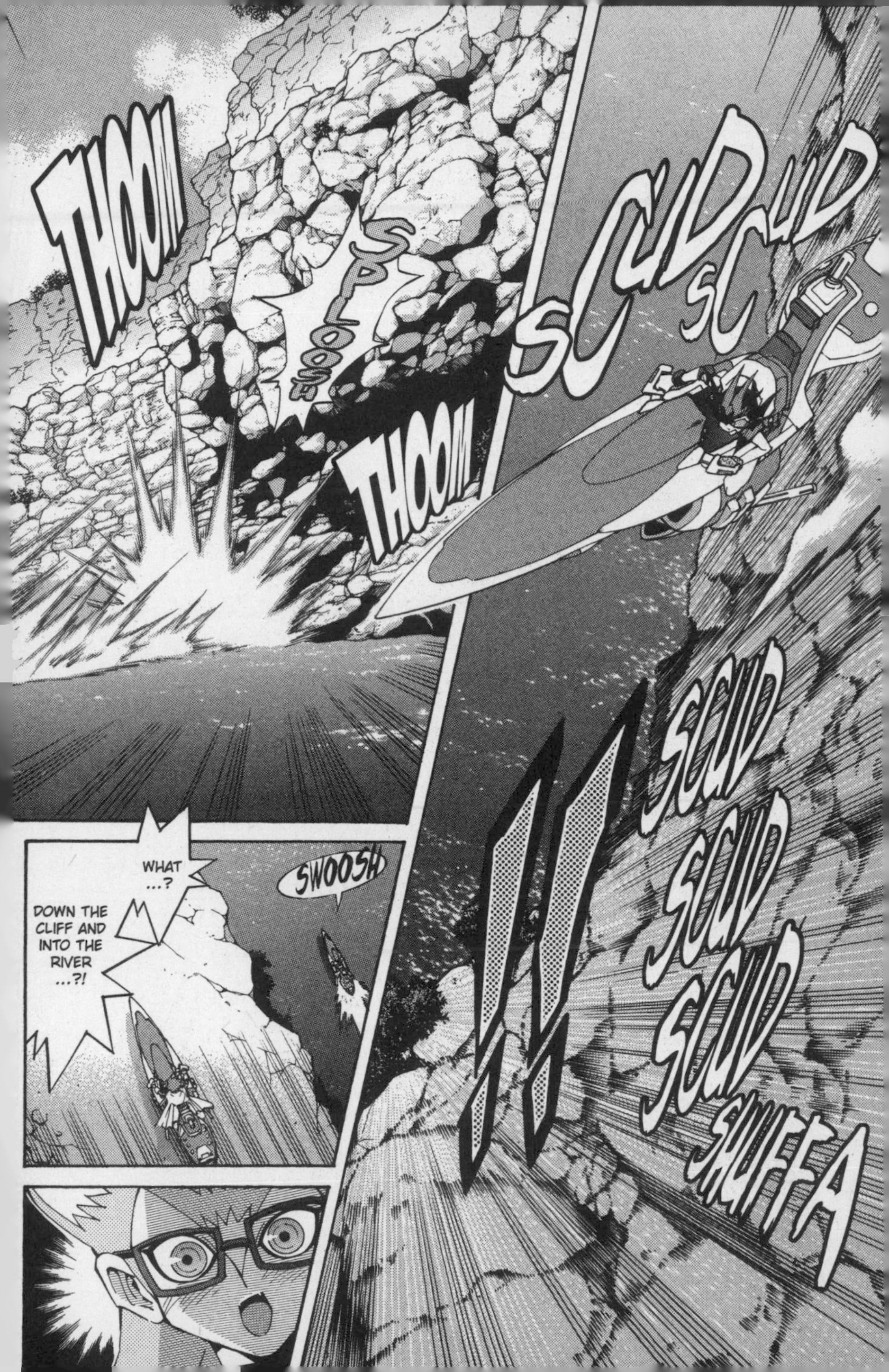
SCUD SCUD
!!
SCUD
SCUD
SCUD
SCUD
SCUFFA
THOOM
SPLOOSH
THOOM
WHAT ...?
SWOOSH
DOWN THE CLIFF AND INTO THE RIVER ...?!

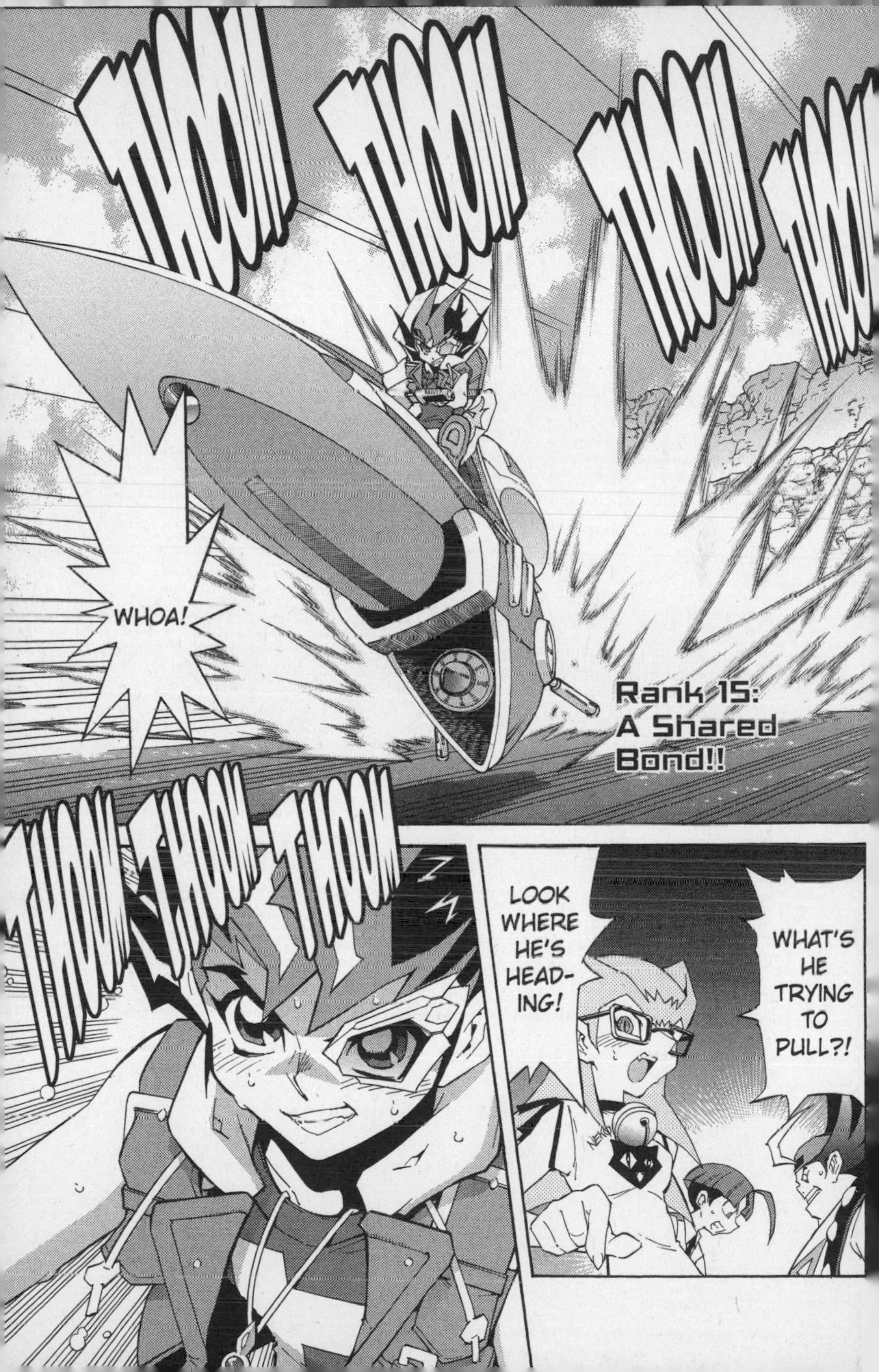
THOOM
THOOM
THOOM
THOOM
Rank 15: A Shared Bond!!
WHOA!
WHAT'S HE TRYING TO PULL?!
LOOK WHERE HE'S HEAD-ING!
THOOM
THOOM
THOOM

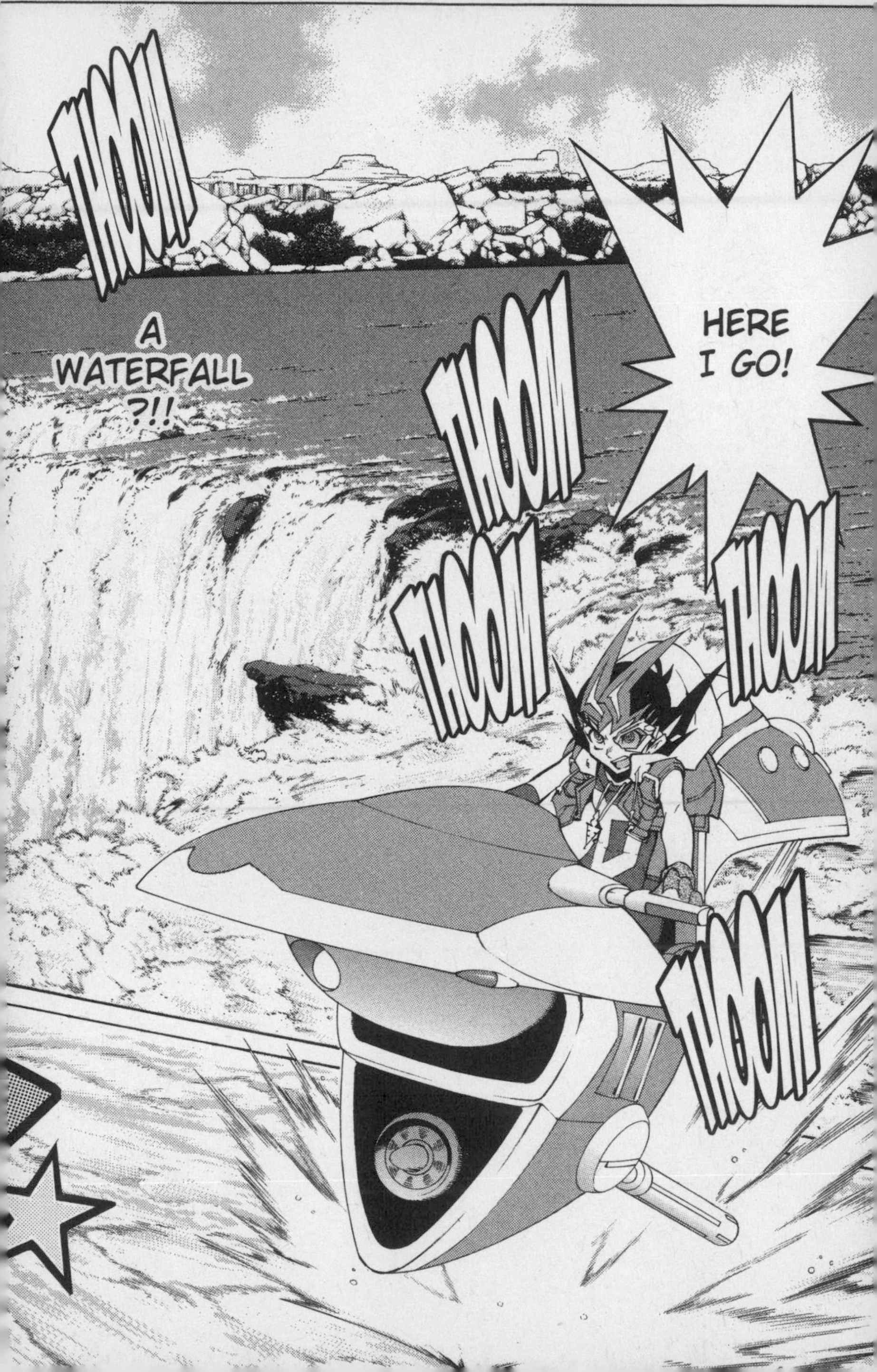
HERE I GO!
THOOM
A WATERFALL ?!!
THOOM
THOOM
THOOM
THOOM

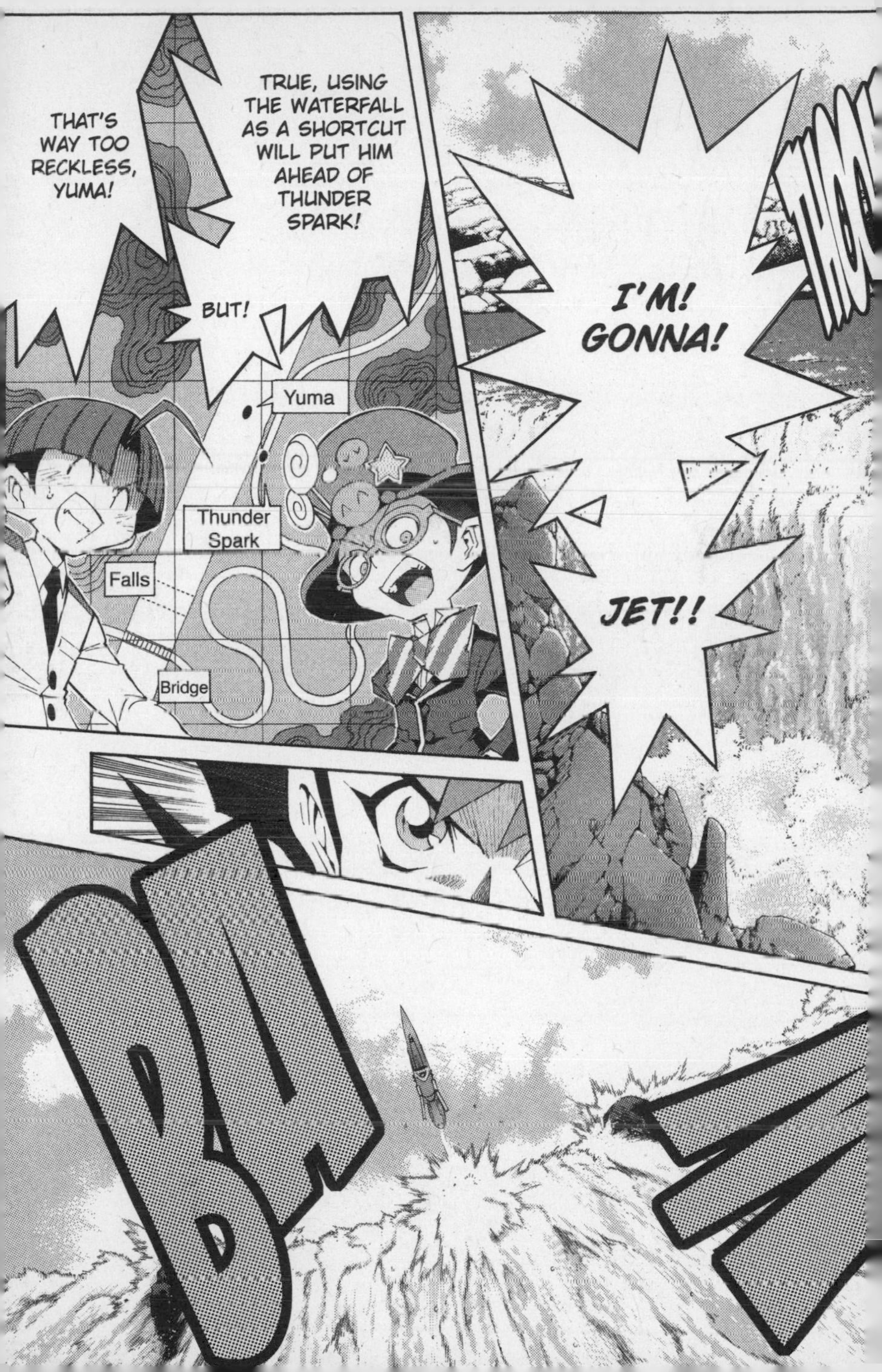
I'M! GONNA!
JET!!
TRUE, USING THE WATERFALL AS A SHORTCUT WILL PUT HIM AHEAD OF THUNDER SPARK!
THAT'S WAY TOO RECKLESS, YUMA!
BUT!
Yuma
Thunder Spark
Falls
Bridge

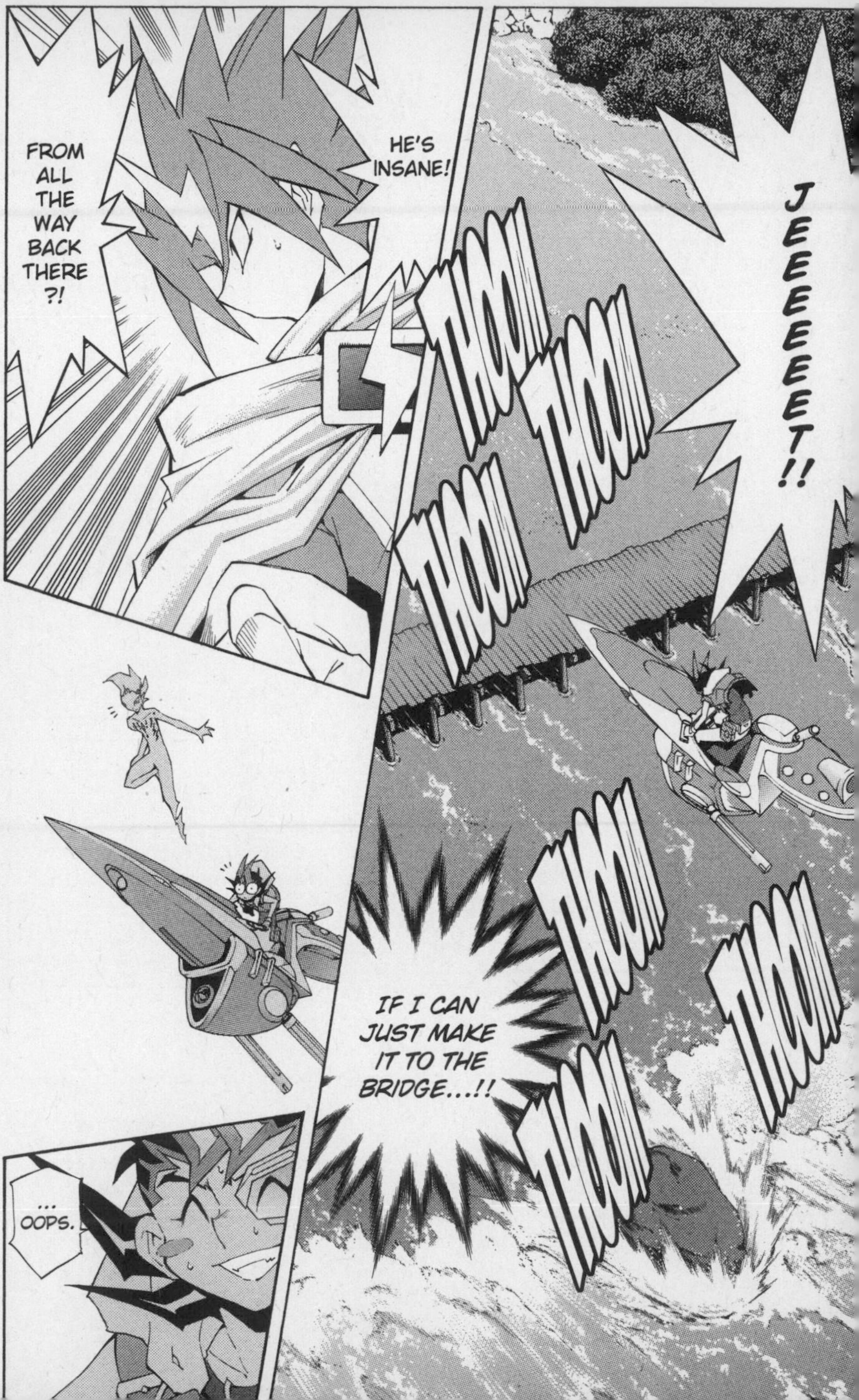
JEEEEEEET!!
THOOM
THOOM
THOOM
THOOM
THOOM
THOOM
IF I CAN JUST MAKE IT TO THE BRIDGE...!!
HE'S INSANE!
FROM ALL THE WAY BACK THERE?!
... OOPS.

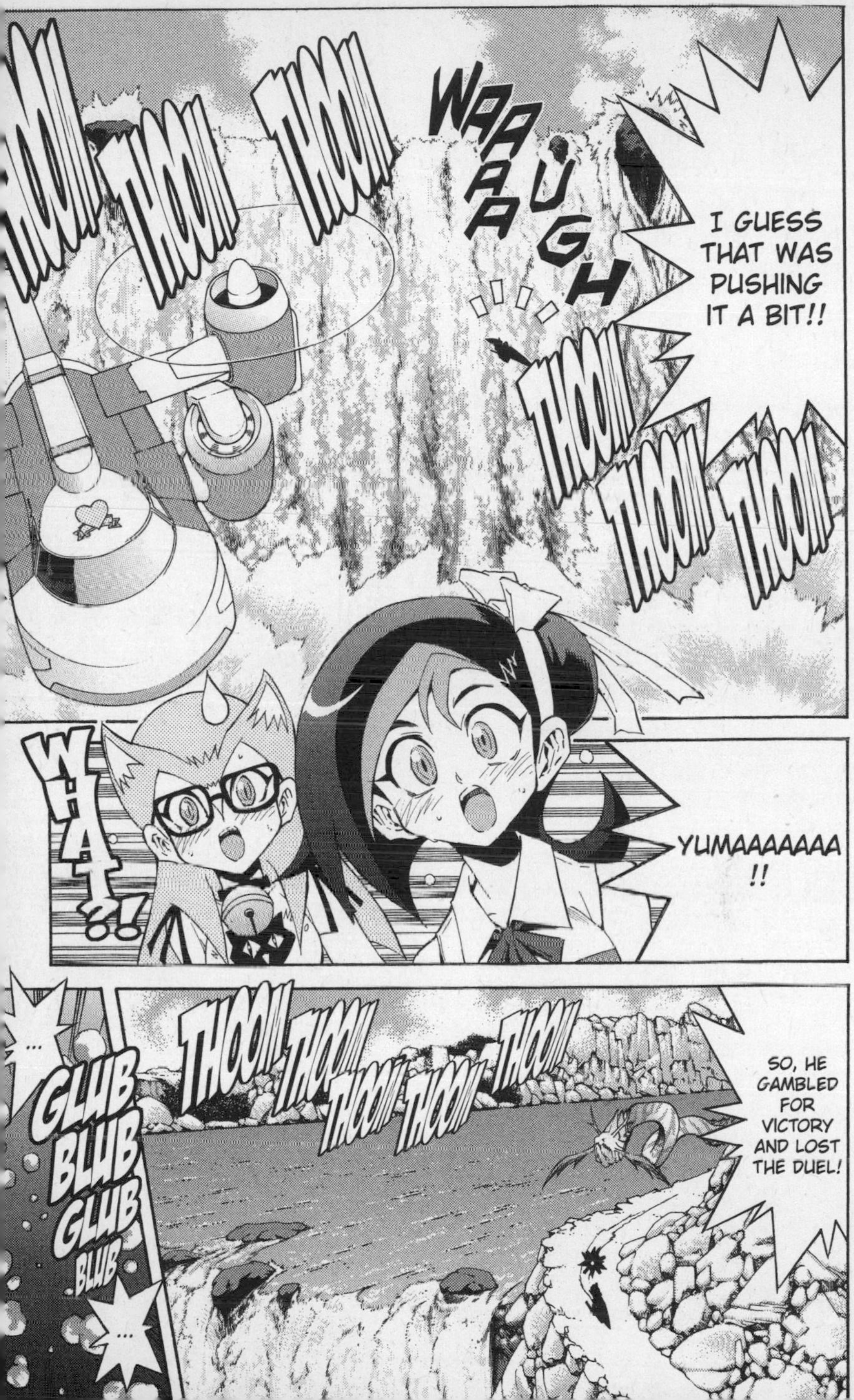
I GUESS THAT WAS PUSHING IT A BIT!!
WAAAAAUGH...!
THOOM
THOOM
THOOM
THOOM
THOOM
THOOM
YUMAAAAAAA!!
WHA?!
SO, HE GAMBLED FOR VICTORY AND LOST THE DUEL!
THOOM
THOOM
THOOM
THOOM
THOOM
...
GLUB
BLUB
GLUB
BLUB
...

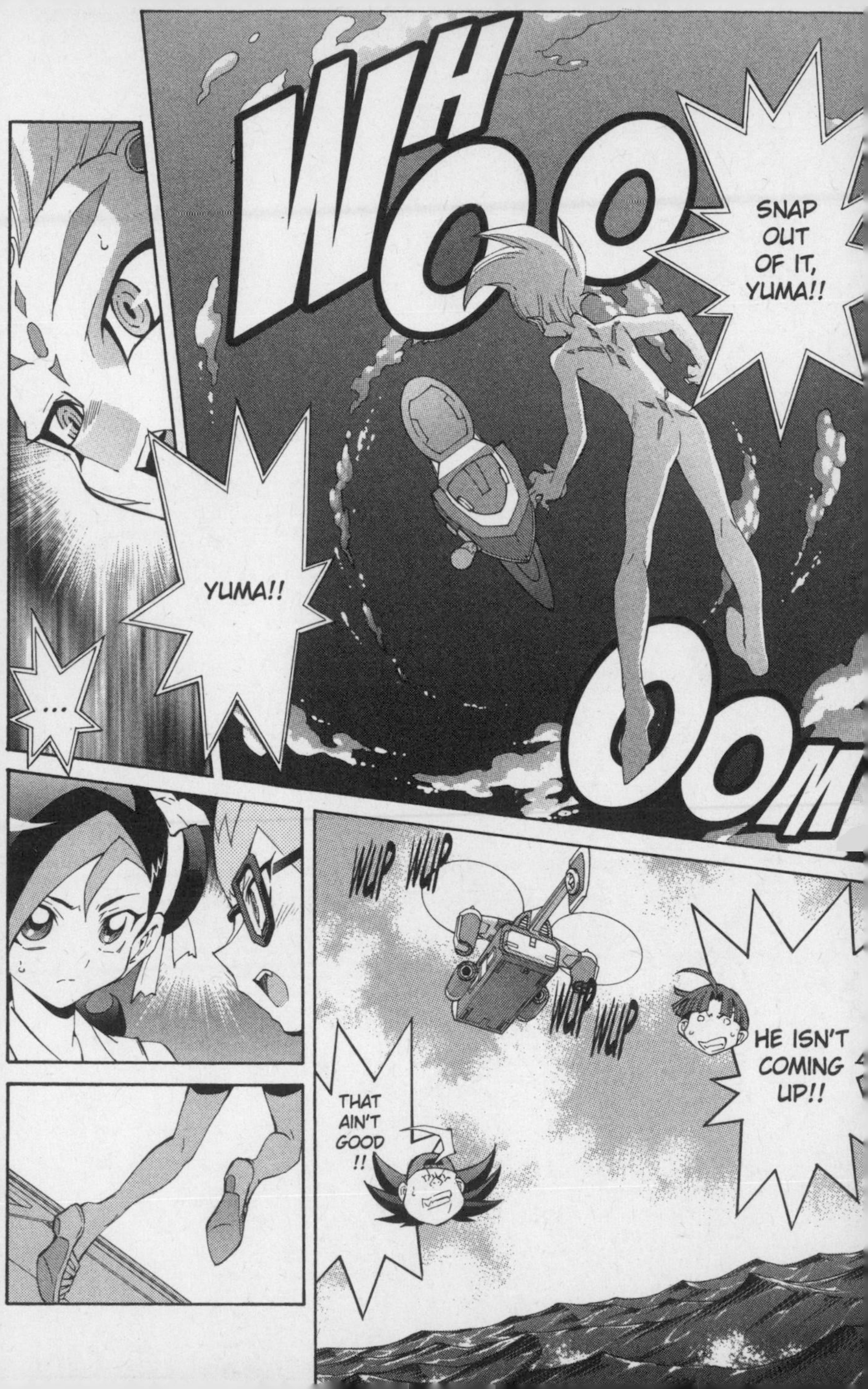
WHOOOOM
SNAP OUT OF IT, YUMA!!
YUMA!!
...
WUP WUP
WUP WUP
HE ISN'T COMING UP!!
THAT AIN'T GOOD!!

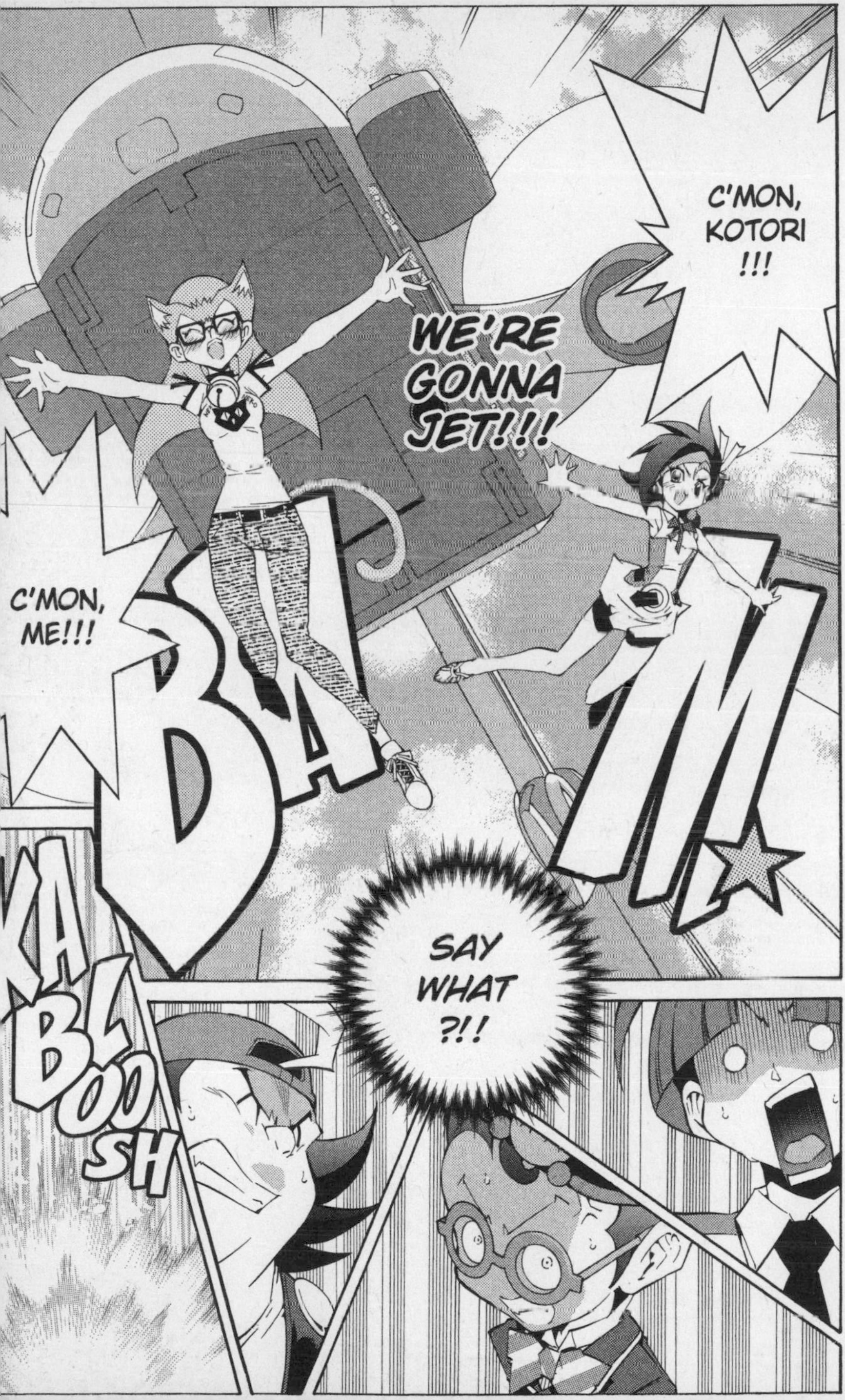
C'MON, KOTORI!!!
WE'RE GONNA JET!!!
C'MON, ME!!!
BAM
SAY WHAT?!!
KABLOOSH

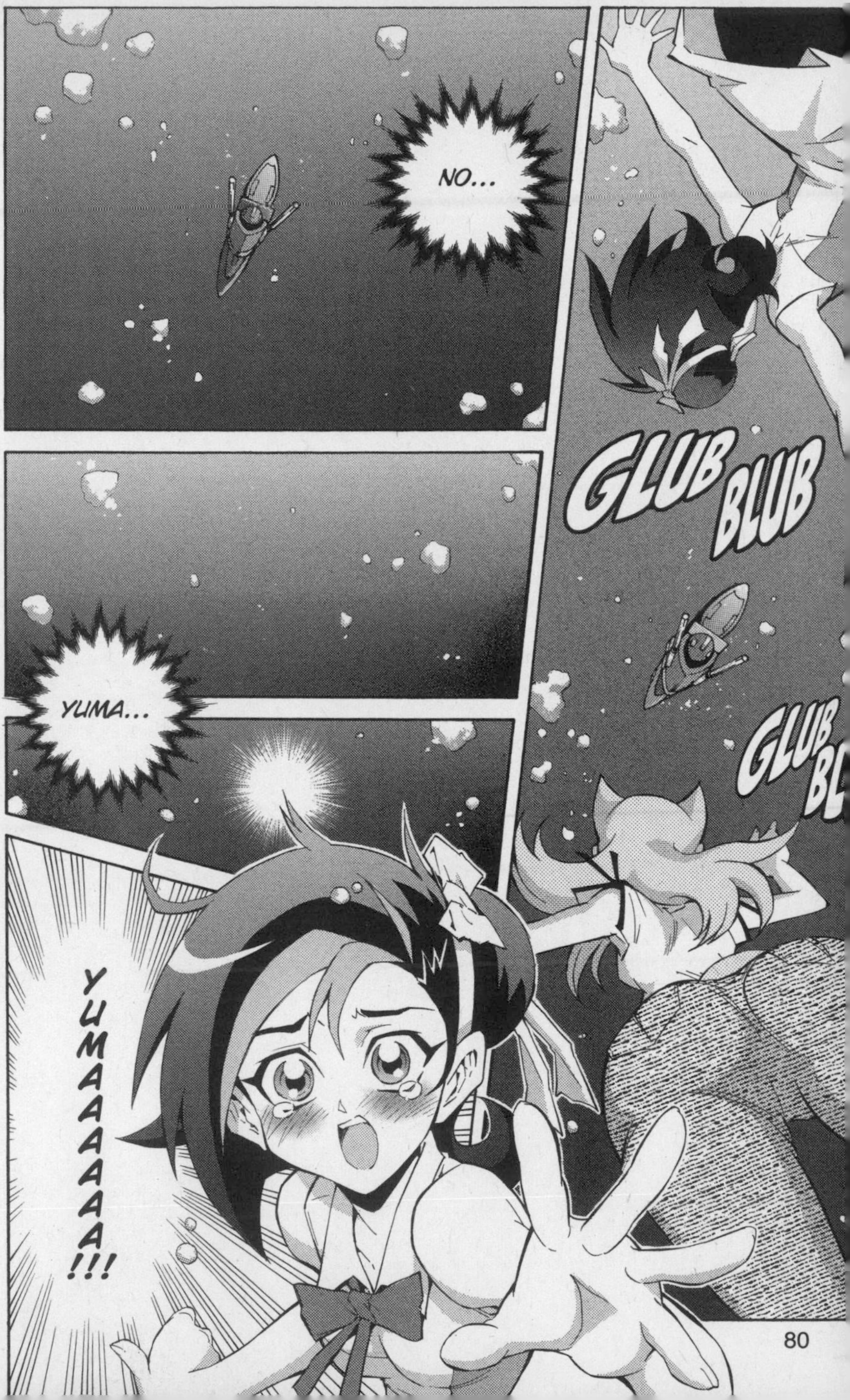
GLUB BLUB
GLUB
NO...
YUMA...
YUMAAAAAAAA!!!

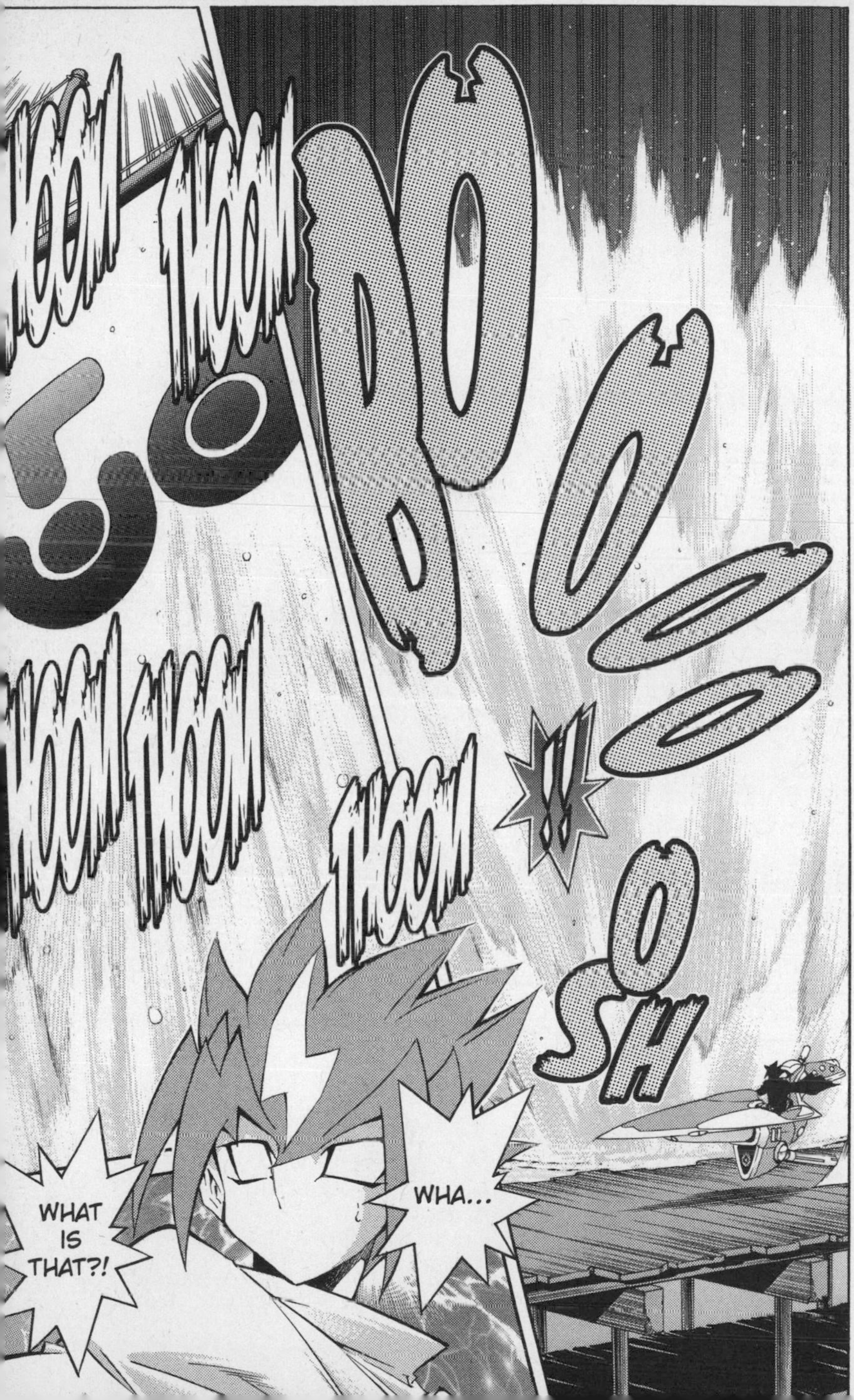
BOOOOOSH
!!
THOOM
THOOM
THOOM
WHA...
WHAT IS THAT?!

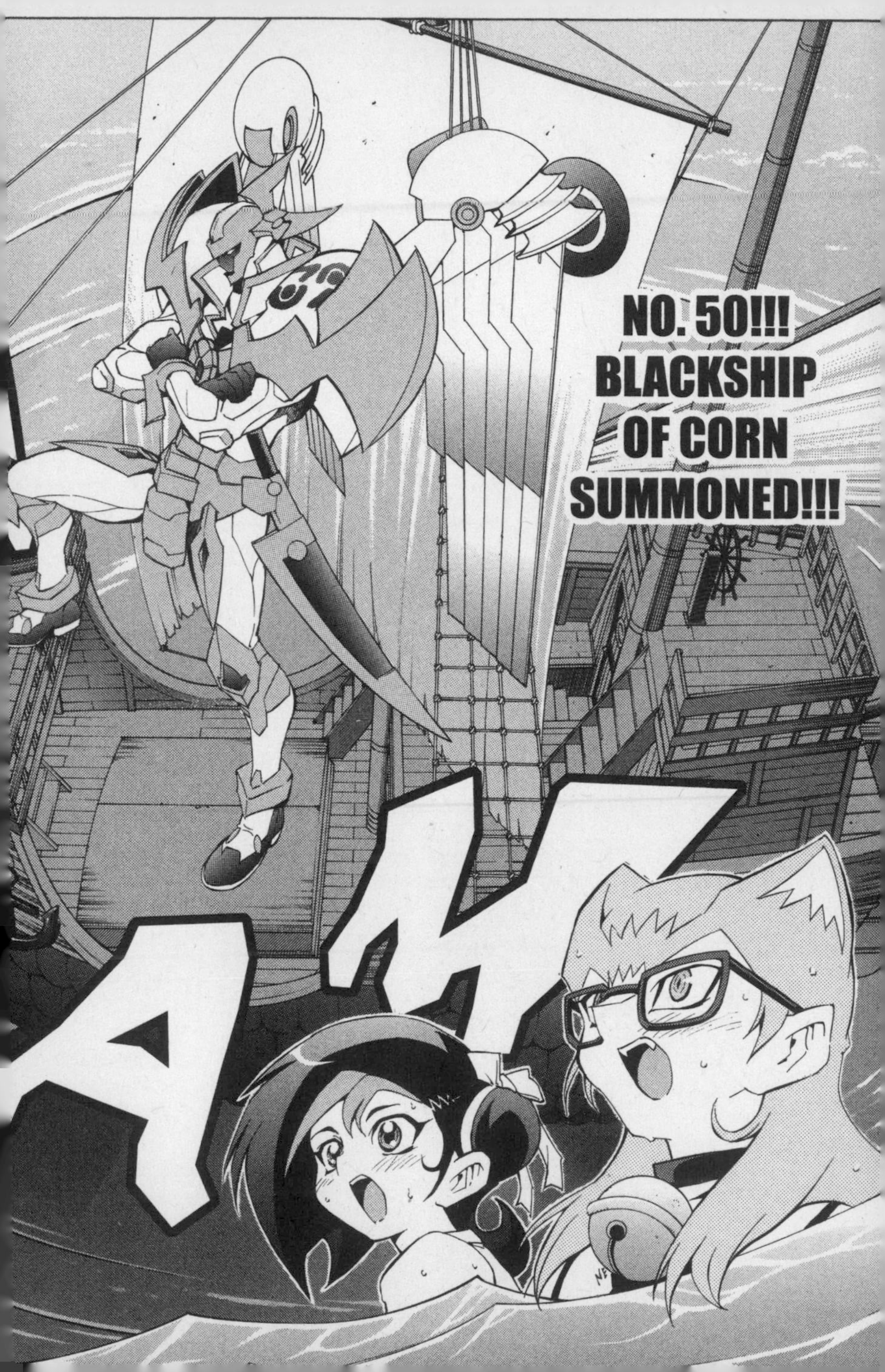
NO. 50!!!
BLACKSHIP
OF CORN
SUMMONED!!!
AH

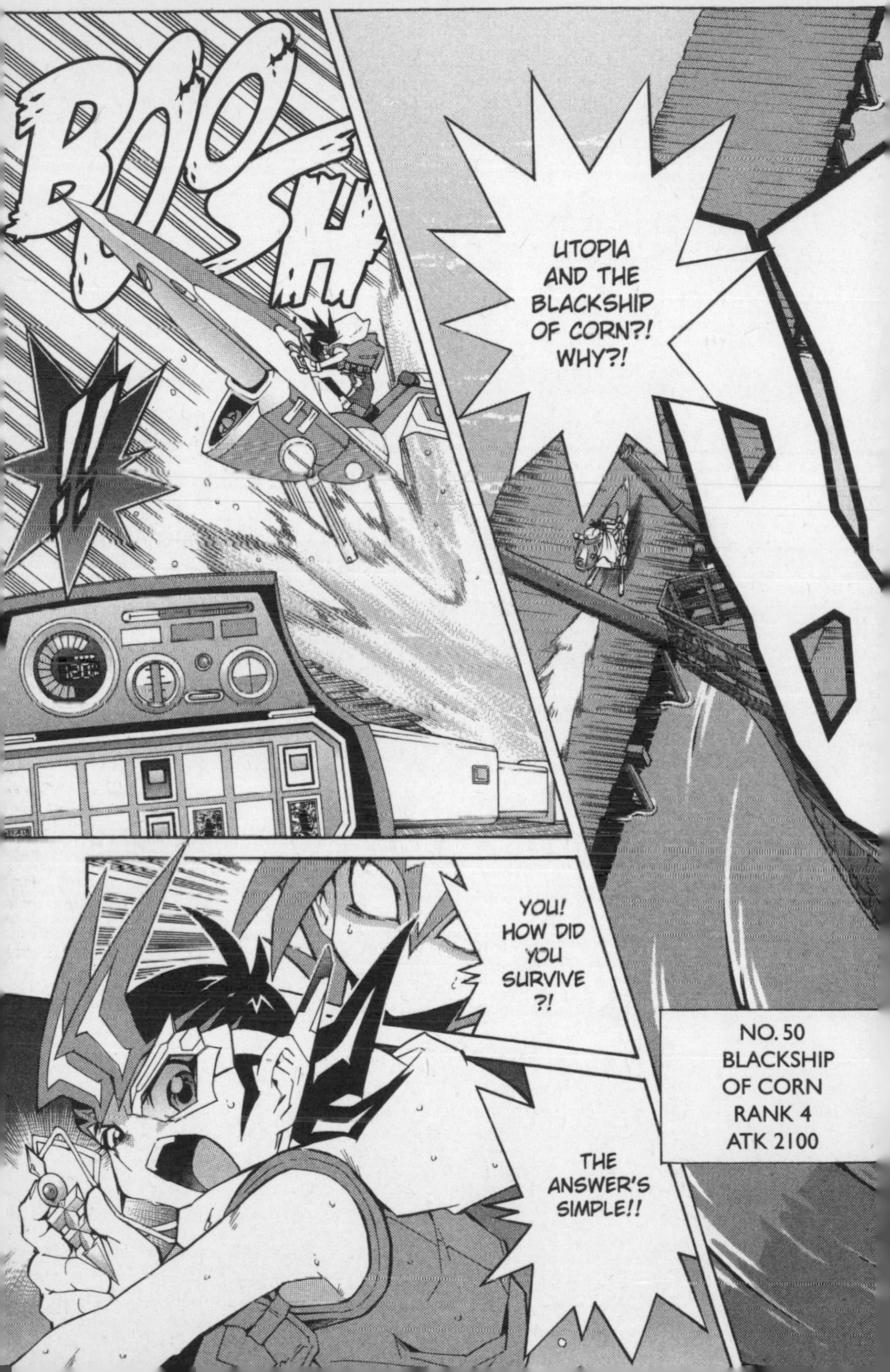
UTOPIA AND THE BLACKSHIP OF CORN?! WHY?!
NO. 50 BLACKSHIP OF CORN RANK 4 ATK 2100
BAOOSH
!
YOU! HOW DID YOU SURVIVE ?!
THE ANSWER'S SIMPLE!!

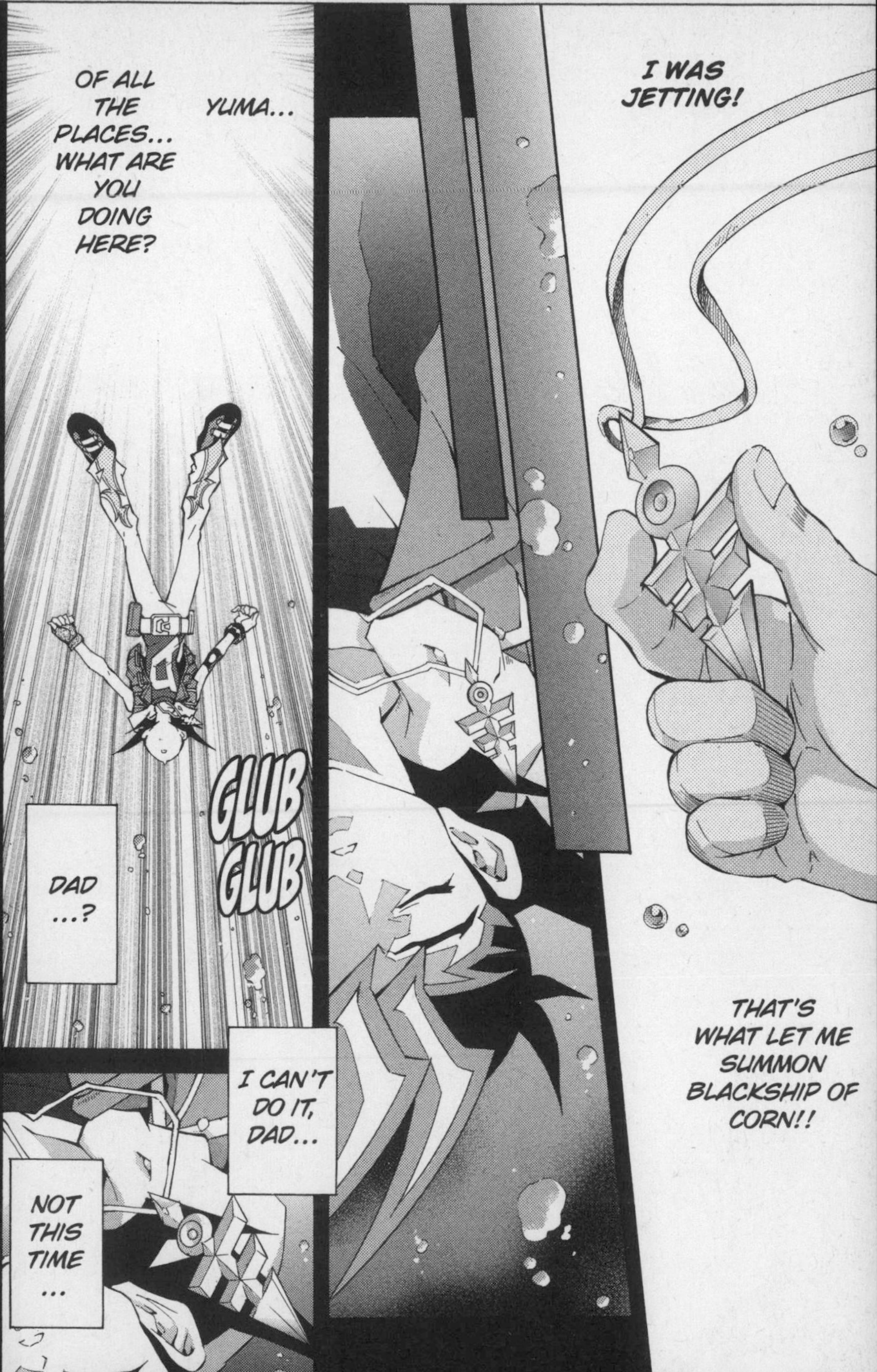

I WAS JETTING!
THAT'S WHAT LET ME SUMMON BLACKSHIP OF CORN!!
YUMA...
OF ALL THE PLACES... WHAT ARE YOU DOING HERE?
GLUB GLUB
DAD ...?
I CAN'T DO IT, DAD...
NOT THIS TIME ...

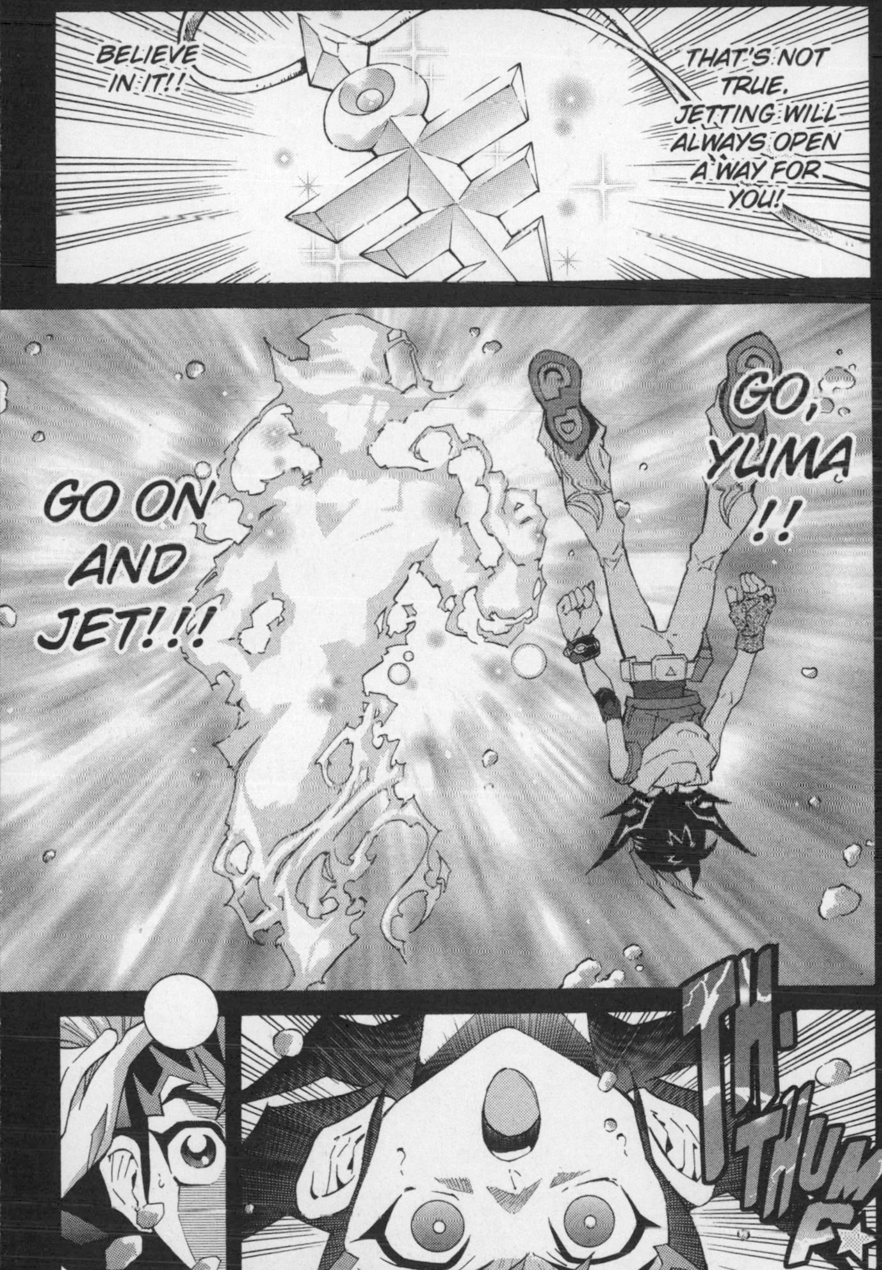
THAT'S NOT TRUE. JETTING WILL ALWAYS OPEN A WAY FOR YOU!
BELIEVE IN IT!!
GO, YUMA!!
GO ON AND JET!!!
TH-THUMP

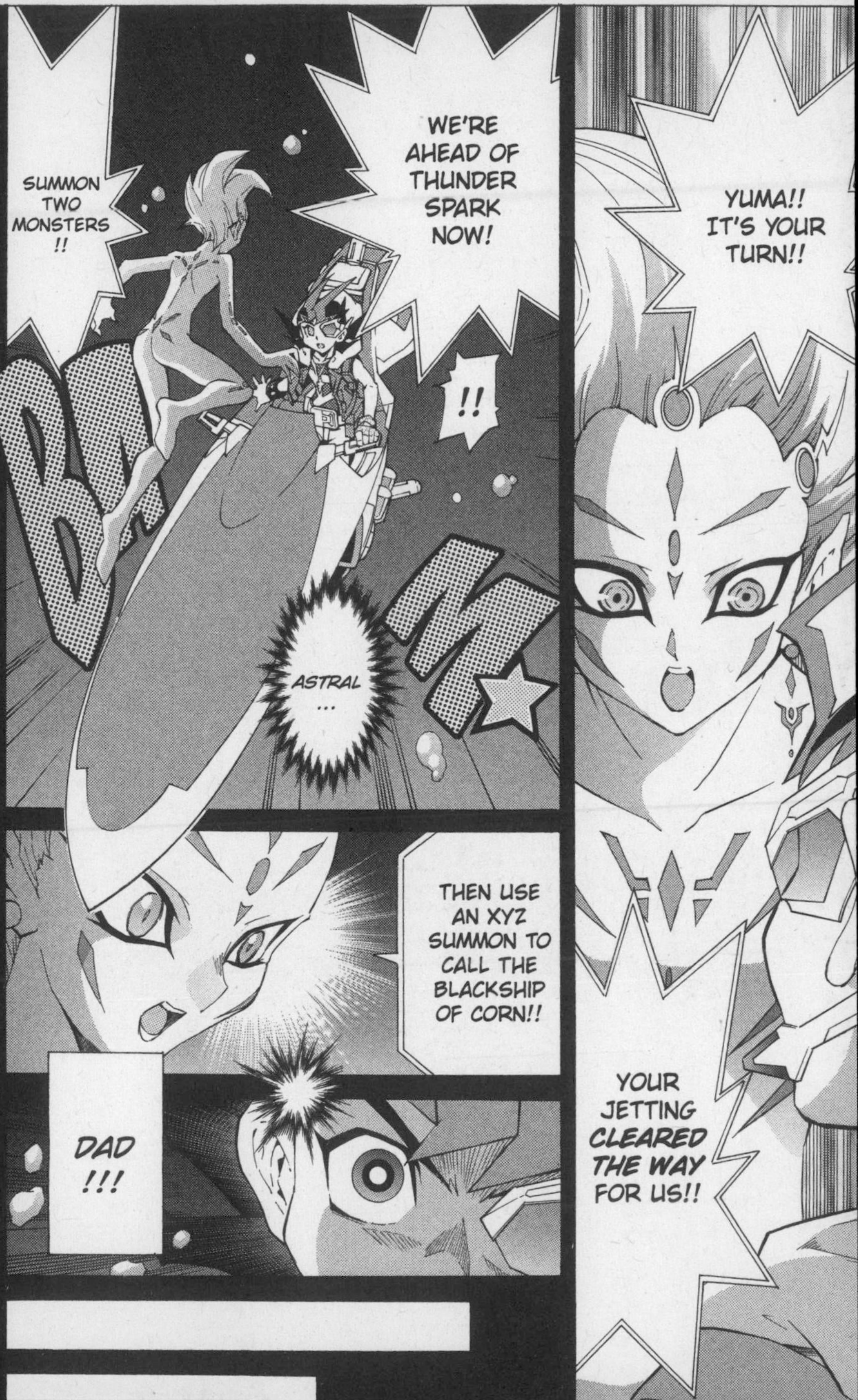
YUMA!! IT'S YOUR TURN!!
YOUR JETTING CLEARED THE WAY FOR US!!
WE'RE AHEAD OF THUNDER SPARK NOW!
SUMMON TWO MONSTERS !!
!!
ASTRAL ...
THEN USE AN XYZ SUMMON TO CALL THE BLACKSHIP OF CORN!!
DAD !!!

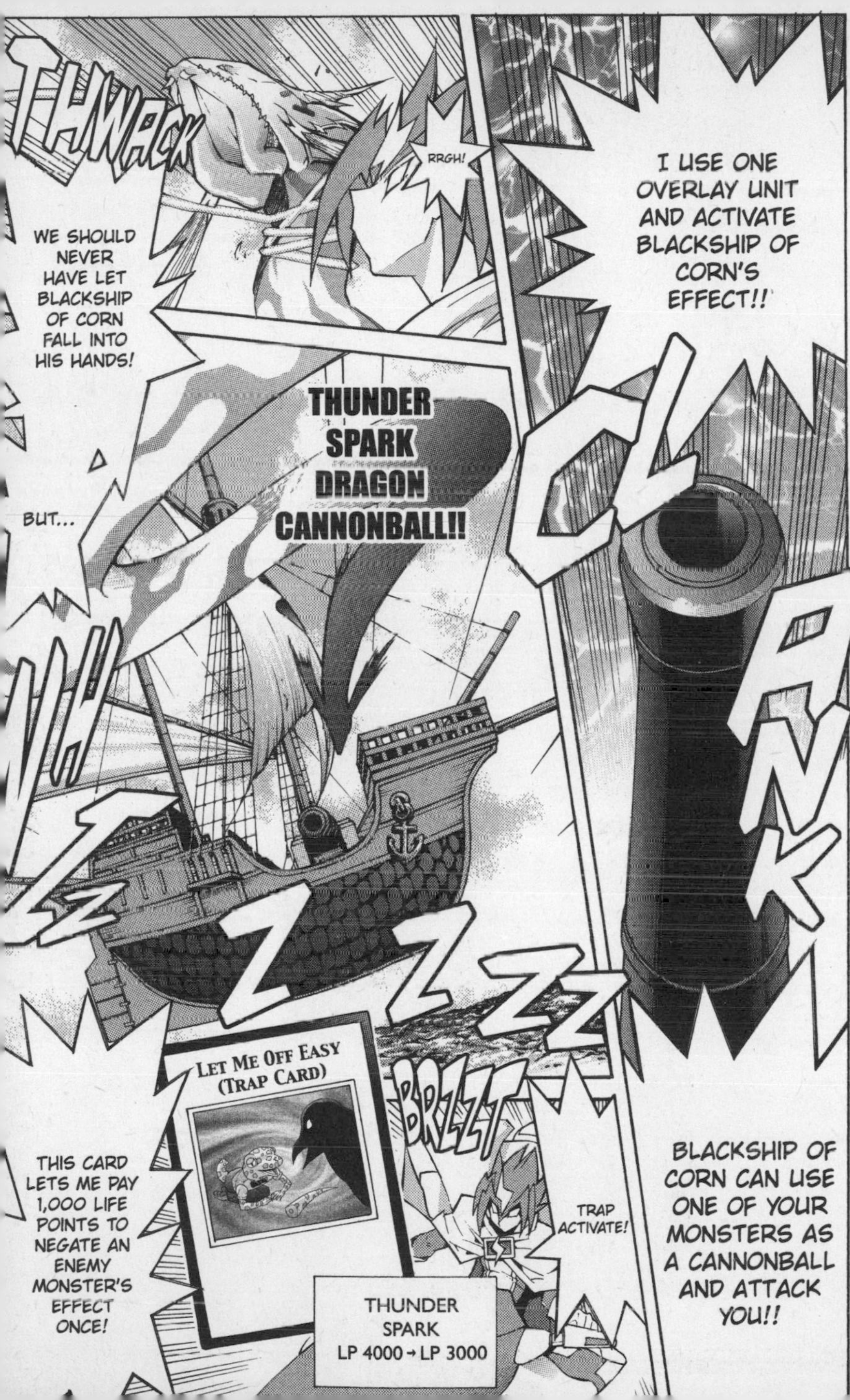
I USE ONE OVERLAY UNIT AND ACTIVATE BLACKSHIP OF CORN'S EFFECT!!
CLANK
THWACK
RRGH!
WE SHOULD NEVER HAVE LET BLACKSHIP OF CORN FALL INTO HIS HANDS!
THUNDER SPARK DRAGON CANNONBALL!!
BUT...
ZZZZZ
BLACKSHIP OF CORN CAN USE ONE OF YOUR MONSTERS AS A CANNONBALL AND ATTACK YOU!!
TRAP ACTIVATE!
BRZZT
LET ME OFF EASY (TRAP CARD)
THIS CARD LETS ME PAY 1,000 LIFE POINTS TO NEGATE AN ENEMY MONSTER'S EFFECT ONCE!
THUNDER SPARK LP 4000→LP 3000

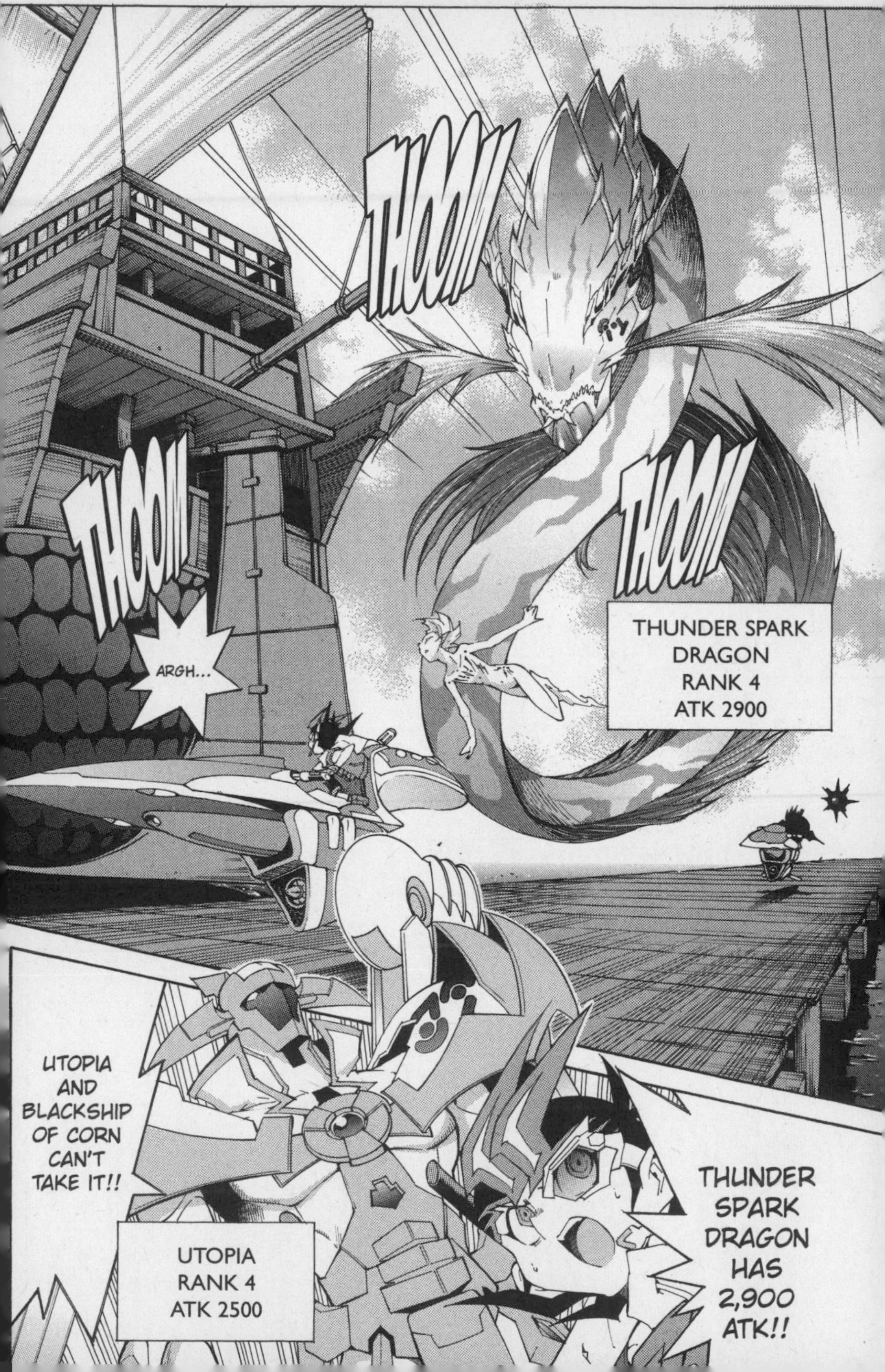
THOOM
THOOM
THUNDER SPARK DRAGON RANK 4 ATK 2900
THOOM
ARGH...
THUNDER SPARK DRAGON HAS 2,900 ATK!!
UTOPIA AND BLACKSHIP OF CORN CAN'T TAKE IT!!
UTOPIA RANK 4 ATK 2500

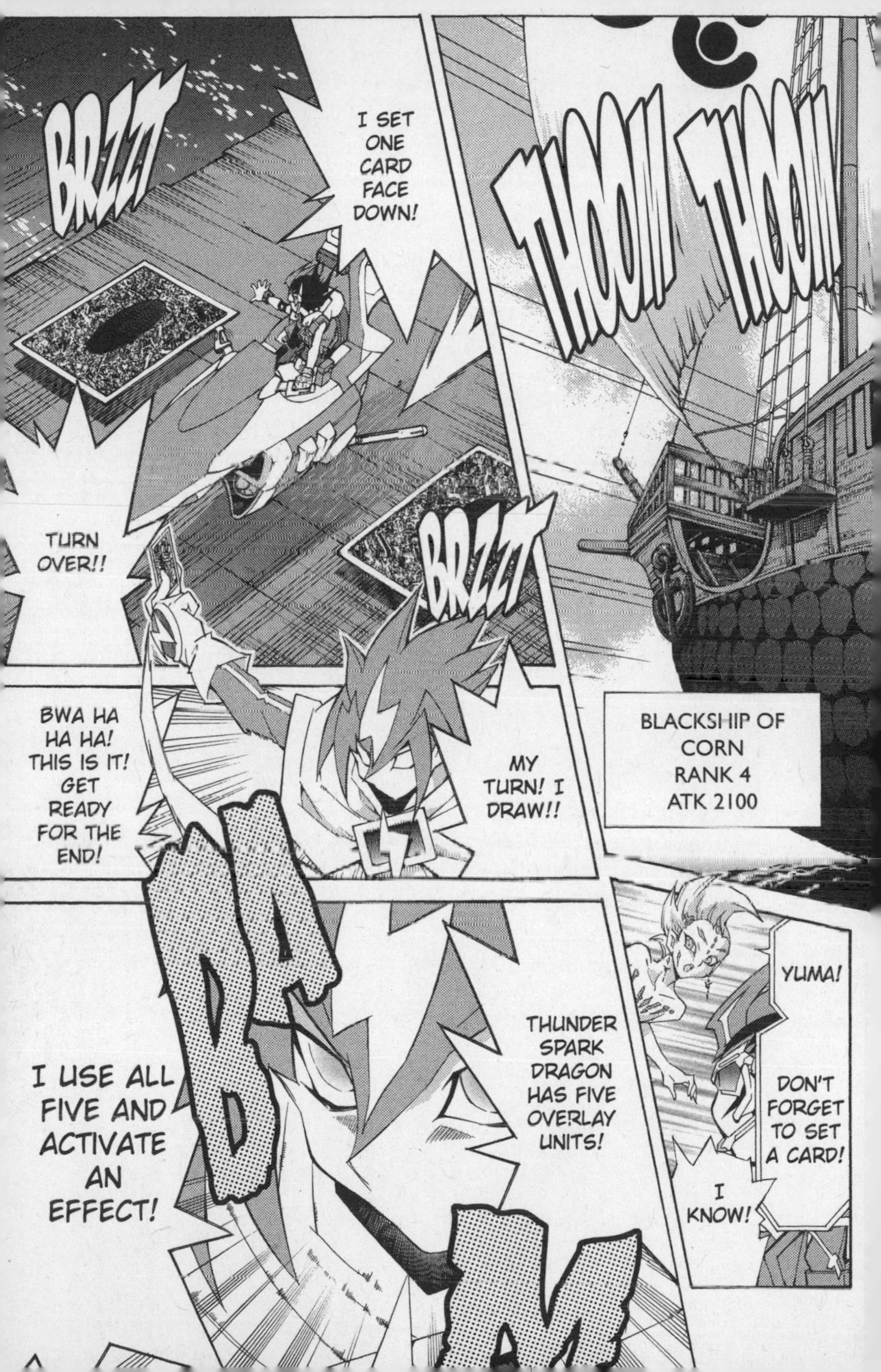
THOOM
THOOM
BLACKSHIP OF CORN RANK 4 ATK 2100
I SET ONE CARD FACE DOWN!
BRZZT
BRZZT
TURN OVER!!
MY TURN! I DRAW!!
BWA HA HA HA! THIS IS IT! GET READY FOR THE END!
YUMA!
DON'T FORGET TO SET A CARD!
I KNOW!
THUNDER SPARK DRAGON HAS FIVE OVERLAY UNITS!
I USE ALL FIVE AND ACTIVATE AN EFFECT!
BAM

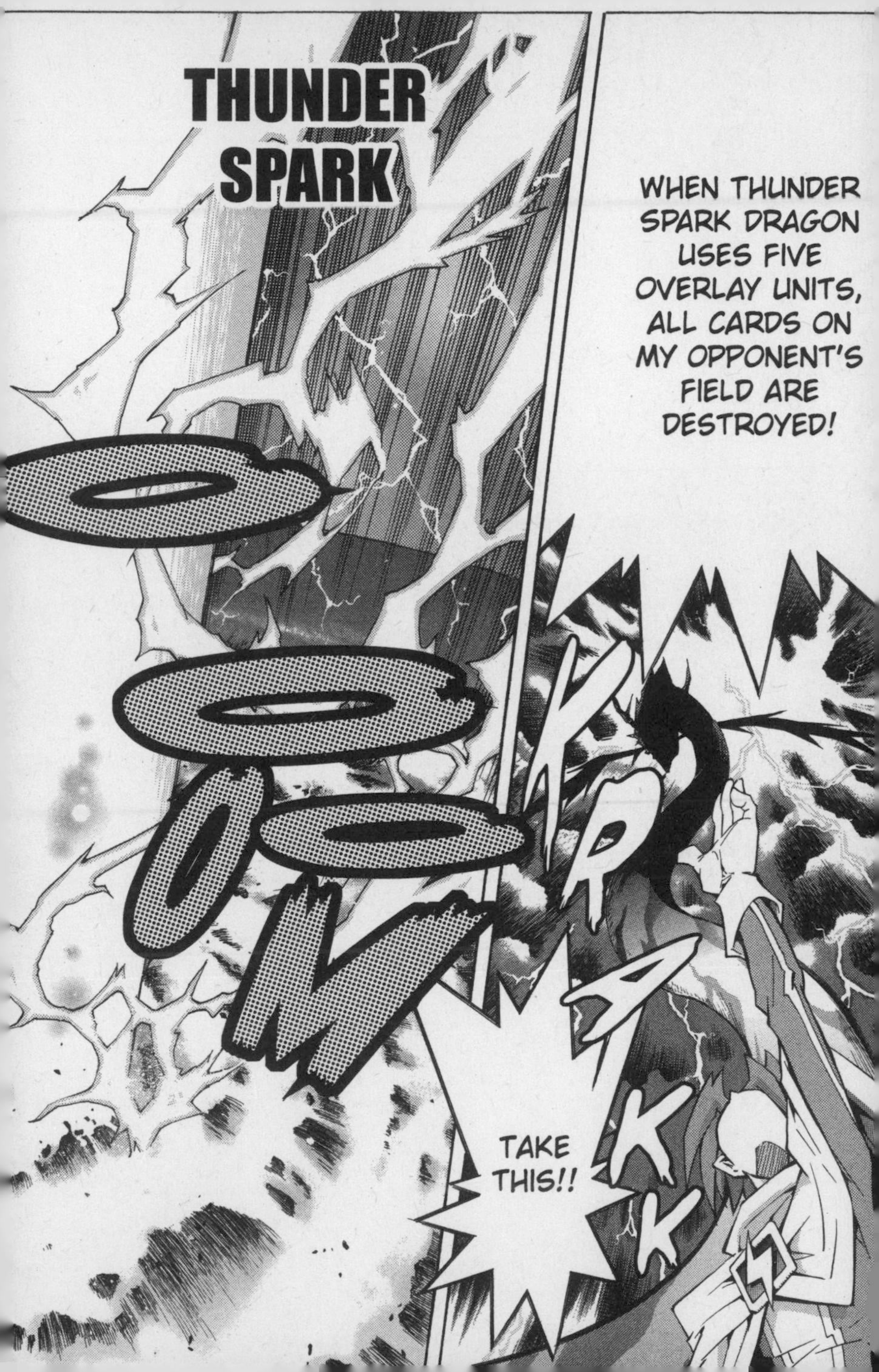

WHEN THUNDER SPARK DRAGON USES FIVE OVERLAY UNITS, ALL CARDS ON MY OPPONENT'S FIELD ARE DESTROYED!
TAKE THIS!!
THUNDER SPARK

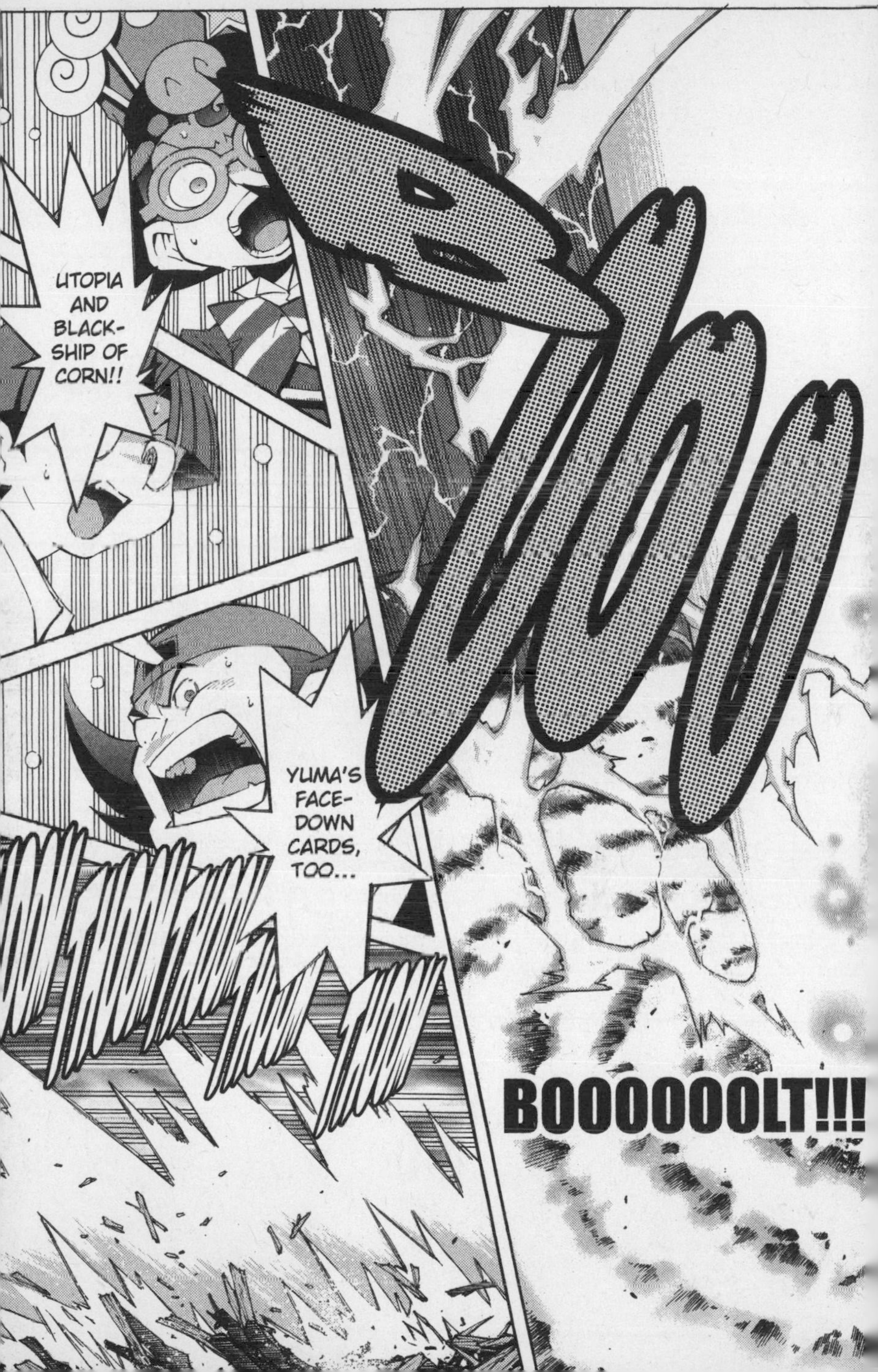
BOOOOOOLT!!!
UTOPIA AND BLACK-SHIP OF CORN!!
YUMA'S FACE-DOWN CARDS, TOO...

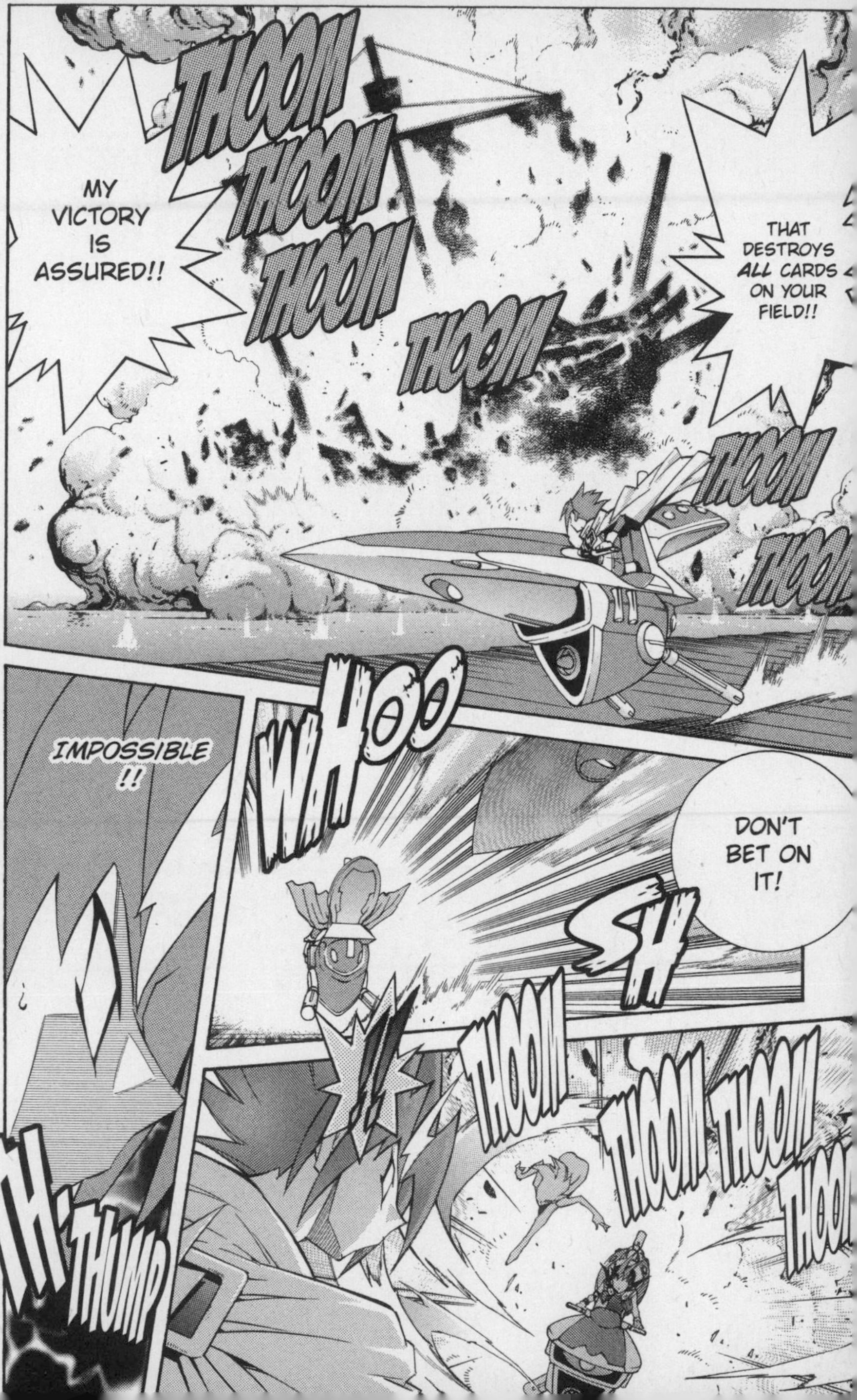
THAT DESTROYS ALL CARDS ON YOUR FIELD!!
THOOM THOOM THOOM
MY VICTORY IS ASSURED!!
THOOM
THOOM
THOOM
DON'T BET ON IT!
WHOOO
SH
IMPOSSIBLE!!
THOOM THOOM THOOM
THOOM
TH-THUMP

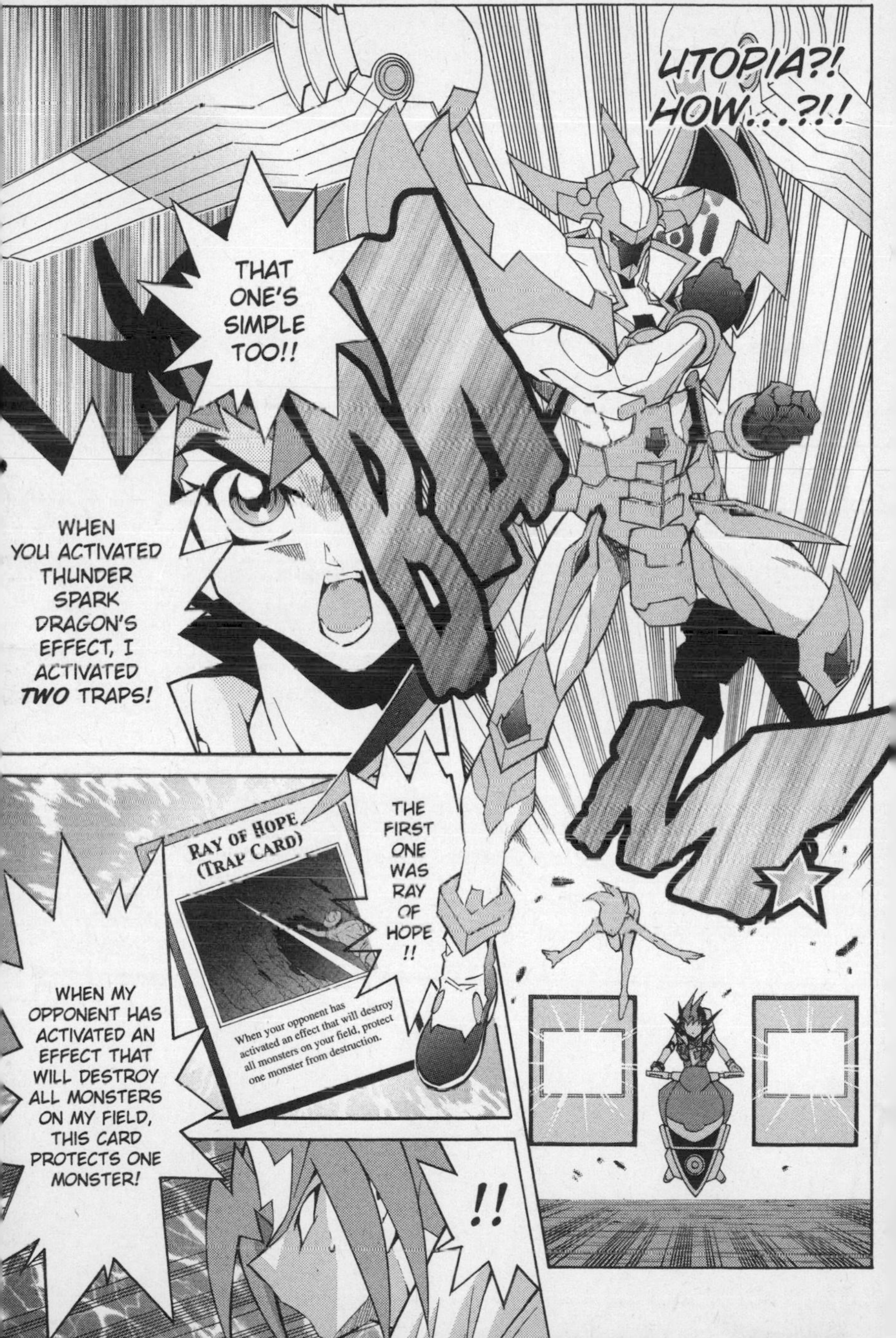

UTOPIA?! HOW...?!!
THAT ONE'S SIMPLE TOO!!
WHEN YOU ACTIVATED THUNDER SPARK DRAGON'S EFFECT, I ACTIVATED **TWO** TRAPS!
THE FIRST ONE WAS RAY OF HOPE!!
RAY OF HOPE (TRAP CARD)
When your opponent has activated an effect that will destroy all monsters on your field, protect one monster from destruction.
WHEN MY OPPONENT HAS ACTIVATED AN EFFECT THAT WILL DESTROY ALL MONSTERS ON MY FIELD, THIS CARD PROTECTS ONE MONSTER!
!!

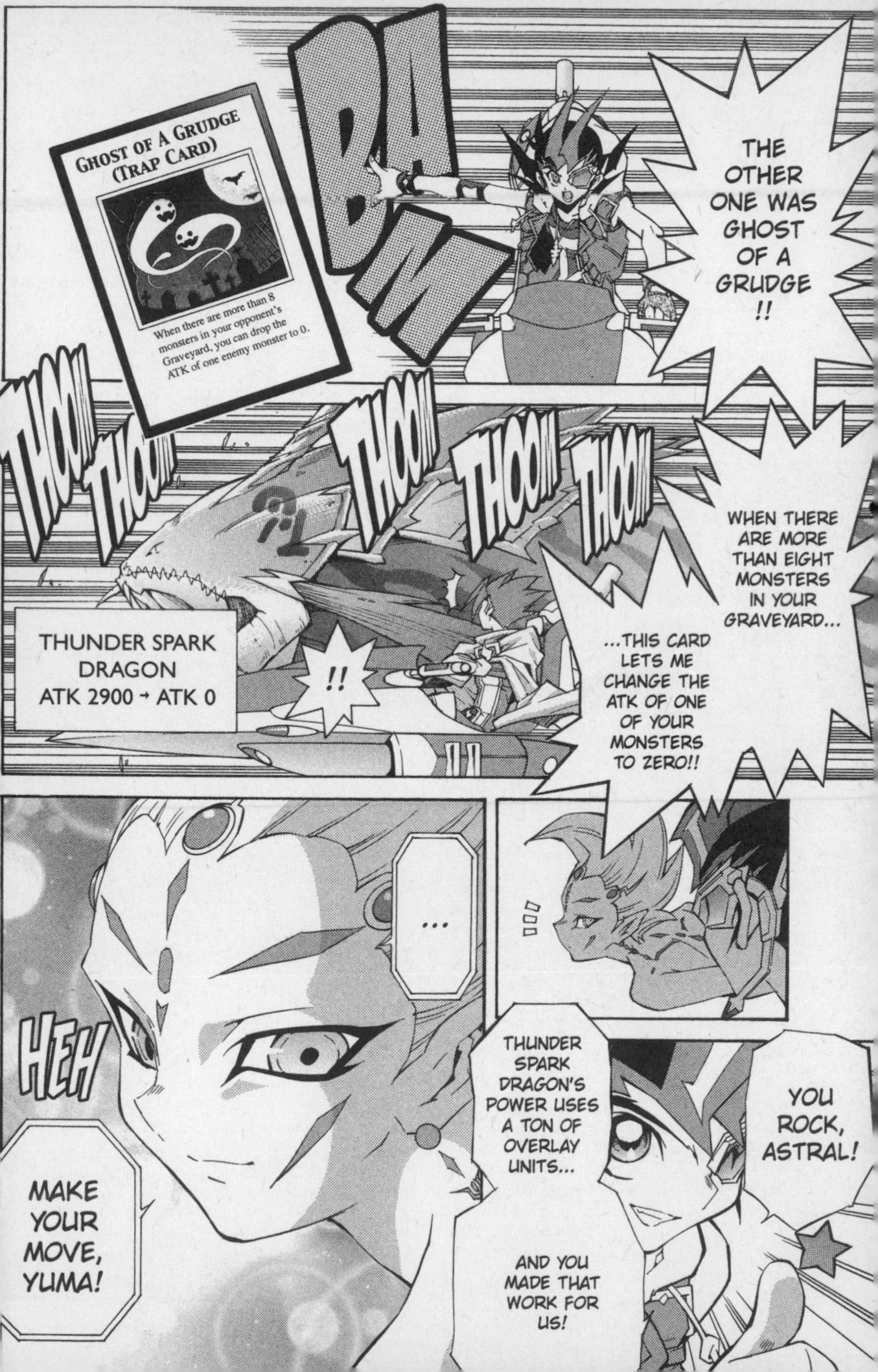

THE OTHER ONE WAS GHOST OF A GRUDGE !!
BAM
GHOST OF A GRUDGE (TRAP CARD)
When there are more than 8 monsters in your opponent's Graveyard, you can drop the ATK of one enemy monster to 0.
THOOM THOOM THOOM THOOM THOOM THOOM
WHEN THERE ARE MORE THAN EIGHT MONSTERS IN YOUR GRAVEYARD...
...THIS CARD LETS ME CHANGE THE ATK OF ONE OF YOUR MONSTERS TO ZERO!!
THUNDER SPARK DRAGON ATK 2900 → ATK 0
!!
YOU ROCK, ASTRAL!
THUNDER SPARK DRAGON'S POWER USES A TON OF OVERLAY UNITS...
AND YOU MADE THAT WORK FOR US!
...
HEH
MAKE YOUR MOVE, YUMA!

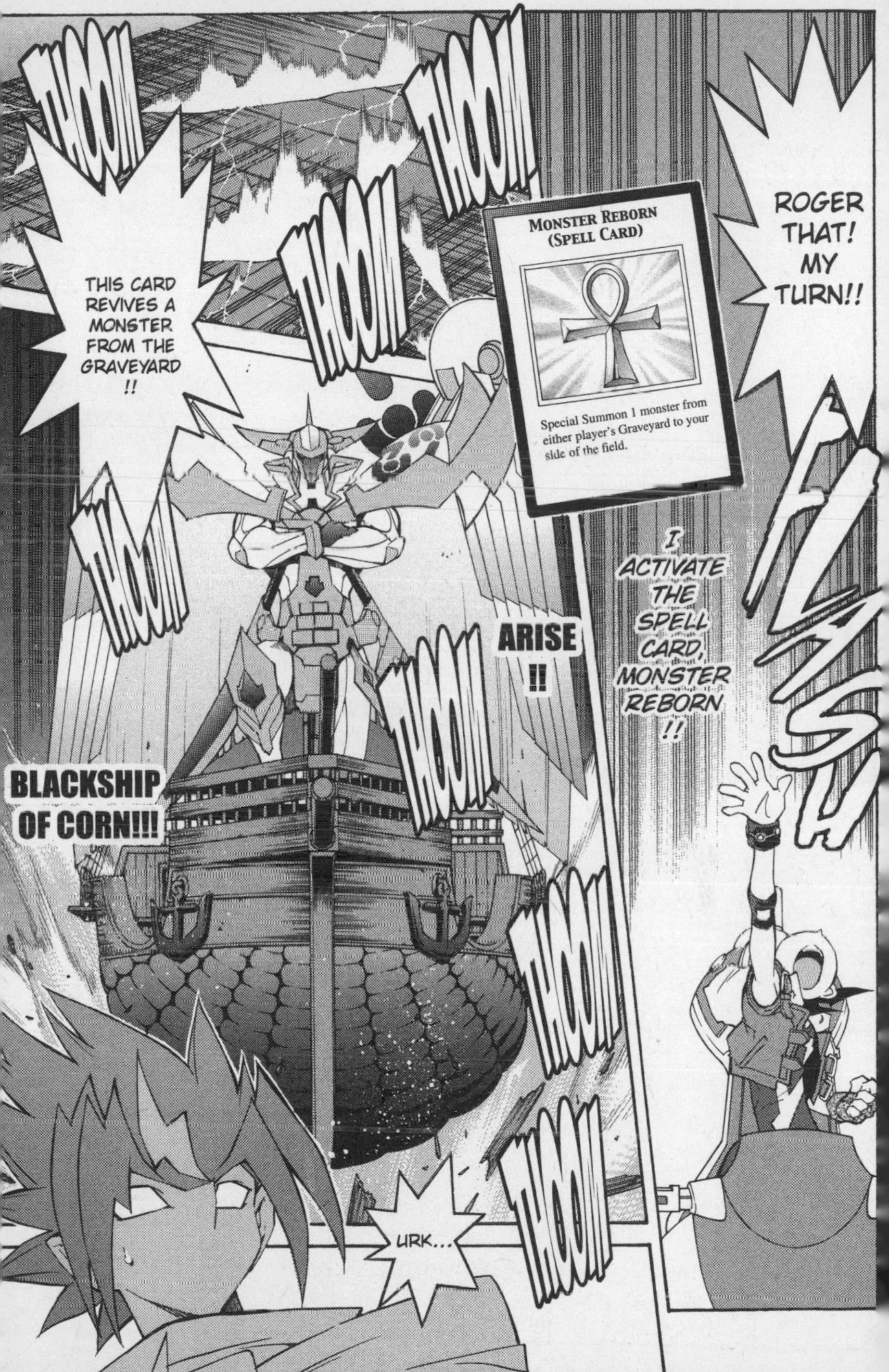

ROGER THAT! MY TURN!!
FLASH
I ACTIVATE THE SPELL CARD, MONSTER REBORN!!
MONSTER REBORN (SPELL CARD)
Special Summon 1 monster from either player's Graveyard to your side of the field.
THOOM
THOOM
THOOM
THOOM
THIS CARD REVIVES A MONSTER FROM THE GRAVEYARD!!
THOOM
ARISE!!
THOOM
BLACKSHIP OF CORN!!!
THOOM
THOOM
URK...

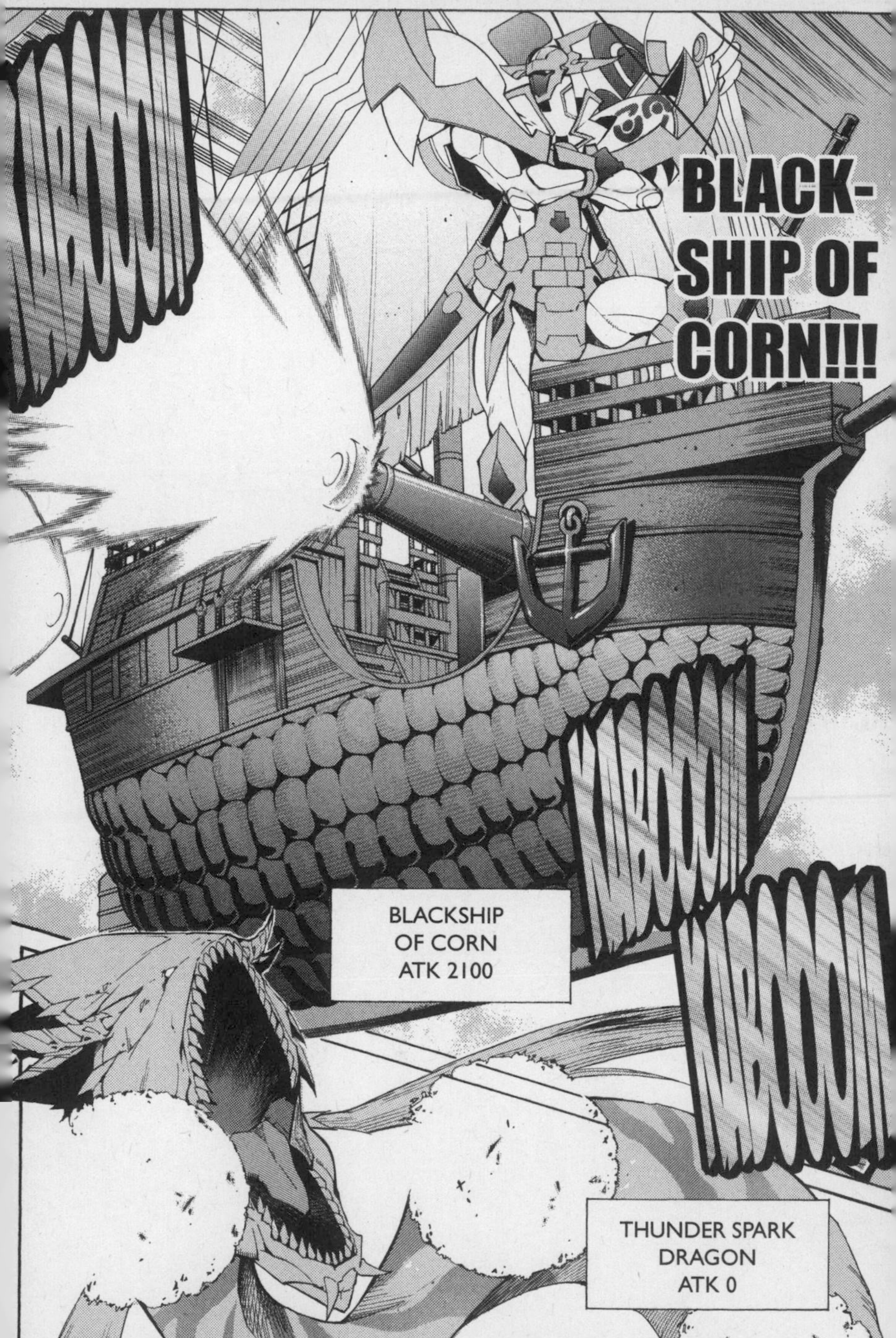
BLACK-SHIP OF CORN!!!
BLACKSHIP OF CORN ATK 2100
THUNDER SPARK DRAGON ATK 0

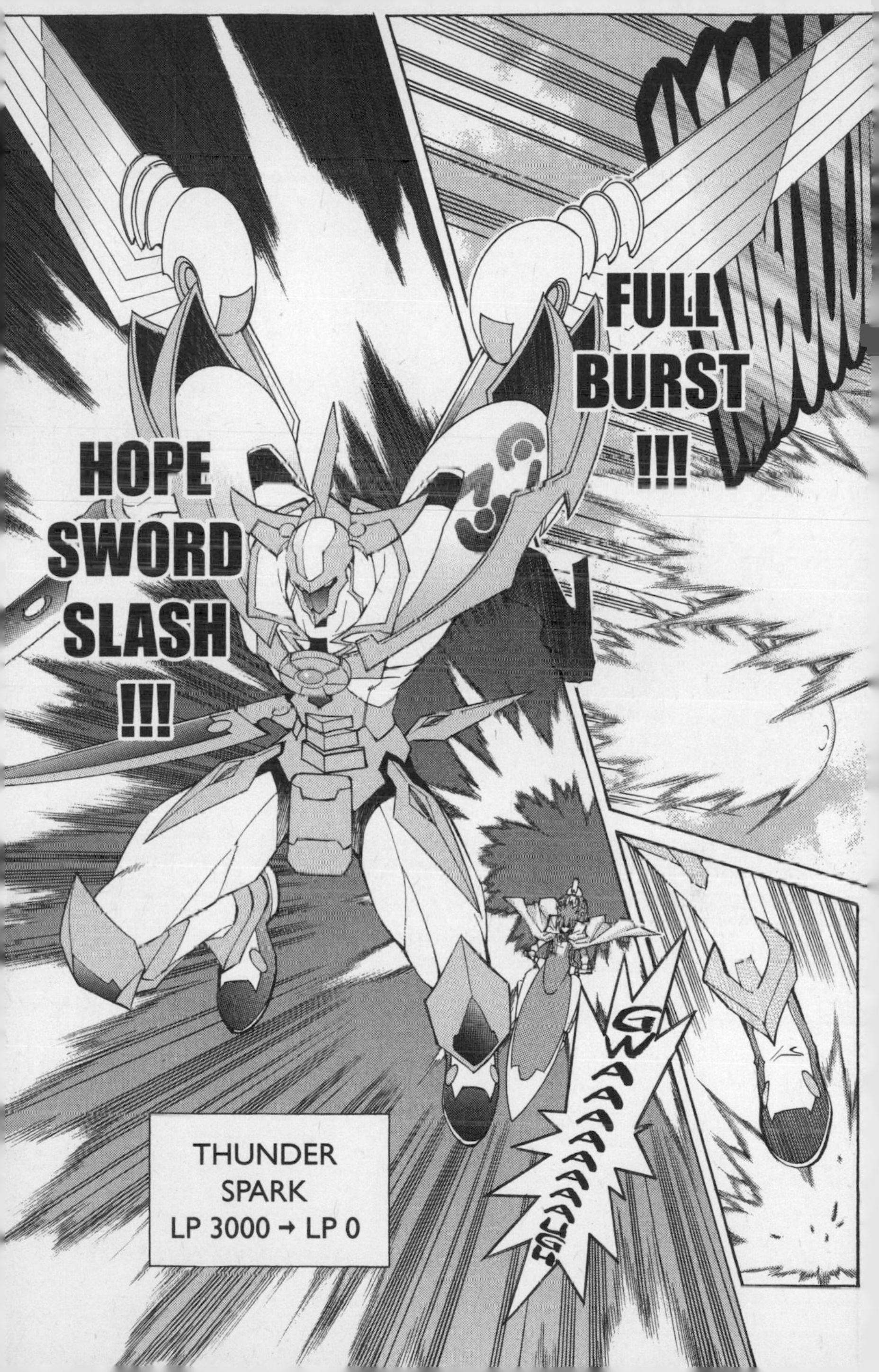
FULL BURST!!!
HOPE SWORD SLASH!!!
THUNDER SPARK LP 3000 → LP 0
GWAAAAAAAUGH!

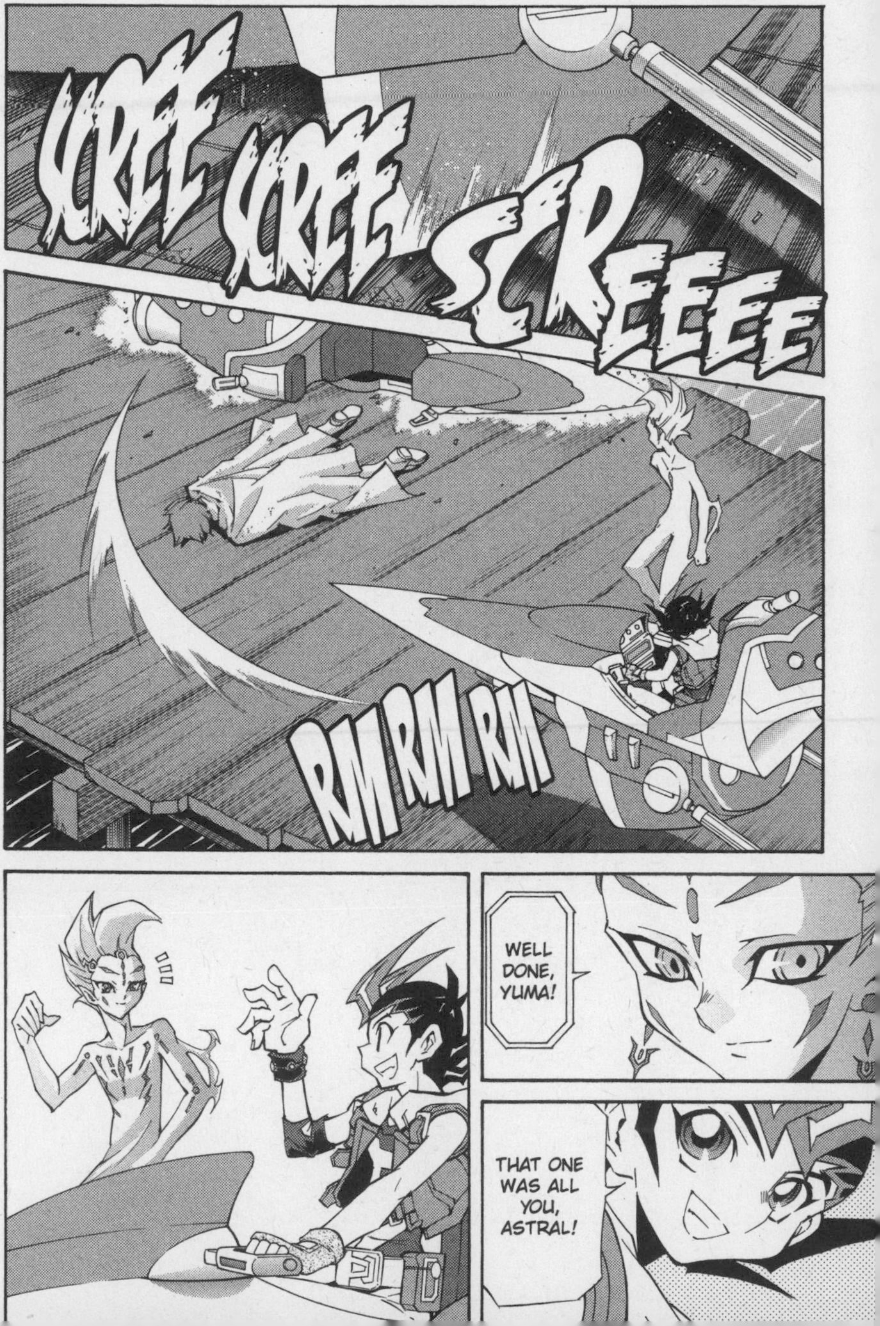
SCREE SCREE SCREEEEE
RM RM RM
WELL DONE, YUMA!
THAT ONE WAS ALL YOU, ASTRAL!

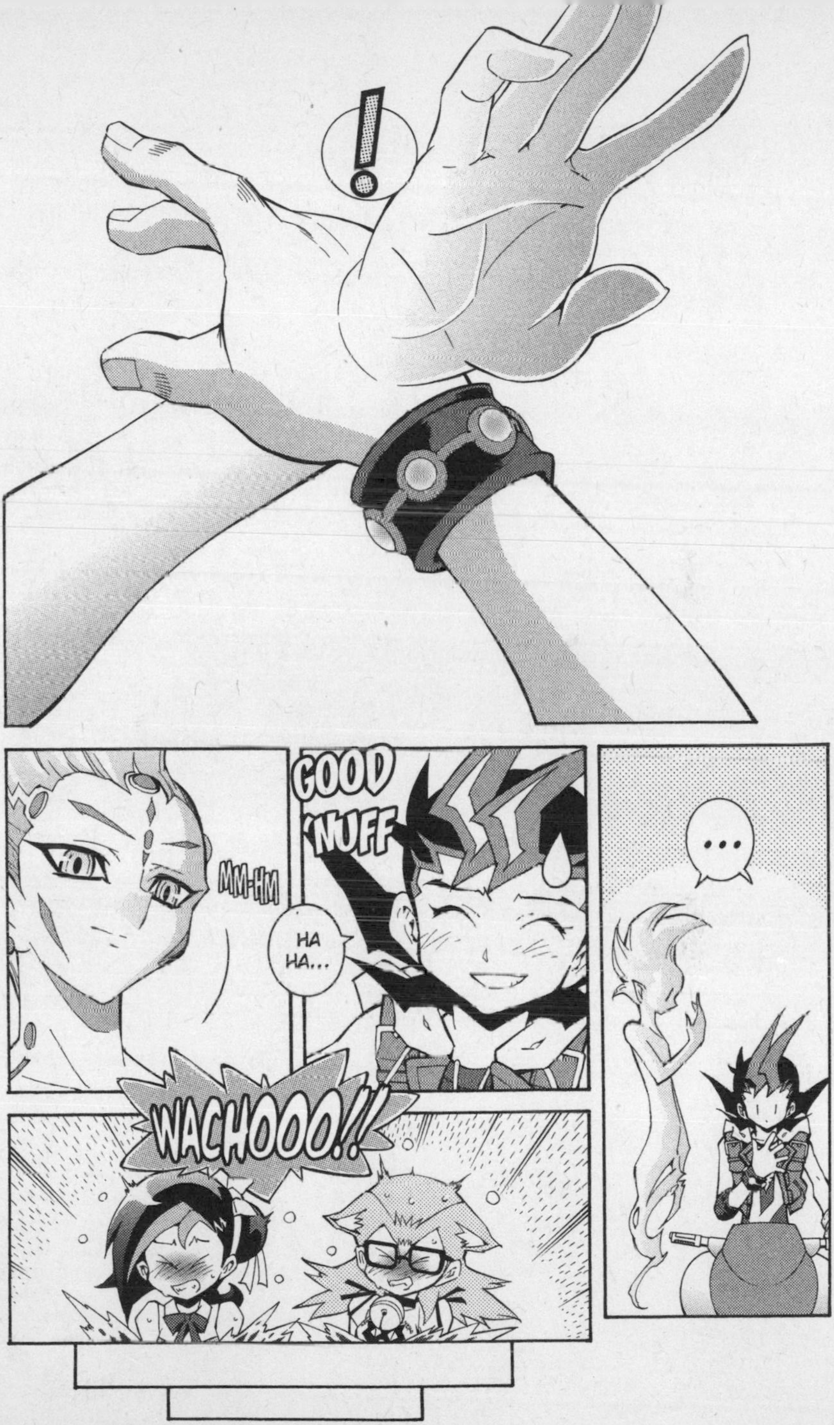
!
...
GOOD 'NUFF
HA HA...
MM-HM
WACHOOO!!

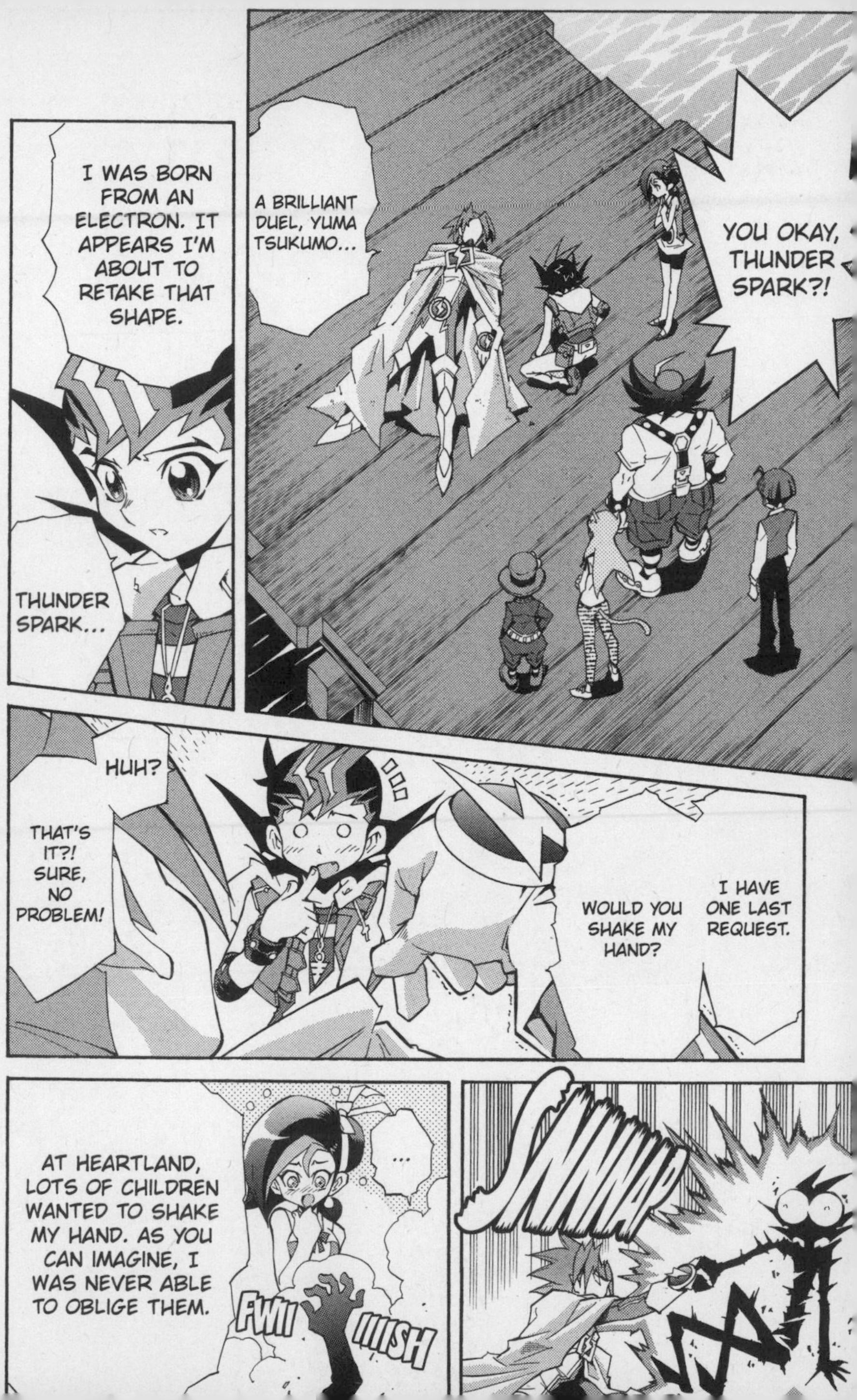
YOU OKAY, THUNDER SPARK?!
A BRILLIANT DUEL, YUMA TSUKUMO...
I WAS BORN FROM AN ELECTRON. IT APPEARS I'M ABOUT TO RETAKE THAT SHAPE.
THUNDER SPARK...
I HAVE ONE LAST REQUEST.
WOULD YOU SHAKE MY HAND?
HUH?
THAT'S IT?! SURE, NO PROBLEM!
SNNNAP
...
AT HEARTLAND, LOTS OF CHILDREN WANTED TO SHAKE MY HAND. AS YOU CAN IMAGINE, I WAS NEVER ABLE TO OBLIGE THEM.
FWIIIIIISH

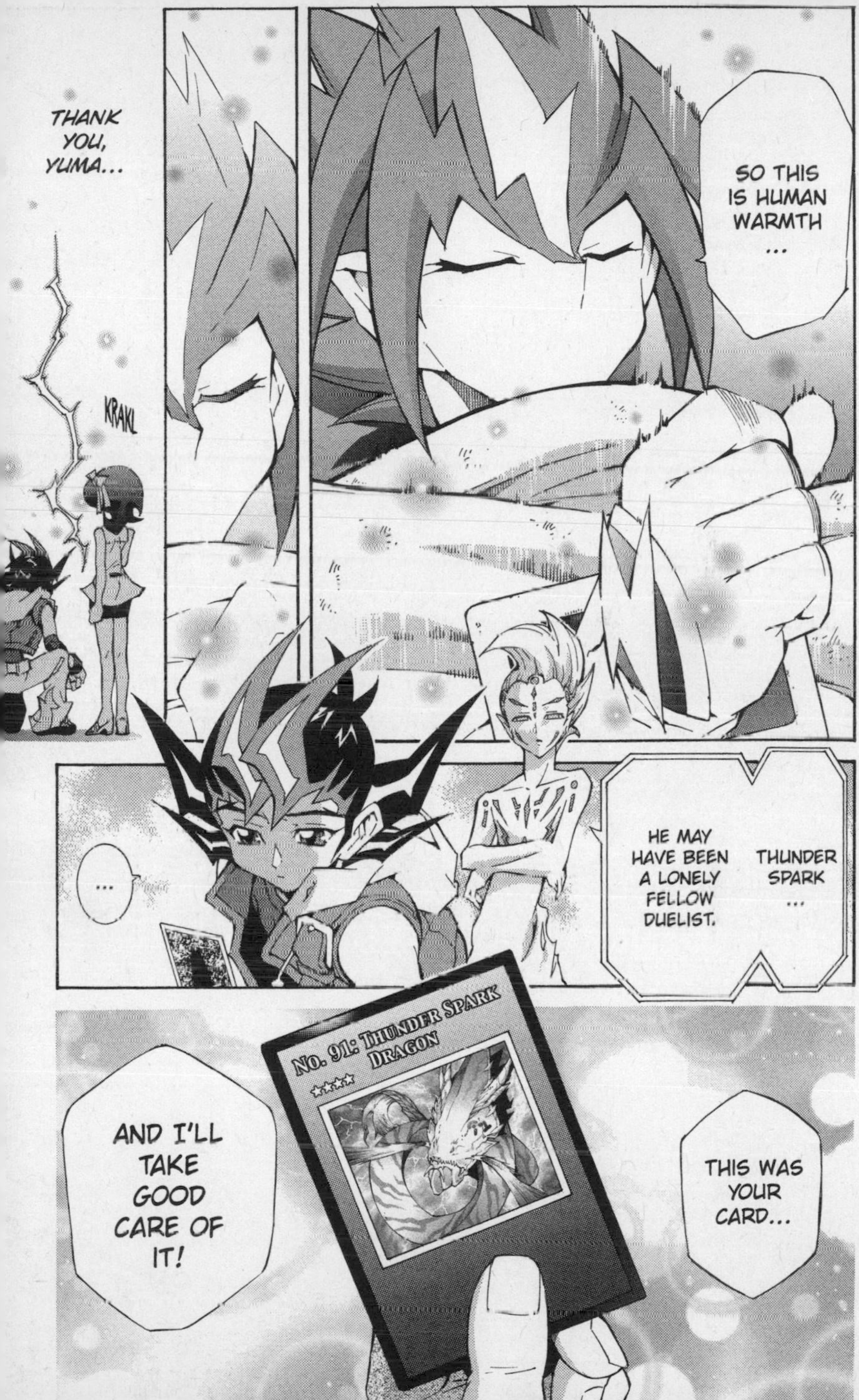
SO THIS IS HUMAN WARMTH ...
THANK YOU, YUMA...
KRAKL
THUNDER SPARK ...
HE MAY HAVE BEEN A LONELY FELLOW DUELIST.
...
No. 91: THUNDER SPARK DRAGON
THIS WAS YOUR CARD...
AND I'LL TAKE GOOD CARE OF IT!

YU-GI-OH!
ZEXAL

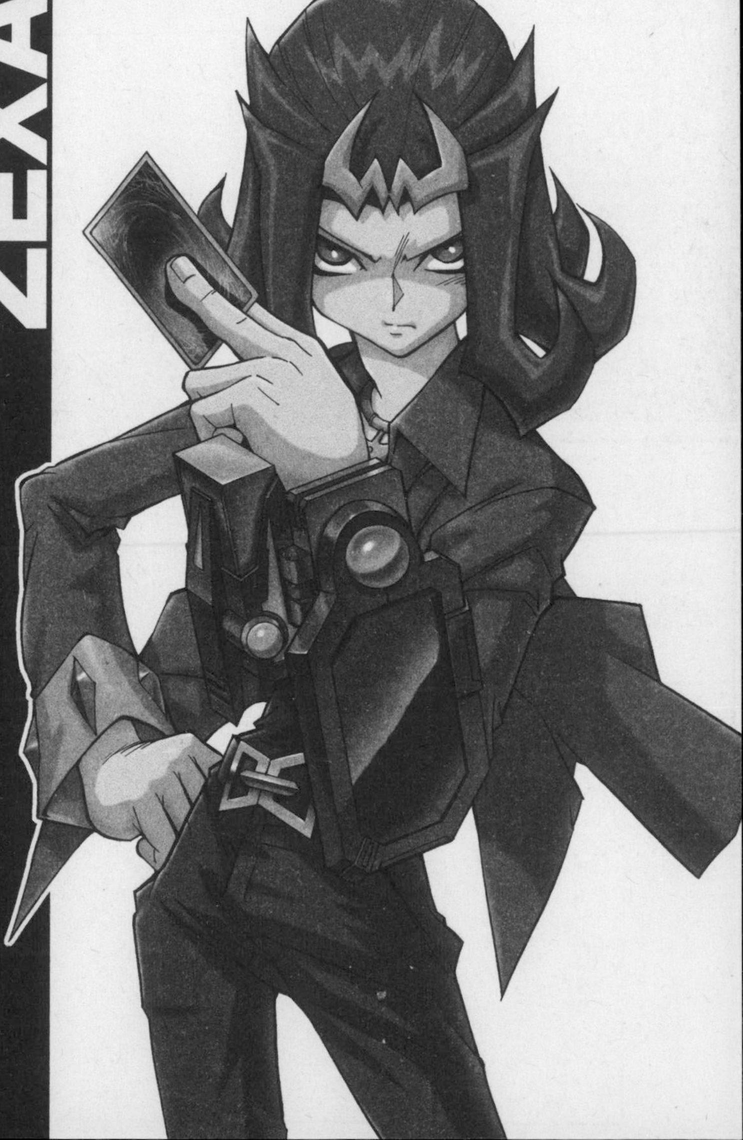

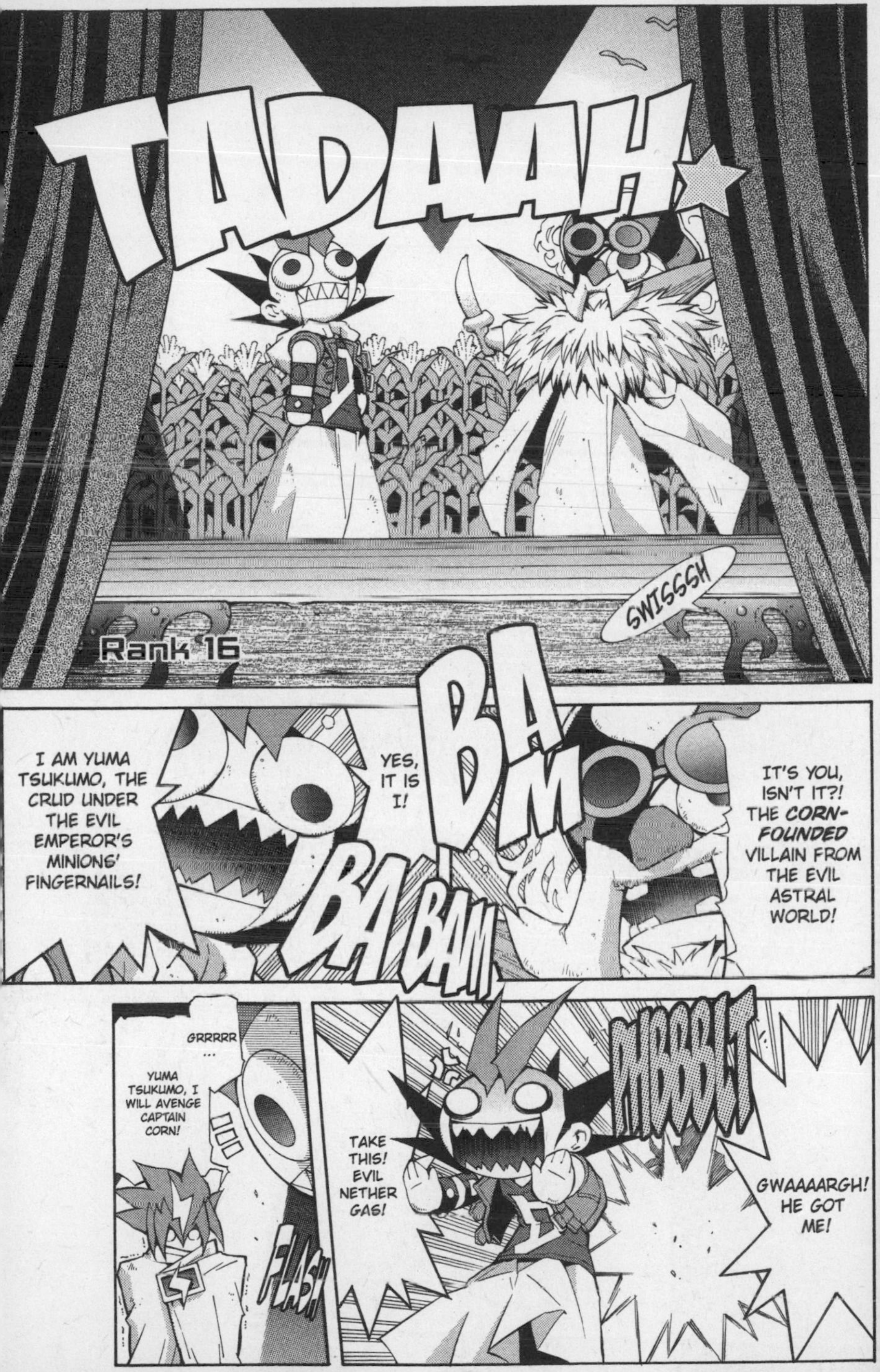
TADAAH!
SWISSSH
Rank 16
IT'S YOU, ISN'T IT?! THE *CORN-FOUNDED* VILLAIN FROM THE EVIL ASTRAL WORLD!
BAM
YES, IT IS I!
I AM YUMA TSUKUMO, THE CRUD UNDER THE EVIL EMPEROR'S MINIONS' FINGERNAILS!
BA BAM
PHBBBLT
GWAAAARGH! HE GOT ME!
TAKE THIS! EVIL NETHER GAS!
GRRRRR ...
YUMA TSUKUMO, I WILL AVENGE CAPTAIN CORN!
FLASH

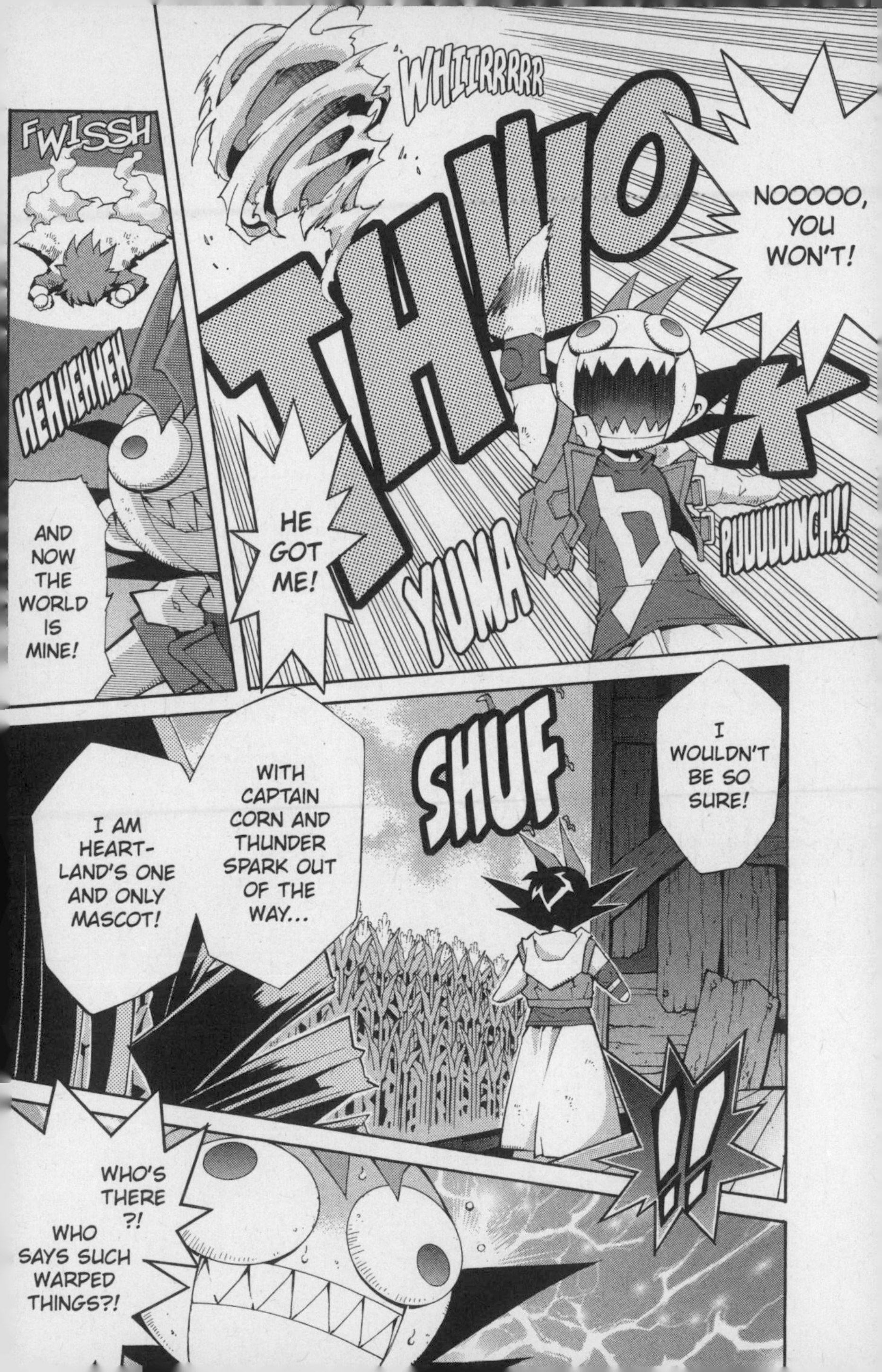
WHIRRRRR
NOOOOO, YOU WON'T!
THWOK
YUMA
PUUUUUNCH!!
HE GOT ME!
FWISSH
HEHHEHHEH
AND NOW THE WORLD IS MINE!
WITH CAPTAIN CORN AND THUNDER SPARK OUT OF THE WAY...
I AM HEART-LAND'S ONE AND ONLY MASCOT!
SHUF
I WOULDN'T BE SO SURE!
!!
WHO'S THERE?!
WHO SAYS SUCH WARPED THINGS?!

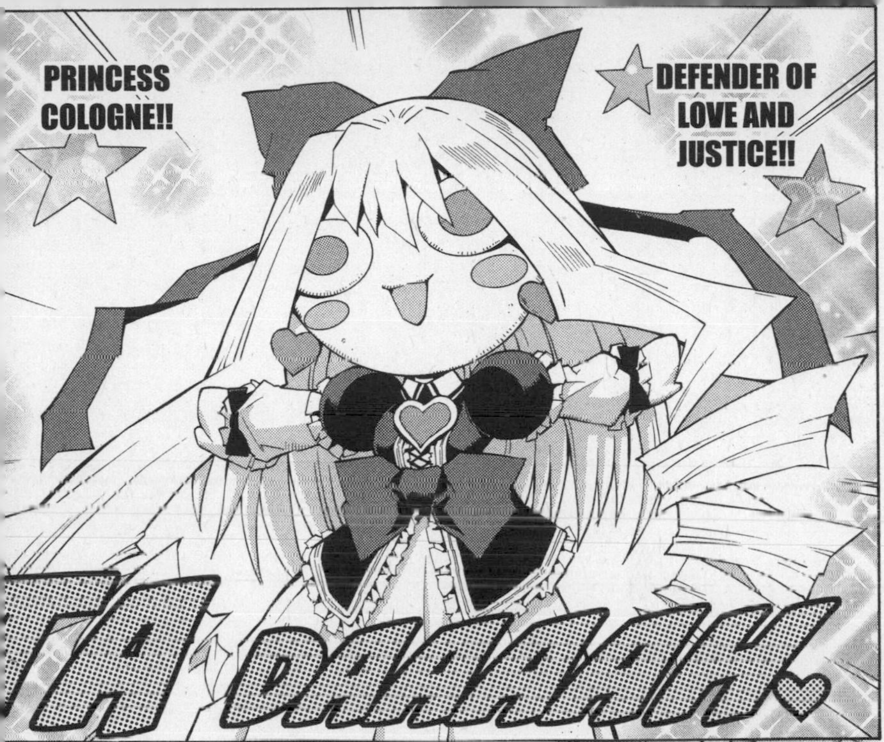
DEFENDER OF LOVE AND JUSTICE!!
PRINCESS COLOGNE!!
TA DAAAAAH.

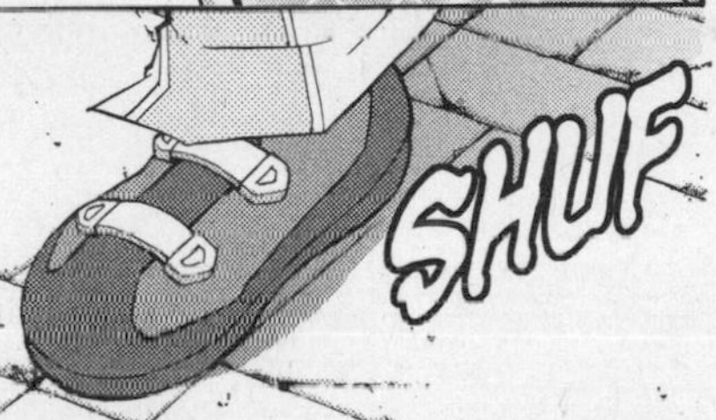
SHUF

Rank 16: The Third Enemy!!

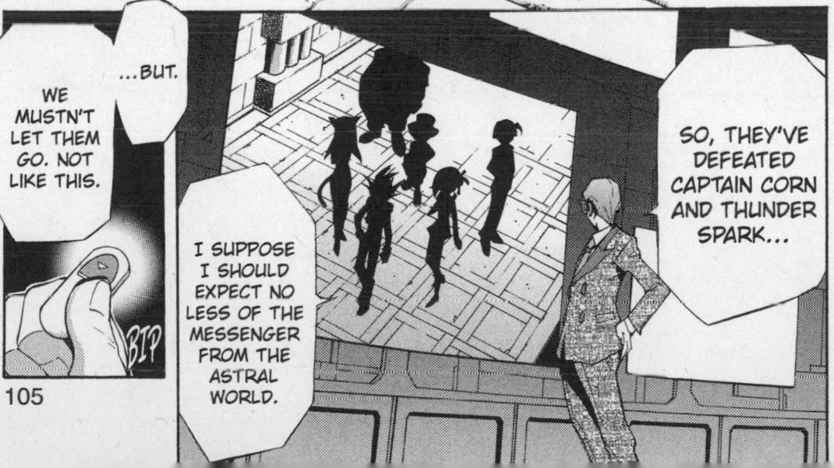
SO, THEY'VE DEFEATED CAPTAIN CORN AND THUNDER SPARK...
I SUPPOSE I SHOULD EXPECT NO LESS OF THE MESSENGER FROM THE ASTRAL WORLD.
...BUT.
WE MUSTN'T LET THEM GO. NOT LIKE THIS.
BIP

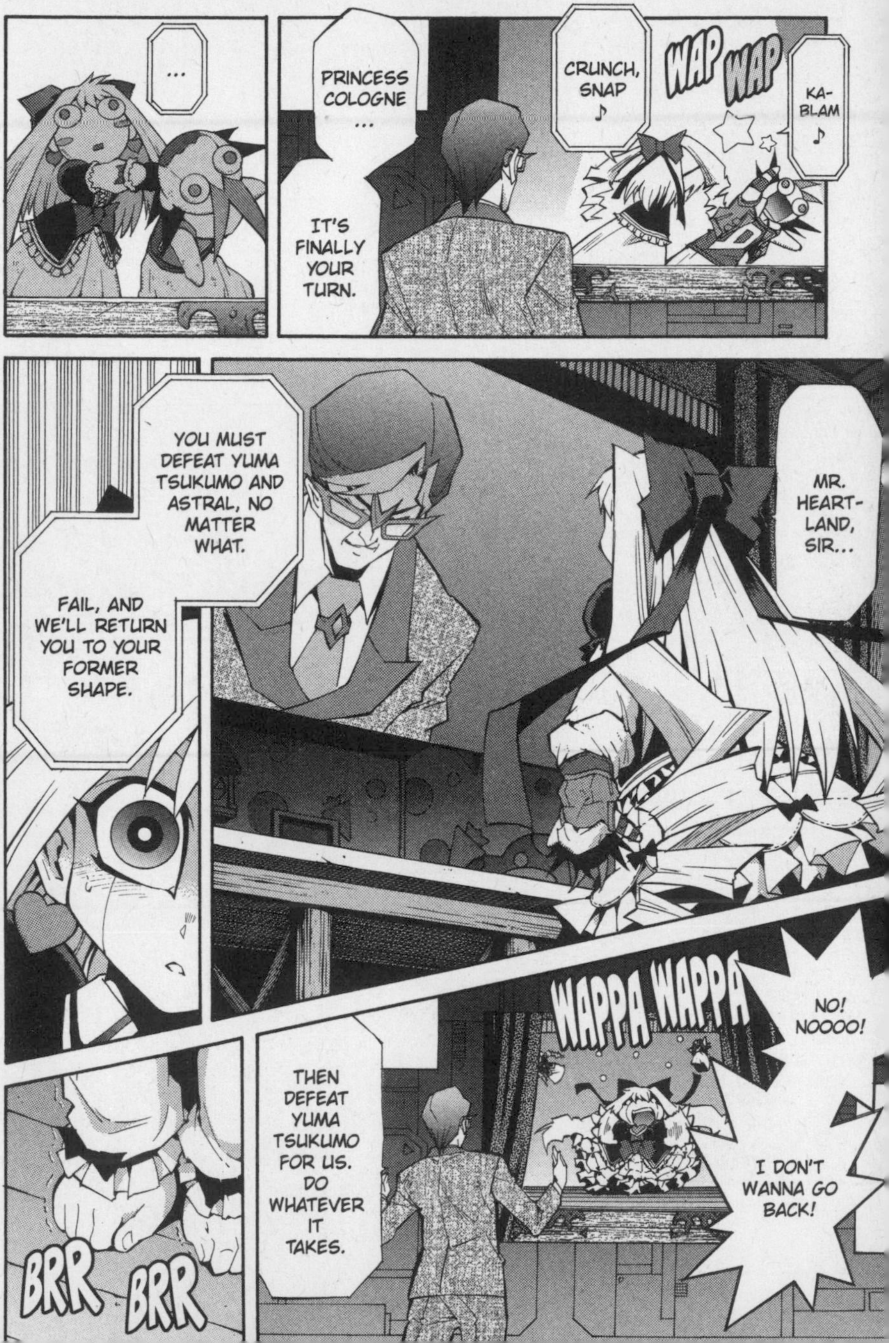
KA-BLAM ♪
WAP WAP
CRUNCH, SNAP ♪
PRINCESS COLOGNE ...
IT'S FINALLY YOUR TURN.
...
MR. HEARTLAND, SIR...
YOU MUST DEFEAT YUMA TSUKUMO AND ASTRAL, NO MATTER WHAT.
FAIL, AND WE'LL RETURN YOU TO YOUR FORMER SHAPE.
NO! NOOOO!
WAPPA WAPPA
I DON'T WANNA GO BACK!
THEN DEFEAT YUMA TSUKUMO FOR US. DO WHATEVER IT TAKES.
BRR BRR

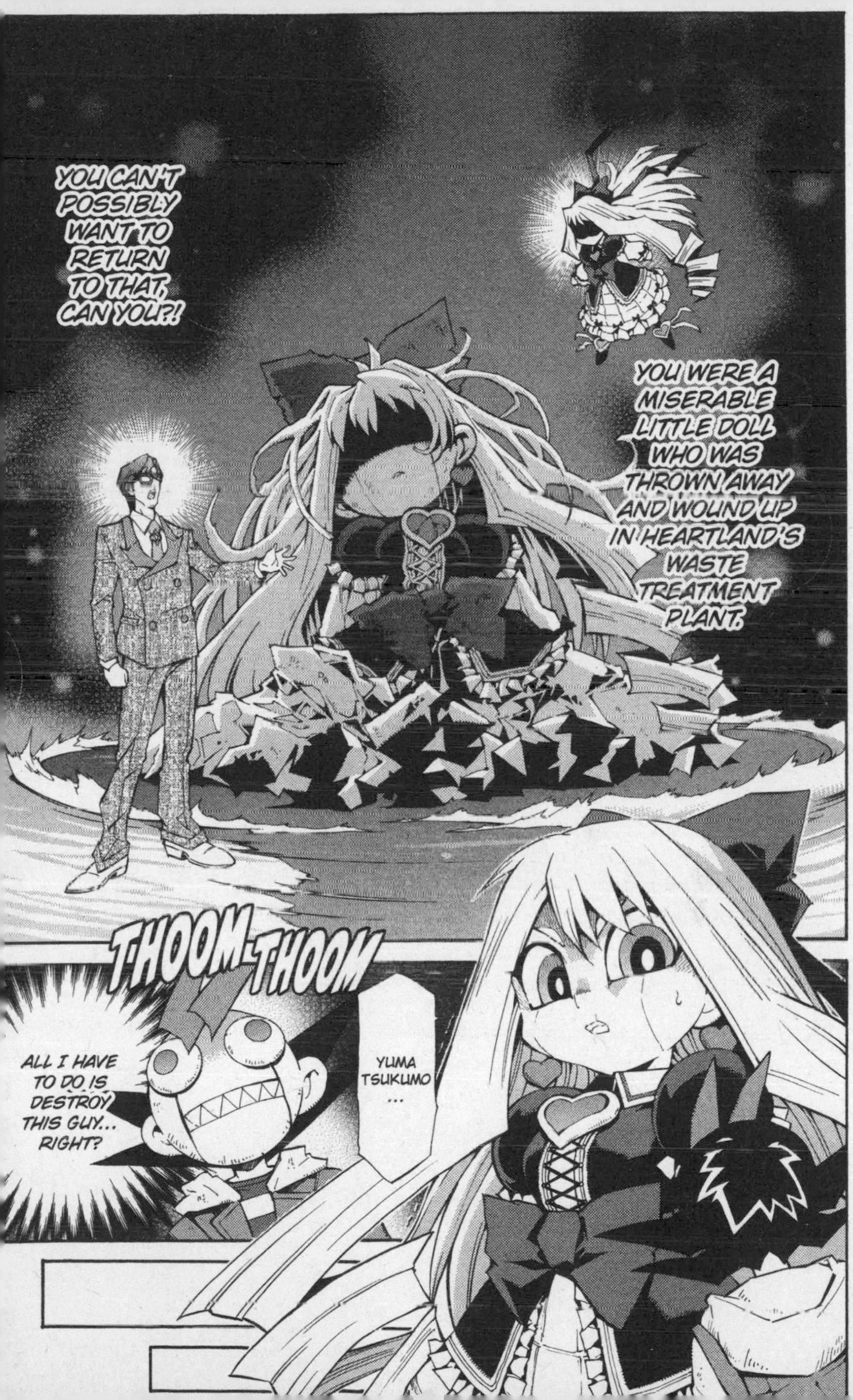
YOU WERE A MISERABLE LITTLE DOLL WHO WAS THROWN AWAY AND WOUND UP IN HEARTLAND'S WASTE TREATMENT PLANT.
YOU CAN'T POSSIBLY WANT TO RETURN TO THAT, CAN YOU?!
THOOM THOOM
YUMA TSUKUMO ...
ALL I HAVE TO DO IS DESTROY THIS GUY... RIGHT?

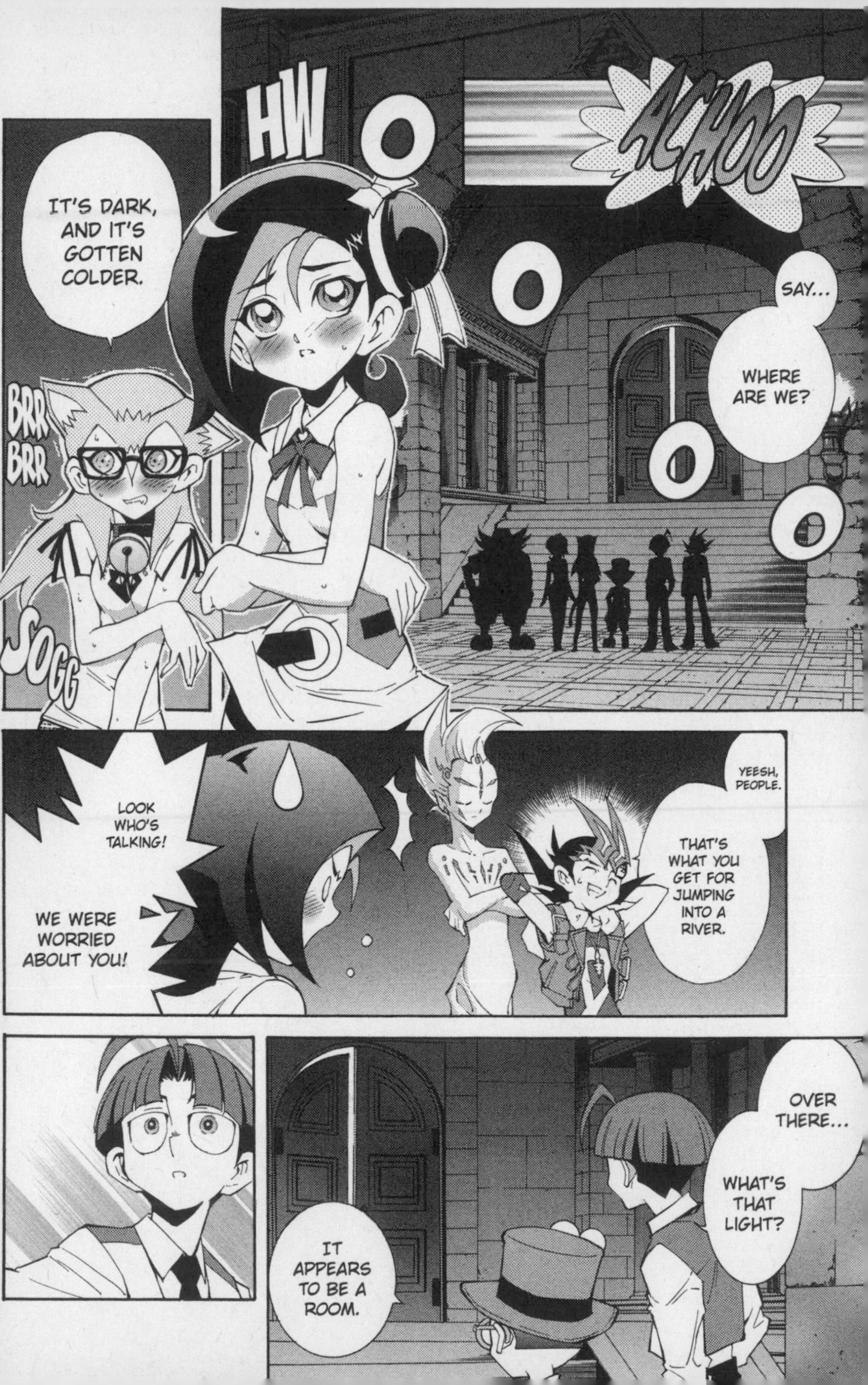
HWOOOOACHOO
SAY...
WHERE ARE WE?
IT'S DARK, AND IT'S GOTTEN COLDER.
BRR BRR
SOGG
YEESH, PEOPLE.
THAT'S WHAT YOU GET FOR JUMPING INTO A RIVER.
LOOK WHO'S TALKING!
WE WERE WORRIED ABOUT YOU!
OVER THERE...
WHAT'S THAT LIGHT?
IT APPEARS TO BE A ROOM.

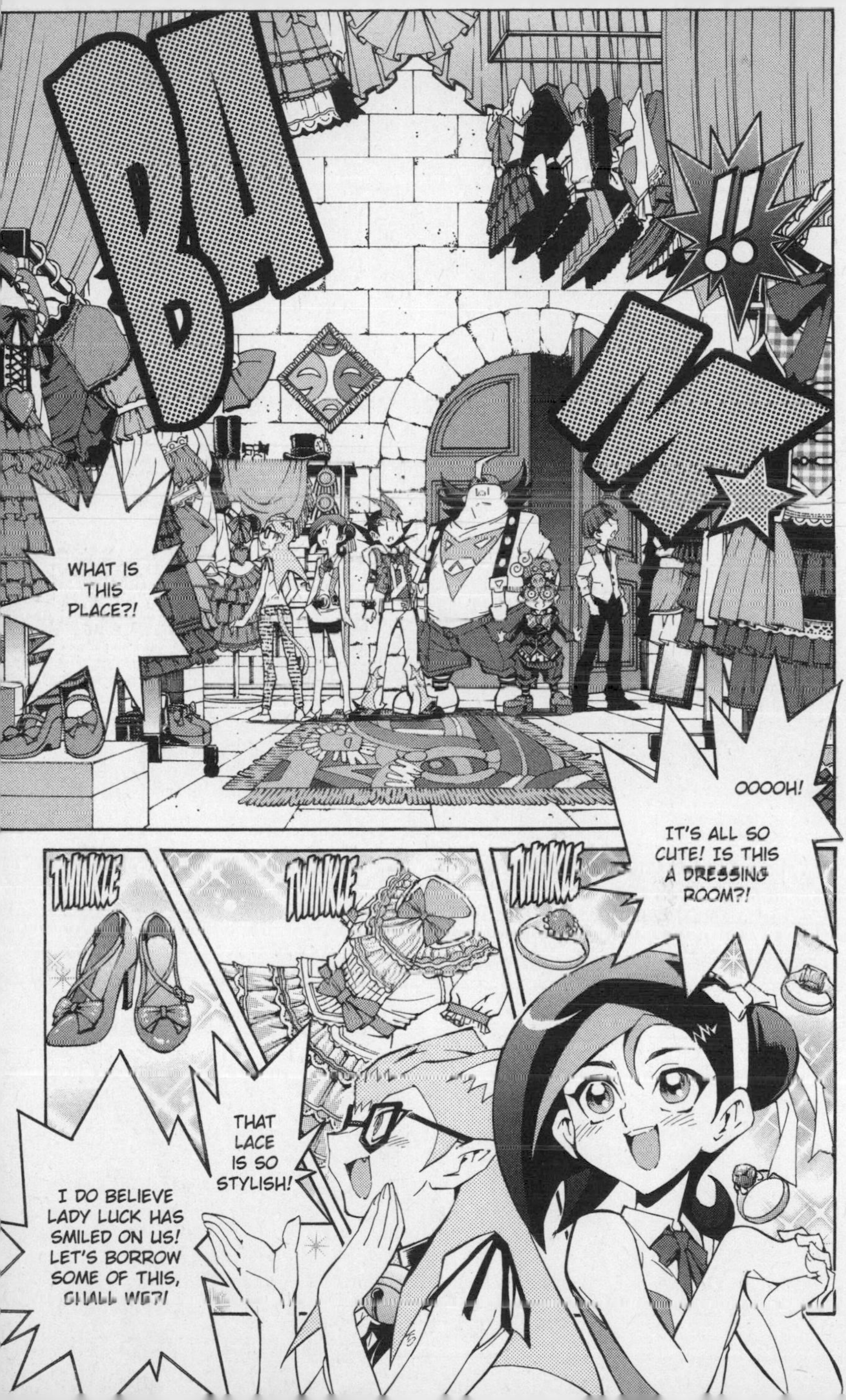
BAM!!
WHAT IS THIS PLACE?!
OOOOH!
IT'S ALL SO CUTE! IS THIS A DRESSING ROOM?!
TWINKLE
TWINKLE
TWINKLE
THAT LACE IS SO STYLISH!
I DO BELIEVE LADY LUCK HAS SMILED ON US! LET'S BORROW SOME OF THIS, SHALL WE?!

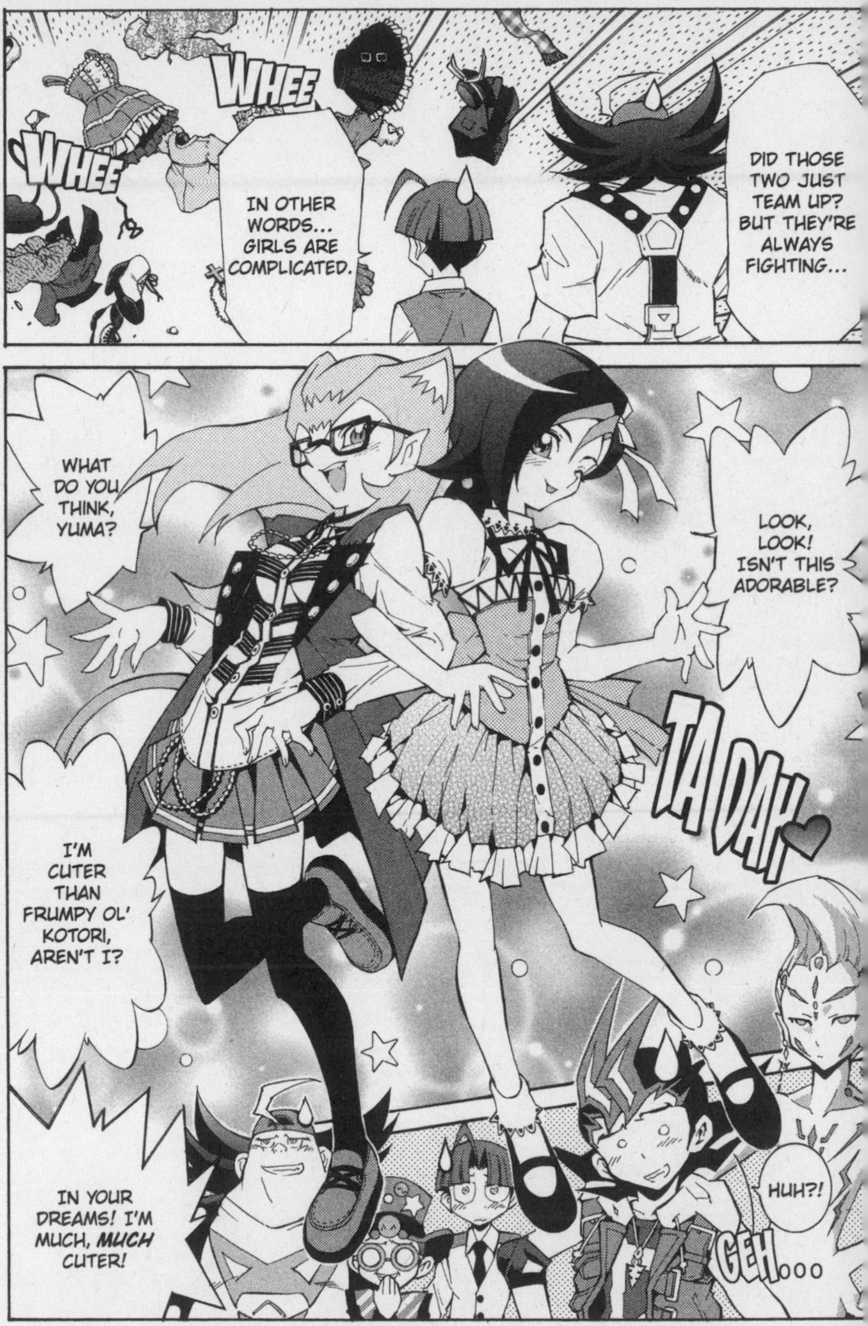
DID THOSE TWO JUST TEAM UP? BUT THEY'RE ALWAYS FIGHTING...
IN OTHER WORDS... GIRLS ARE COMPLICATED.
WHEE
WHEE
LOOK, LOOK! ISN'T THIS ADORABLE?
TA DAH♥
WHAT DO YOU THINK, YUMA?
I'M CUTER THAN FRUMPY OL' KOTORI, AREN'T I?
HUH?!
GEH...
IN YOUR DREAMS! I'M MUCH, *MUCH* CUTER!

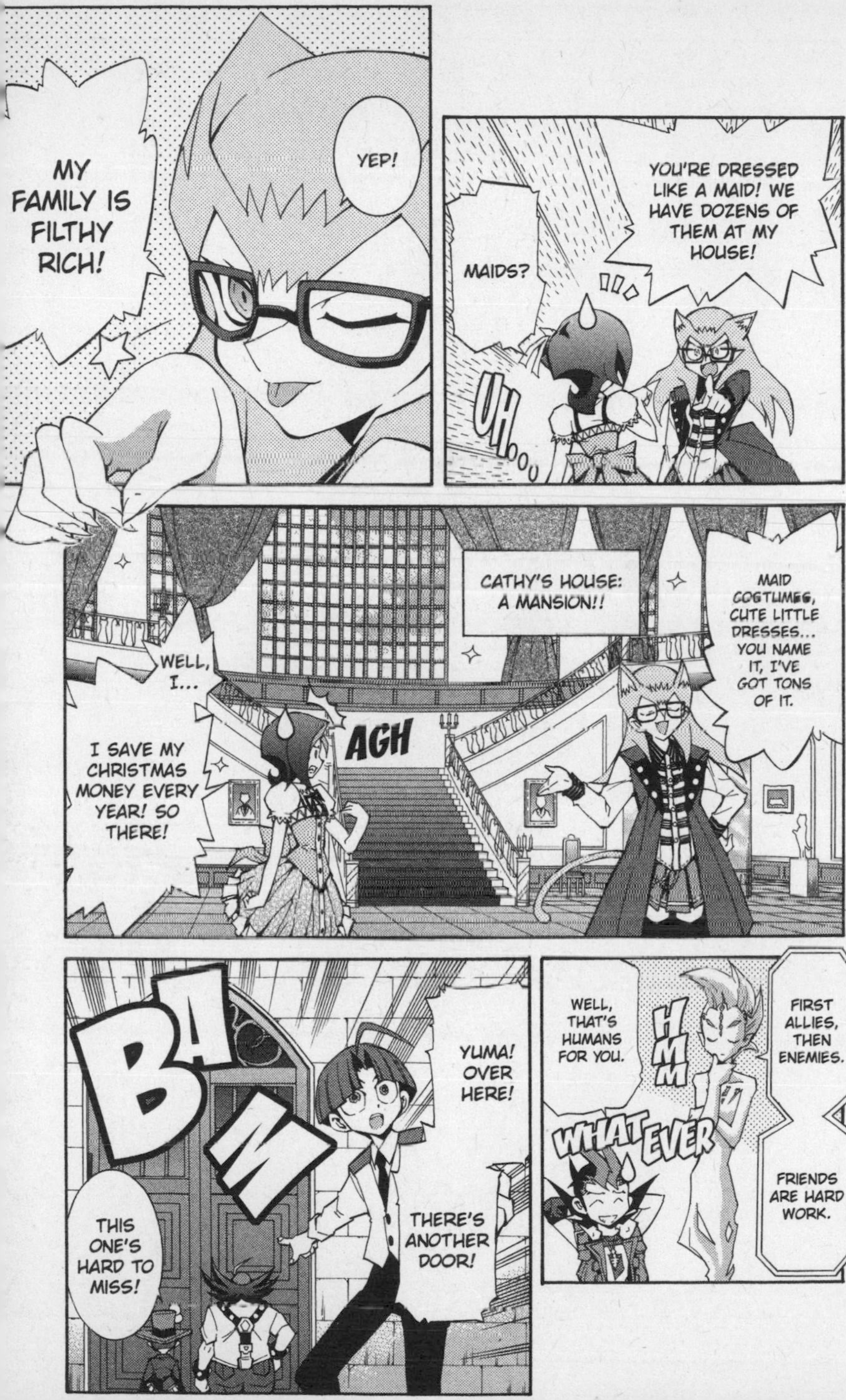
YOU'RE DRESSED LIKE A MAID! WE HAVE DOZENS OF THEM AT MY HOUSE!
MAIDS?
UH...
YEP!
MY FAMILY IS FILTHY RICH!
MAID COSTUMES, CUTE LITTLE DRESSES... YOU NAME IT, I'VE GOT TONS OF IT.
CATHY'S HOUSE: A MANSION!!
WELL, I...
AGH
I SAVE MY CHRISTMAS MONEY EVERY YEAR! SO THERE!
FIRST ALLIES, THEN ENEMIES.
FRIENDS ARE HARD WORK.
HMM
WELL, THAT'S HUMANS FOR YOU.
WHATEVER
BAM
YUMA! OVER HERE!
THERE'S ANOTHER DOOR!
THIS ONE'S HARD TO MISS!

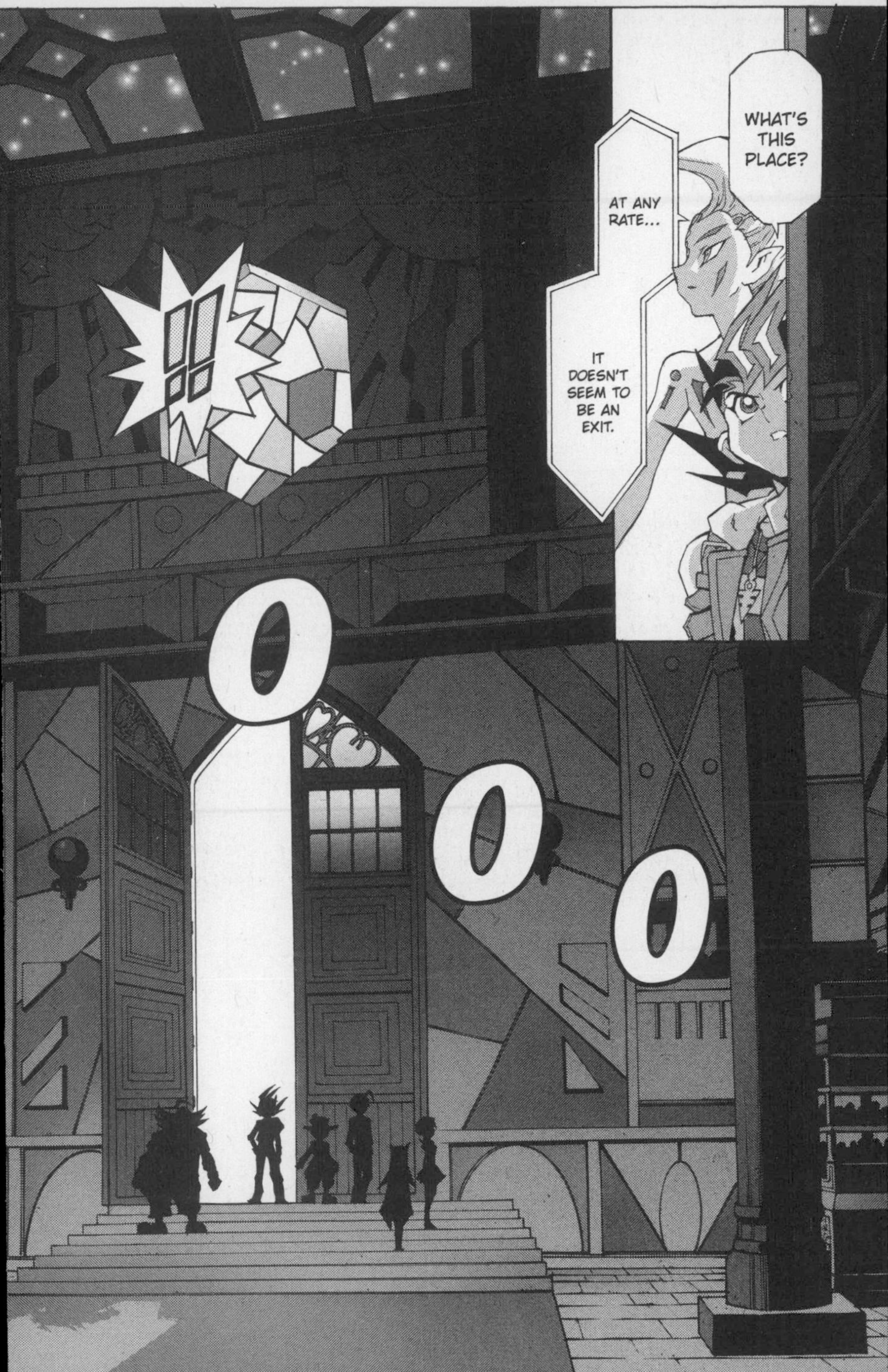
WHAT'S THIS PLACE?
AT ANY RATE...
IT DOESN'T SEEM TO BE AN EXIT.
!!
OOO

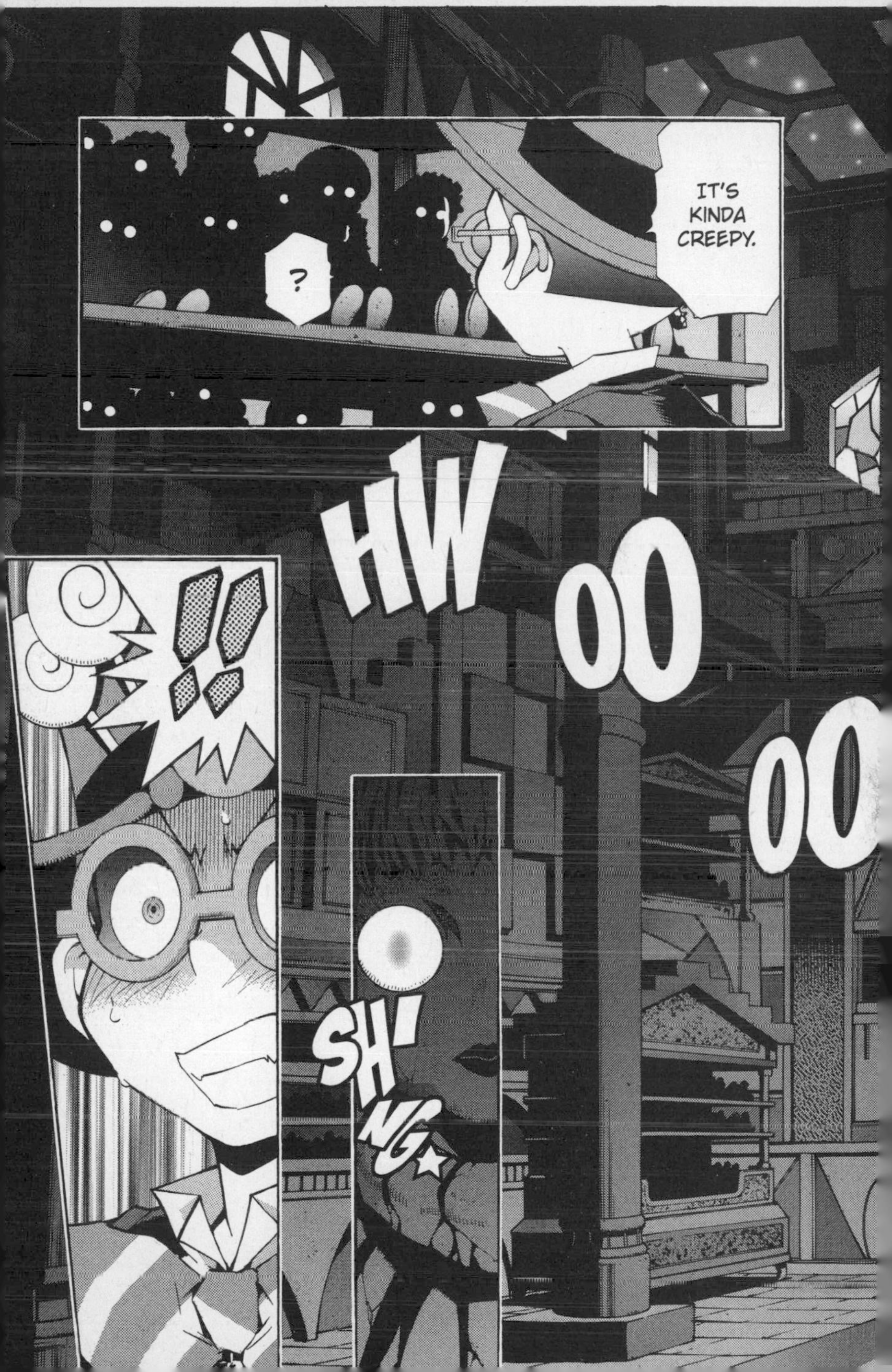
IT'S KINDA CREEPY.
?
HWOOOO
SHING☆
!!

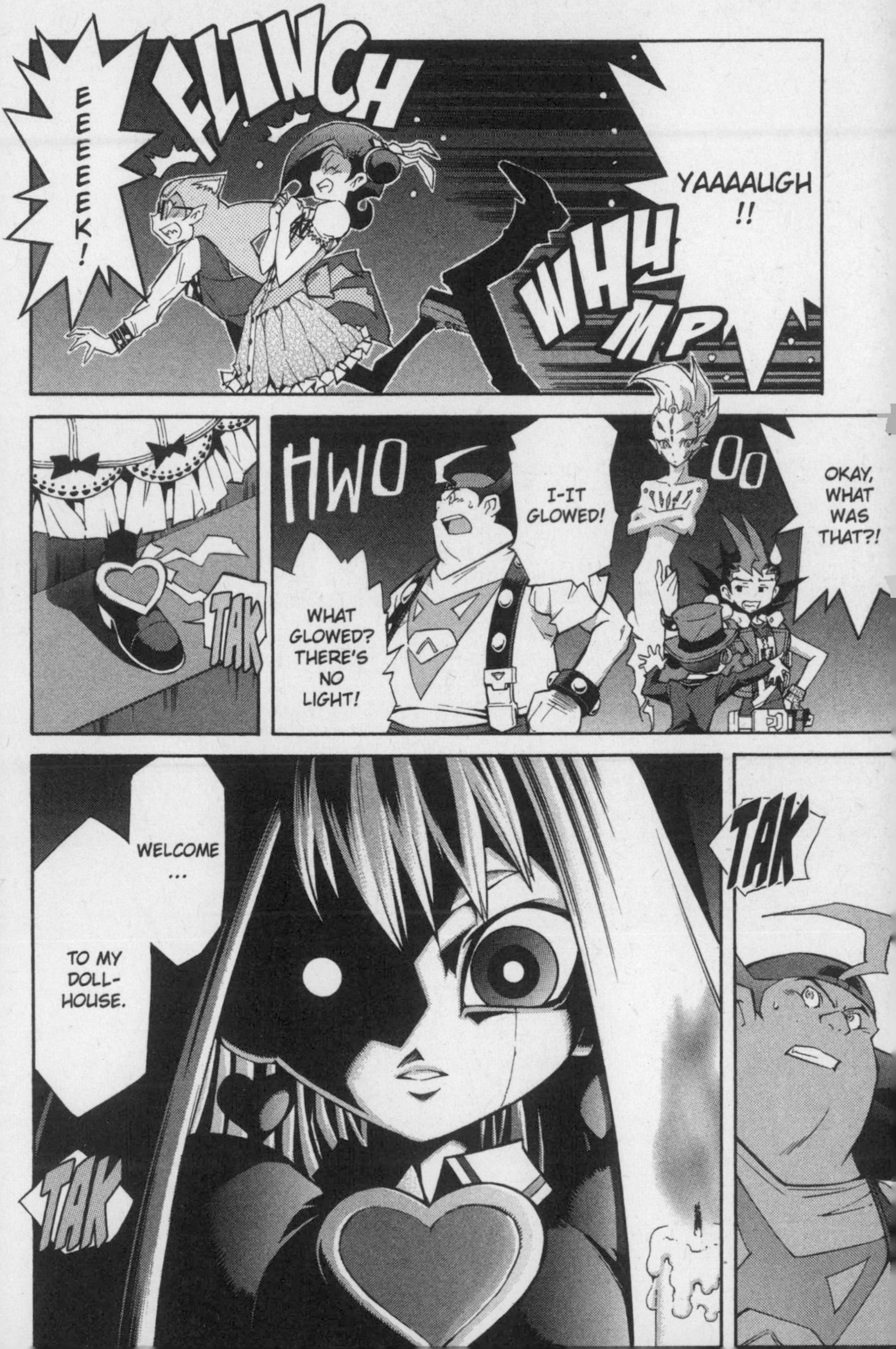
YAAAAUGH !!
WHUMP
FLINCH
EEEEEEK!
OKAY, WHAT WAS THAT?!
HWOOO
I-IT GLOWED!
WHAT GLOWED? THERE'S NO LIGHT!
TAK
TAK
WELCOME ...
TO MY DOLL-HOUSE.
TAK

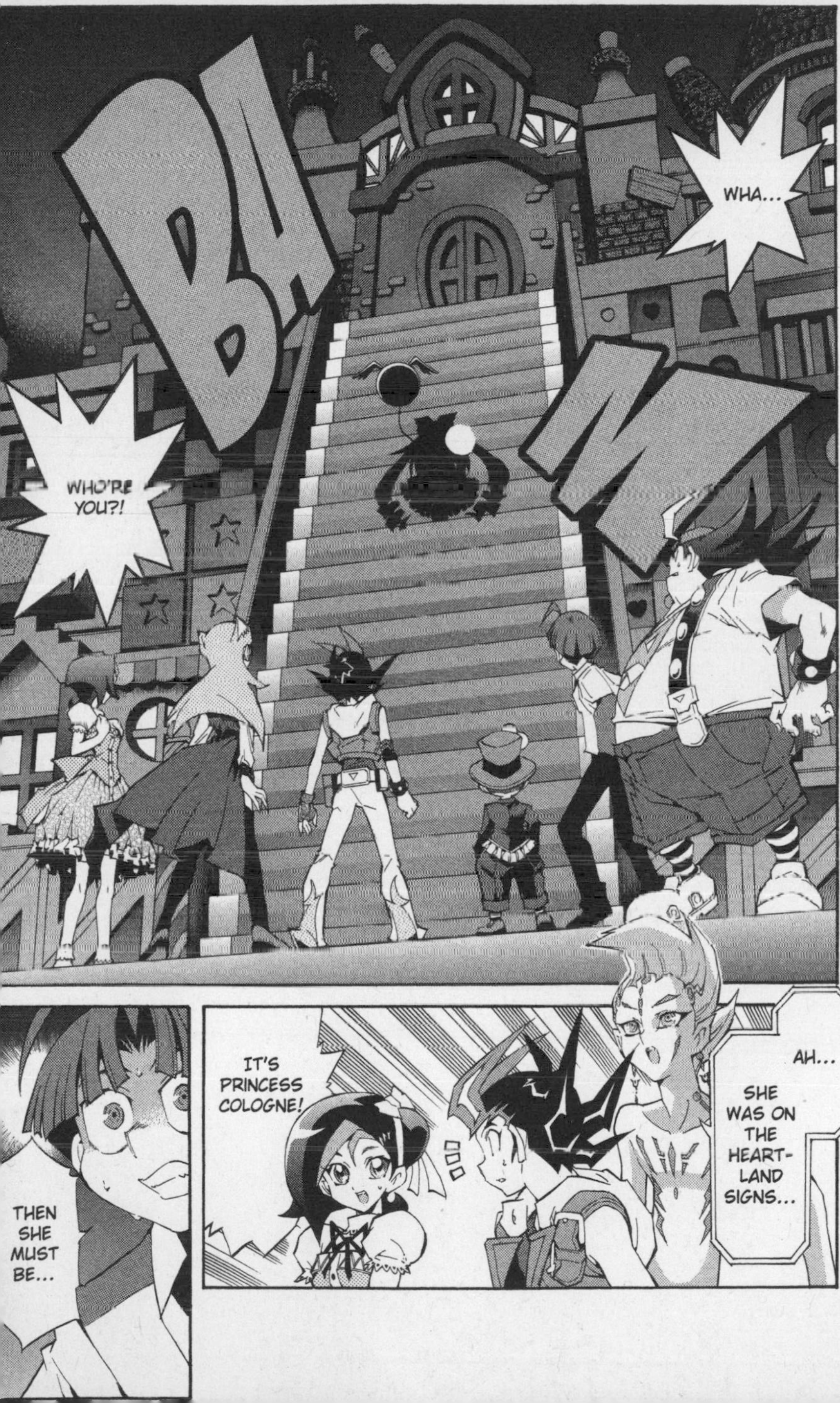
BAM
WHA...
WHO'RE YOU?!
AH...
SHE WAS ON THE HEART-LAND SIGNS...
IT'S PRINCESS COLOGNE!
THEN SHE MUST BE...

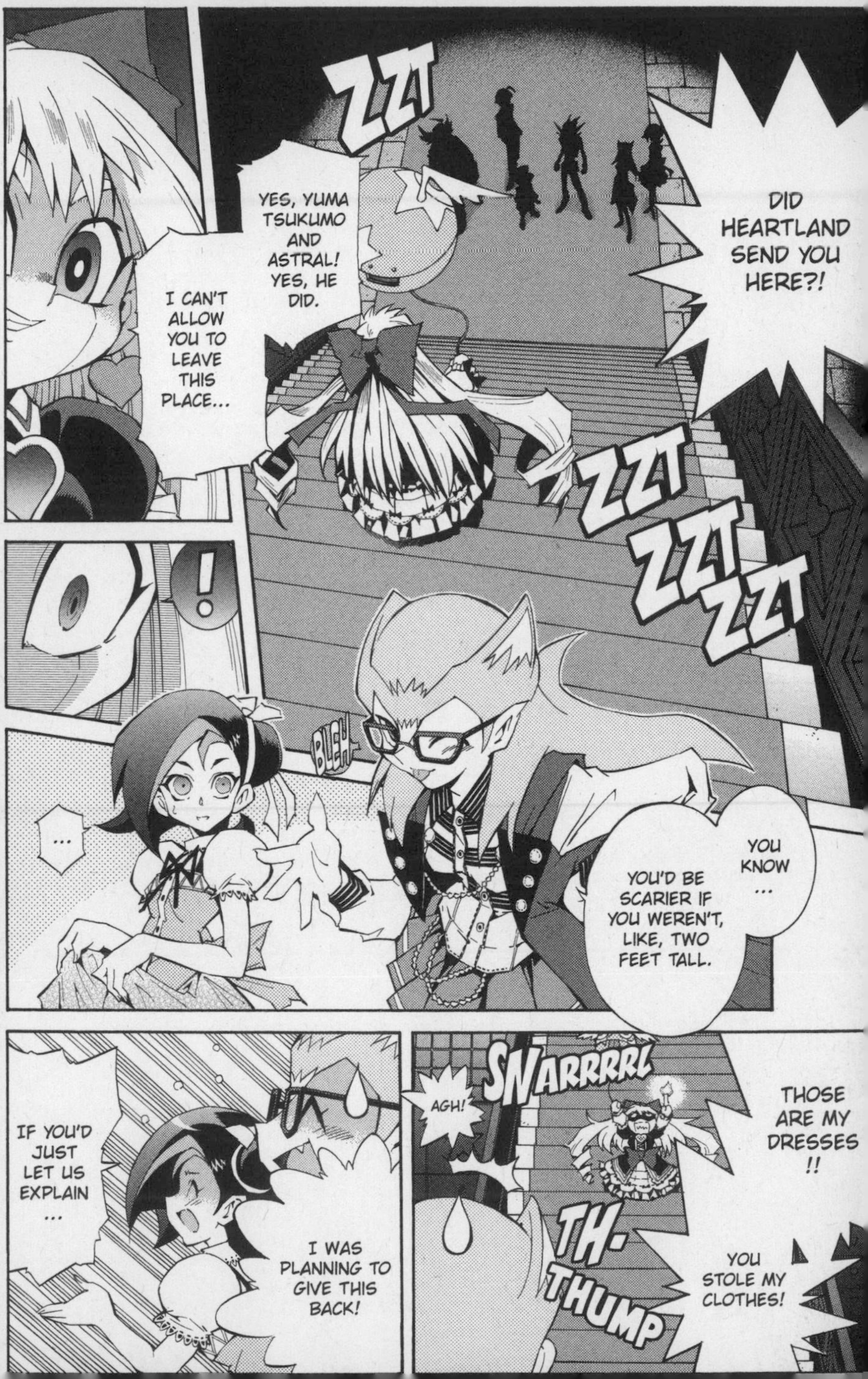
ZZT
DID HEARTLAND SEND YOU HERE?!
YES, YUMA TSUKUMO AND ASTRAL! YES, HE DID.
ZZT
ZZT
ZZT
I CAN'T ALLOW YOU TO LEAVE THIS PLACE...
!
YOU KNOW...
YOU'D BE SCARIER IF YOU WEREN'T, LIKE, TWO FEET TALL.
BLEH
...
SNARRRRL
THOSE ARE MY DRESSES!!
AGH!
YOU STOLE MY CLOTHES!
TH-THUMP
IF YOU'D JUST LET US EXPLAIN...
I WAS PLANNING TO GIVE THIS BACK!

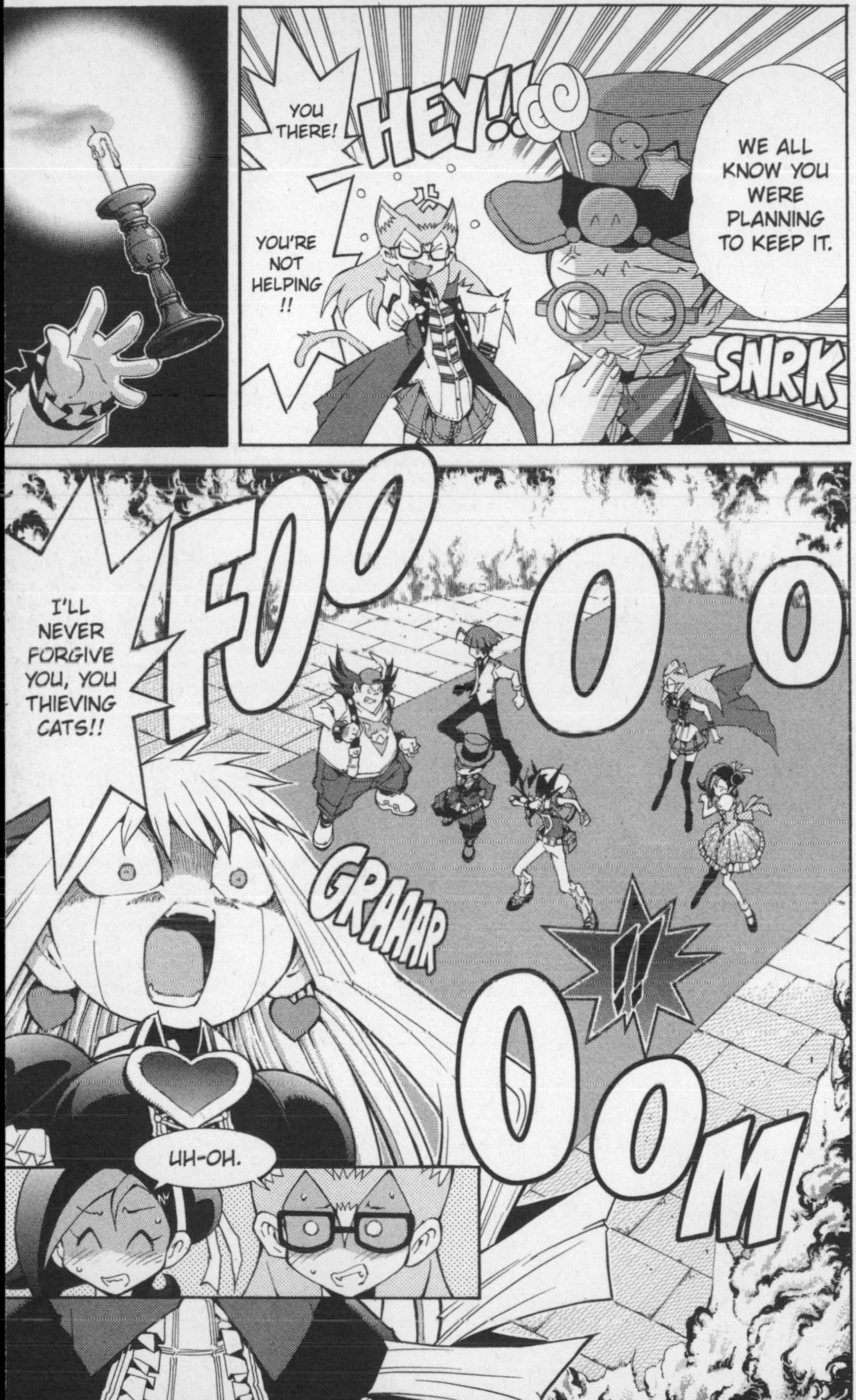
WE ALL KNOW YOU WERE PLANNING TO KEEP IT.
HEY!!
YOU THERE!
YOU'RE NOT HELPING!!
SNRK
FOOOOOOM
I'LL NEVER FORGIVE YOU, YOU THIEVING CATS!!
GRAAAR
!!
UH-OH.

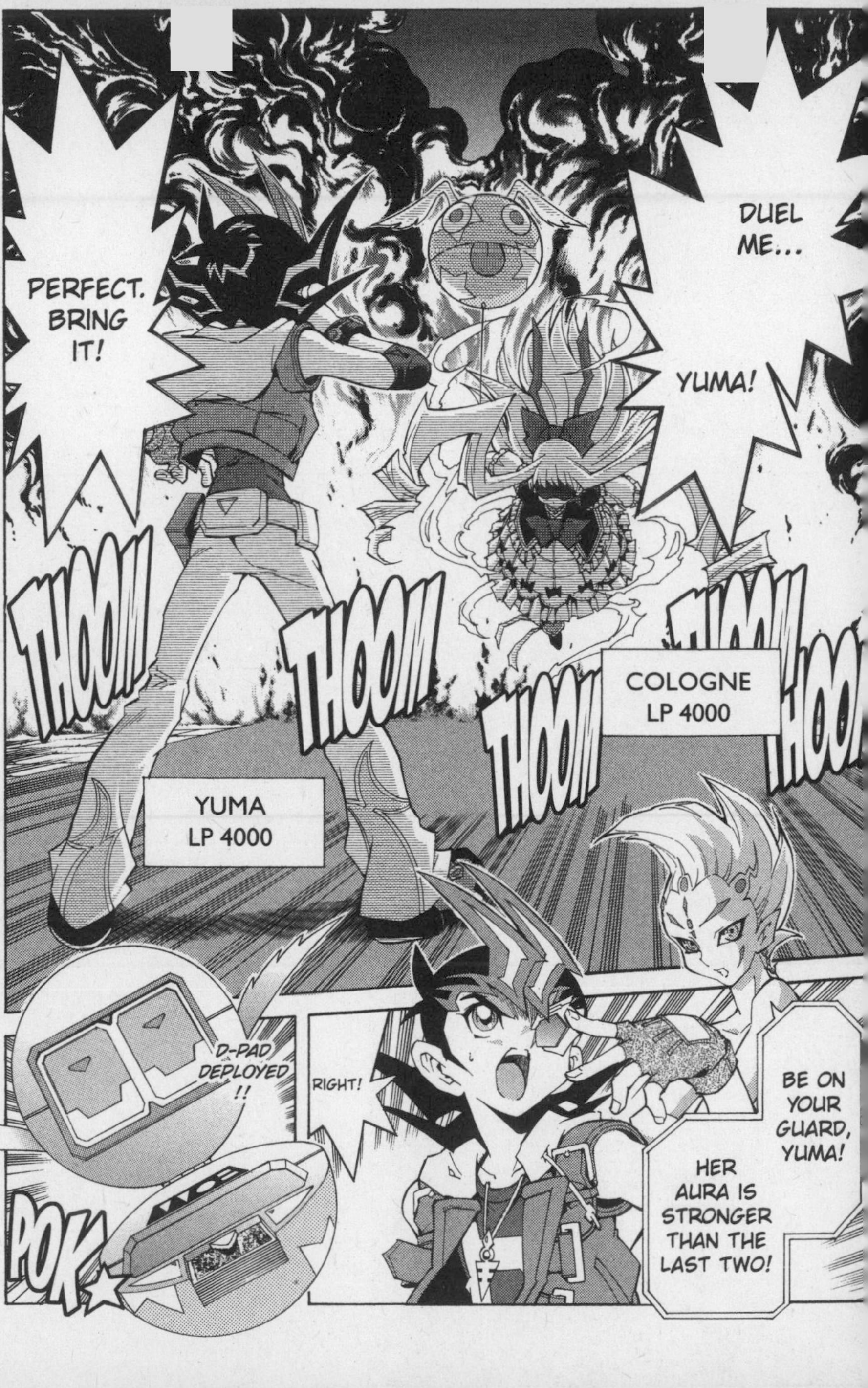
DUEL ME...
YUMA!
PERFECT. BRING IT!
THOOM
THOOM
THOOM
THOOM
COLOGNE LP 4000
YUMA LP 4000
BE ON YOUR GUARD, YUMA!
HER AURA IS STRONGER THAN THE LAST TWO!
RIGHT!
D-PAD DEPLOYED!!
POK

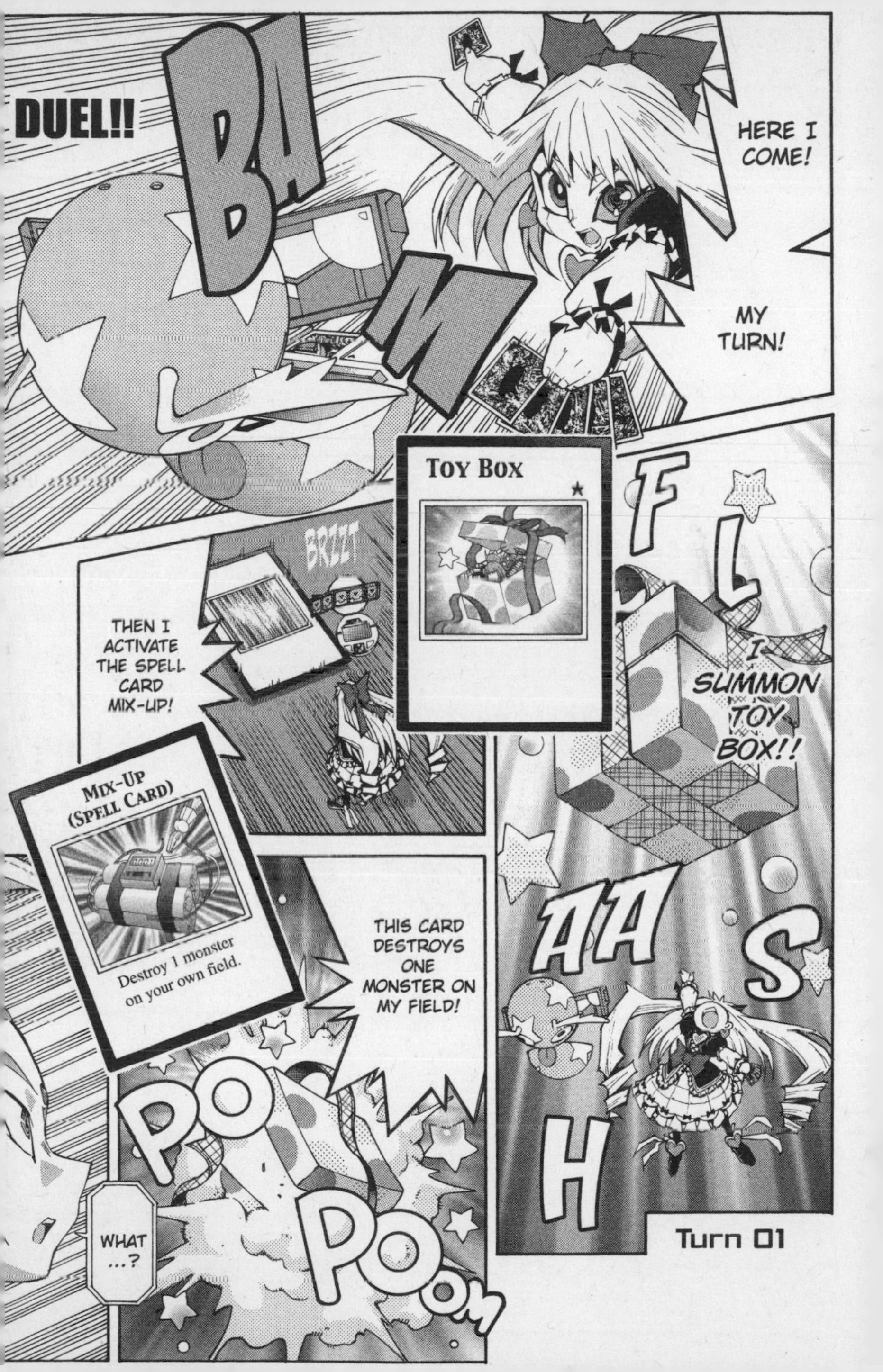
HERE I COME!
MY TURN!
BAM
DUEL!!
TOY BOX
FLAASH
I SUMMON TOY BOX!!
Turn 01
BRZZT
THEN I ACTIVATE THE SPELL CARD MIX-UP!
MIX-UP (SPELL CARD)
Destroy 1 monster on your own field.
THIS CARD DESTROYS ONE MONSTER ON MY FIELD!
POOM
POOOOM
WHAT ...?

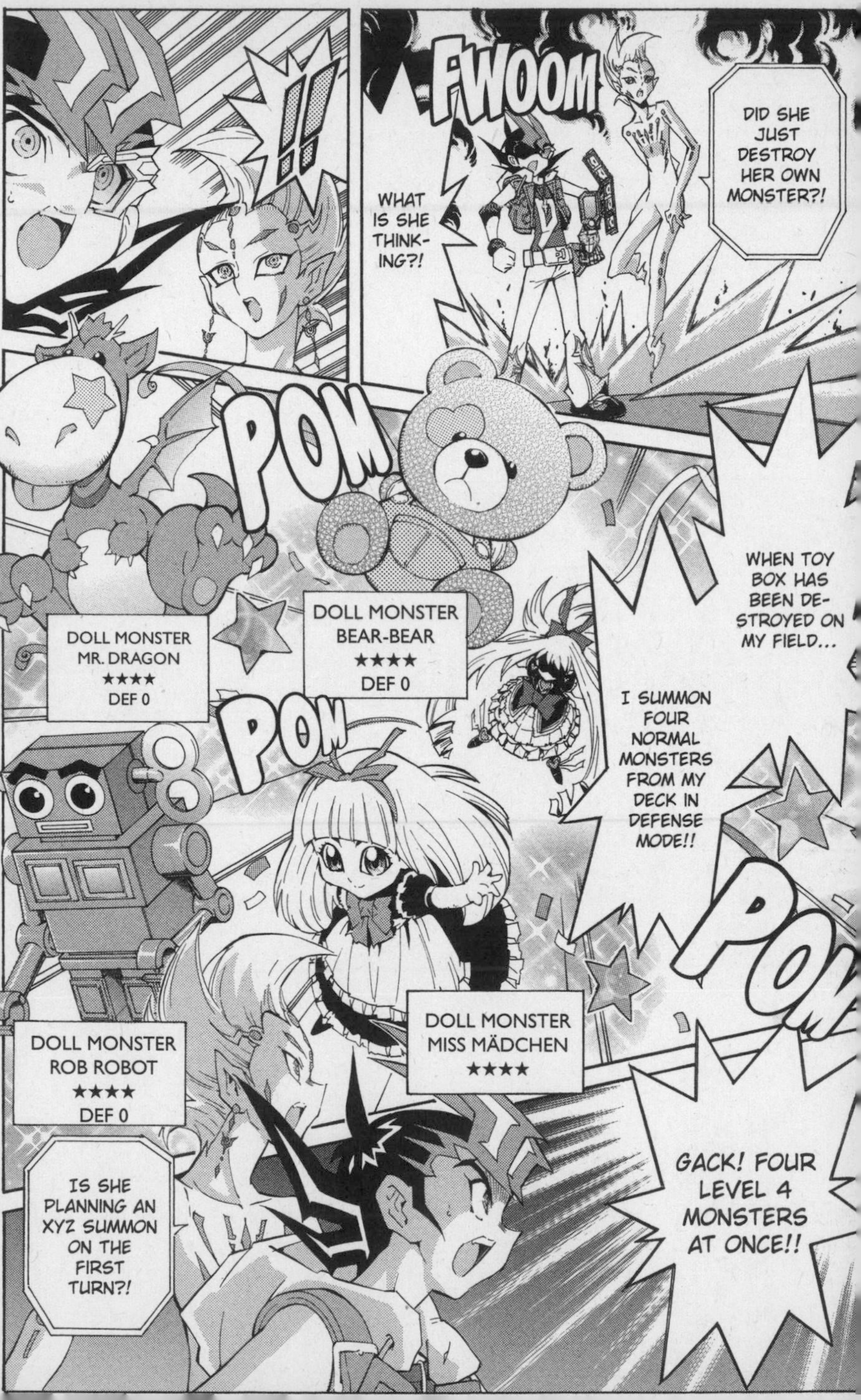
FWOOM
DID SHE JUST DESTROY HER OWN MONSTER?!
WHAT IS SHE THINKING?!
!!
WHEN TOY BOX HAS BEEN DESTROYED ON MY FIELD...
I SUMMON FOUR NORMAL MONSTERS FROM MY DECK IN DEFENSE MODE!!
POM
DOLL MONSTER BEAR-BEAR ★★★★ DEF 0
DOLL MONSTER MR. DRAGON ★★★★ DEF 0
POM
PO
DOLL MONSTER MISS MÄDCHEN ★★★★
DOLL MONSTER ROB ROBOT ★★★★ DEF 0
GACK! FOUR LEVEL 4 MONSTERS AT ONCE!!
IS SHE PLANNING AN XYZ SUMMON ON THE FIRST TURN?!

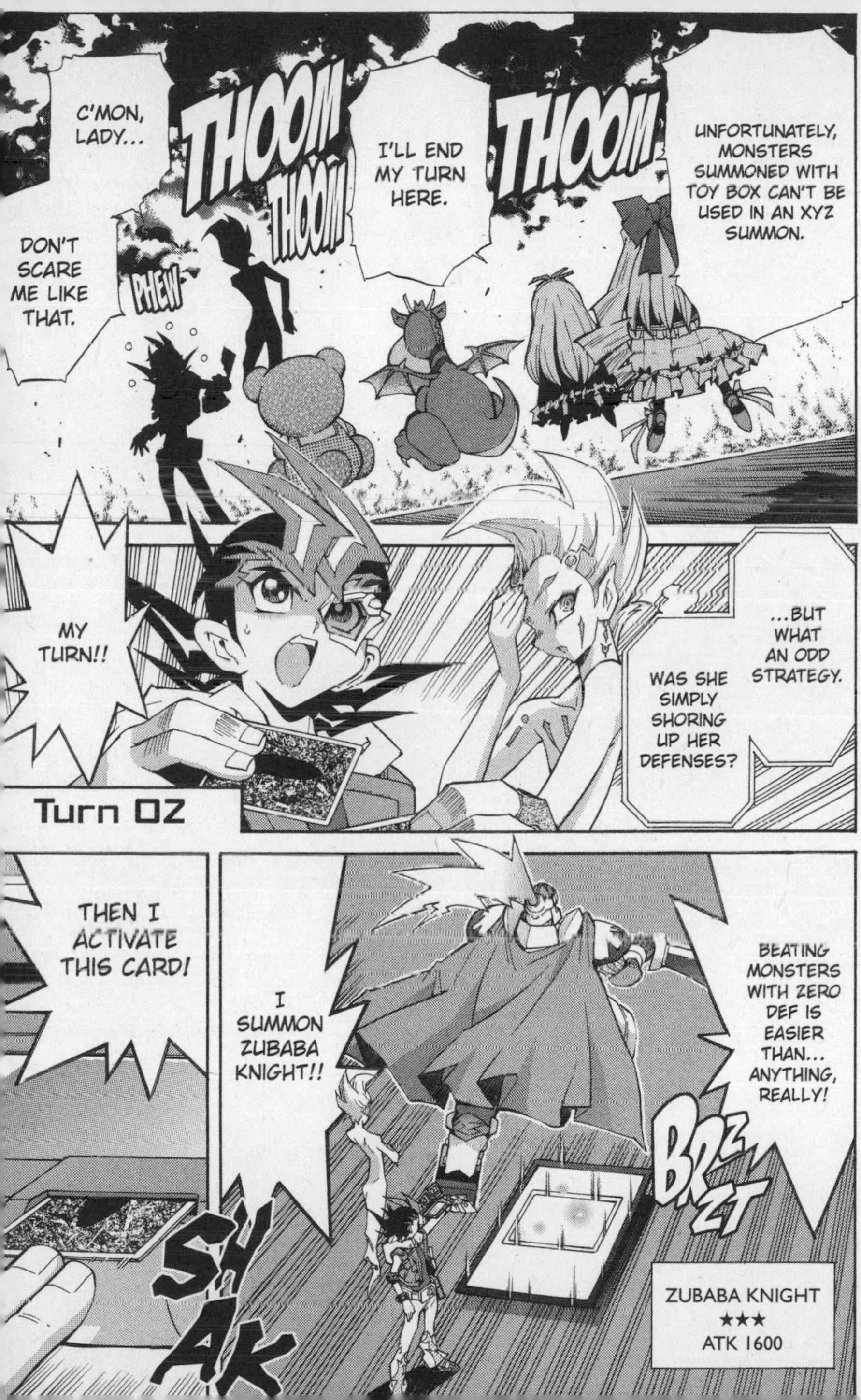
UNFORTUNATELY, MONSTERS SUMMONED WITH TOY BOX CAN'T BE USED IN AN XYZ SUMMON.
THOOM
I'LL END MY TURN HERE.
THOOM THOOM
C'MON, LADY...
PHEW
DON'T SCARE ME LIKE THAT.
...BUT WHAT AN ODD STRATEGY.
WAS SHE SIMPLY SHORING UP HER DEFENSES?
MY TURN!!
Turn 02
BEATING MONSTERS WITH ZERO DEF IS EASIER THAN... ANYTHING, REALLY!
I SUMMON ZUBABA KNIGHT!!
BZZZT
ZUBABA KNIGHT
★★★
ATK 1600
THEN I ACTIVATE THIS CARD!
SHAK

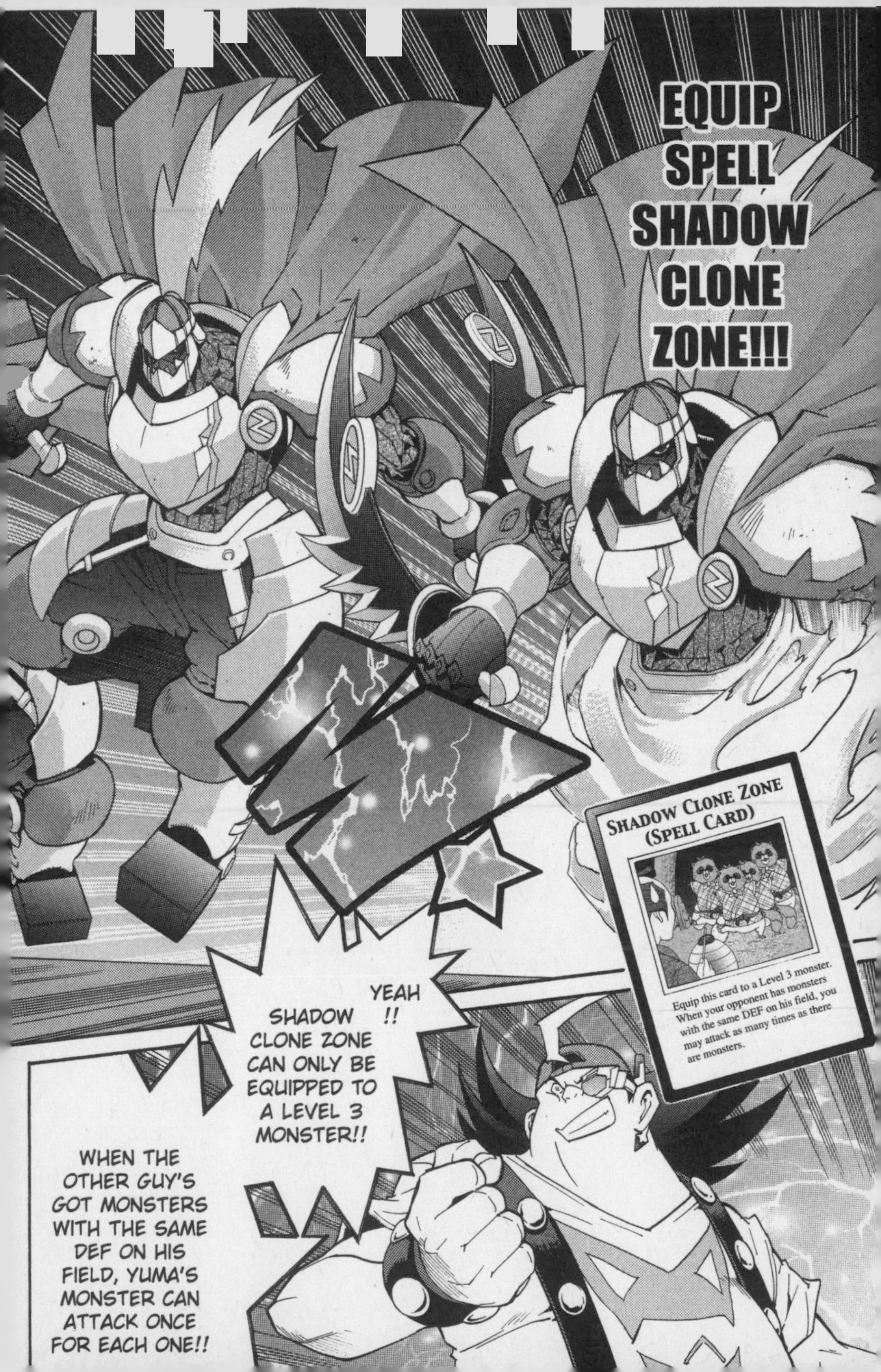
EQUIP SPELL SHADOW CLONE ZONE!!!!
SHADOW CLONE ZONE (SPELL CARD)
Equip this card to a Level 3 monster. When your opponent has monsters with the same DEF on his field, you may attack as many times as there are monsters.
YEAH!!
SHADOW CLONE ZONE CAN ONLY BE EQUIPPED TO A LEVEL 3 MONSTER!!
WHEN THE OTHER GUY'S GOT MONSTERS WITH THE SAME DEF ON HIS FIELD, YUMA'S MONSTER CAN ATTACK ONCE FOR EACH ONE!!

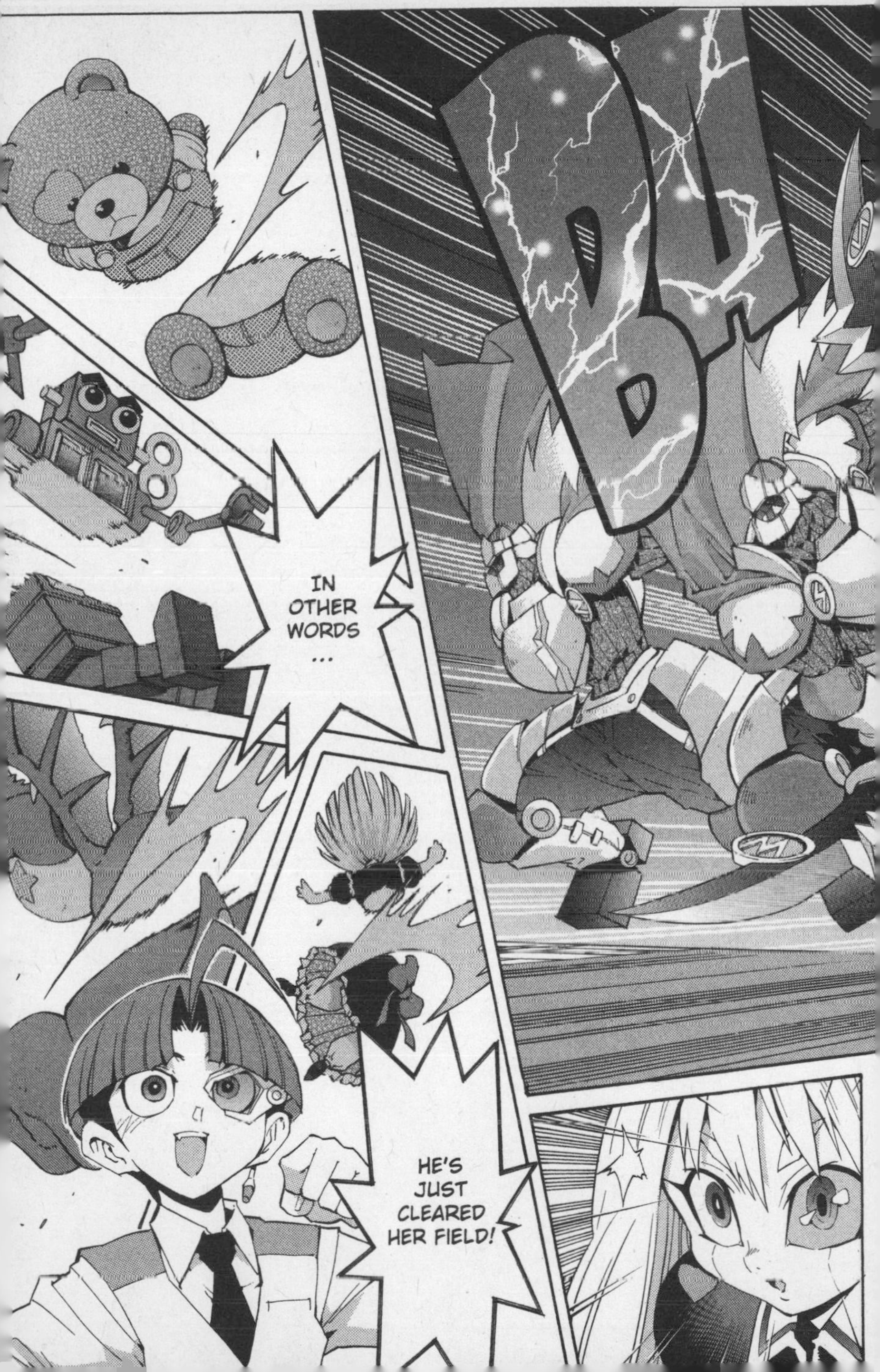
IN OTHER WORDS ...
HE'S JUST CLEARED HER FIELD!

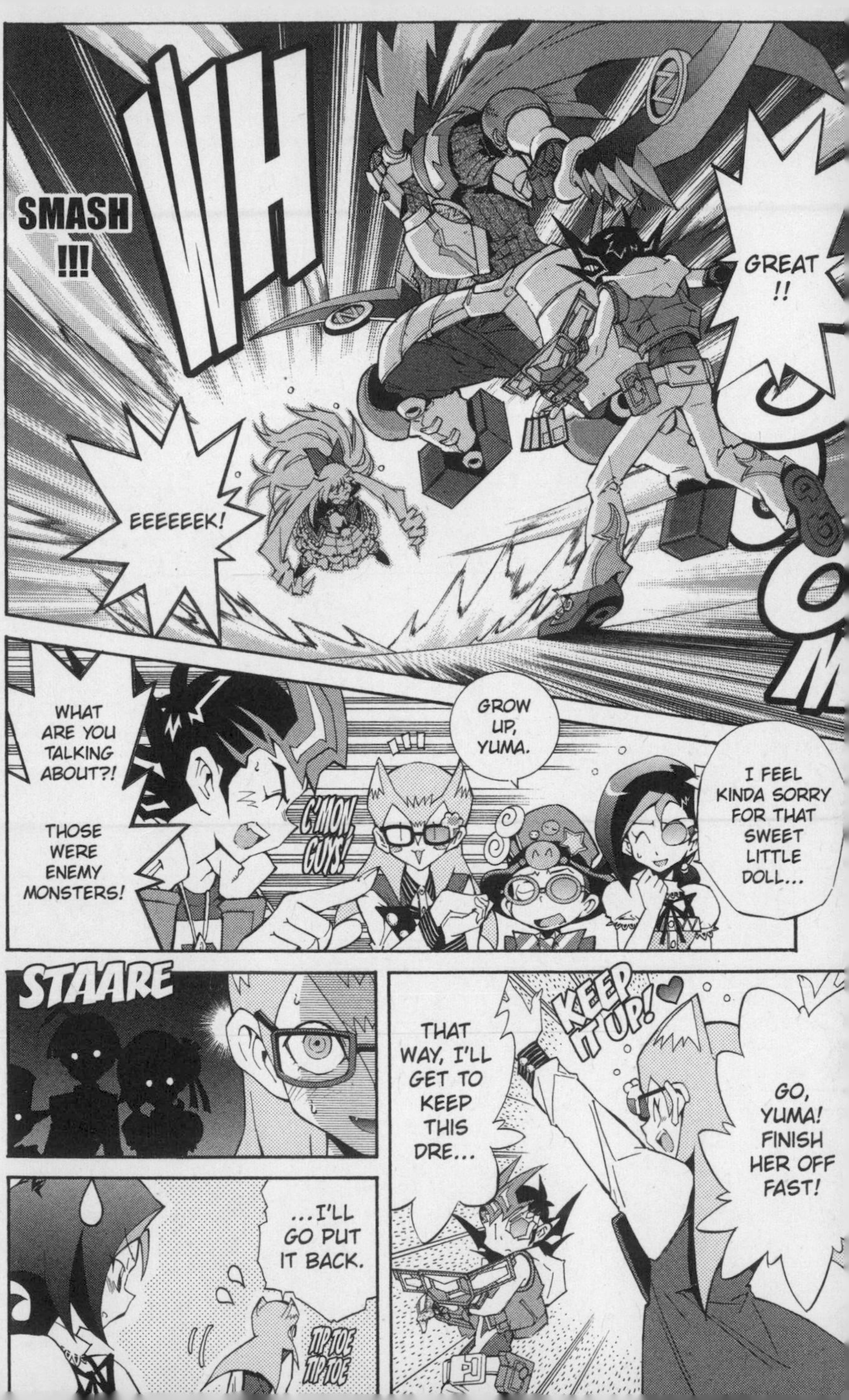
GREAT!!
WH
SMASH!!!
EEEEEEK!
I FEEL KINDA SORRY FOR THAT SWEET LITTLE DOLL...
GROW UP, YUMA.
C'MON GUYS!
WHAT ARE YOU TALKING ABOUT?!
THOSE WERE ENEMY MONSTERS!
GO, YUMA! FINISH HER OFF FAST!
KEEP IT UP!
THAT WAY, I'LL GET TO KEEP THIS DRE...
STAARE
...I'LL GO PUT IT BACK.
TIP TOE TIP TOE

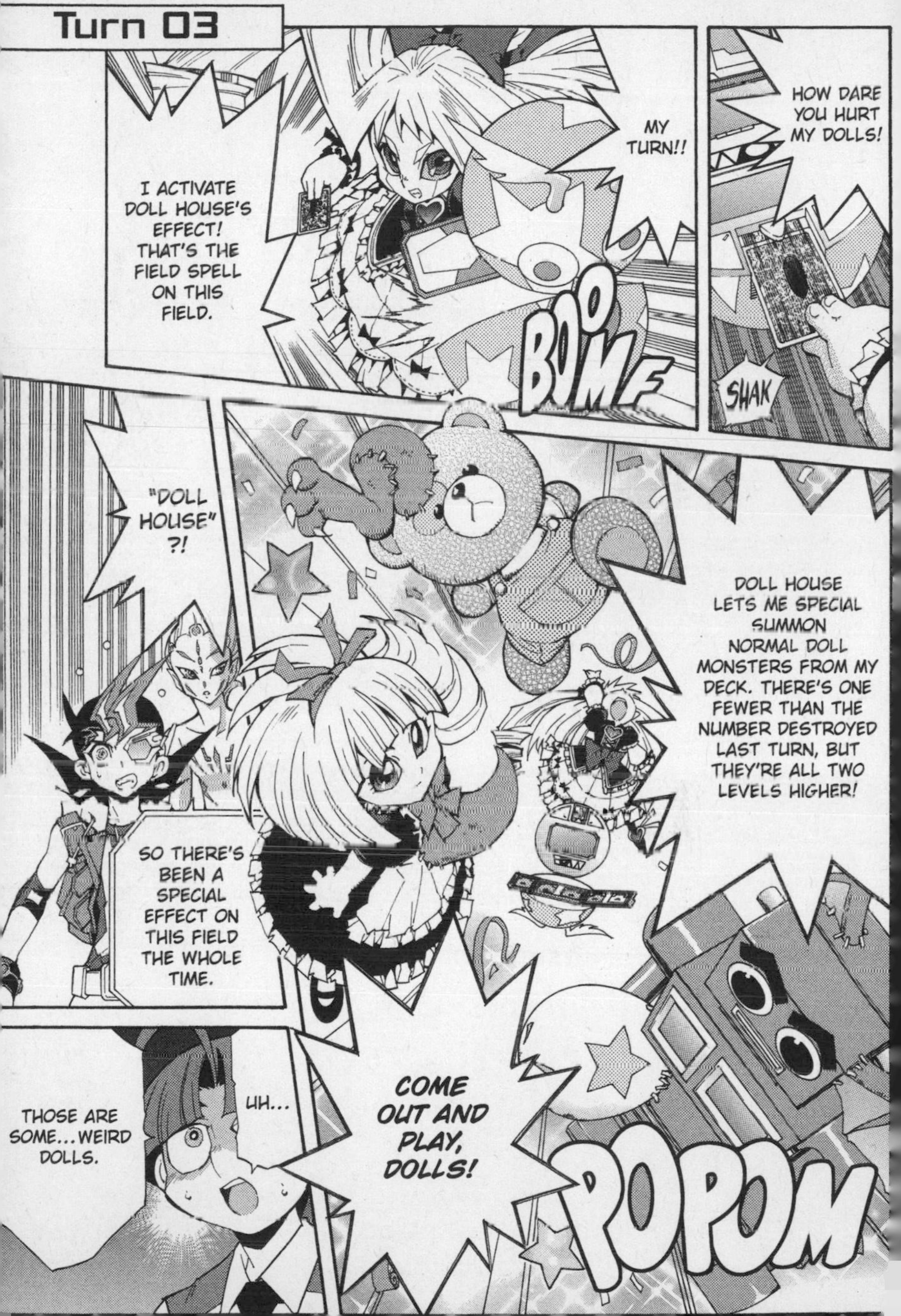
Turn 03
HOW DARE YOU HURT MY DOLLS!
SHAK
MY TURN!!
BOOMF
I ACTIVATE DOLL HOUSE'S EFFECT! THAT'S THE FIELD SPELL ON THIS FIELD.
DOLL HOUSE LETS ME SPECIAL SUMMON NORMAL DOLL MONSTERS FROM MY DECK. THERE'S ONE FEWER THAN THE NUMBER DESTROYED LAST TURN, BUT THEY'RE ALL TWO LEVELS HIGHER!
"DOLL HOUSE" ?!
SO THERE'S BEEN A SPECIAL EFFECT ON THIS FIELD THE WHOLE TIME.
POPOM
COME OUT AND PLAY, DOLLS!
UH...
THOSE ARE SOME...WEIRD DOLLS.

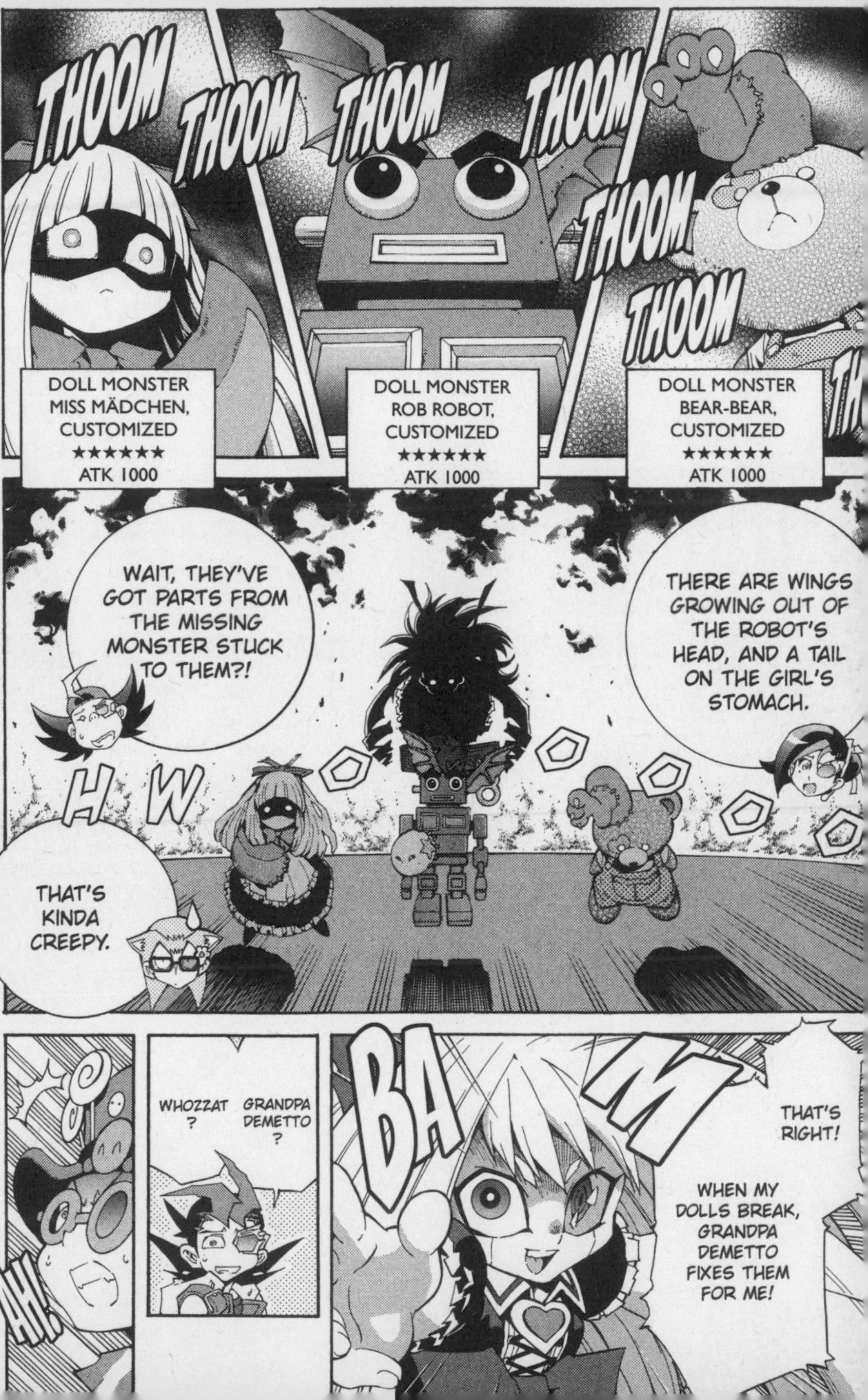
THOOM
THOOM
THOOM
DOLL MONSTER
BEAR-BEAR,
CUSTOMIZED
★★★★★★
ATK 1000
THOOM
DOLL MONSTER
ROB ROBOT,
CUSTOMIZED
★★★★★★
ATK 1000
THOOM
THOOM
DOLL MONSTER
MISS MÄDCHEN,
CUSTOMIZED
★★★★★★
ATK 1000
THERE ARE WINGS GROWING OUT OF THE ROBOT'S HEAD, AND A TAIL ON THE GIRL'S STOMACH.
WAIT, THEY'VE GOT PARTS FROM THE MISSING MONSTER STUCK TO THEM?!
THAT'S KINDA CREEPY.
BAM
THAT'S RIGHT!
WHEN MY DOLLS BREAK, GRANDPA DEMETTO FIXES THEM FOR ME!
GRANDPA DEMETTO?
WHOZZAT?
AH!

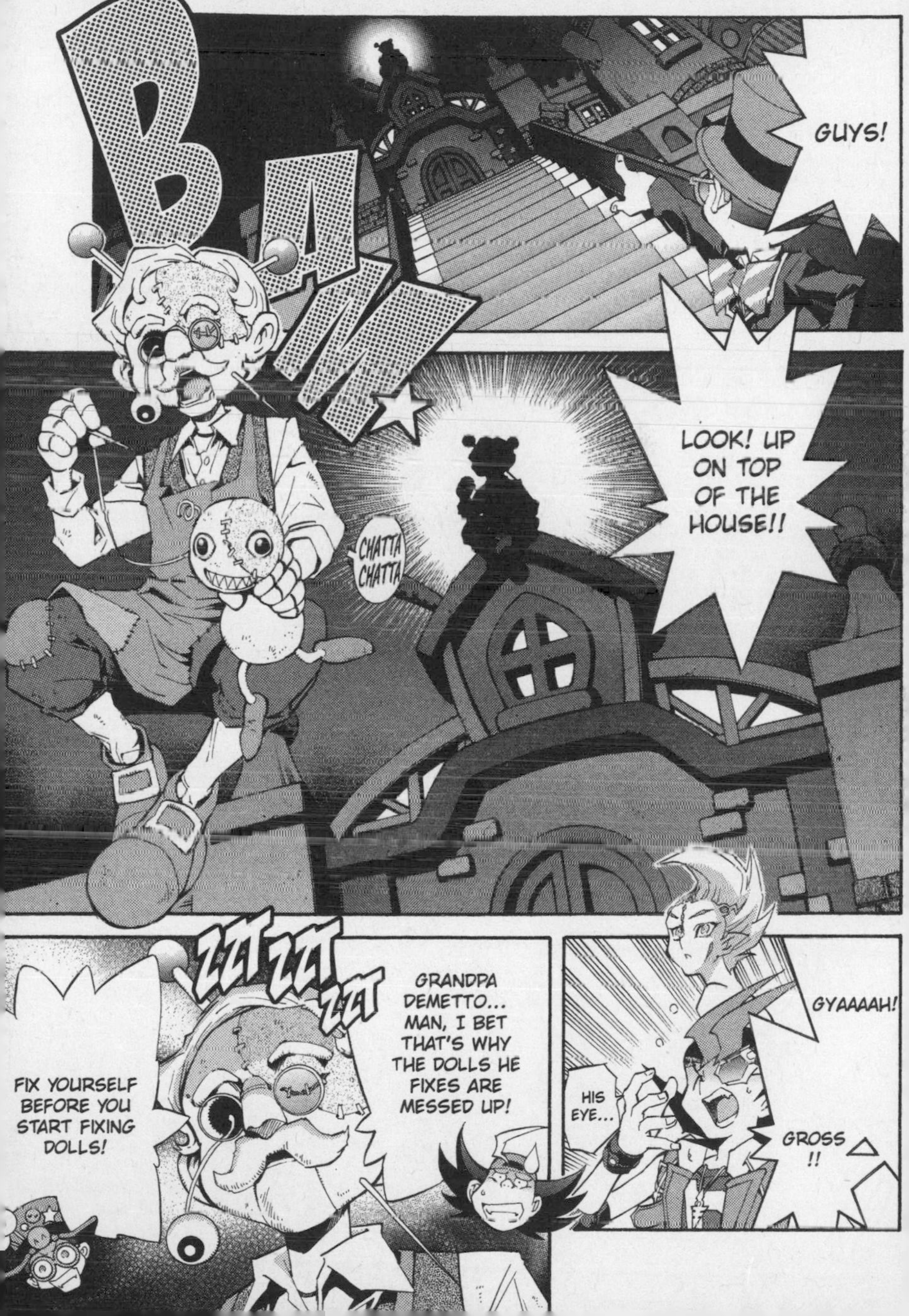
GUYS!
BAM
LOOK! UP ON TOP OF THE HOUSE!!
CHATTA CHATTA
GYAAAAH!
HIS EYE...
GROSS !!
ZZT ZZT ZZT
GRANDPA DEMETTO... MAN, I BET THAT'S WHY THE DOLLS HE FIXES ARE MESSED UP!
FIX YOURSELF BEFORE YOU START FIXING DOLLS!

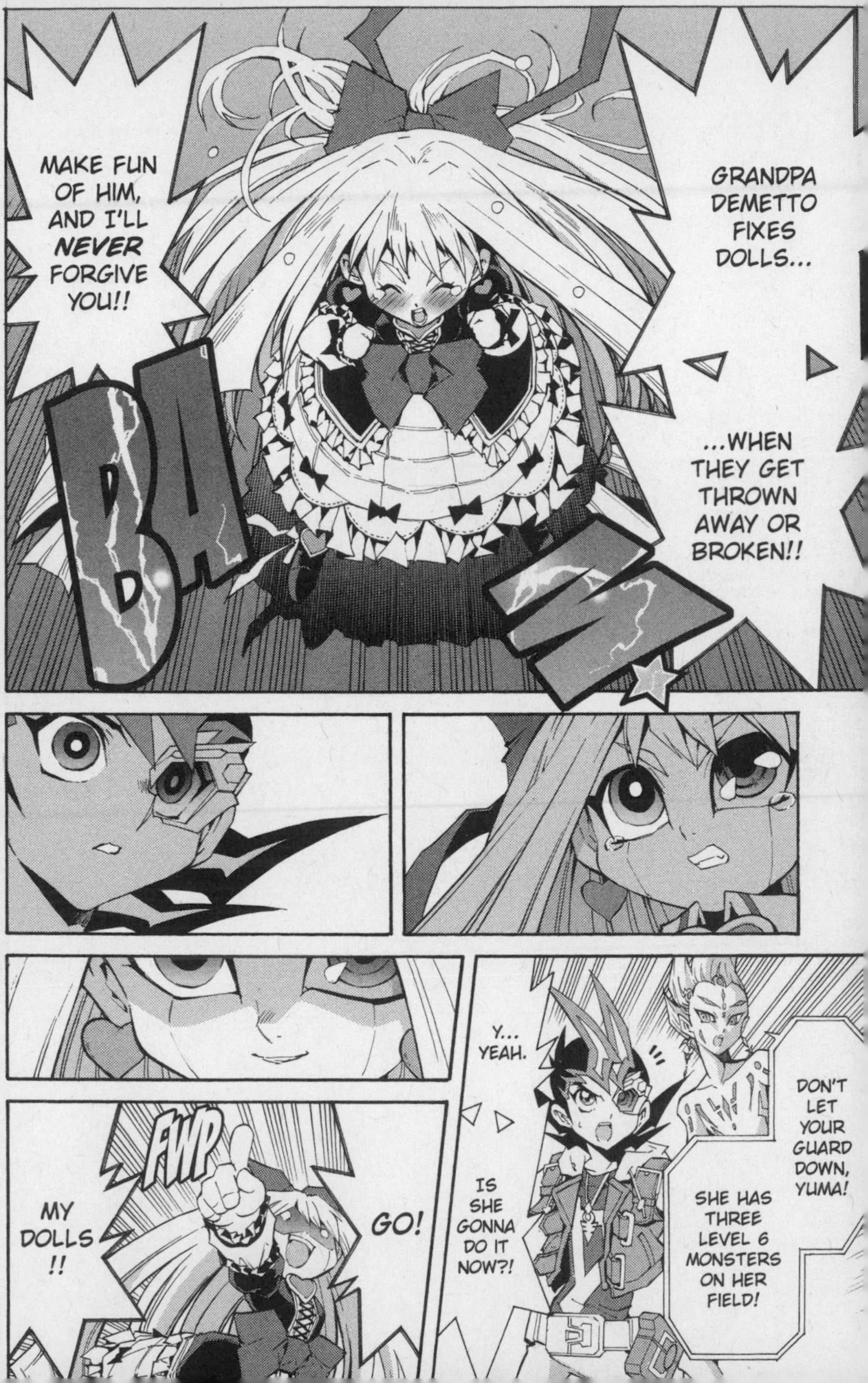
GRANDPA DEMETTO FIXES DOLLS...
...WHEN THEY GET THROWN AWAY OR BROKEN!!
MAKE FUN OF HIM, AND I'LL *NEVER* FORGIVE YOU!!
BA
DON'T LET YOUR GUARD DOWN, YUMA!
SHE HAS THREE LEVEL 6 MONSTERS ON HER FIELD!
Y... YEAH.
IS SHE GONNA DO IT NOW?!
GO!
FWP
MY DOLLS !!

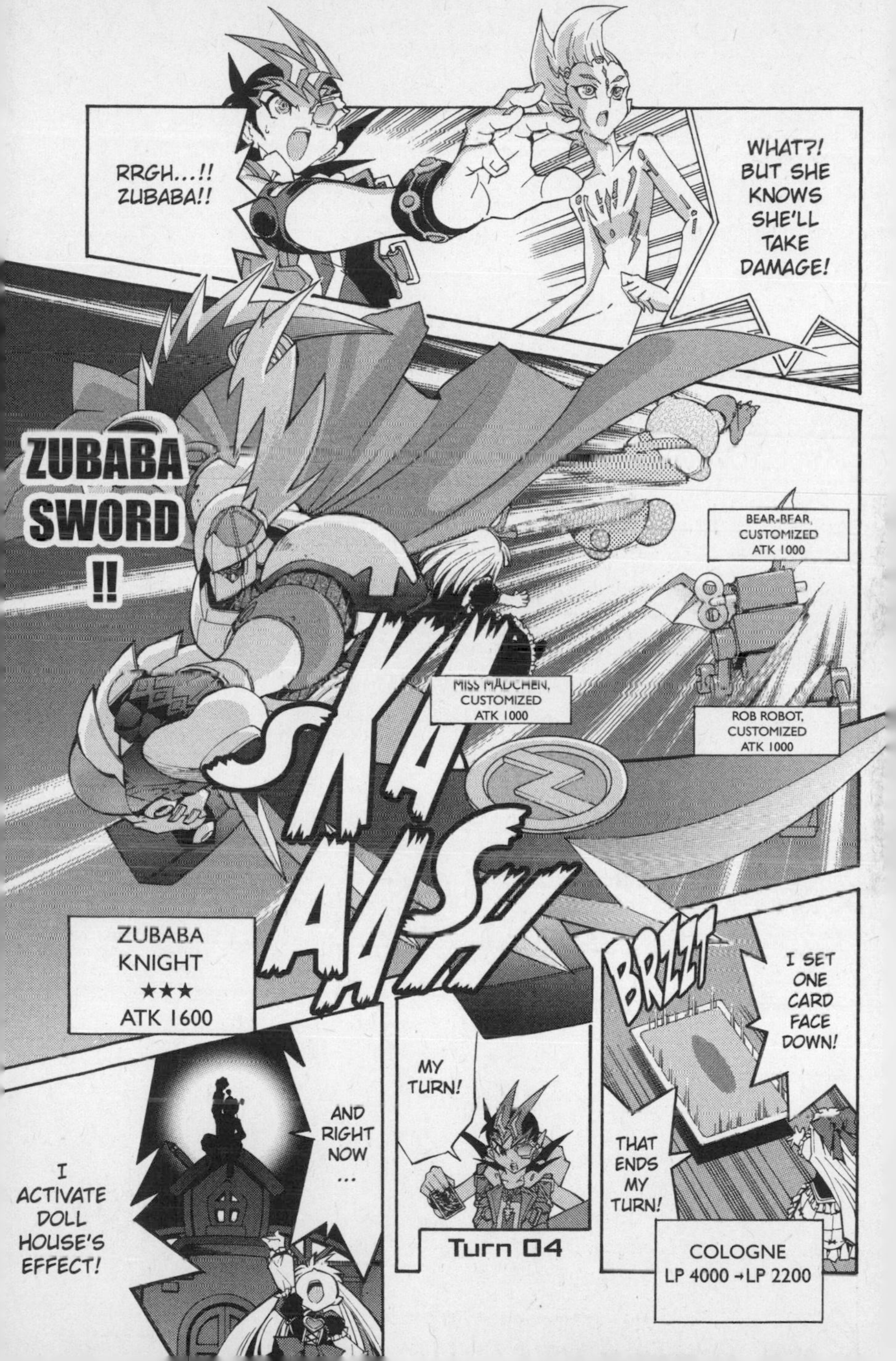
WHAT?! BUT SHE KNOWS SHE'LL TAKE DAMAGE!
RRGH...!! ZUBABA!!
BEAR-BEAR, CUSTOMIZED ATK 1000
ROB ROBOT, CUSTOMIZED ATK 1000
MISS MÄDCHEN, CUSTOMIZED ATK 1000
ZUBABA SWORD !!
KA AASH
ZUBABA KNIGHT ★★★ ATK 1600
BRZZT
I SET ONE CARD FACE DOWN!
THAT ENDS MY TURN!
COLOGNE LP 4000 → LP 2200
MY TURN!
Turn 04
AND RIGHT NOW ...
I ACTIVATE DOLL HOUSE'S EFFECT!

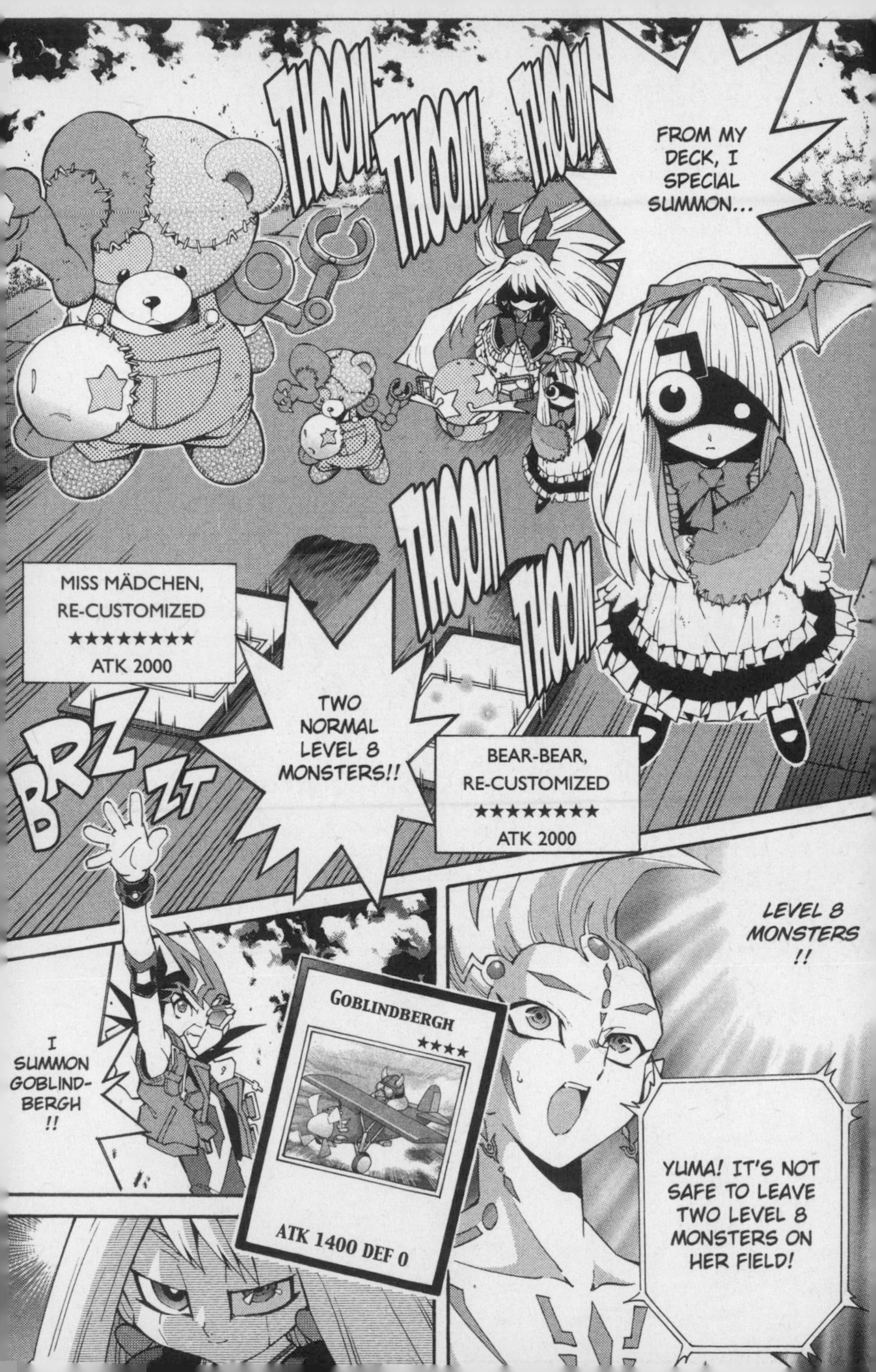
FROM MY DECK, I SPECIAL SUMMON...
THOOM THOOM THOOM
THOOM THOOM
BEAR-BEAR, RE-CUSTOMIZED ★★★★★★★★ ATK 2000
TWO NORMAL LEVEL 8 MONSTERS!!
MISS MÄDCHEN, RE-CUSTOMIZED ★★★★★★★★ ATK 2000
BRZZT
LEVEL 8 MONSTERS !!
YUMA! IT'S NOT SAFE TO LEAVE TWO LEVEL 8 MONSTERS ON HER FIELD!
I SUMMON GOBLINDBERGH !!
GOBLINDBERGH ★★★★
ATK 1400 DEF 0

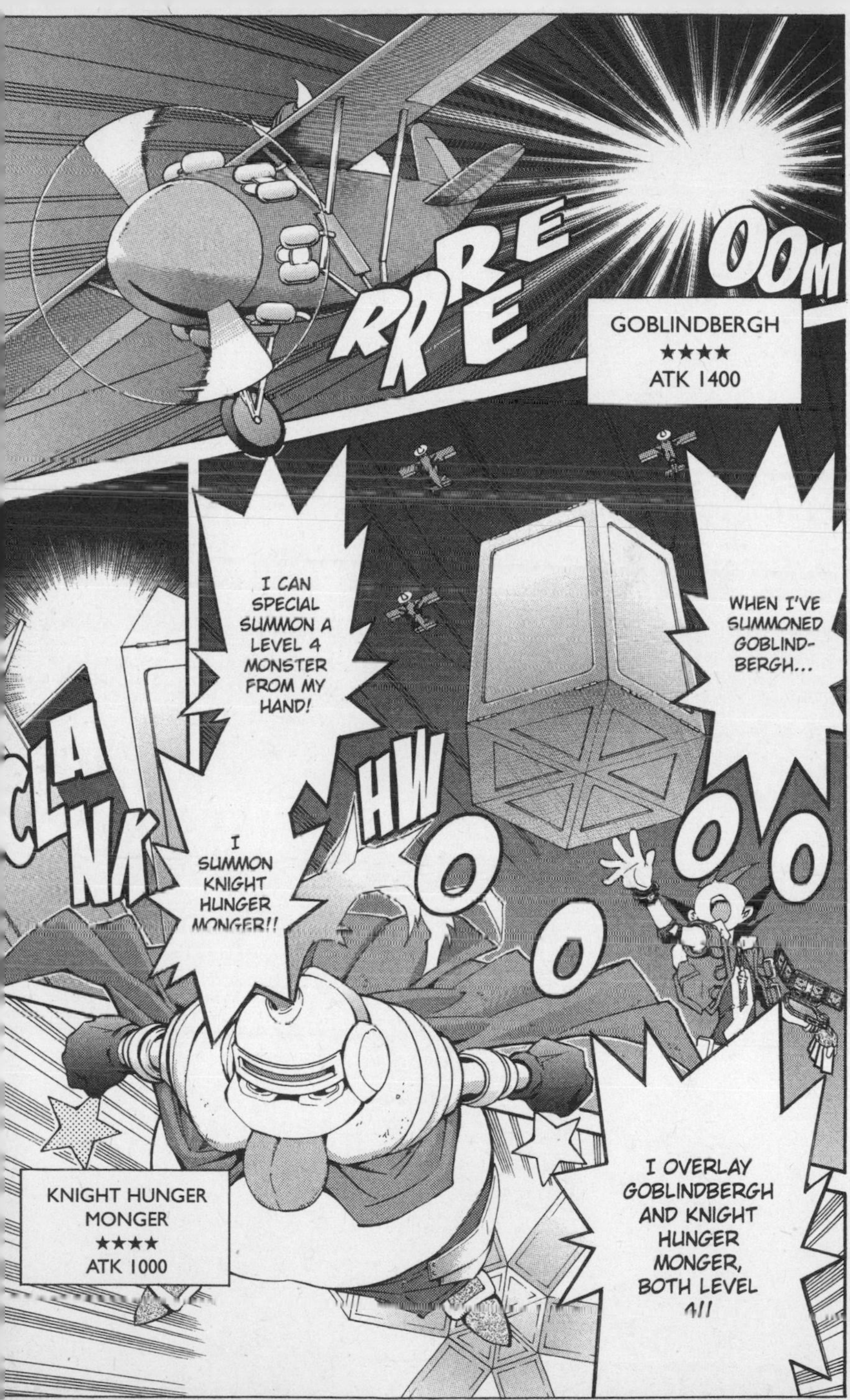
RRREE OOM
GOBLINDBERGH
★★★★
ATK 1400
WHEN I'VE SUMMONED GOBLIND-BERGH...
I CAN SPECIAL SUMMON A LEVEL 4 MONSTER FROM MY HAND!
CLANK
HWOOOO
I SUMMON KNIGHT HUNGER MONGER!!
I OVERLAY GOBLINDBERGH AND KNIGHT HUNGER MONGER, BOTH LEVEL 4!!
KNIGHT HUNGER MONGER
★★★★
ATK 1000

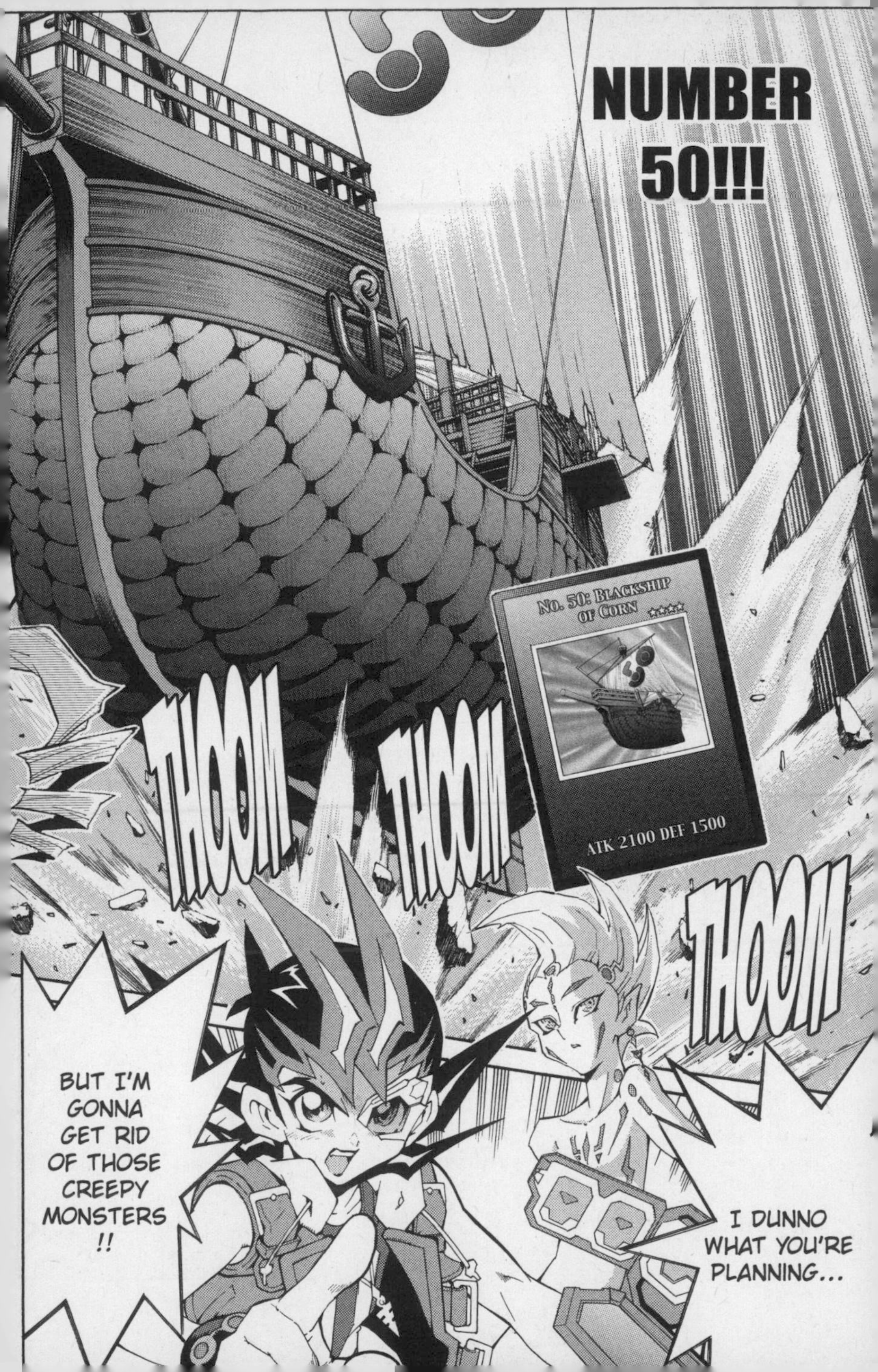
NUMBER 50!!!
No. 50: Blackship of Corn
ATK 2100 DEF 1500
THOOM
THOOM
THOOM
I DUNNO WHAT YOU'RE PLANNING...
BUT I'M GONNA GET RID OF THOSE CREEPY MONSTERS!!

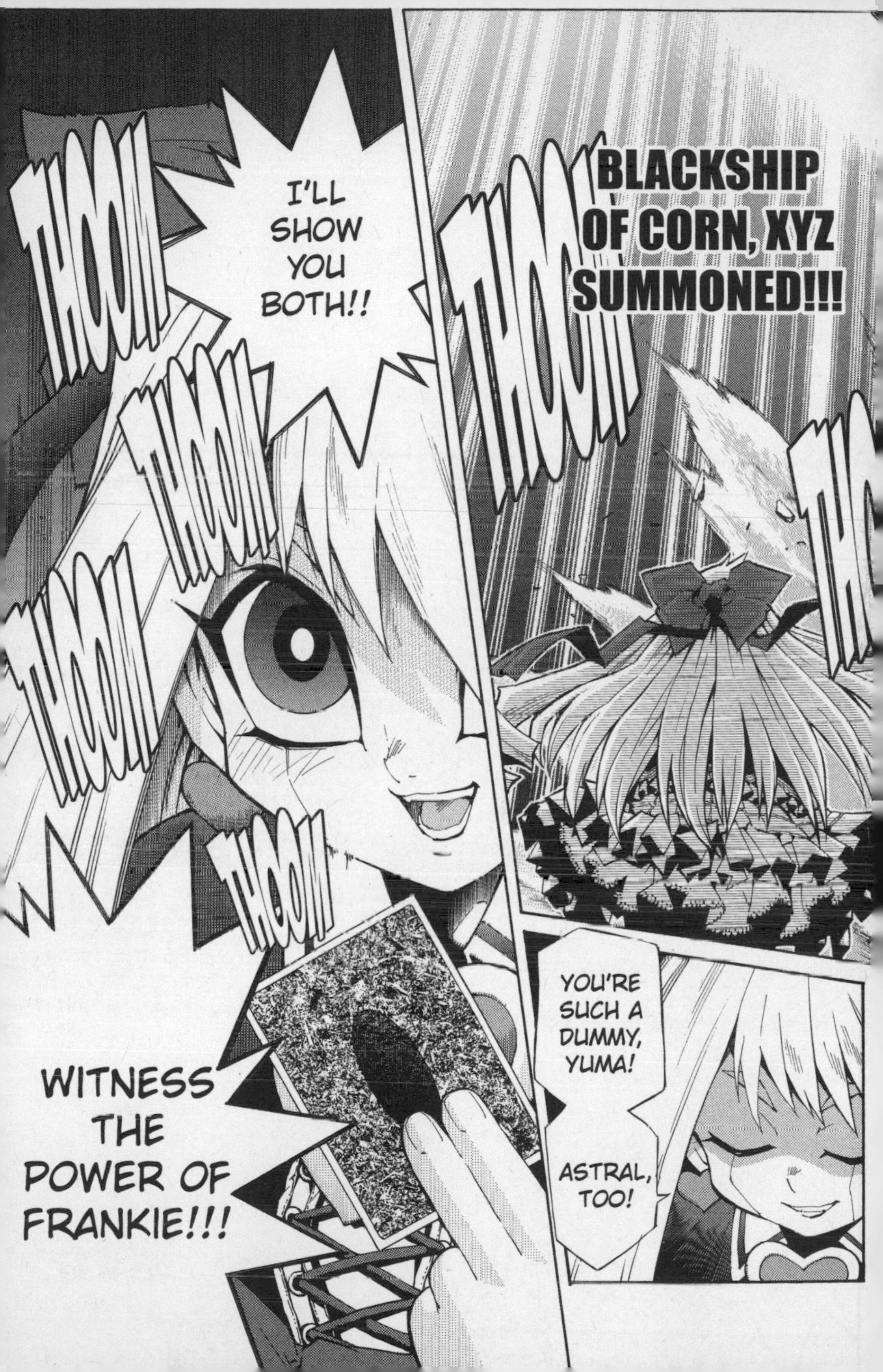
THOOM
BLACKSHIP OF CORN, XYZ SUMMONED!!!
THO
YOU'RE SUCH A DUMMY, YUMA!
ASTRAL, TOO!
I'LL SHOW YOU BOTH!!
THOOM
THOOM
THOOM
THOOM
WITNESS THE POWER OF FRANKIE!!!

YU-GI-OH!
ZEXAL

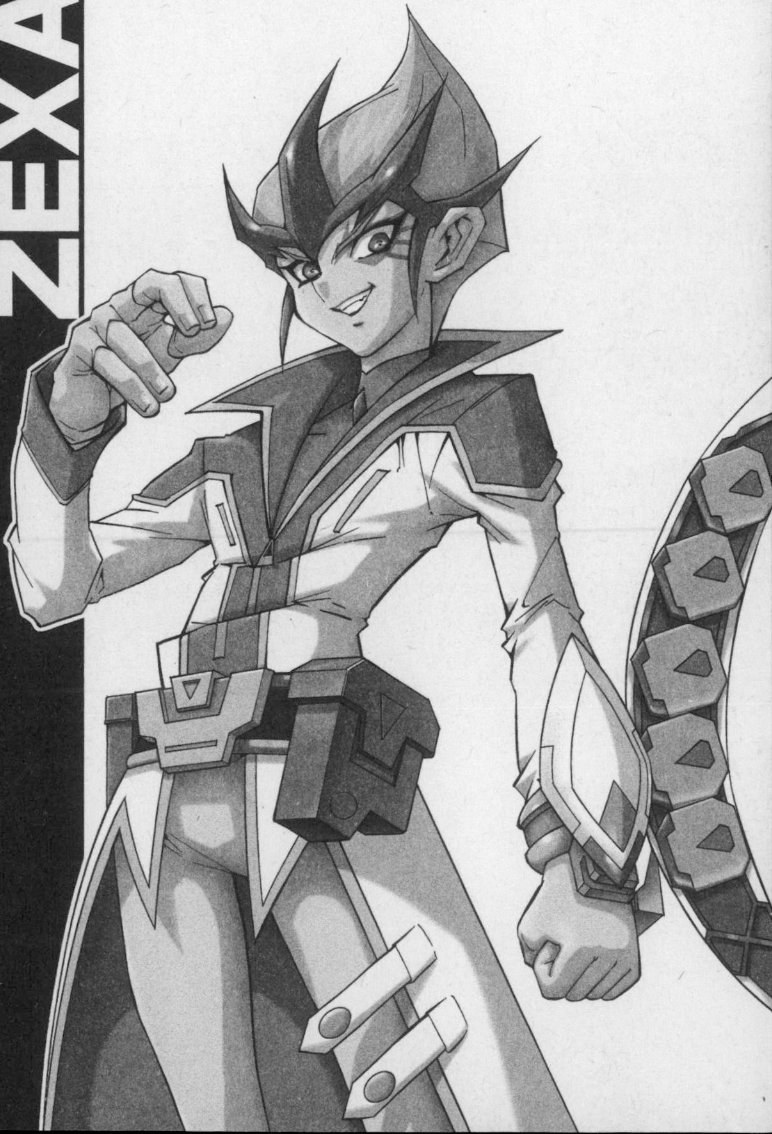

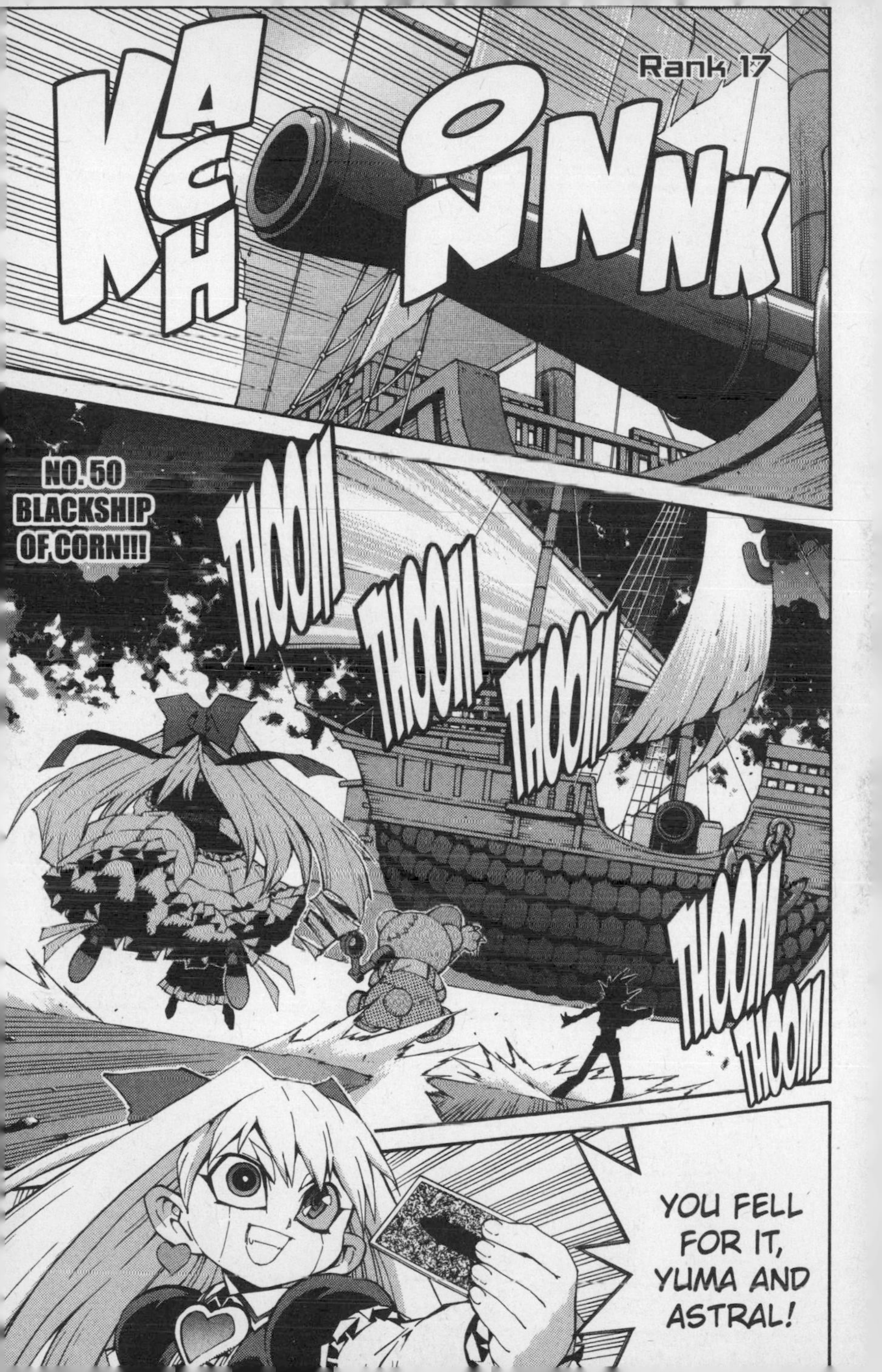
Rank 17
KACHONNNK
THOOM THOOM
THOOM
THOOM
THOOM
THOOM
NO. 50 BLACKSHIP OF CORN!!!
YOU FELL FOR IT, YUMA AND ASTRAL!

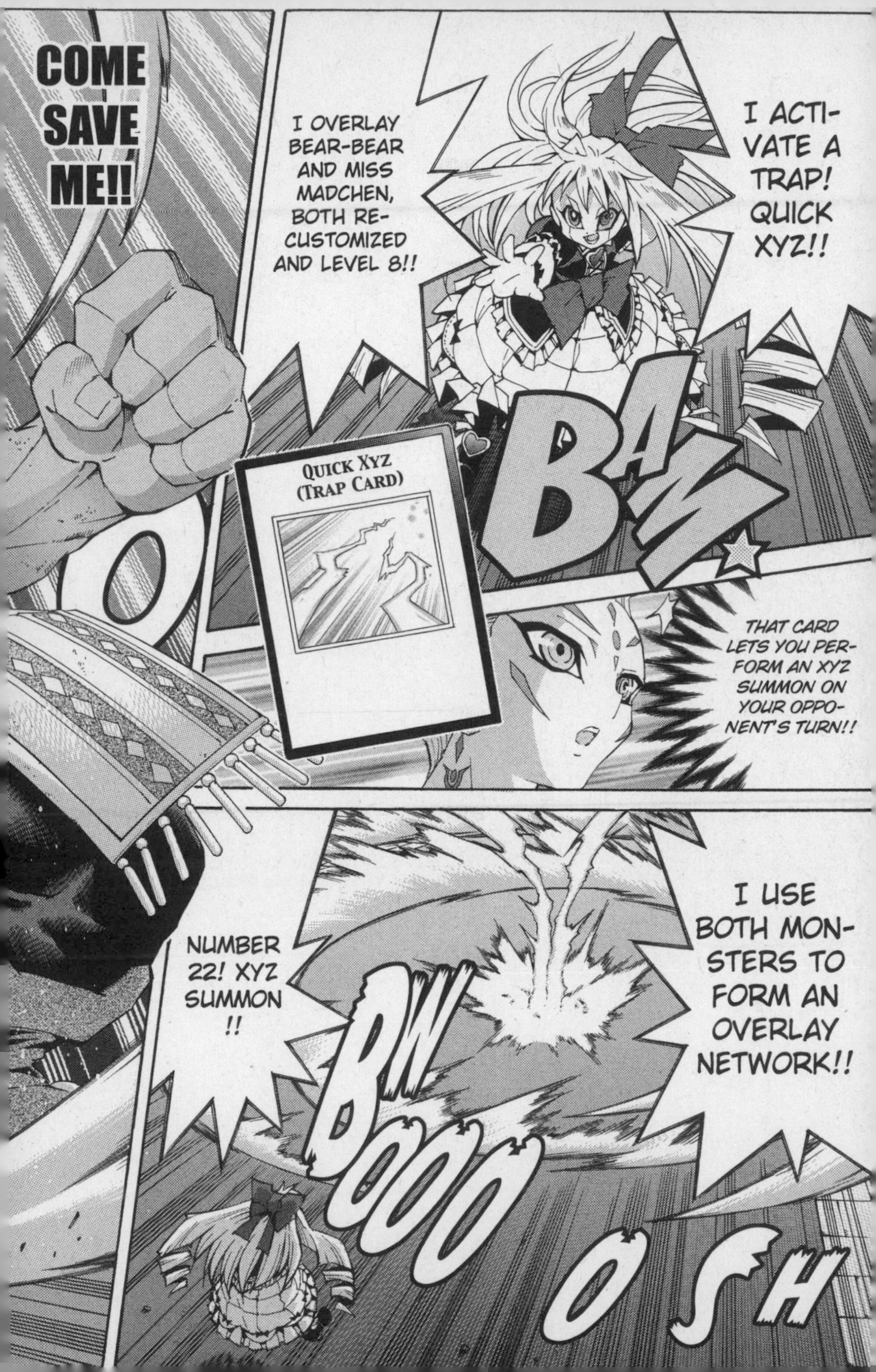
I ACTI-
VATE A
TRAP!
QUICK
XYZ!!
I OVERLAY
BEAR-BEAR
AND MISS
MADCHEN,
BOTH RE-
CUSTOMIZED
AND LEVEL 8!!
BAM
QUICK XYZ
(TRAP CARD)
THAT CARD
LETS YOU PER-
FORM AN XYZ
SUMMON ON
YOUR OPPO-
NENT'S TURN!!
COME
SAVE
ME!!
I USE
BOTH MON-
STERS TO
FORM AN
OVERLAY
NETWORK!!
NUMBER
22! XYZ
SUMMON
!!
BWOOOOOSH

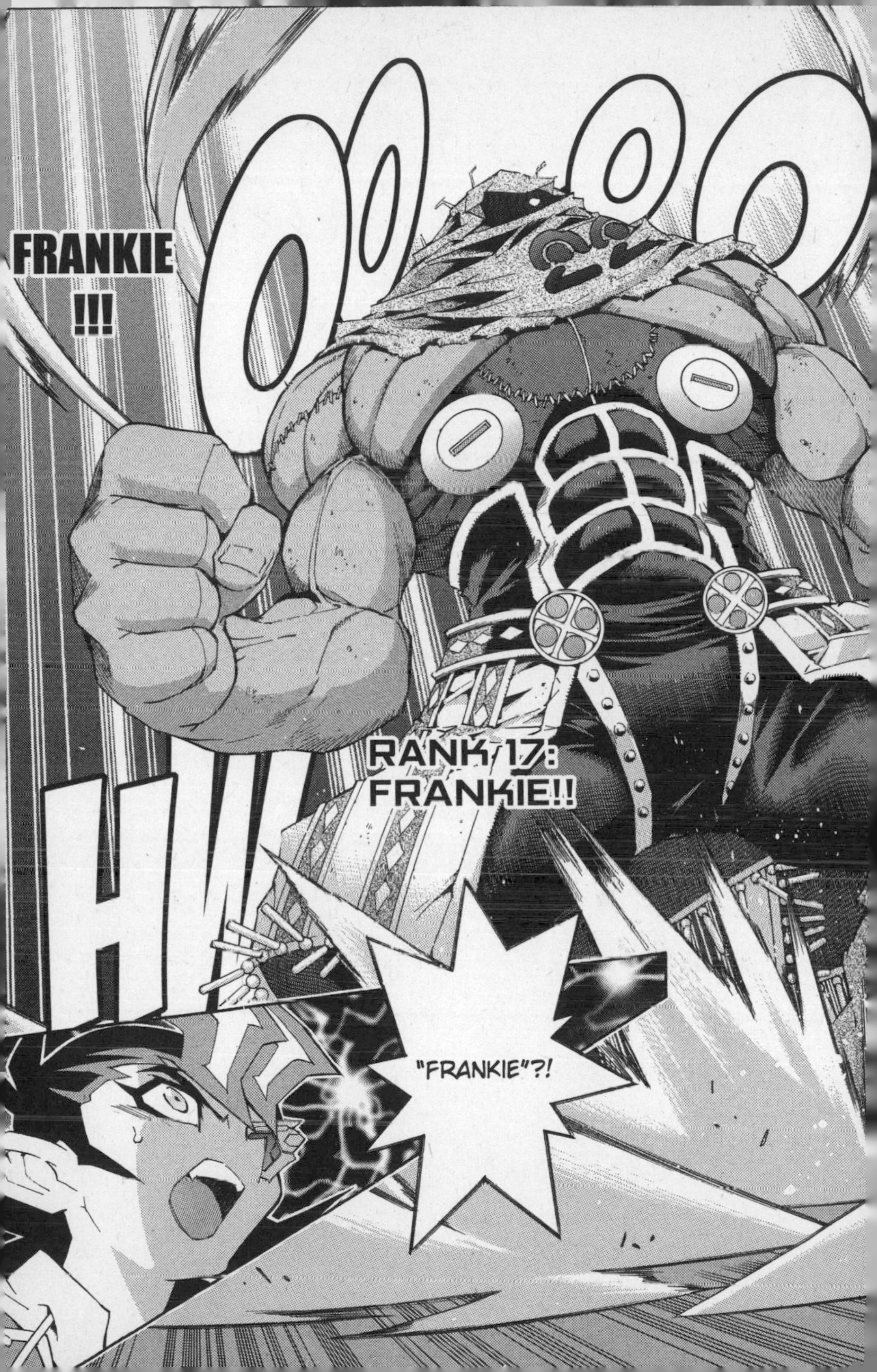
FRANKIE !!!
RANK 17: FRANKIE!!
"FRANKIE"?!

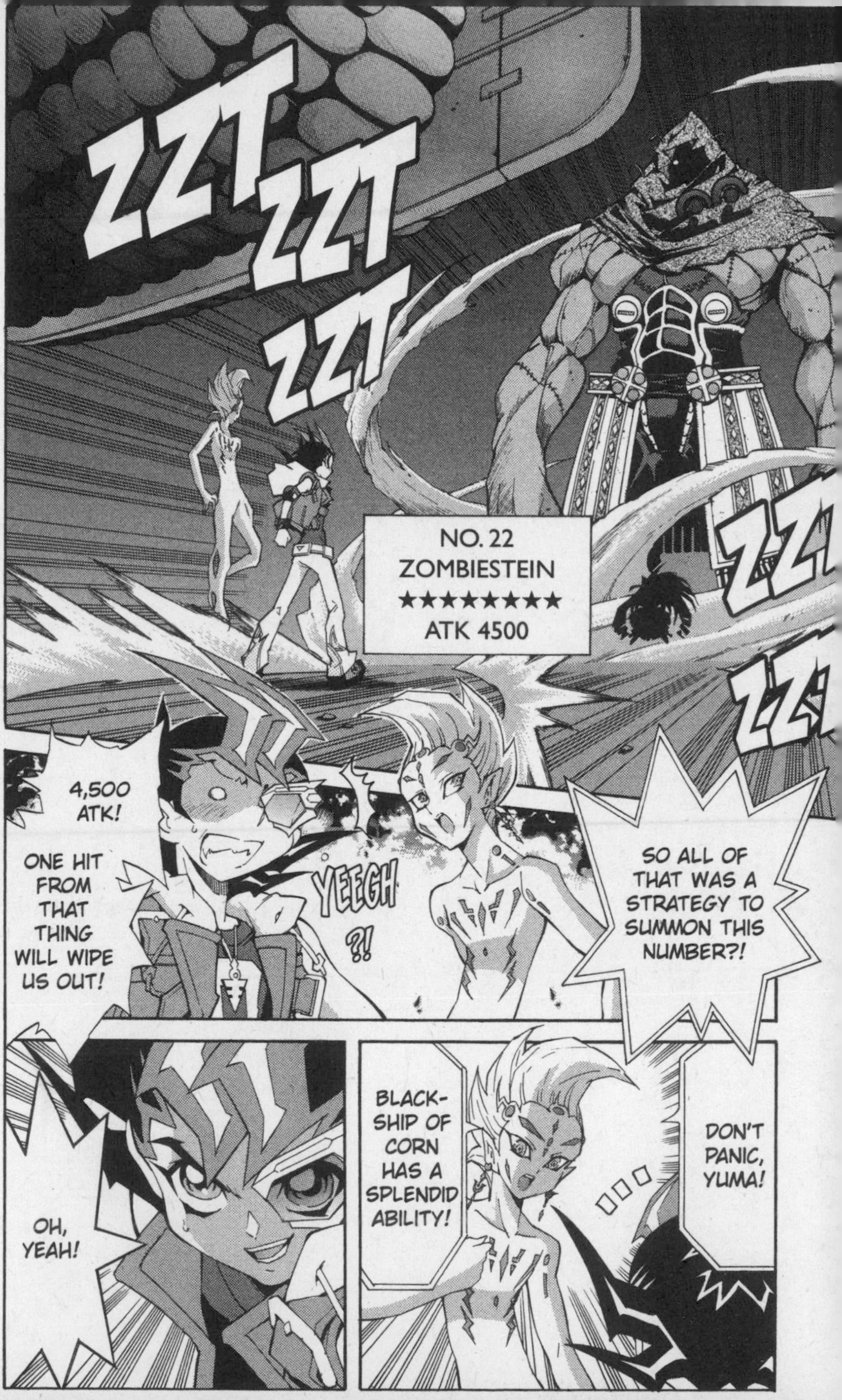
ZZT ZZT ZZT
ZZ
ZZ
NO. 22 ZOMBIESTEIN ★★★★★★★★ ATK 4500
SO ALL OF THAT WAS A STRATEGY TO SUMMON THIS NUMBER?!
YEEGH ?!
4,500 ATK!
ONE HIT FROM THAT THING WILL WIPE US OUT!
DON'T PANIC, YUMA!
...
BLACK-SHIP OF CORN HAS A SPLENDID ABILITY!
OH, YEAH!

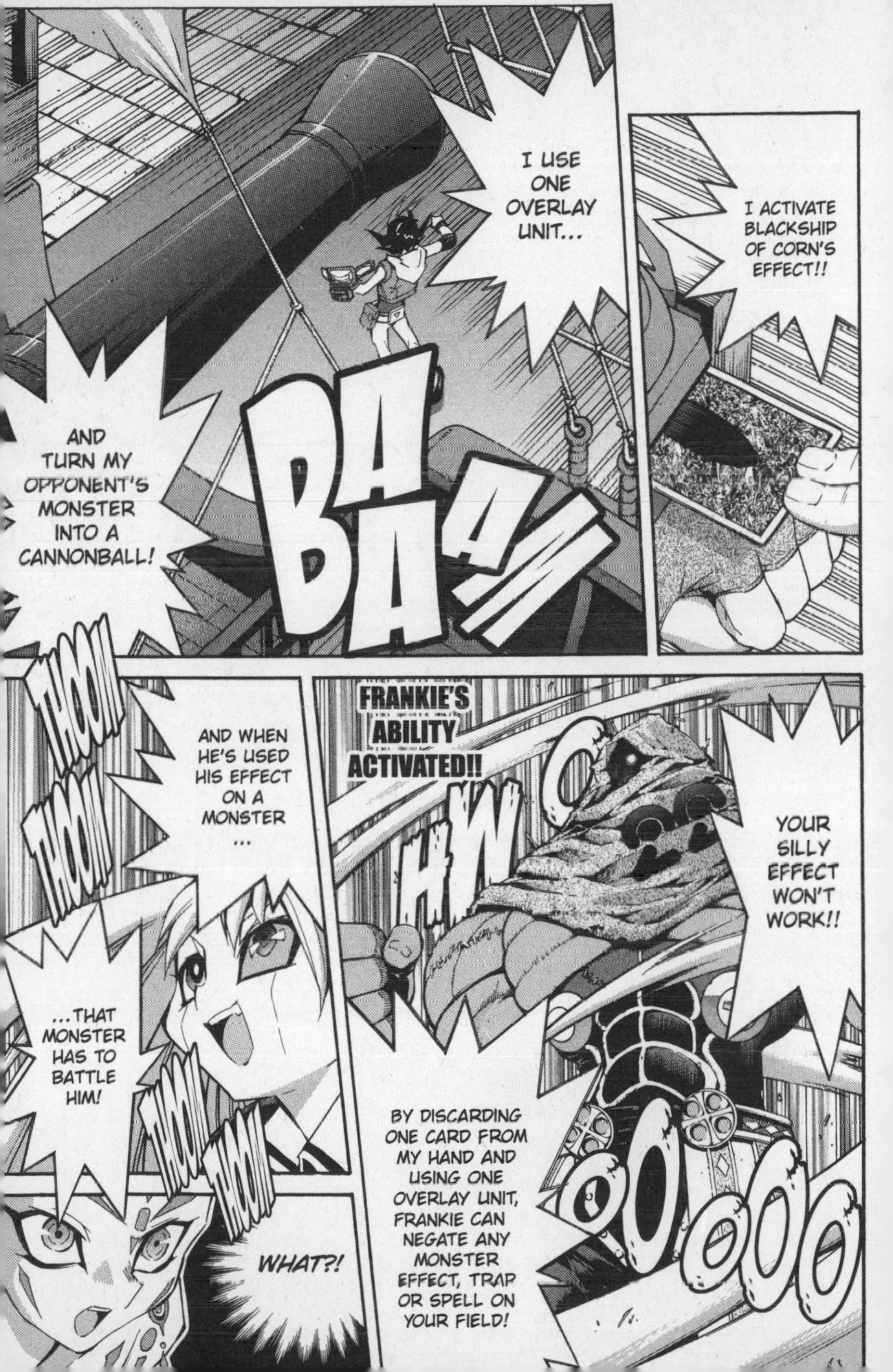
I ACTIVATE BLACKSHIP OF CORN'S EFFECT!!
I USE ONE OVERLAY UNIT...
AND TURN MY OPPONENT'S MONSTER INTO A CANNONBALL!
FRANKIE'S ABILITY ACTIVATED!!
YOUR SILLY EFFECT WON'T WORK!!
BY DISCARDING ONE CARD FROM MY HAND AND USING ONE OVERLAY UNIT, FRANKIE CAN NEGATE ANY MONSTER EFFECT, TRAP OR SPELL ON YOUR FIELD!
AND WHEN HE'S USED HIS EFFECT ON A MONSTER ...
THOOM THOOM
...THAT MONSTER HAS TO BATTLE HIM!
THOOM THOOM
WHAT?!

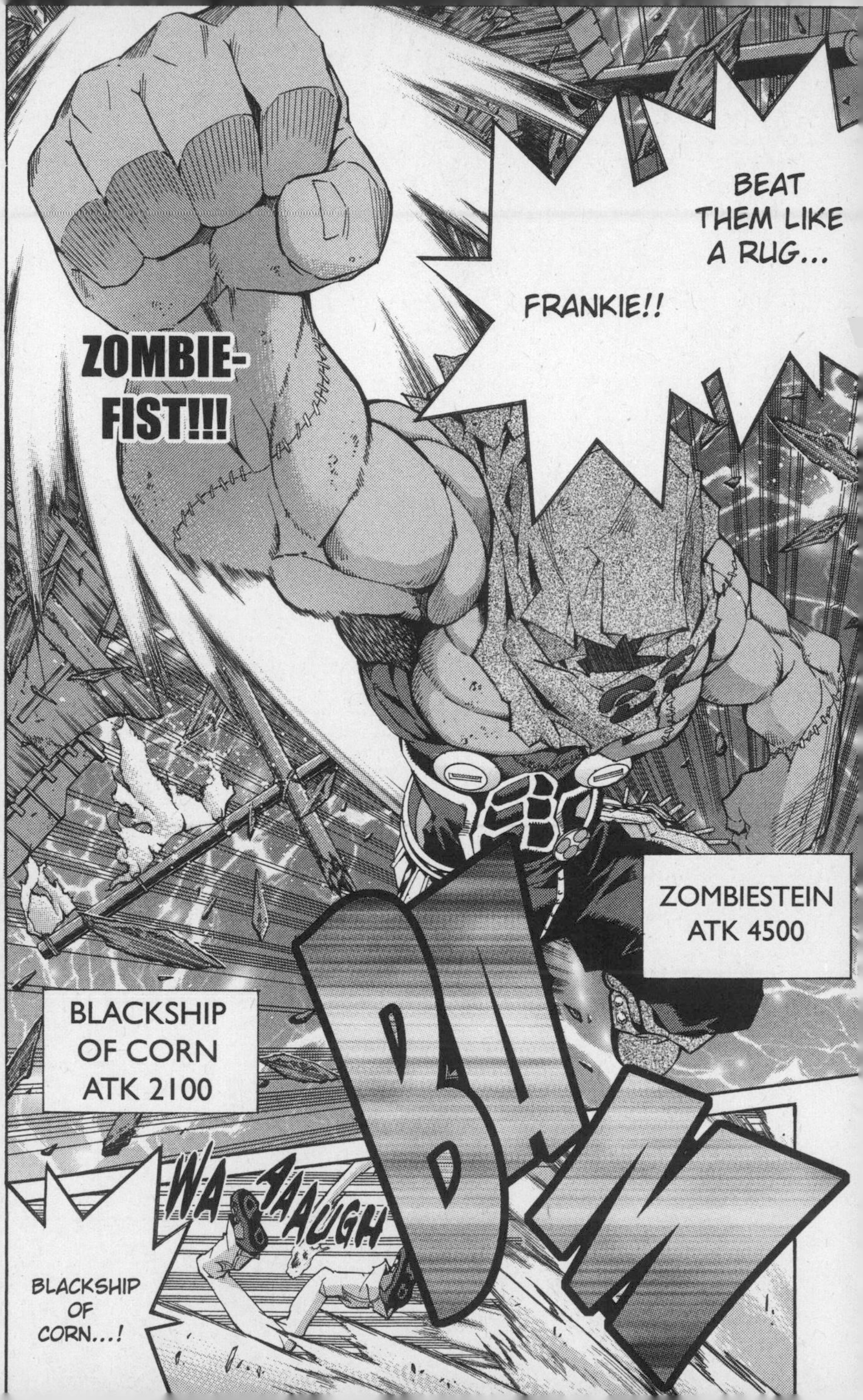
BEAT THEM LIKE A RUG...
FRANKIE!!
ZOMBIE-FIST!!!
ZOMBIESTEIN ATK 4500
BLACKSHIP OF CORN ATK 2100
WAAAAUGH
BLACKSHIP OF CORN...!

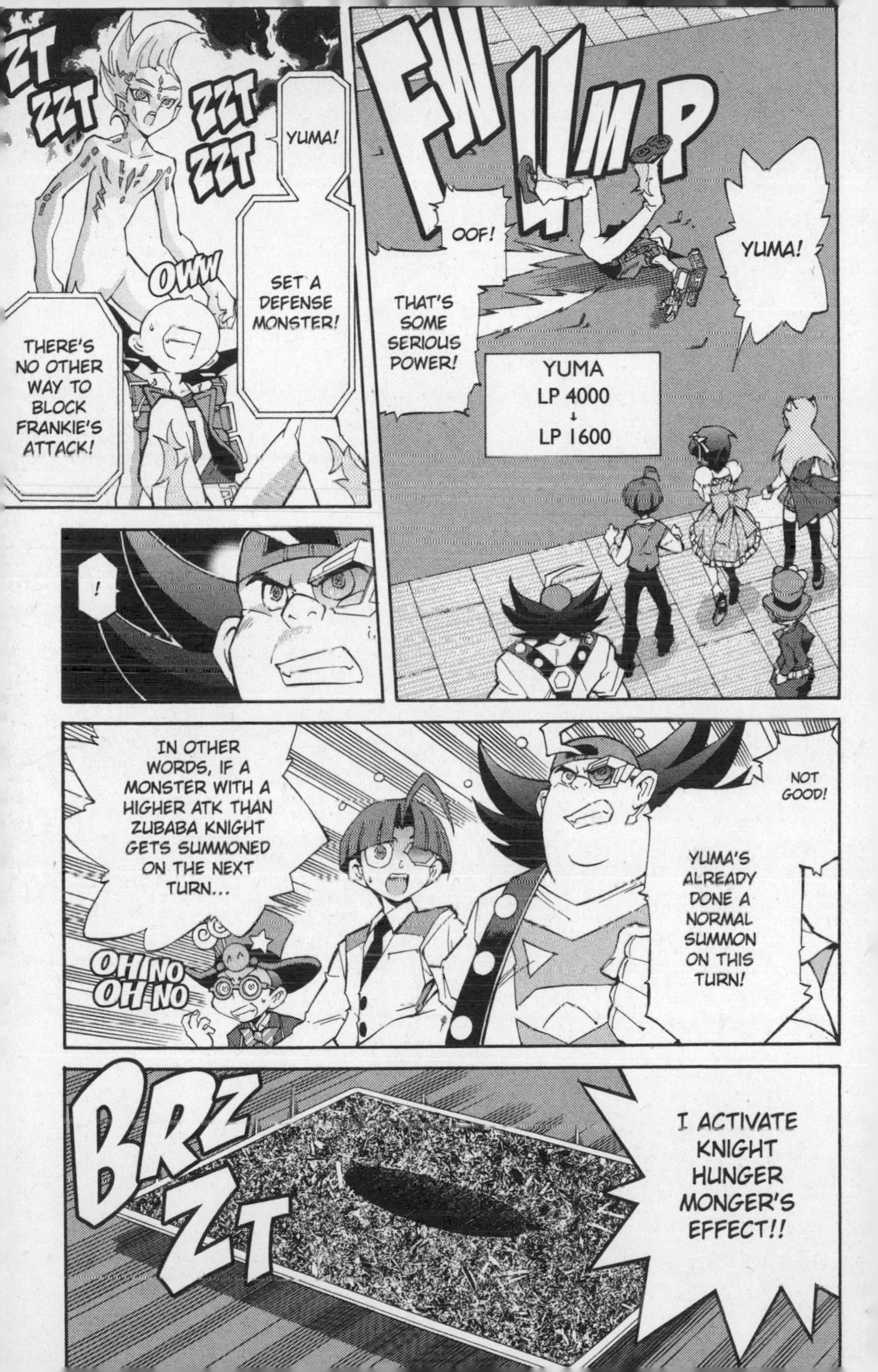
YUMA!
FWUMP
OOF!
YUMA
LP 4000
↓
LP 1600
THAT'S SOME SERIOUS POWER!
YUMA!
ZZT ZZT
ZT ZZT
SET A DEFENSE MONSTER!
OWW
THERE'S NO OTHER WAY TO BLOCK FRANKIE'S ATTACK!
!
NOT GOOD!
YUMA'S ALREADY DONE A NORMAL SUMMON ON THIS TURN!
IN OTHER WORDS, IF A MONSTER WITH A HIGHER ATK THAN ZUBABA KNIGHT GETS SUMMONED ON THE NEXT TURN...
OH NO OH NO
I ACTIVATE KNIGHT HUNGER MONGER'S EFFECT!!
BRZ ZT

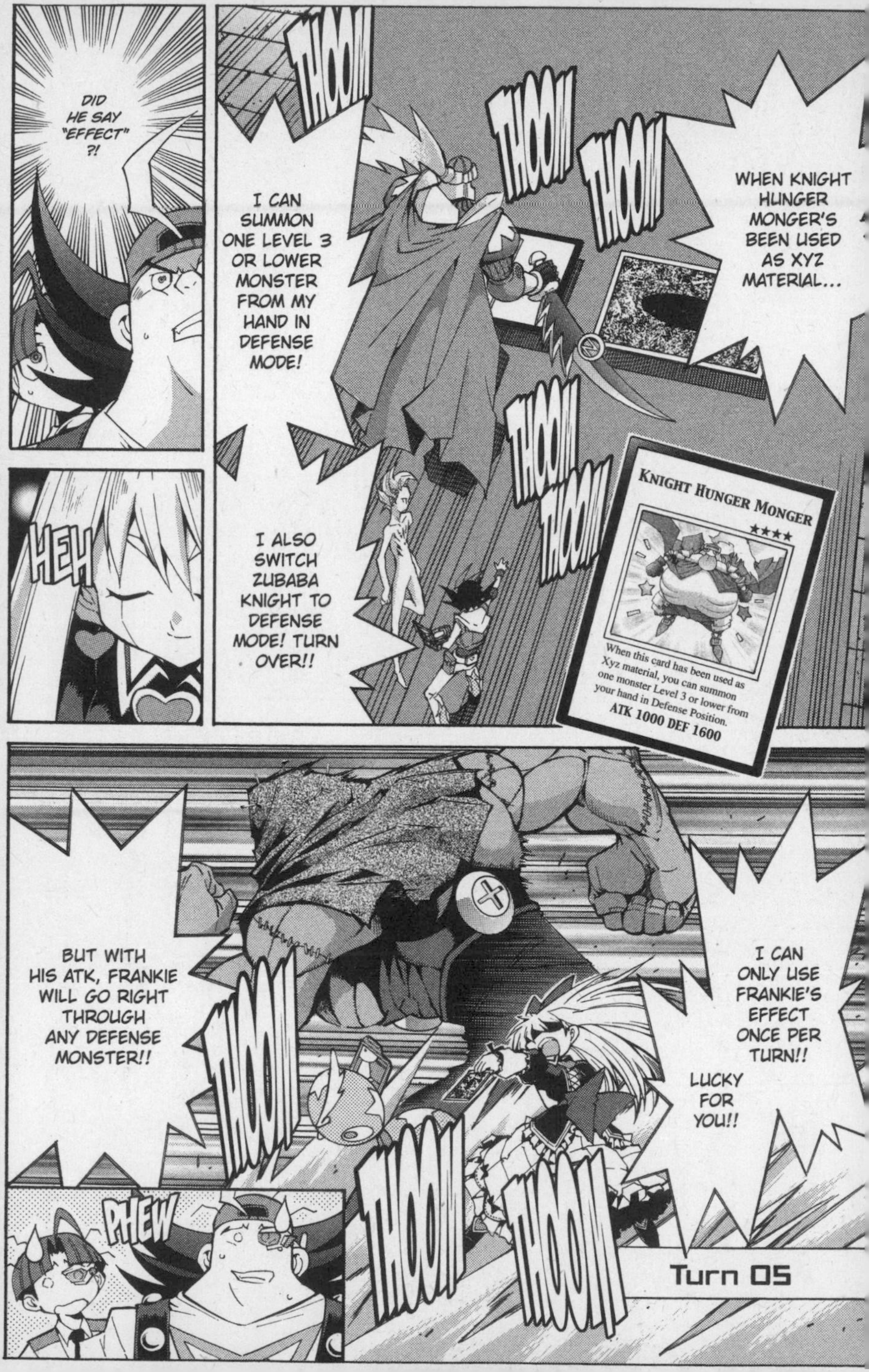
THOOM
THOOM
THOOM
WHEN KNIGHT HUNGER MONGER'S BEEN USED AS XYZ MATERIAL...
I CAN SUMMON ONE LEVEL 3 OR LOWER MONSTER FROM MY HAND IN DEFENSE MODE!
THOOM
THOOM
KNIGHT HUNGER MONGER
When this card has been used as Xyz material, you can summon one monster Level 3 or lower from your hand in Defense Position.
ATK 1000 DEF 1600
I ALSO SWITCH ZUBABA KNIGHT TO DEFENSE MODE! TURN OVER!!
DID HE SAY "EFFECT" ?!
HEH
I CAN ONLY USE FRANKIE'S EFFECT ONCE PER TURN!!
LUCKY FOR YOU!!
BUT WITH HIS ATK, FRANKIE WILL GO RIGHT THROUGH ANY DEFENSE MONSTER!!
THOOM
THOOM
THOOM
Turn 05
PHEW

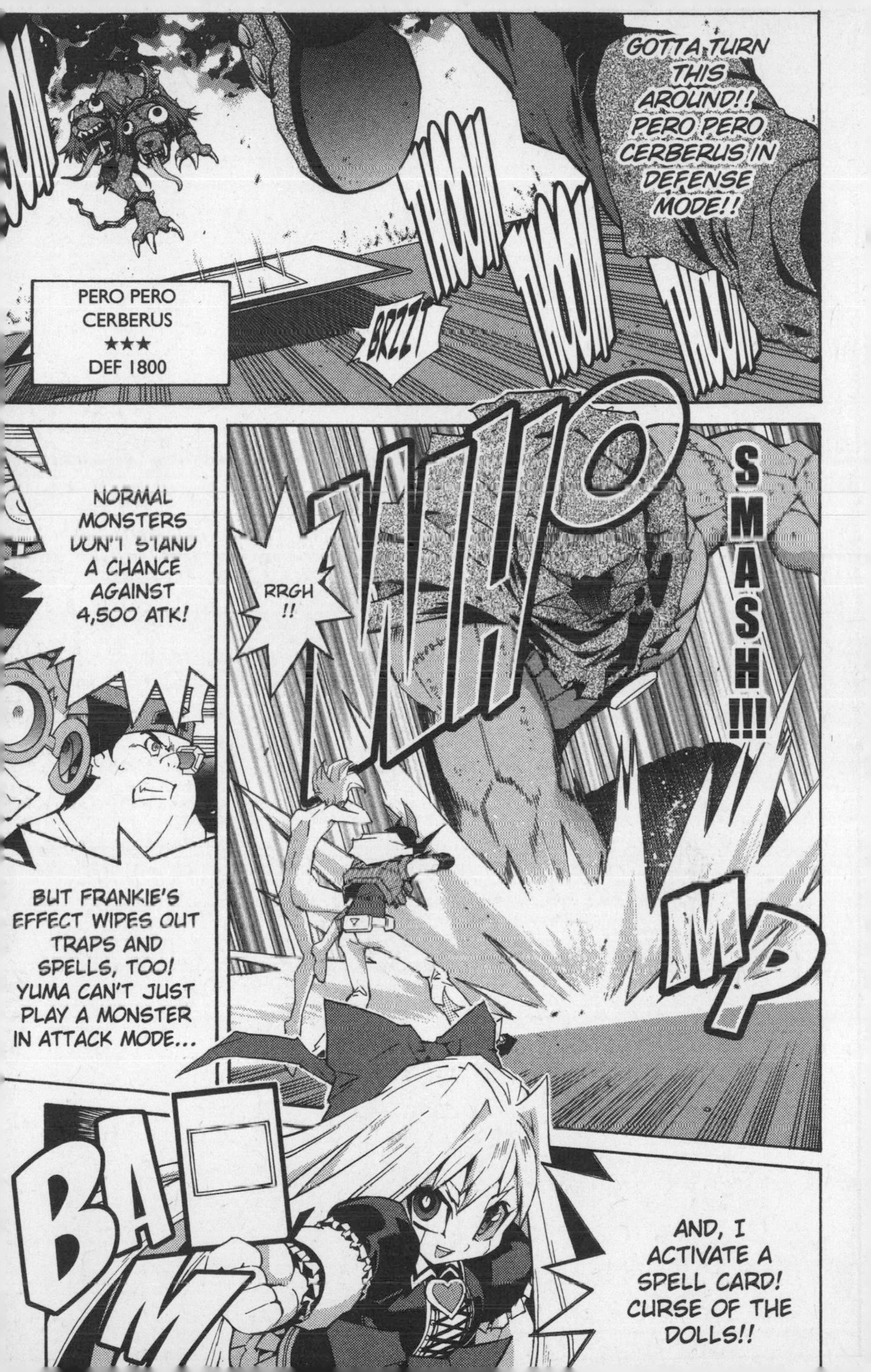
GOTTA TURN THIS AROUND!! PERO PERO CERBERUS IN DEFENSE MODE!!
THOOM
THOOM
THOOM
BRZZT
PERO PERO CERBERUS ★★★ DEF 1800
SMASH!!!
RRGH!!
NORMAL MONSTERS DON'T STAND A CHANCE AGAINST 4,500 ATK!
BUT FRANKIE'S EFFECT WIPES OUT TRAPS AND SPELLS, TOO! YUMA CAN'T JUST PLAY A MONSTER IN ATTACK MODE...
AND, I ACTIVATE A SPELL CARD! CURSE OF THE DOLLS!!
BAM

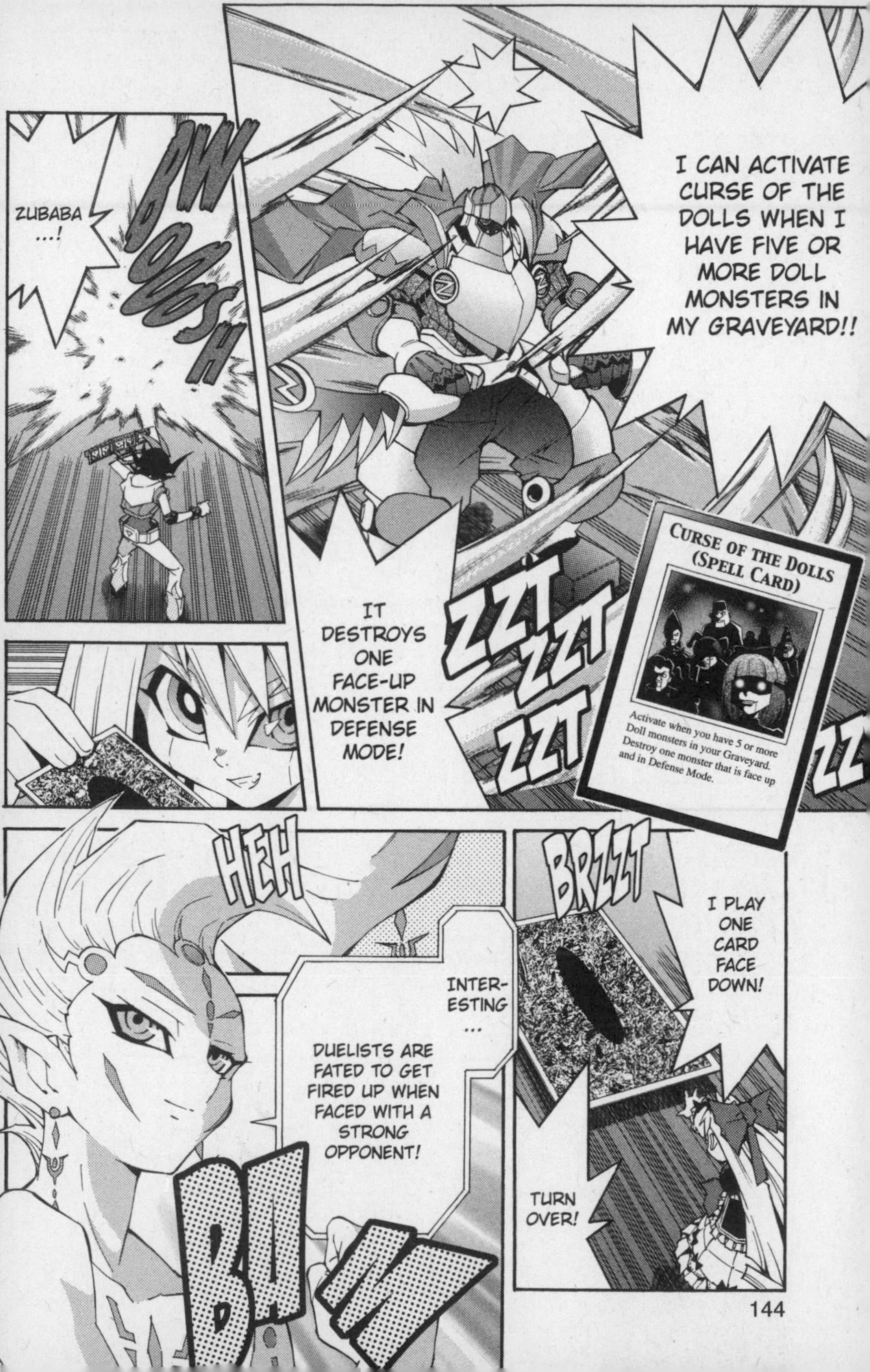
I CAN ACTIVATE CURSE OF THE DOLLS WHEN I HAVE FIVE OR MORE DOLL MONSTERS IN MY GRAVEYARD!!
IT DESTROYS ONE FACE-UP MONSTER IN DEFENSE MODE!
ZZT ZZT ZZT
CURSE OF THE DOLLS (SPELL CARD)
Activate when you have 5 or more Doll monsters in your Graveyard. Destroy one monster that is face up and in Defense Mode.
BWOOOOSH
ZUBABA ...!
BRZZT
I PLAY ONE CARD FACE DOWN!
TURN OVER!
HEH
INTER-ESTING ...
DUELISTS ARE FATED TO GET FIRED UP WHEN FACED WITH A STRONG OPPONENT!
BA!!

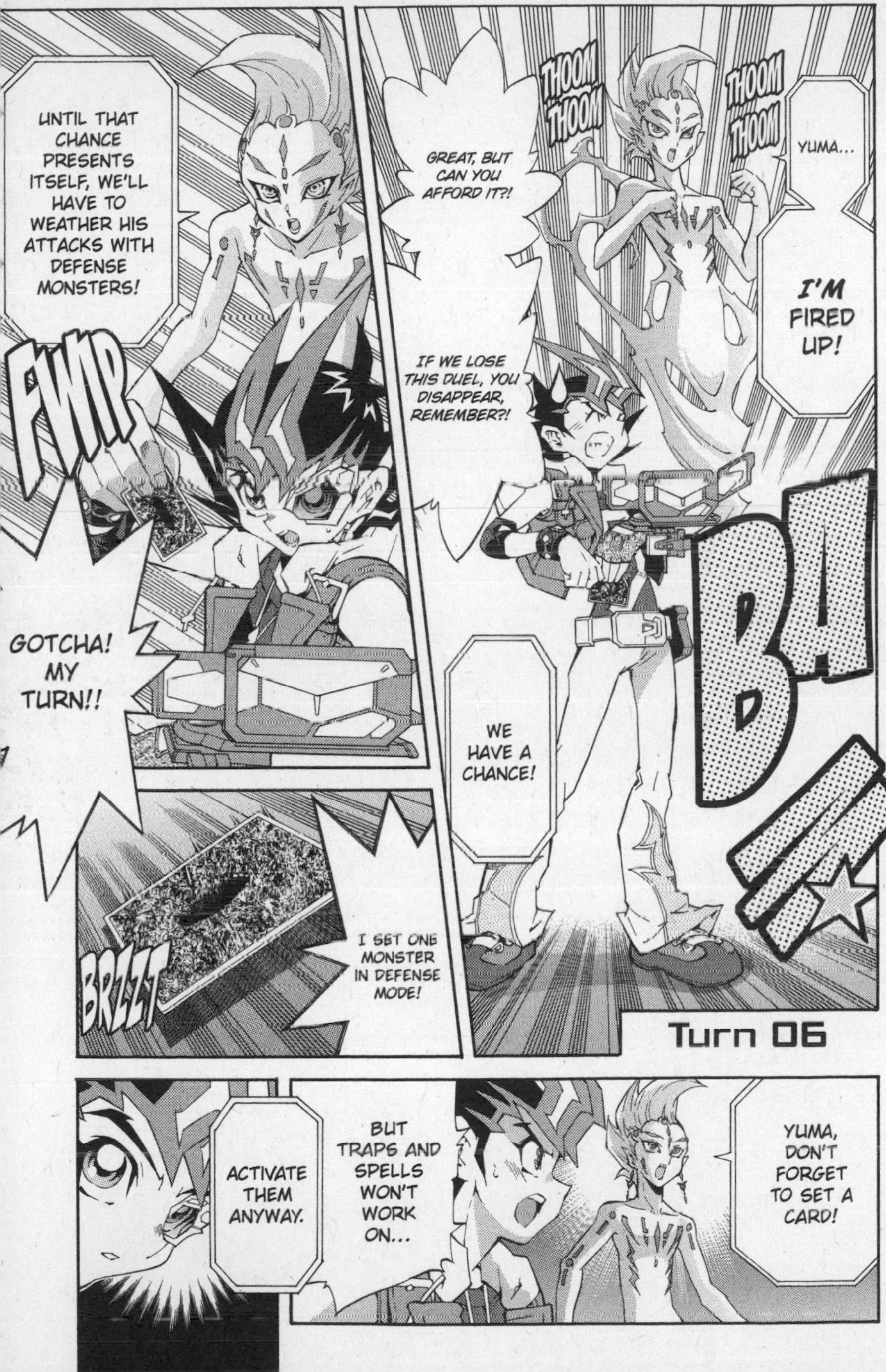
THOOM THOOM
YUMA...
I'M FIRED UP!
THOOM THOOM
GREAT, BUT CAN YOU AFFORD IT?!
IF WE LOSE THIS DUEL, YOU DISAPPEAR, REMEMBER?!
BA-
WE HAVE A CHANCE!
UNTIL THAT CHANCE PRESENTS ITSELF, WE'LL HAVE TO WEATHER HIS ATTACKS WITH DEFENSE MONSTERS!
FWIP
GOTCHA! MY TURN!!
I SET ONE MONSTER IN DEFENSE MODE!
BRZZT
Turn 06
YUMA, DON'T FORGET TO SET A CARD!
BUT TRAPS AND SPELLS WON'T WORK ON...
ACTIVATE THEM ANYWAY.

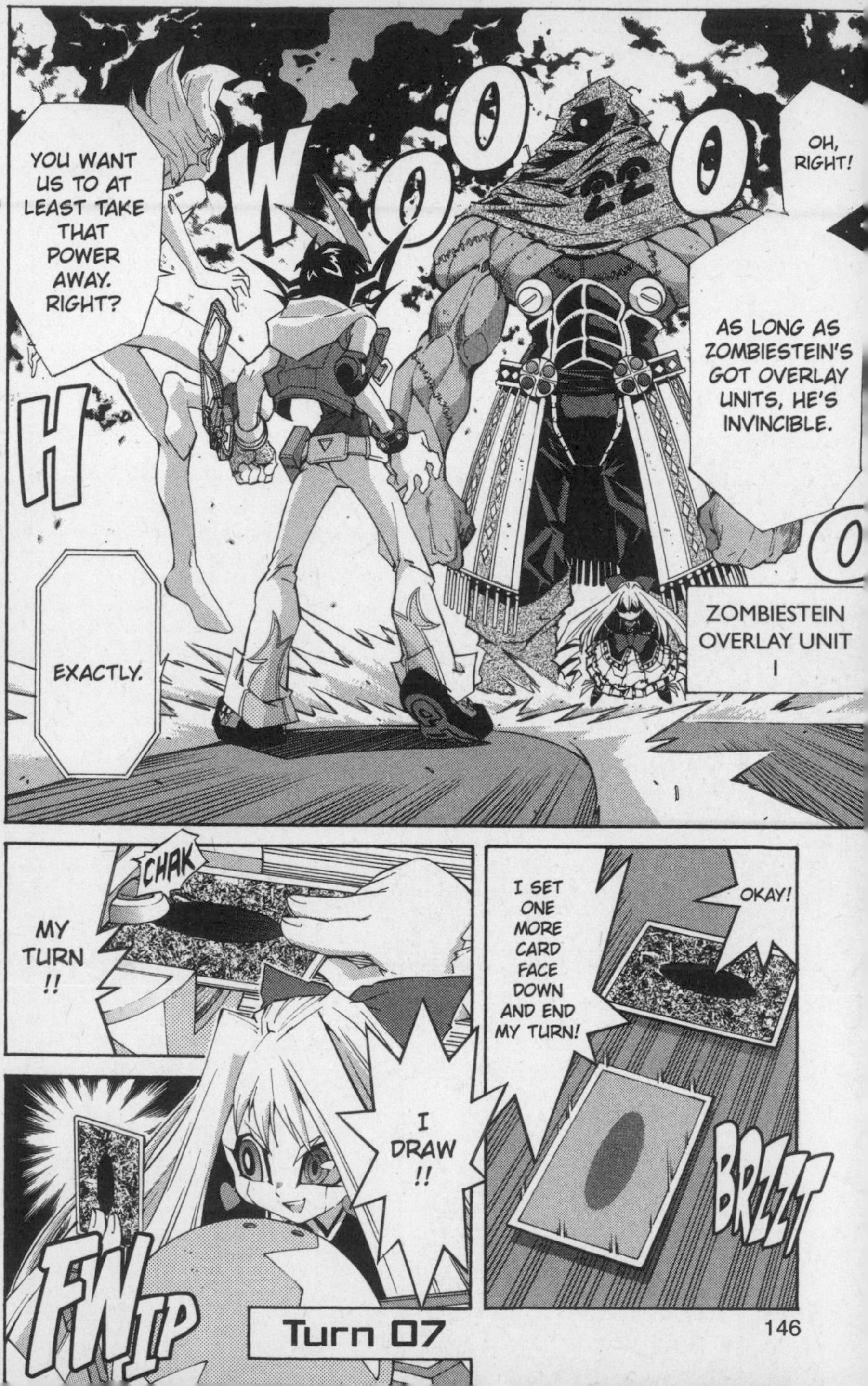
OH, RIGHT!
AS LONG AS ZOMBIESTEIN'S GOT OVERLAY UNITS, HE'S INVINCIBLE.
WOOOO
YOU WANT US TO AT LEAST TAKE THAT POWER AWAY. RIGHT?
ZOMBIESTEIN OVERLAY UNIT 1
EXACTLY.
OKAY!
I SET ONE MORE CARD FACE DOWN AND END MY TURN!
BRZZT
CHAK
MY TURN !!
I DRAW !!
FWIP
Turn 07

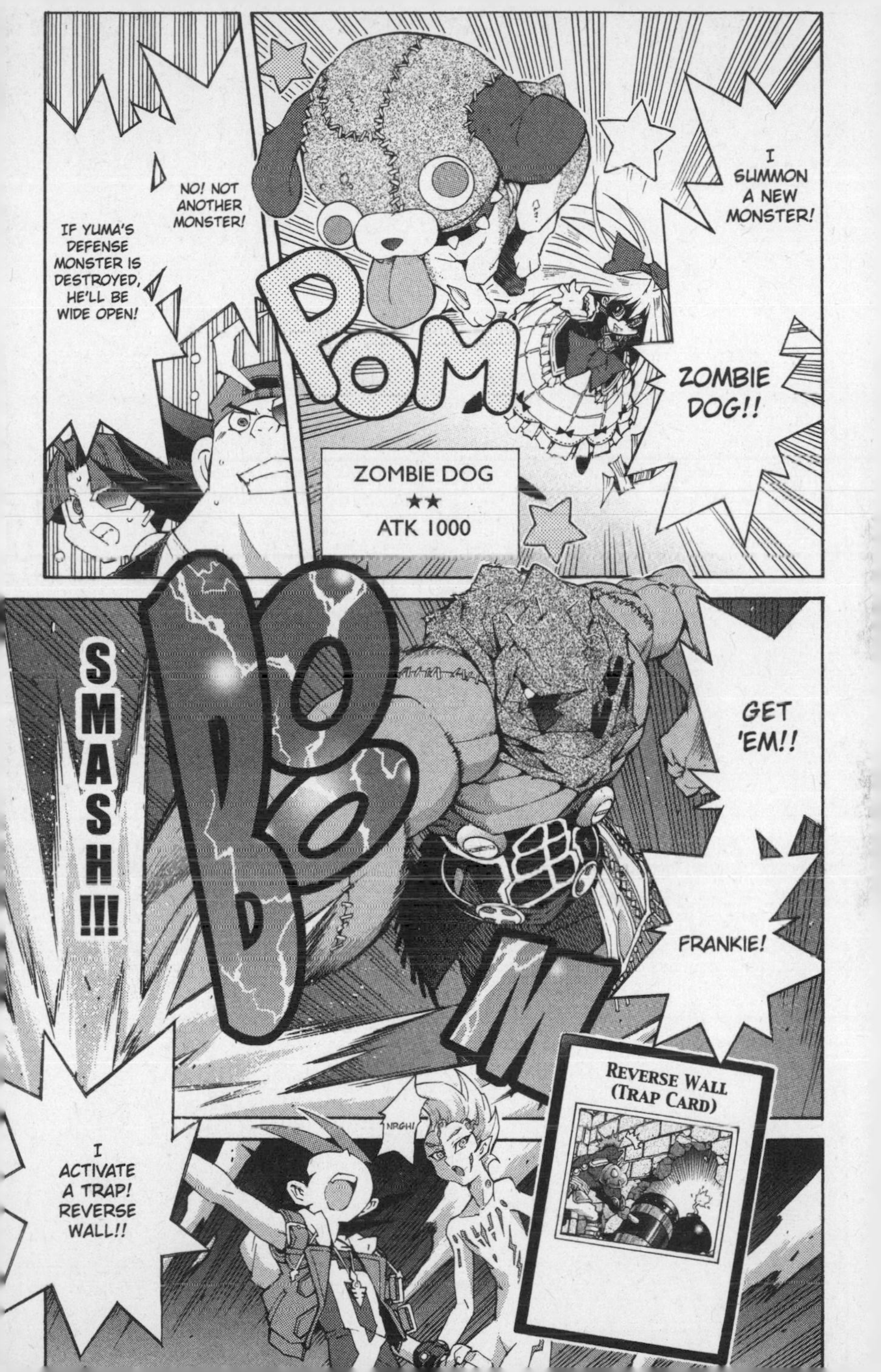
I SUMMON A NEW MONSTER!
POM
ZOMBIE DOG!!
NO! NOT ANOTHER MONSTER!
IF YUMA'S DEFENSE MONSTER IS DESTROYED, HE'LL BE WIDE OPEN!
ZOMBIE DOG
★★
ATK 1000
GET 'EM!!
FRANKIE!
BOOM
SMASH!!!
REVERSE WALL
(TRAP CARD)
NRGH!
I ACTIVATE A TRAP! REVERSE WALL!!

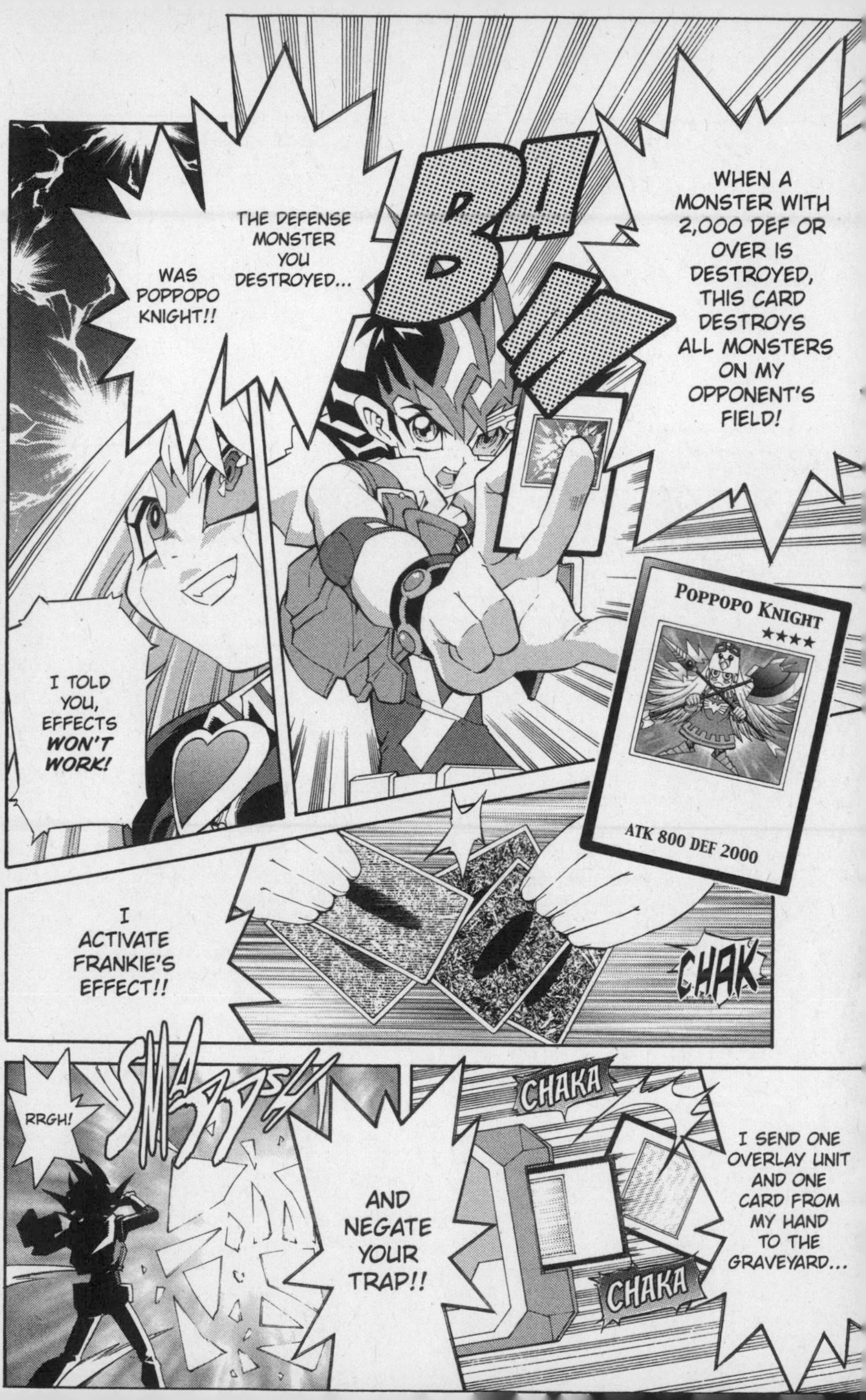

THE DEFENSE MONSTER YOU DESTROYED...
WAS POPPOPO KNIGHT!!
BAM
WHEN A MONSTER WITH 2,000 DEF OR OVER IS DESTROYED, THIS CARD DESTROYS ALL MONSTERS ON MY OPPONENT'S FIELD!
POPPOPO KNIGHT
★★★★
ATK 800 DEF 2000
I TOLD YOU, EFFECTS *WON'T WORK!*
CHAK
I ACTIVATE FRANKIE'S EFFECT!!
CHAKA
I SEND ONE OVERLAY UNIT AND ONE CARD FROM MY HAND TO THE GRAVEYARD...
CHAKA
AND NEGATE YOUR TRAP!!
SMAAASH!!
RRGH!

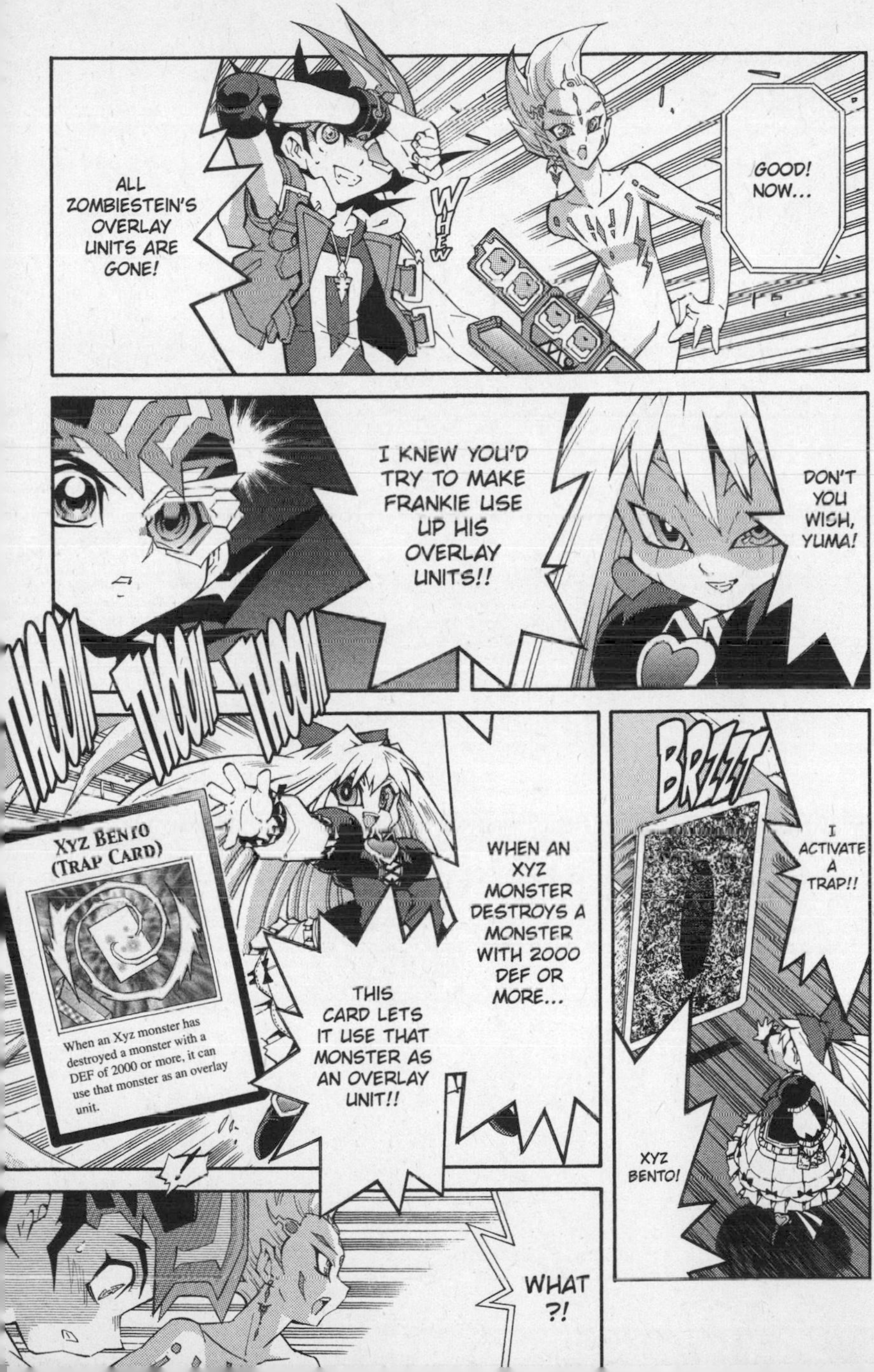
GOOD! NOW...
WHEW
ALL ZOMBIESTEIN'S OVERLAY UNITS ARE GONE!
DON'T YOU WISH, YUMA!
I KNEW YOU'D TRY TO MAKE FRANKIE USE UP HIS OVERLAY UNITS!!
BRZZZT
I ACTIVATE A TRAP!!
XYZ BENTO!
THOOM THOOM THOOM
WHEN AN XYZ MONSTER DESTROYS A MONSTER WITH 2000 DEF OR MORE...
THIS CARD LETS IT USE THAT MONSTER AS AN OVERLAY UNIT!!
XYZ BENTO (TRAP CARD)
When an Xyz monster has destroyed a monster with a DEF of 2000 or more, it can use that monster as an overlay unit.
WHAT ?!

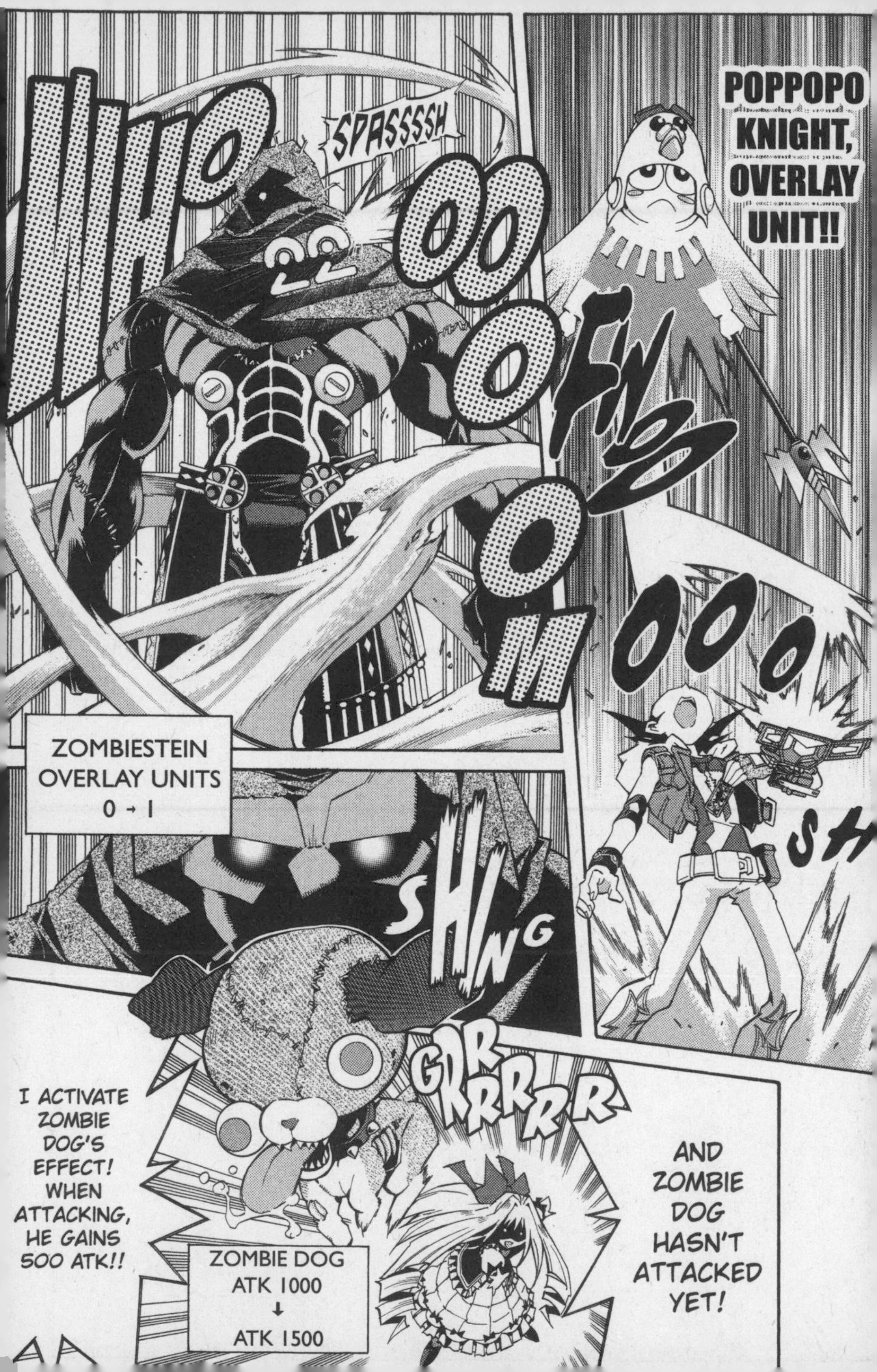
POPPOPO KNIGHT, OVERLAY UNIT!!
SPASSSSH
ZOMBIESTEIN OVERLAY UNITS 0 → 1
SHING
AND ZOMBIE DOG HASN'T ATTACKED YET!
GRRRRRR
I ACTIVATE ZOMBIE DOG'S EFFECT! WHEN ATTACKING, HE GAINS 500 ATK!!
ZOMBIE DOG ATK 1000 ↓ ATK 1500

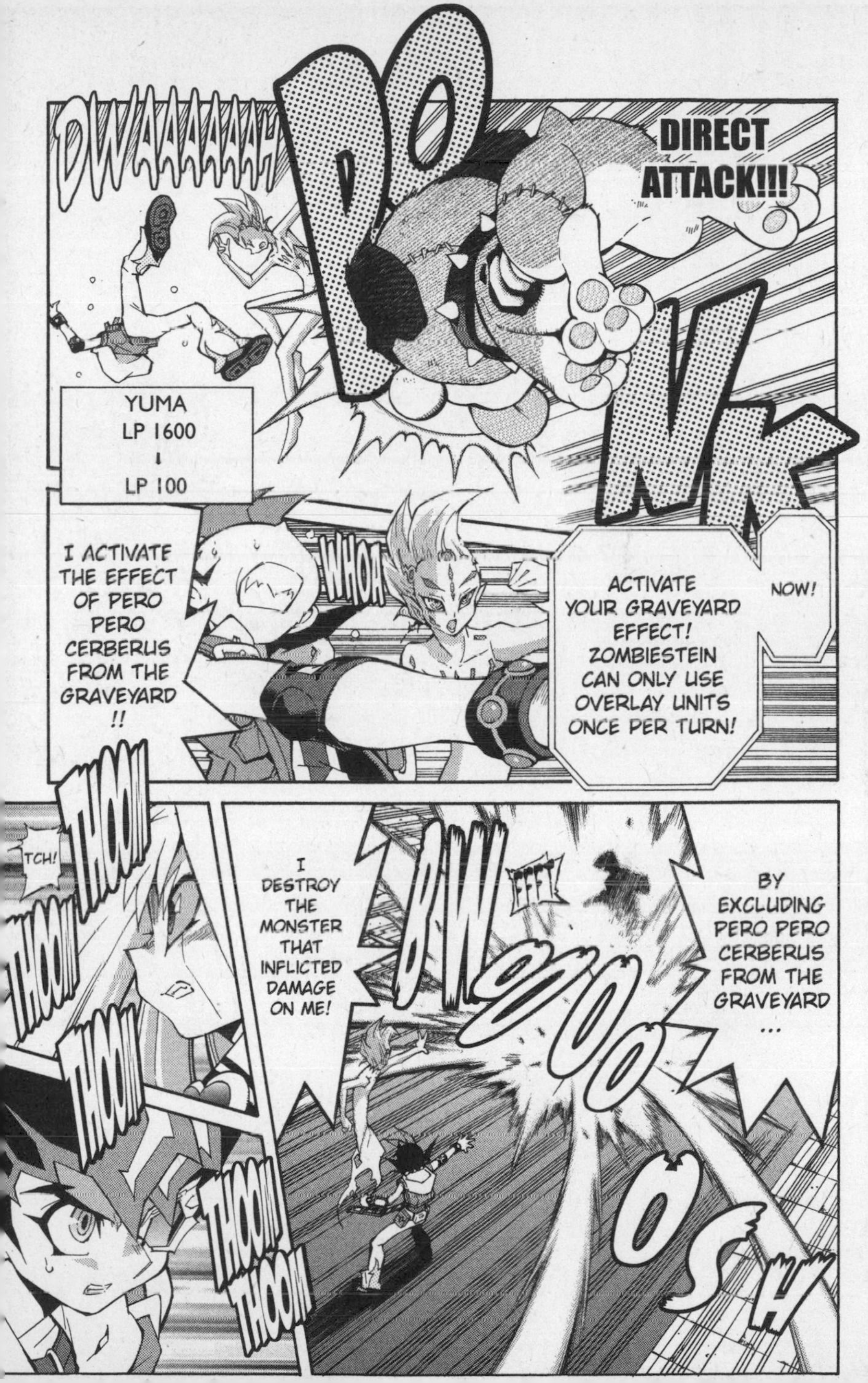
DIRECT ATTACK!!!
DONK
DWAAAAAAAH
YUMA
LP 1600
↓
LP 100
NOW!
ACTIVATE YOUR GRAVEYARD EFFECT! ZOMBIESTEIN CAN ONLY USE OVERLAY UNITS ONCE PER TURN!
WHOA
I ACTIVATE THE EFFECT OF PERO PERO CERBERUS FROM THE GRAVEYARD !!
BY EXCLUDING PERO PERO CERBERUS FROM THE GRAVEYARD ...
FFFT
BWOOOOOOSH
I DESTROY THE MONSTER THAT INFLICTED DAMAGE ON ME!
THOOM
TCH!
THOOM
THOOM
THOOM
THOOM

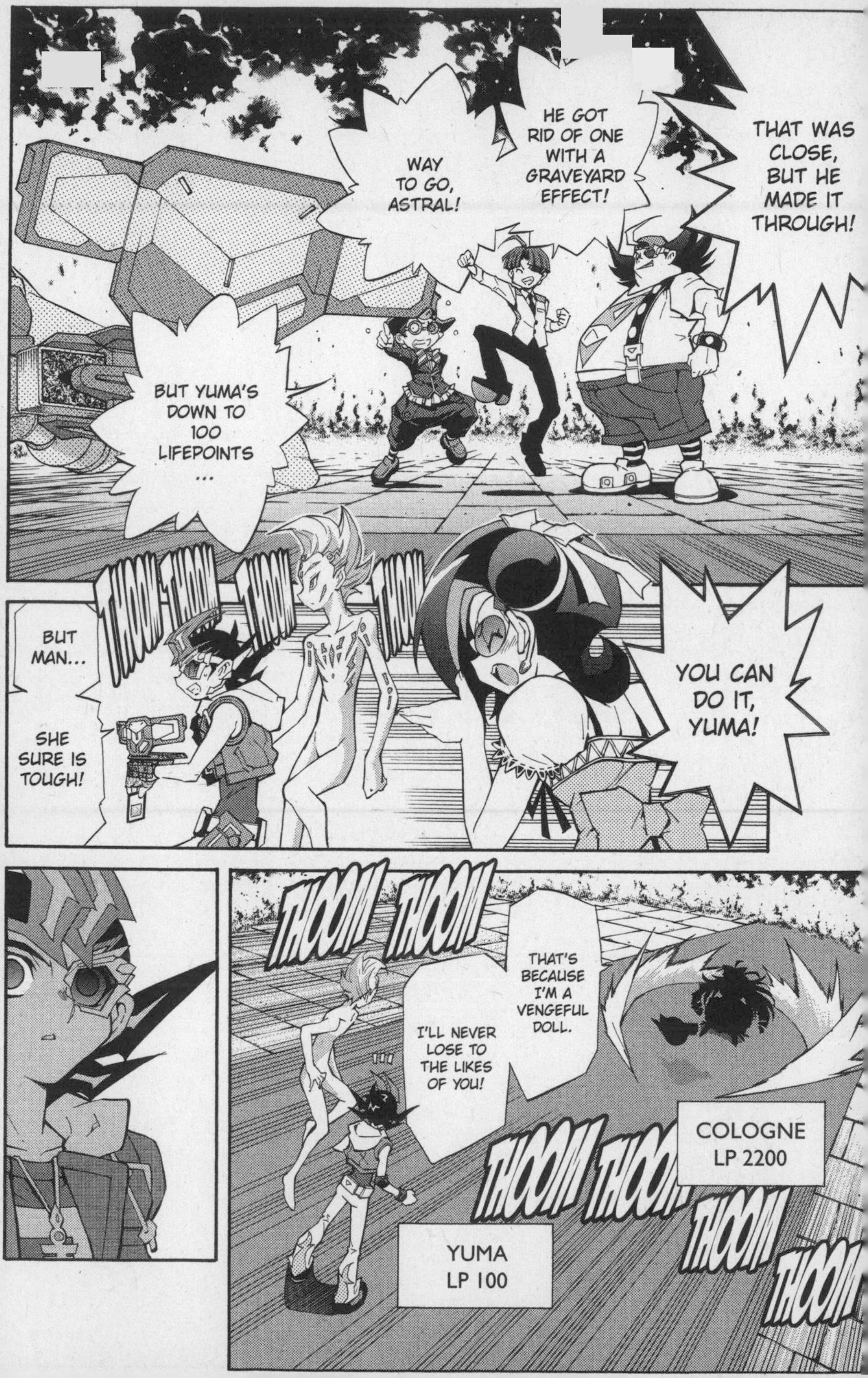
THAT WAS CLOSE, BUT HE MADE IT THROUGH!
HE GOT RID OF ONE WITH A GRAVEYARD EFFECT!
WAY TO GO, ASTRAL!
BUT YUMA'S DOWN TO 100 LIFEPOINTS ...
YOU CAN DO IT, YUMA!
THOOM
THOOM
THOOM
THOOM
BUT MAN...
SHE SURE IS TOUGH!
THOOM
THOOM
THAT'S BECAUSE I'M A VENGEFUL DOLL.
I'LL NEVER LOSE TO THE LIKES OF YOU!
COLOGNE
LP 2200
THOOM
THOOM
THOOM
THOOM
YUMA
LP 100

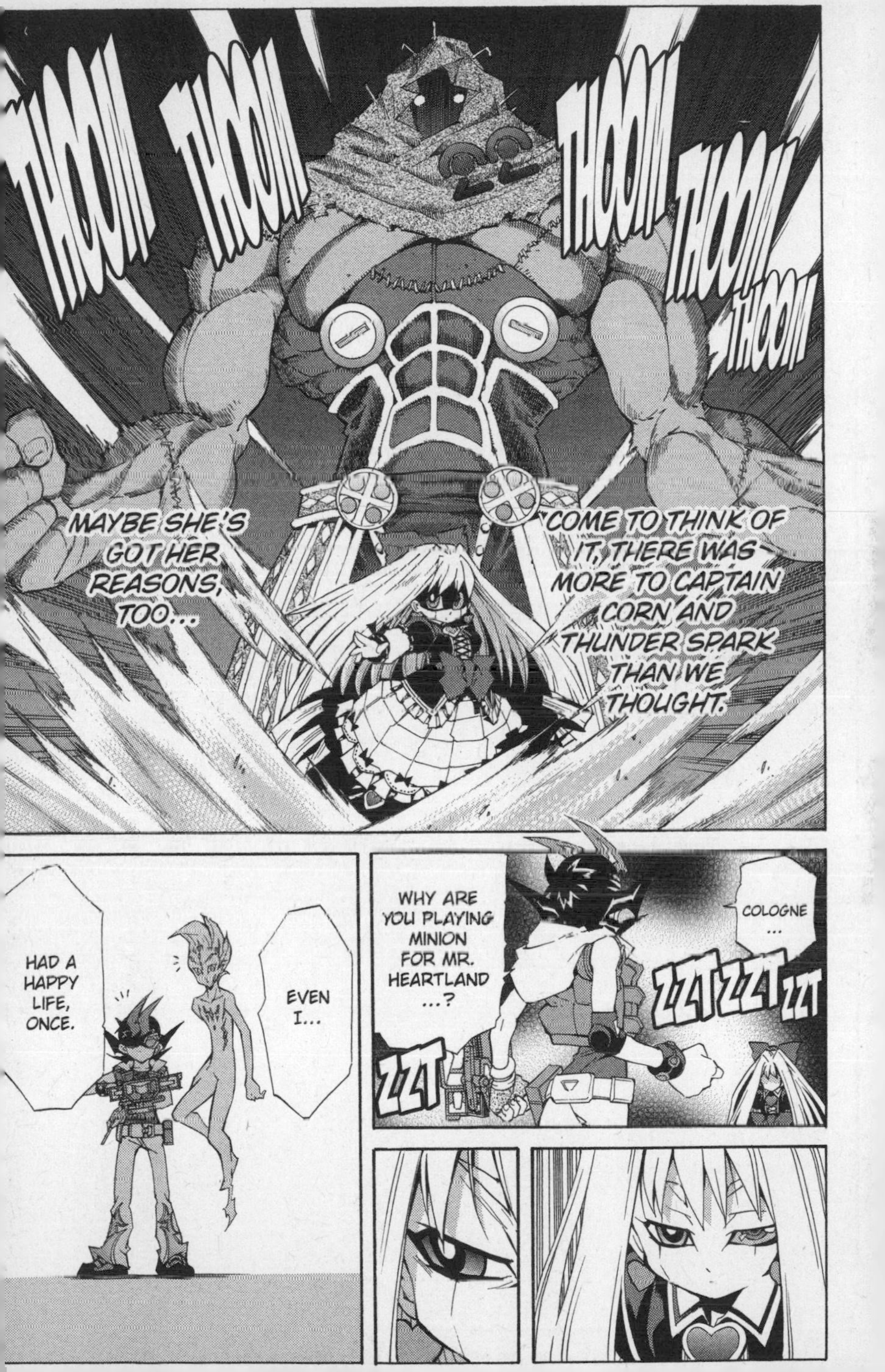
THOOM
THOOM
THOOM
THOOM
THOOM
THOOM
COME TO THINK OF IT, THERE WAS MORE TO CAPTAIN CORN AND THUNDER SPARK THAN WE THOUGHT.
MAYBE SHE'S GOT HER REASONS, TOO...
COLOGNE ...
WHY ARE YOU PLAYING MINION FOR MR. HEARTLAND ...?
ZZT ZZT ZZT
ZZT
EVEN I...
HAD A HAPPY LIFE, ONCE.

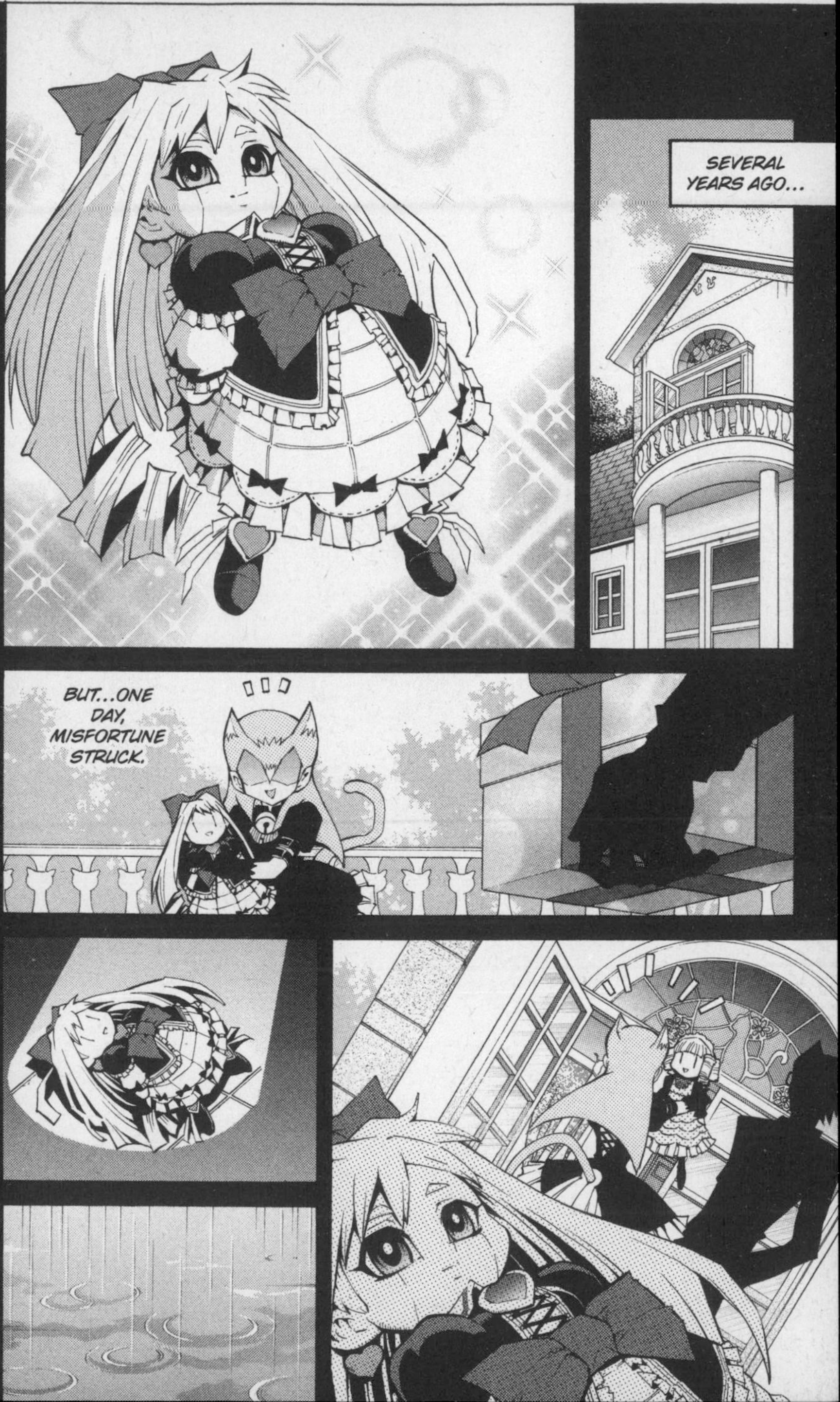
SEVERAL YEARS AGO...
BUT...ONE DAY, MISFORTUNE STRUCK.

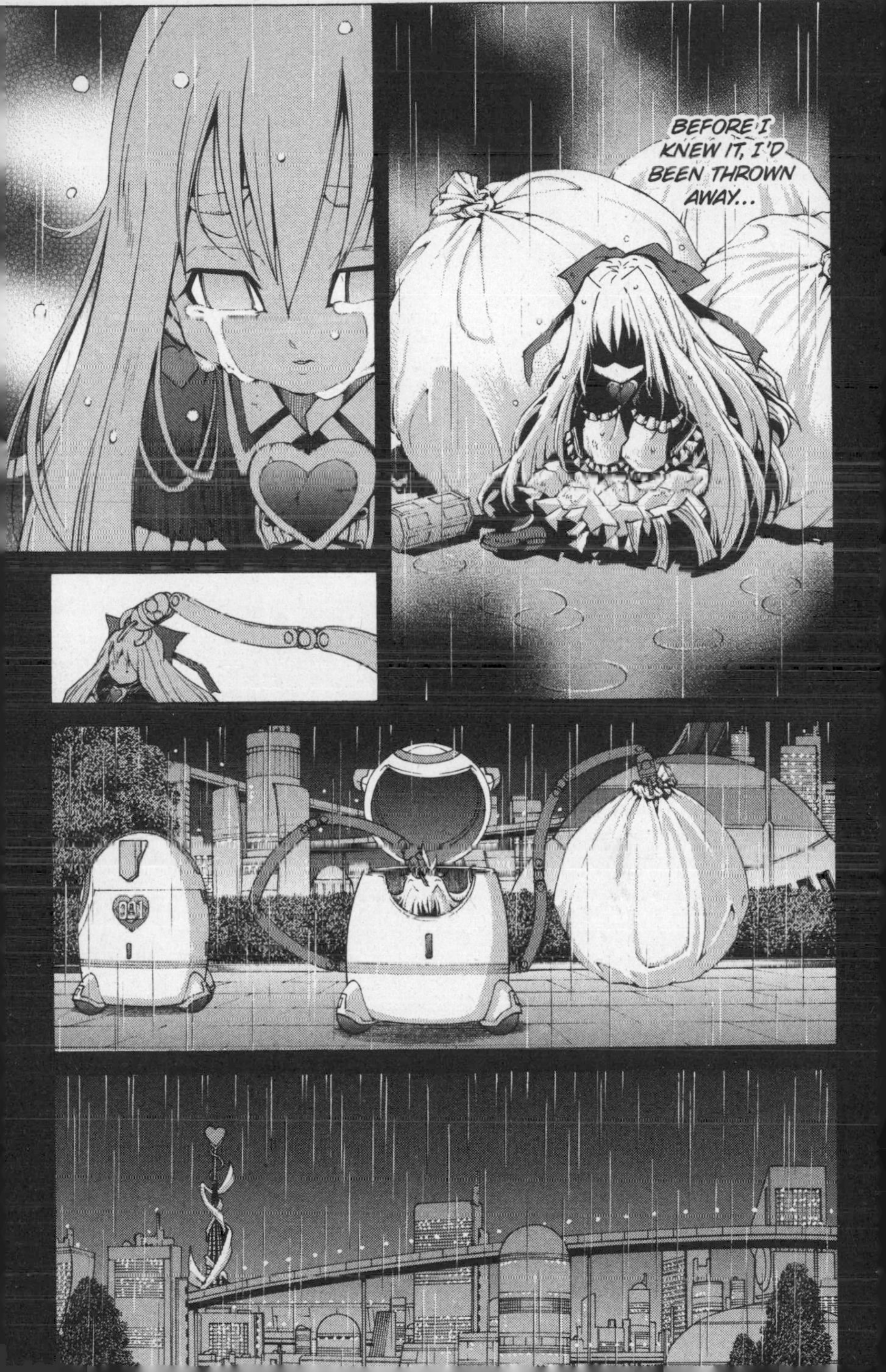
BEFORE I KNEW IT, I'D BEEN THROWN AWAY...

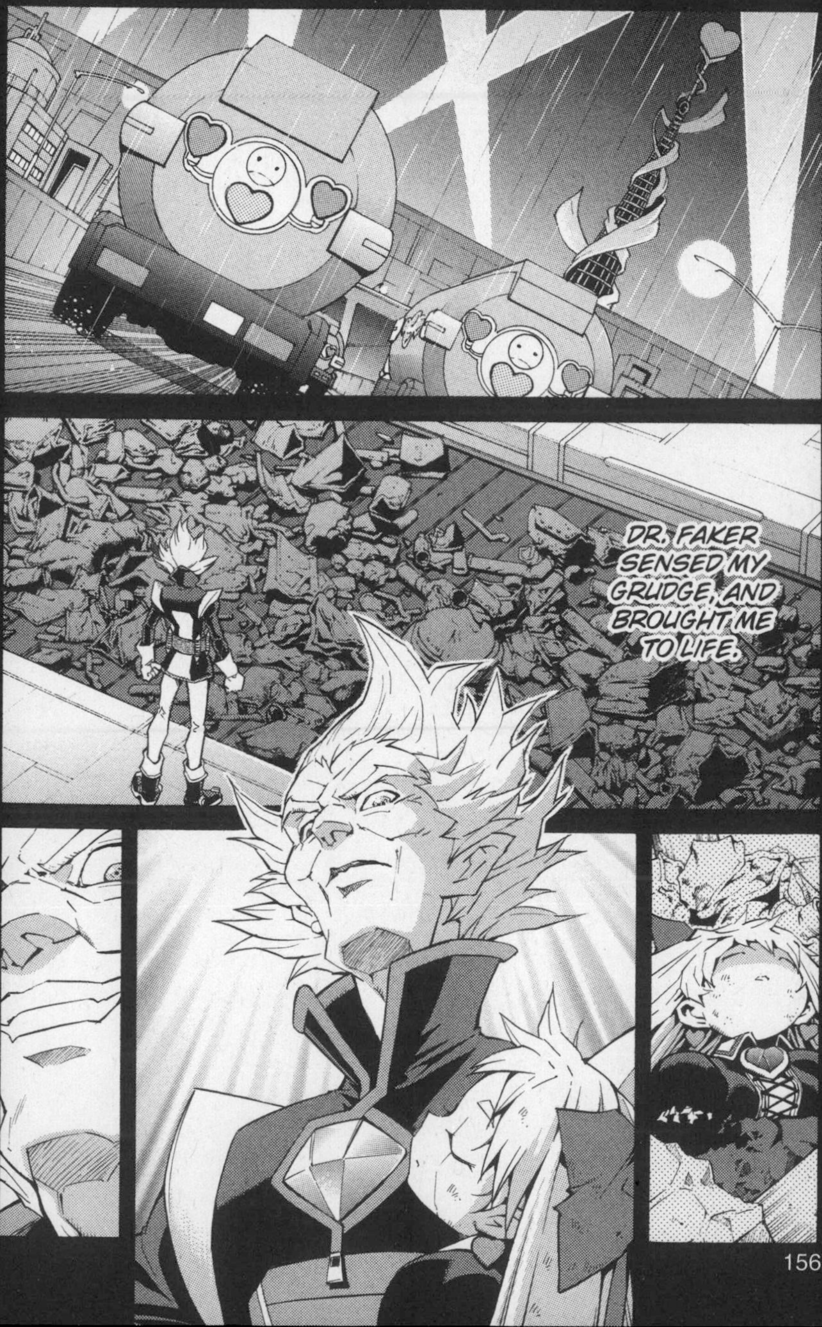
DR. FAKER SENSED MY GRUDGE, AND BROUGHT ME TO LIFE.

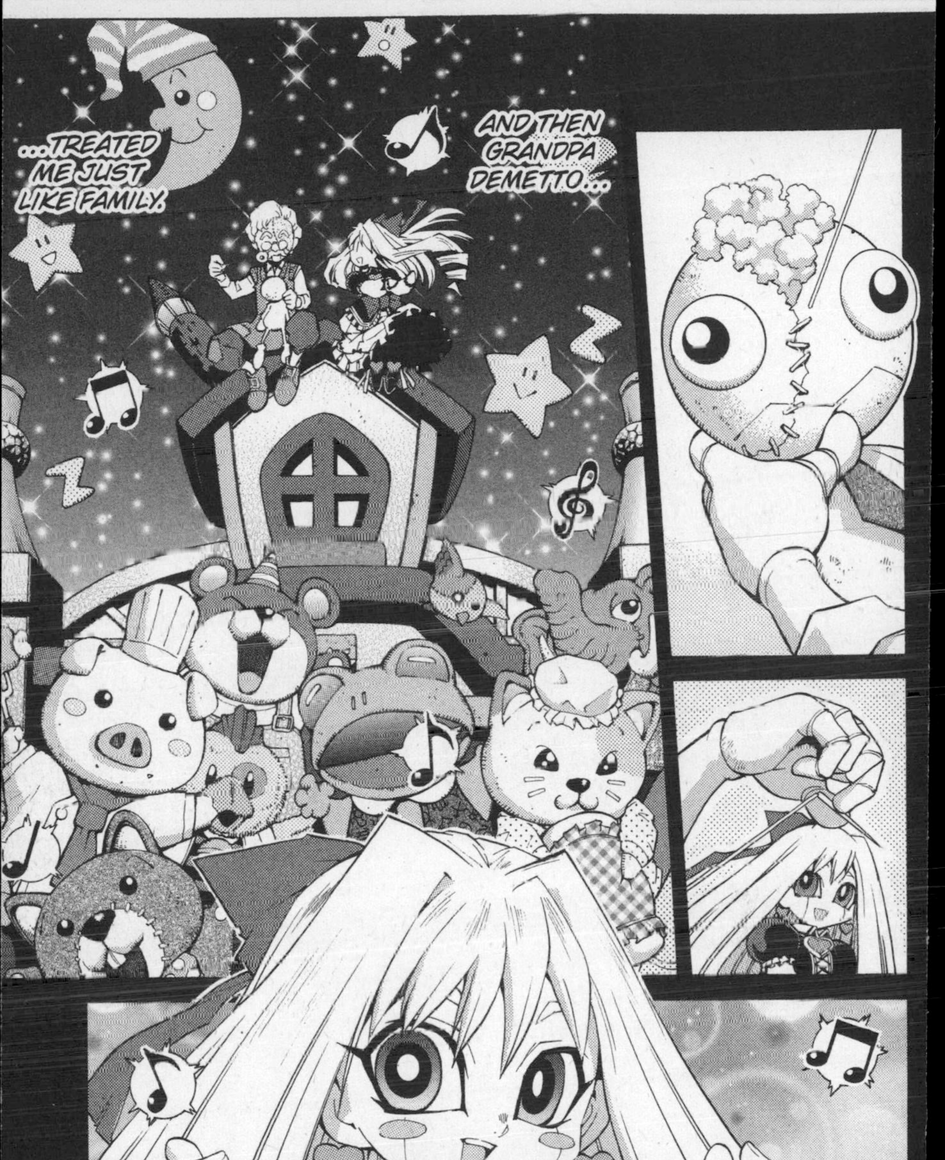
AND THEN GRANDPA DEMETTO...
...TREATED ME JUST LIKE FAMILY.

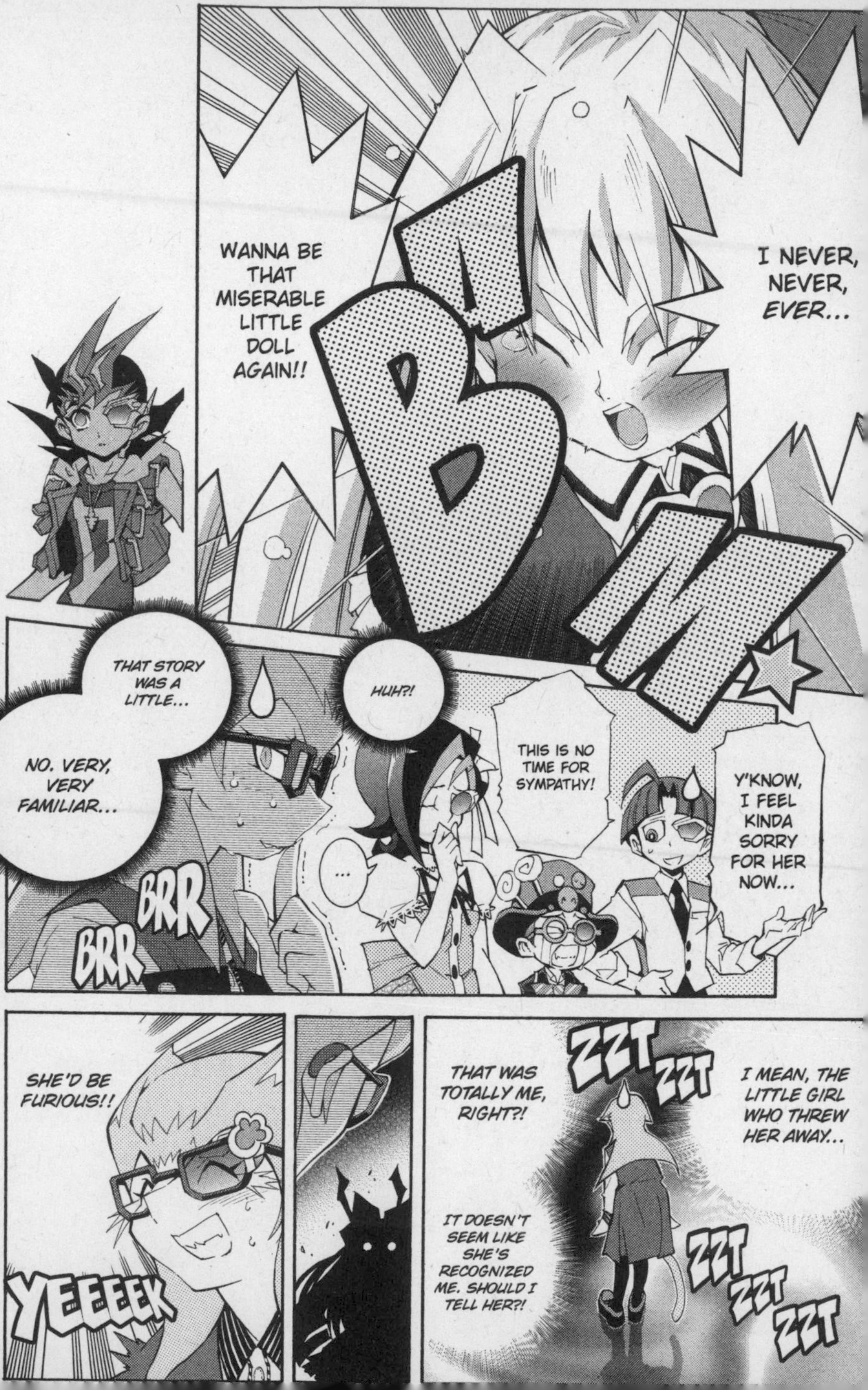

I NEVER, NEVER, EVER...
WANNA BE THAT MISERABLE LITTLE DOLL AGAIN!!
Y'KNOW, I FEEL KINDA SORRY FOR HER NOW...
THIS IS NO TIME FOR SYMPATHY!
HUH?!
...
THAT STORY WAS A LITTLE...
NO. VERY, VERY FAMILIAR...
BRR
BRR
I MEAN, THE LITTLE GIRL WHO THREW HER AWAY...
ZZT ZZT
THAT WAS TOTALLY ME, RIGHT?!
IT DOESN'T SEEM LIKE SHE'S RECOGNIZED ME. SHOULD I TELL HER?!
ZZT ZZT ZZT
SHE'D BE FURIOUS!!
YEEEEK

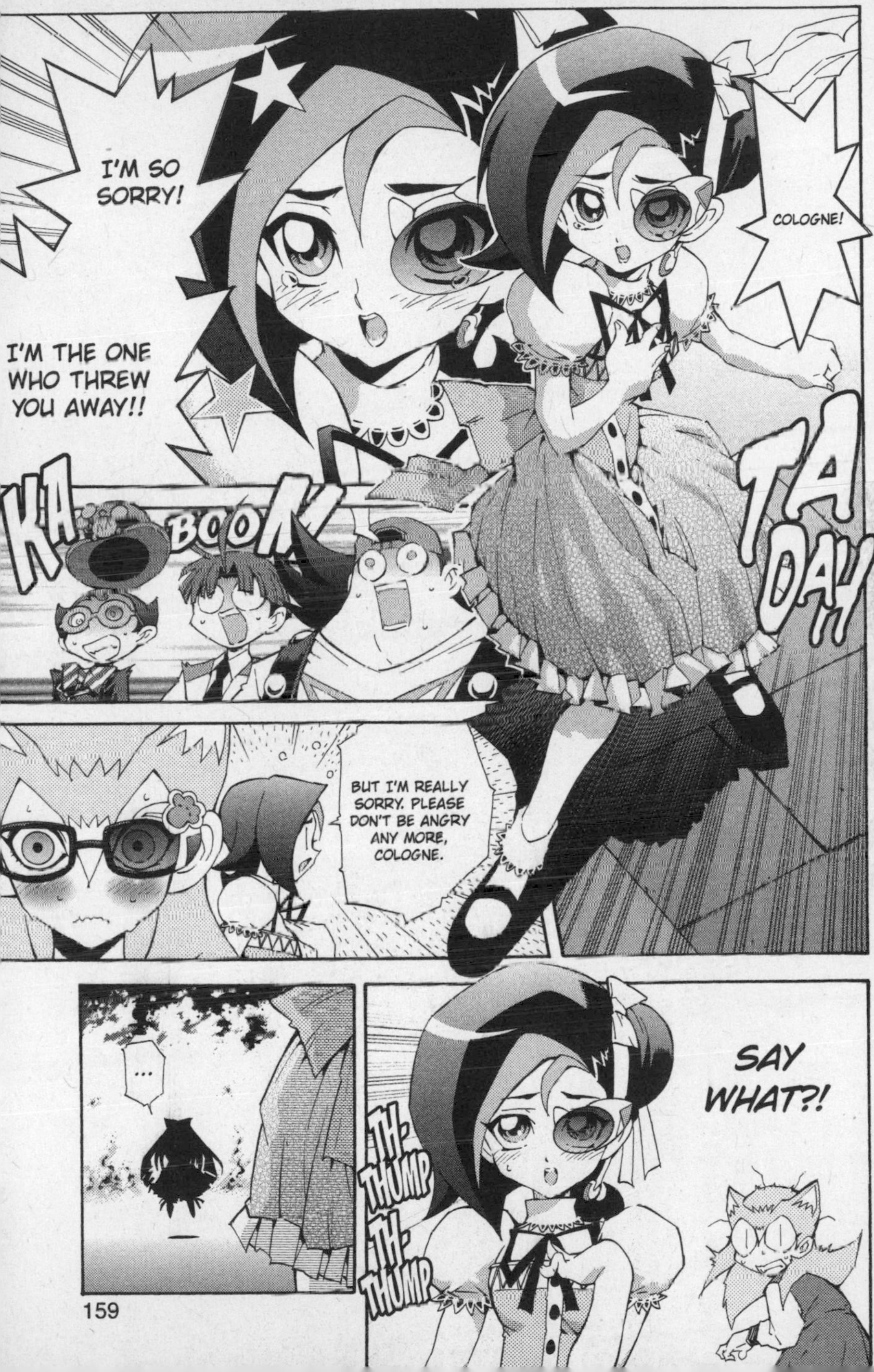
COLOGNE!
I'M SO SORRY!
I'M THE ONE WHO THREW YOU AWAY!!
TA DAH
KA BOOM
BUT I'M REALLY SORRY. PLEASE DON'T BE ANGRY ANY MORE, COLOGNE.
SAY WHAT?!
TH-THUMP TH-THUMP
...

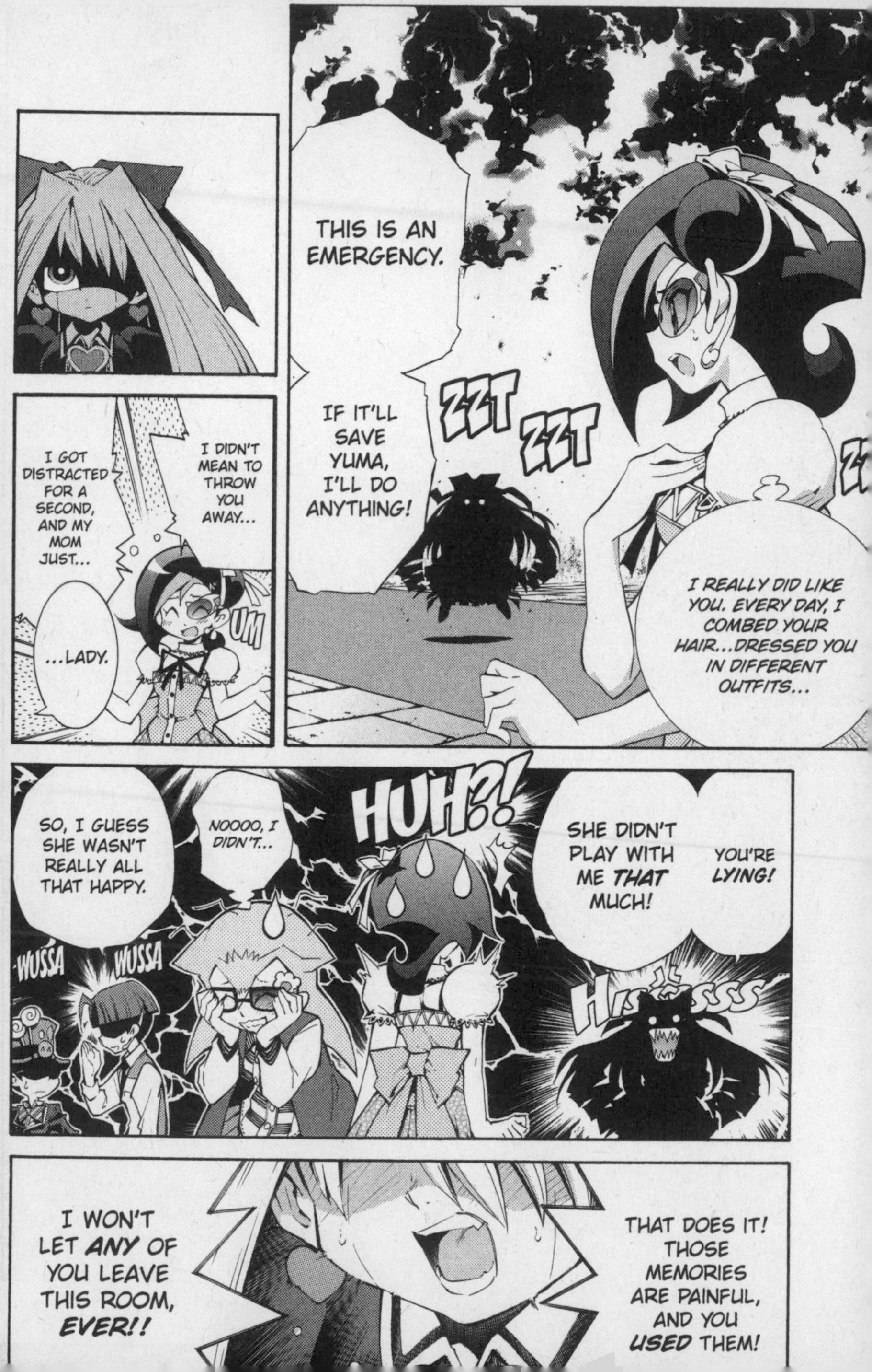

ZZT
ZZT
THIS IS AN EMERGENCY.
IF IT'LL SAVE YUMA, I'LL DO ANYTHING!
I REALLY DID LIKE YOU. EVERY DAY, I COMBED YOUR HAIR...DRESSED YOU IN DIFFERENT OUTFITS...
I DIDN'T MEAN TO THROW YOU AWAY...
I GOT DISTRACTED FOR A SECOND, AND MY MOM JUST...
UM
...LADY.
YOU'RE LYING!
SHE DIDN'T PLAY WITH ME THAT MUCH!
HISSSS
HUH?!
NOOOO, I DIDN'T...
SO, I GUESS SHE WASN'T REALLY ALL THAT HAPPY.
WUSSA
WUSSA
THAT DOES IT! THOSE MEMORIES ARE PAINFUL, AND YOU USED THEM!
I WON'T LET ANY OF YOU LEAVE THIS ROOM, EVER!!

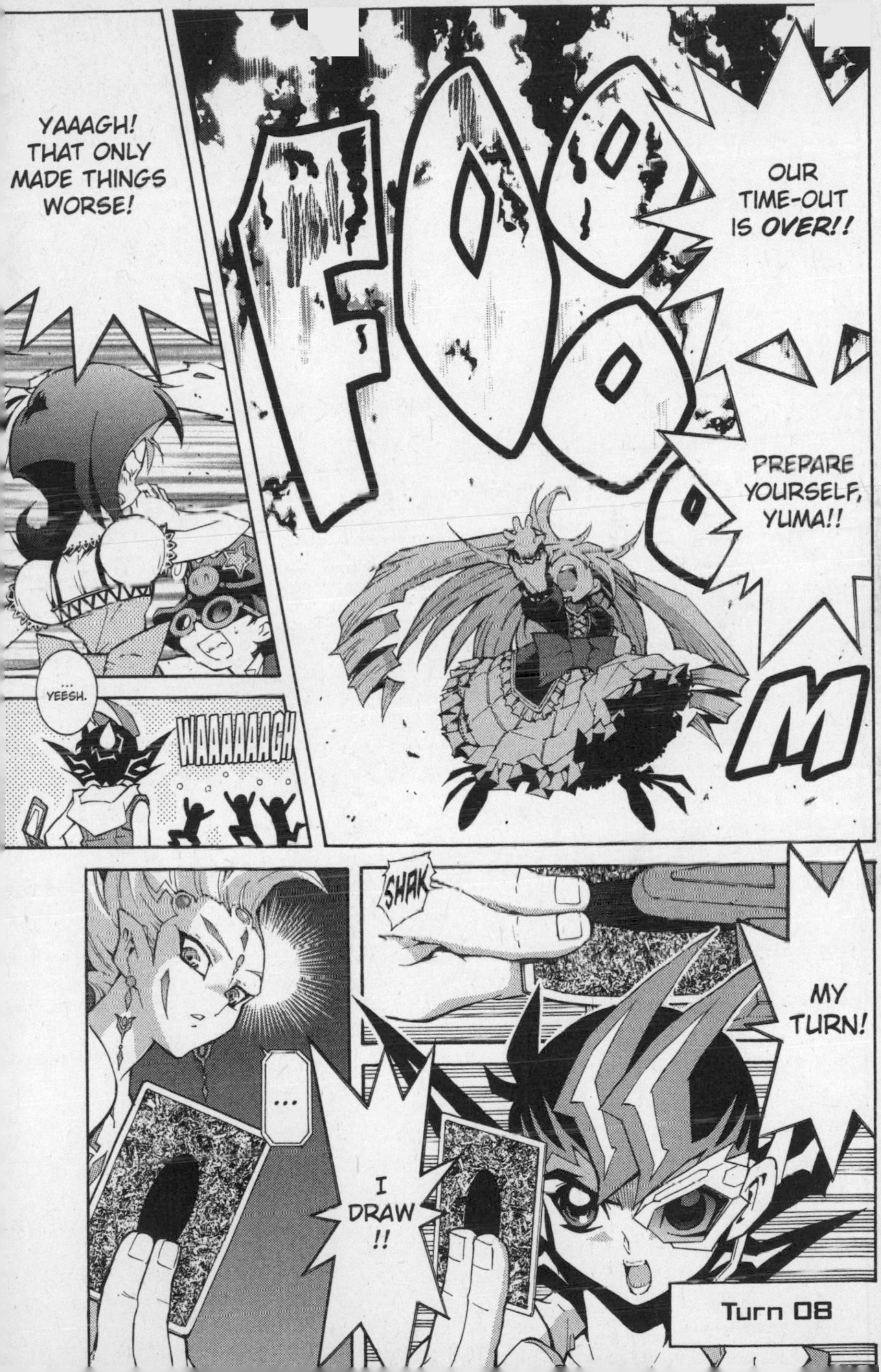
OUR TIME-OUT IS *OVER!!*
FOOOOM
PREPARE YOURSELF, YUMA!!
YAAAGH! THAT ONLY MADE THINGS WORSE!
... YEESH.
WAAAAAAGH
SHAK
MY TURN!
I DRAW!!
Turn 08
...

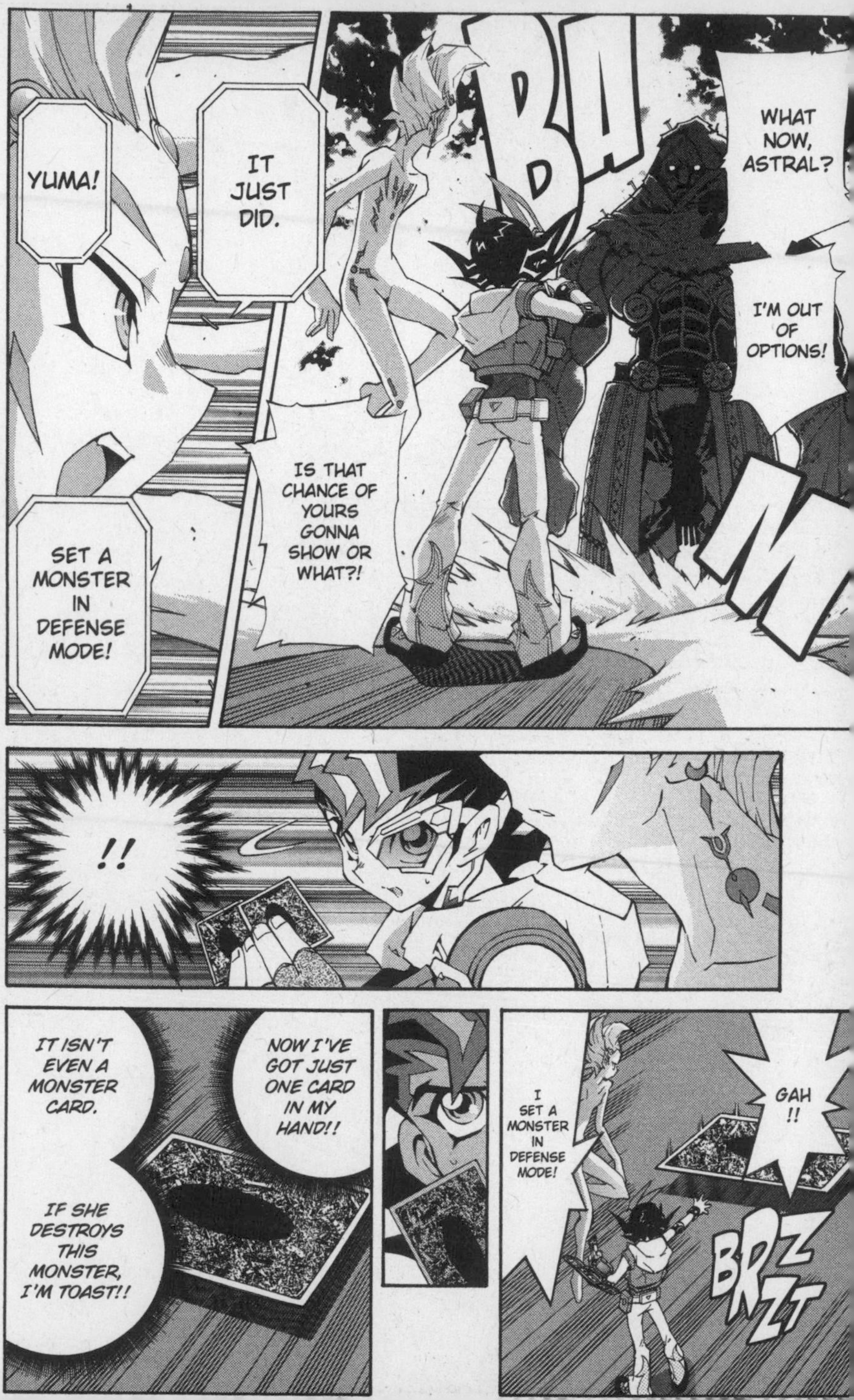
WHAT NOW, ASTRAL?
I'M OUT OF OPTIONS!
IS THAT CHANCE OF YOURS GONNA SHOW OR WHAT?!
IT JUST DID.
YUMA!
SET A MONSTER IN DEFENSE MODE!
!!
GAH!!
I SET A MONSTER IN DEFENSE MODE!
BRZZT
NOW I'VE GOT JUST ONE CARD IN MY HAND!!
IT ISN'T EVEN A MONSTER CARD.
IF SHE DESTROYS THIS MONSTER, I'M TOAST!!

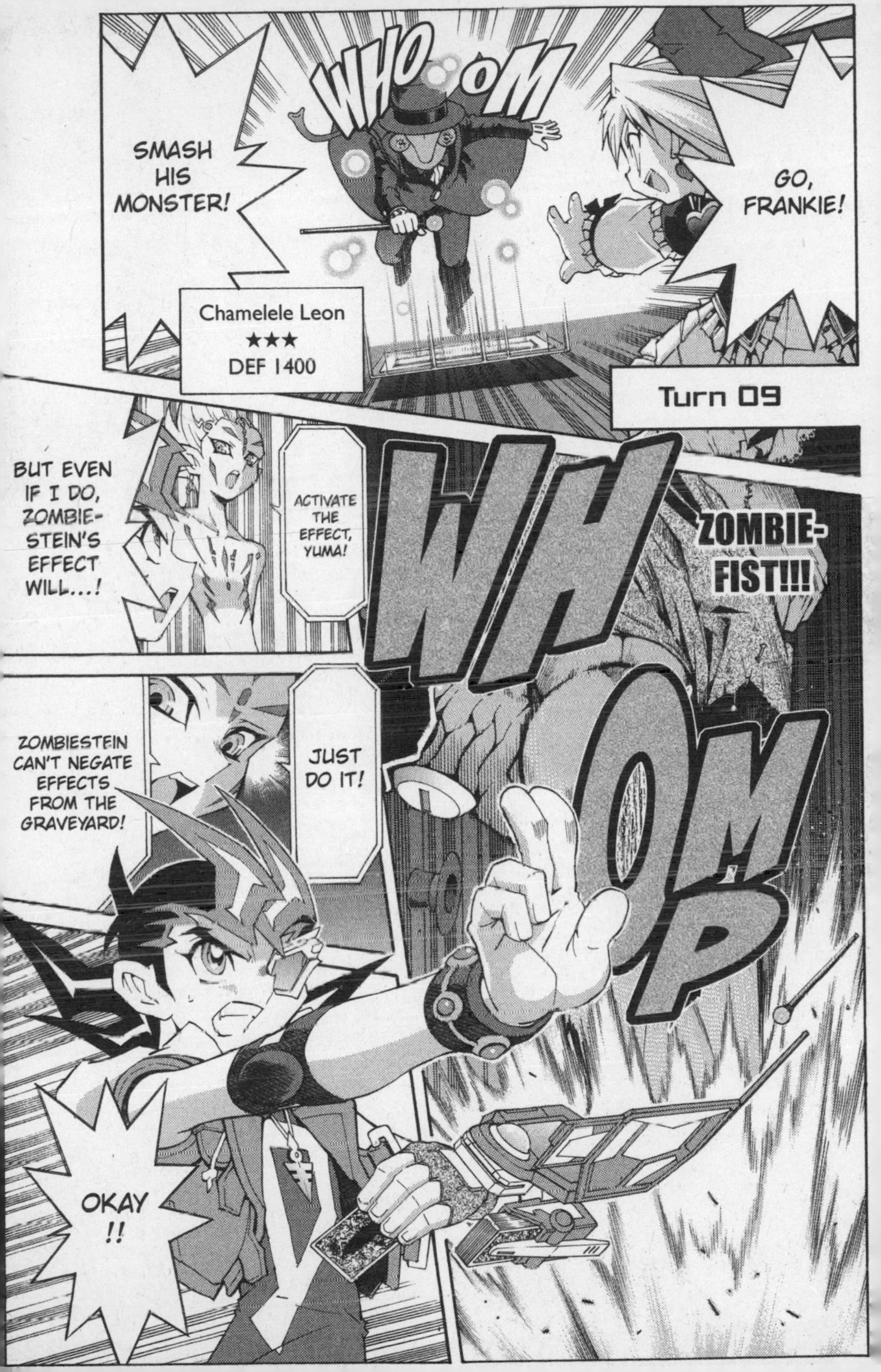
GO, FRANKIE!
WHOOM
SMASH HIS MONSTER!
Chamelele Leon
★★★
DEF 1400
Turn 09
ZOMBIE-FIST!!!
WHOMP
ACTIVATE THE EFFECT, YUMA!
BUT EVEN IF I DO, ZOMBIE-STEIN'S EFFECT WILL...!
JUST DO IT!
ZOMBIESTEIN CAN'T NEGATE EFFECTS FROM THE GRAVEYARD!
OKAY !!

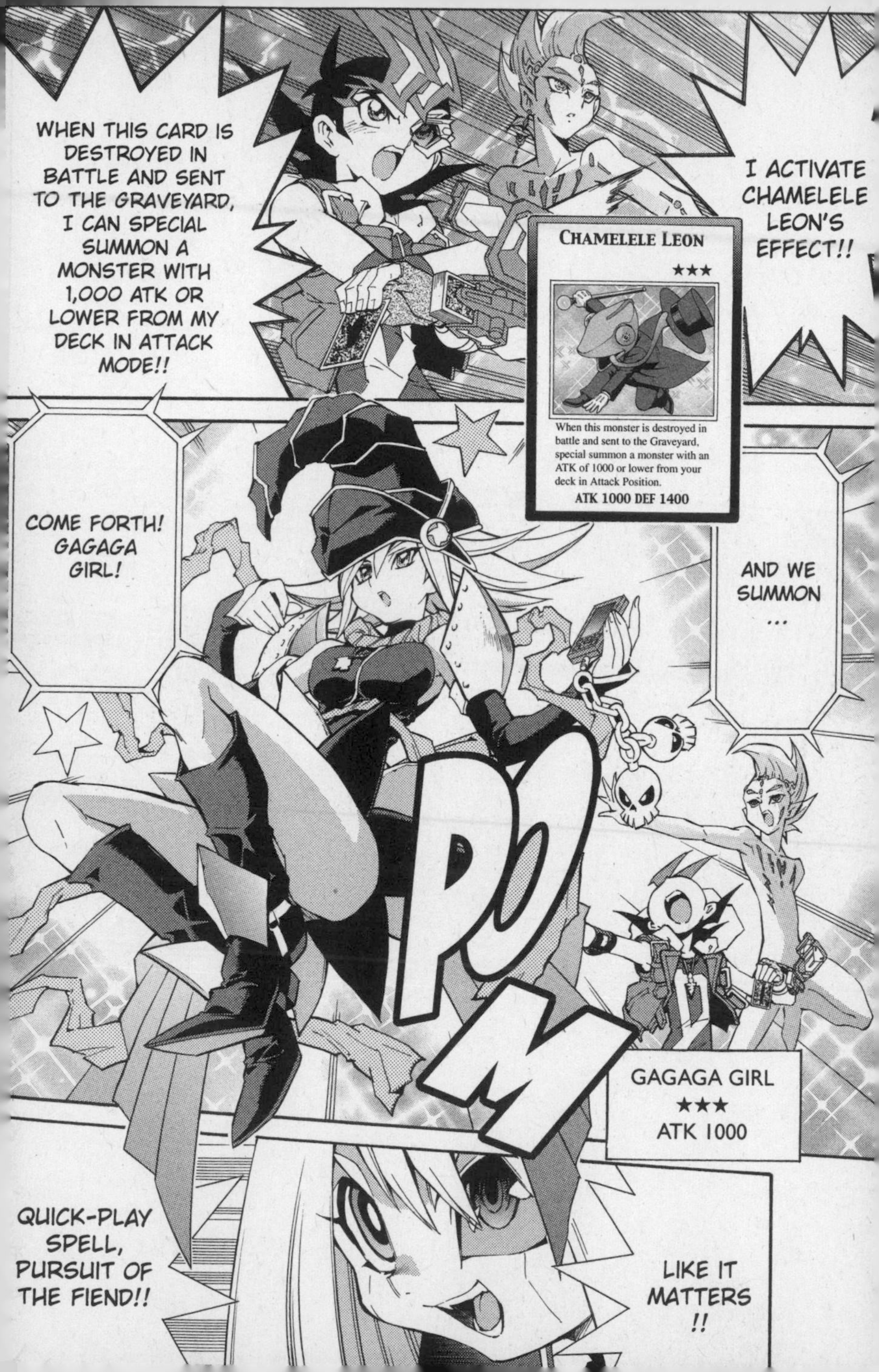
I ACTIVATE CHAMELELE LEON'S EFFECT!!
CHAMELELE LEON
★★★
When this monster is destroyed in battle and sent to the Graveyard, special summon a monster with an ATK of 1000 or lower from your deck in Attack Position.
ATK 1000 DEF 1400
WHEN THIS CARD IS DESTROYED IN BATTLE AND SENT TO THE GRAVEYARD, I CAN SPECIAL SUMMON A MONSTER WITH 1,000 ATK OR LOWER FROM MY DECK IN ATTACK MODE!!
AND WE SUMMON ...
COME FORTH! GAGAGA GIRL!
POM
GAGAGA GIRL
★★★
ATK 1000
LIKE IT MATTERS !!
QUICK-PLAY SPELL, PURSUIT OF THE FIEND!!

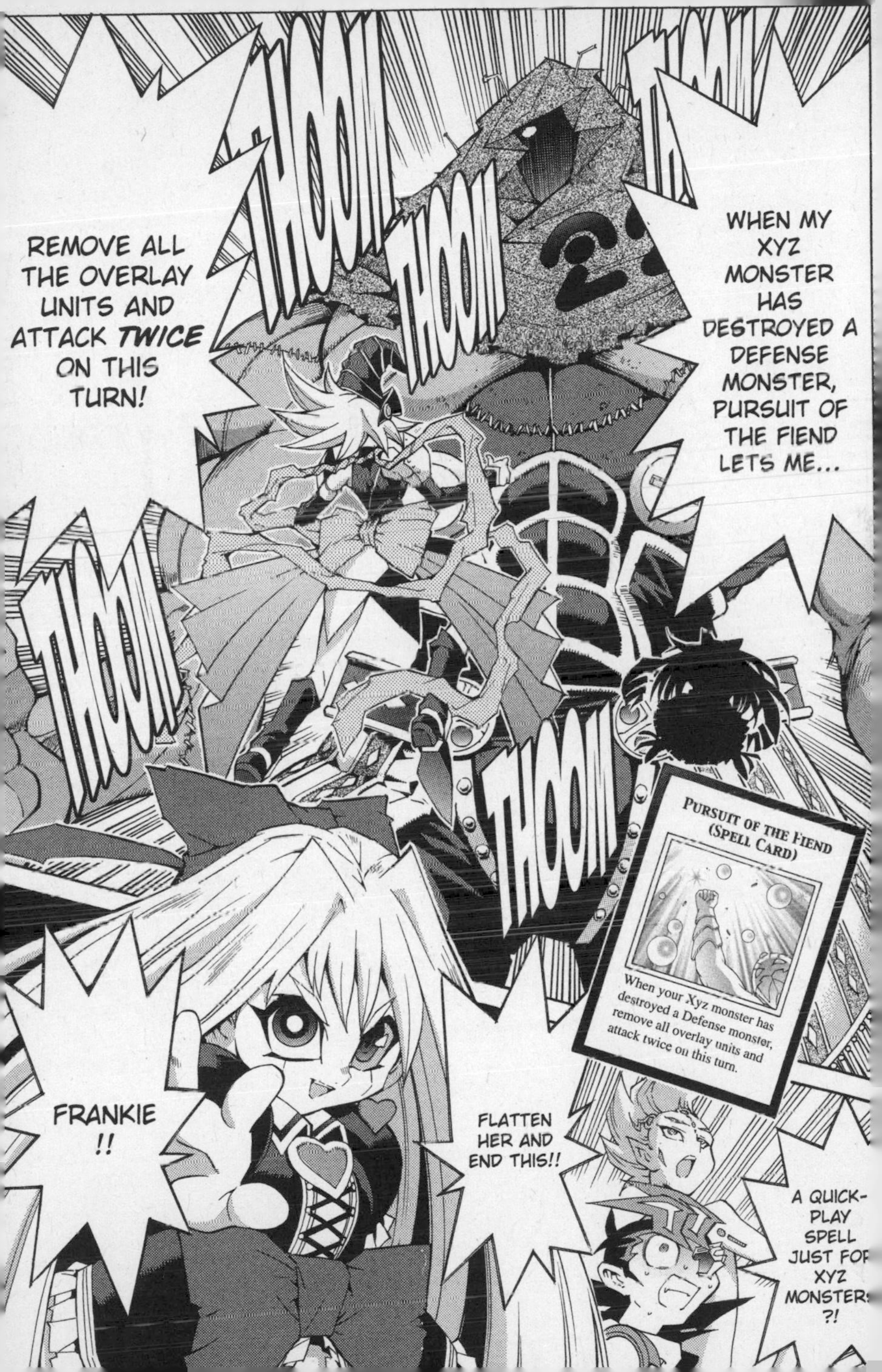

WHEN MY XYZ MONSTER HAS DESTROYED A DEFENSE MONSTER, PURSUIT OF THE FIEND LETS ME...
REMOVE ALL THE OVERLAY UNITS AND ATTACK *TWICE* ON THIS TURN!
THOOM
THOOM
THOOM
THOOM
THOOM
PURSUIT OF THE FIEND (SPELL CARD)
When your Xyz monster has destroyed a Defense monster, remove all overlay units and attack twice on this turn.
A QUICK-PLAY SPELL JUST FOR XYZ MONSTERS ?!
FLATTEN HER AND END THIS!!
FRANKIE !!

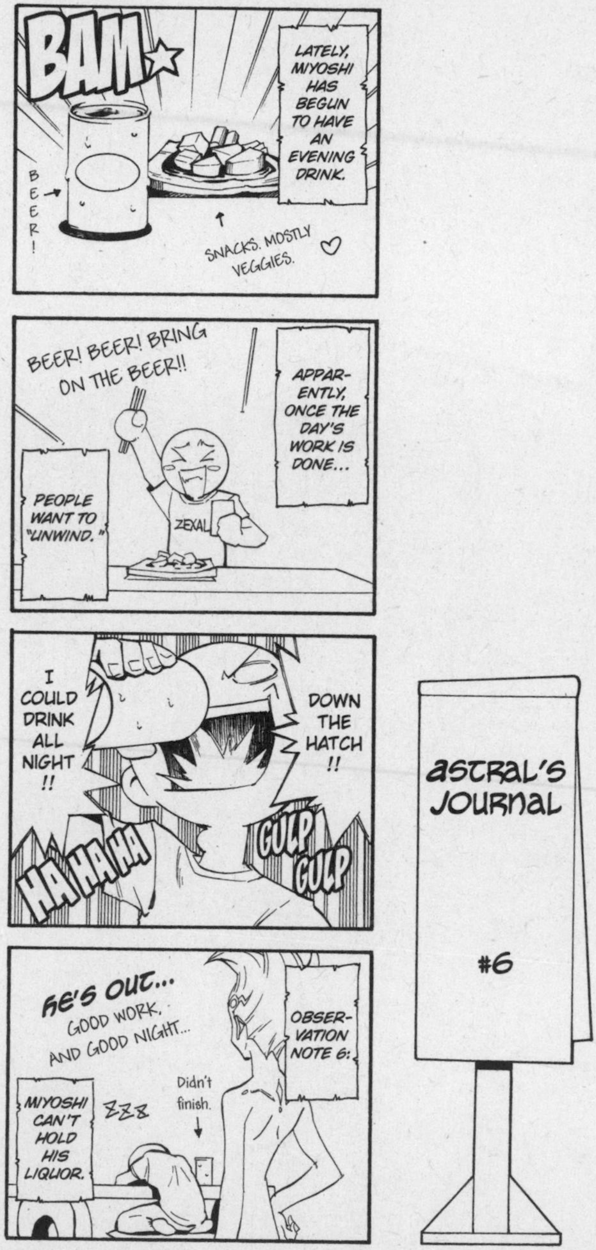
ASTRAL'S JOURNAL
#6
LATELY, MIYOSHI HAS BEGUN TO HAVE AN EVENING DRINK.
BAM
SNACKS. MOSTLY VEGGIES.
BEER!
APPARENTLY, ONCE THE DAY'S WORK IS DONE...
BEER! BEER! BRING ON THE BEER!!
ZEXAL
PEOPLE WANT TO "UNWIND."
DOWN THE HATCH!!
I COULD DRINK ALL NIGHT!!
GULP GULP
HA HA HA
OBSERVATION NOTE 6:
HE'S OUT...
GOOD WORK, AND GOOD NIGHT...
Didn't finish.
ZZZ
MIYOSHI CAN'T HOLD HIS LIQUOR.

Rank 18

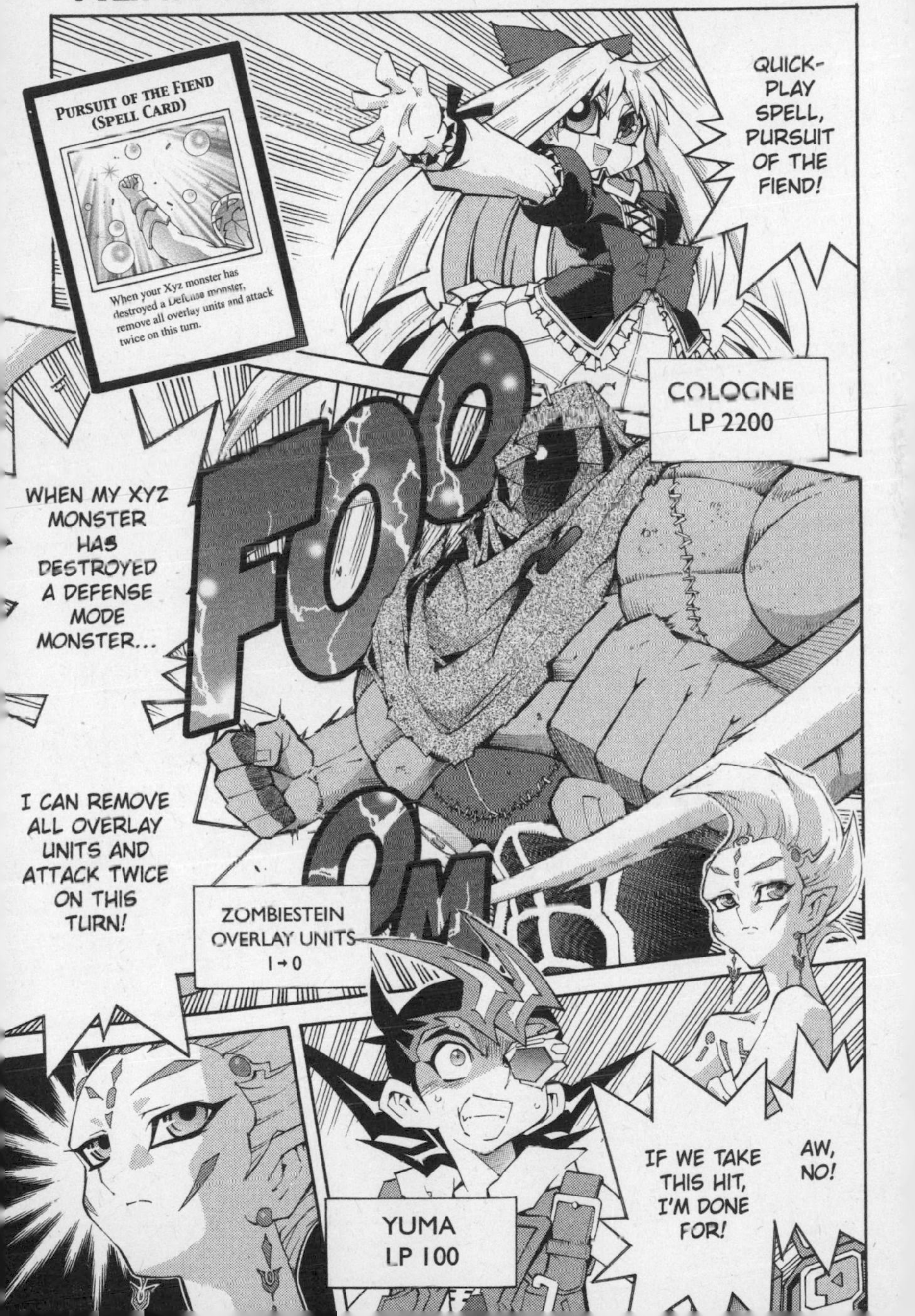
QUICK-PLAY SPELL, PURSUIT OF THE FIEND!
PURSUIT OF THE FIEND (SPELL CARD)
When your Xyz monster has destroyed a Defense monster, remove all overlay units and attack twice on this turn.
COLOGNE LP 2200
FOOOM
WHEN MY XYZ MONSTER HAS DESTROYED A DEFENSE MODE MONSTER...
I CAN REMOVE ALL OVERLAY UNITS AND ATTACK TWICE ON THIS TURN!
ZOMBIESTEIN OVERLAY UNITS 1→0
AW, NO!
IF WE TAKE THIS HIT, I'M DONE FOR!
YUMA LP 100

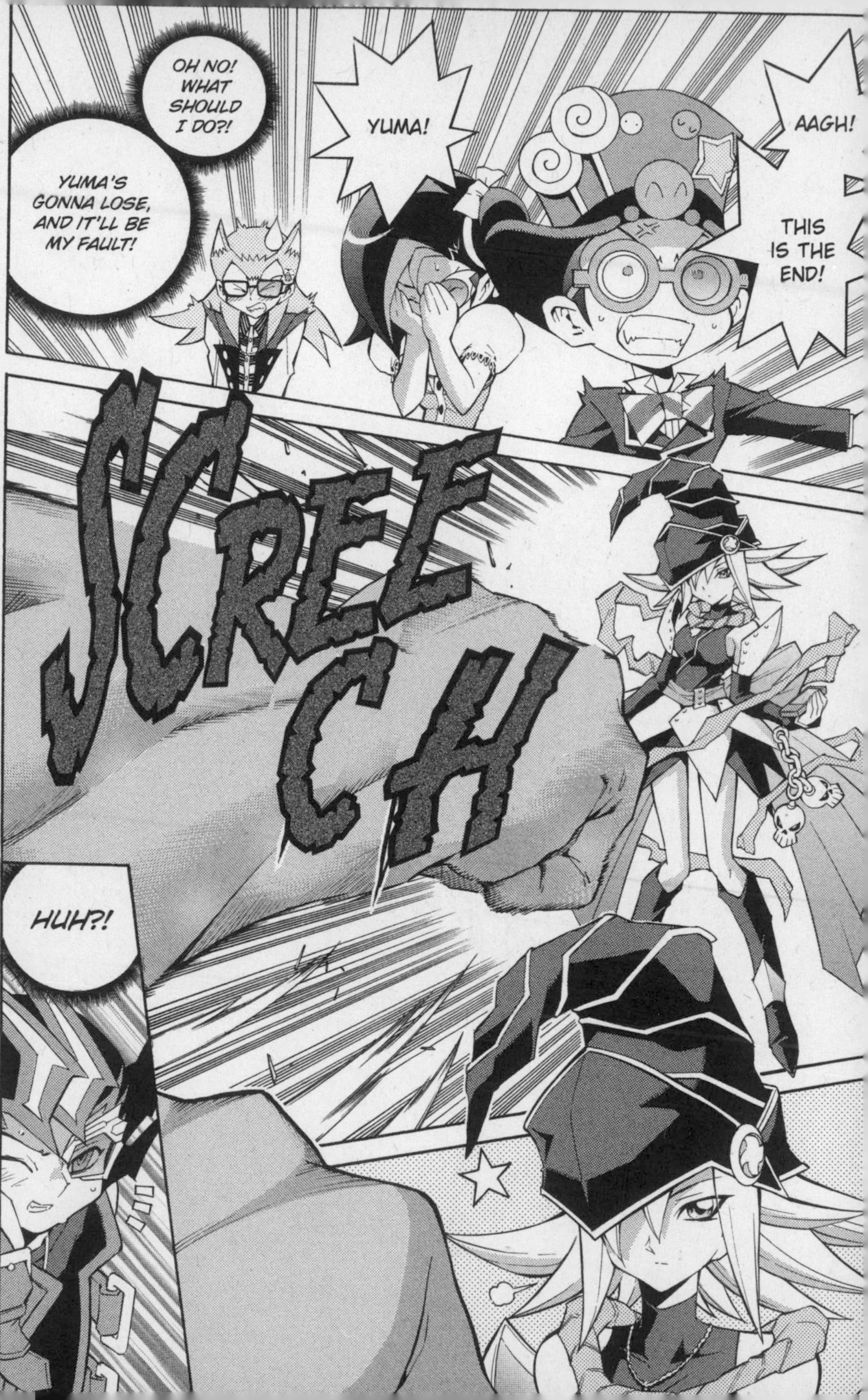
AAGH!
THIS IS THE END!
YUMA!
OH NO! WHAT SHOULD I DO?!
YUMA'S GONNA LOSE, AND IT'LL BE MY FAULT!
SCREECH
HUH?!

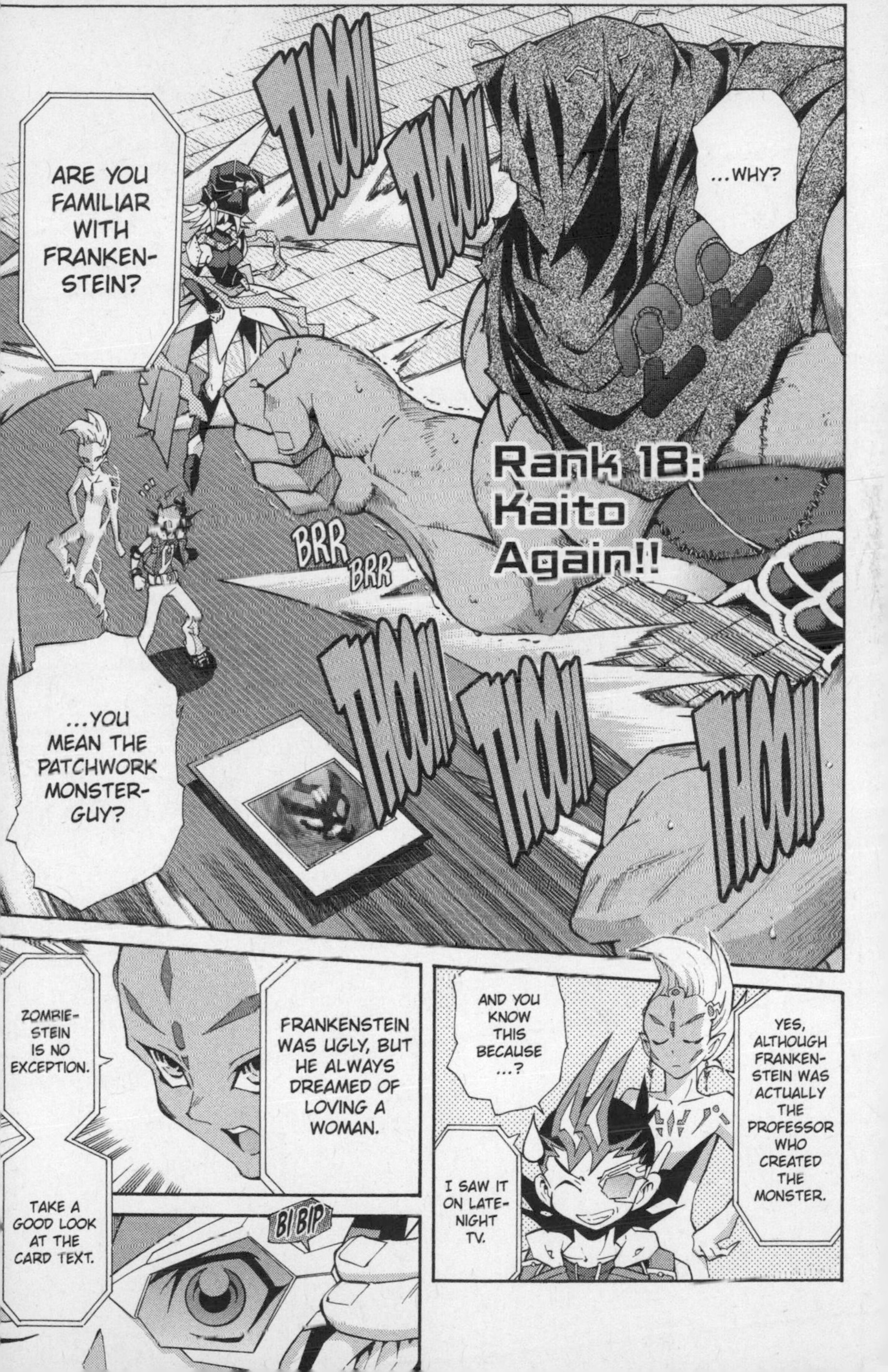
...WHY?
THOOM
THOOM
ARE YOU FAMILIAR WITH FRANKEN-STEIN?
Rank 18: Kaito Again!!
BRR
BRR
THOOM
THOOM
THOOM
...YOU MEAN THE PATCHWORK MONSTER-GUY?
YES, ALTHOUGH FRANKEN-STEIN WAS ACTUALLY THE PROFESSOR WHO CREATED THE MONSTER.
AND YOU KNOW THIS BECAUSE ...?
I SAW IT ON LATE-NIGHT TV.
FRANKENSTEIN WAS UGLY, BUT HE ALWAYS DREAMED OF LOVING A WOMAN.
ZOMBIE-STEIN IS NO EXCEPTION.
BI BIP
TAKE A GOOD LOOK AT THE CARD TEXT.

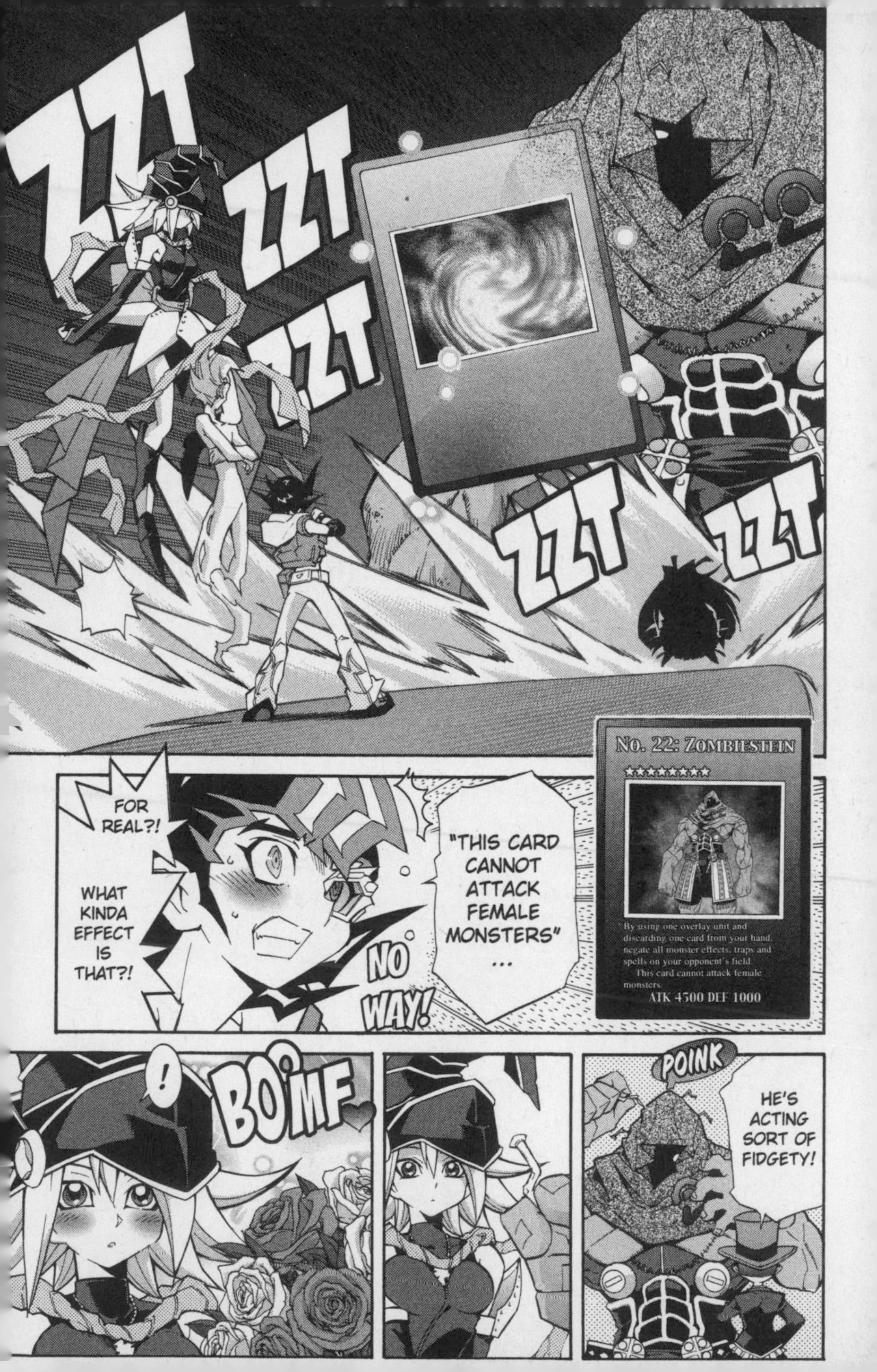
ZZZT
ZZZT
ZZZT
ZZZT
ZZZT
No. 22: Zombiestein
By using one overlay unit and discarding one card from your hand, negate all monster effects, traps and spells on your opponent's field.
This card cannot attack female monsters.
ATK 4500 DEF 1000
"THIS CARD CANNOT ATTACK FEMALE MONSTERS" ...
NO WAY!
FOR REAL?!
WHAT KINDA EFFECT IS THAT?!
POINK
HE'S ACTING SORT OF FIDGETY!
BOOMF
!

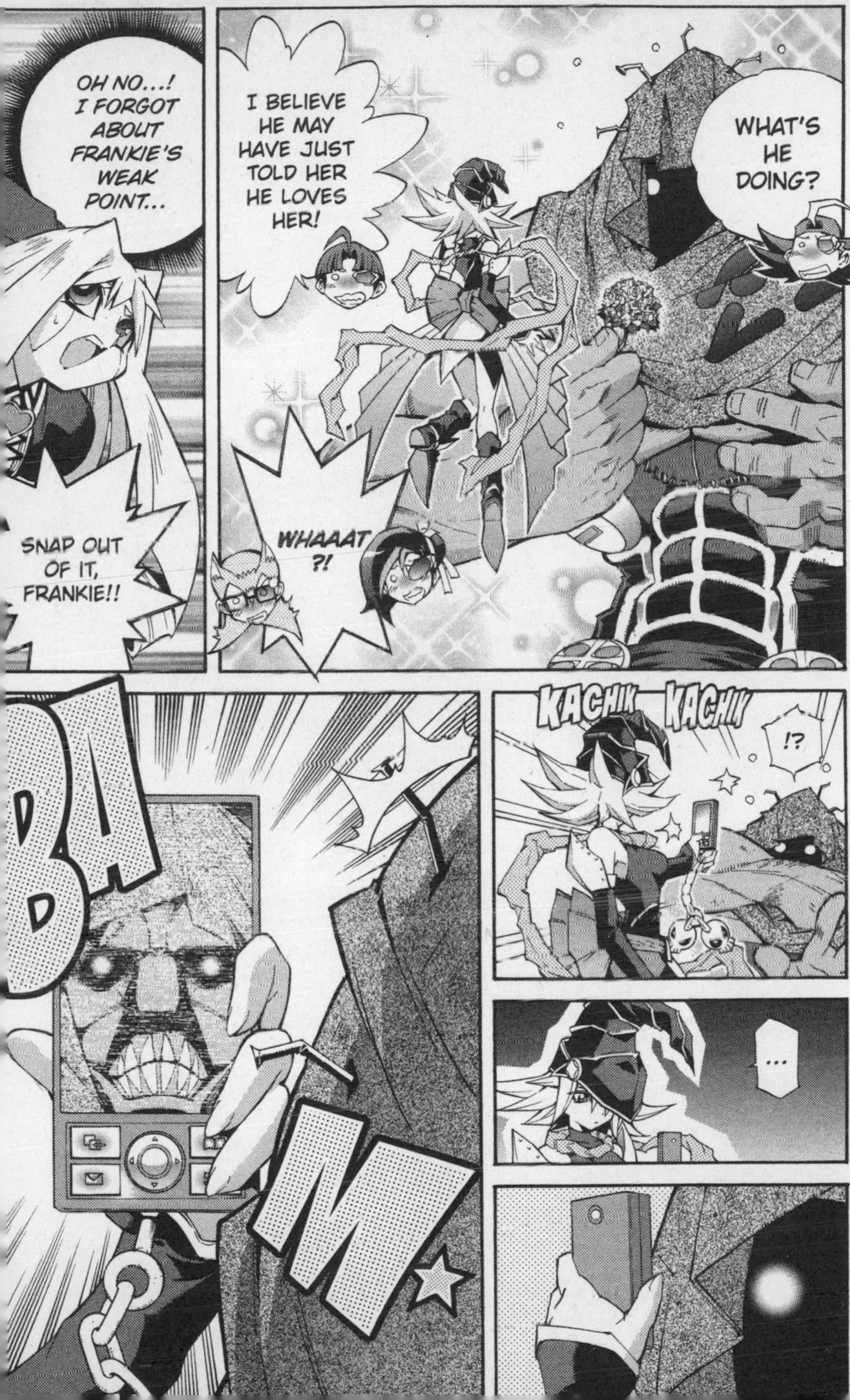
WHAT'S HE DOING?
I BELIEVE HE MAY HAVE JUST TOLD HER HE LOVES HER!
WHAAAT?!
OH NO...! I FORGOT ABOUT FRANKIE'S WEAK POINT...
SNAP OUT OF IT, FRANKIE!!
KACHIK KACHIK
!?
...
BA
D D
M

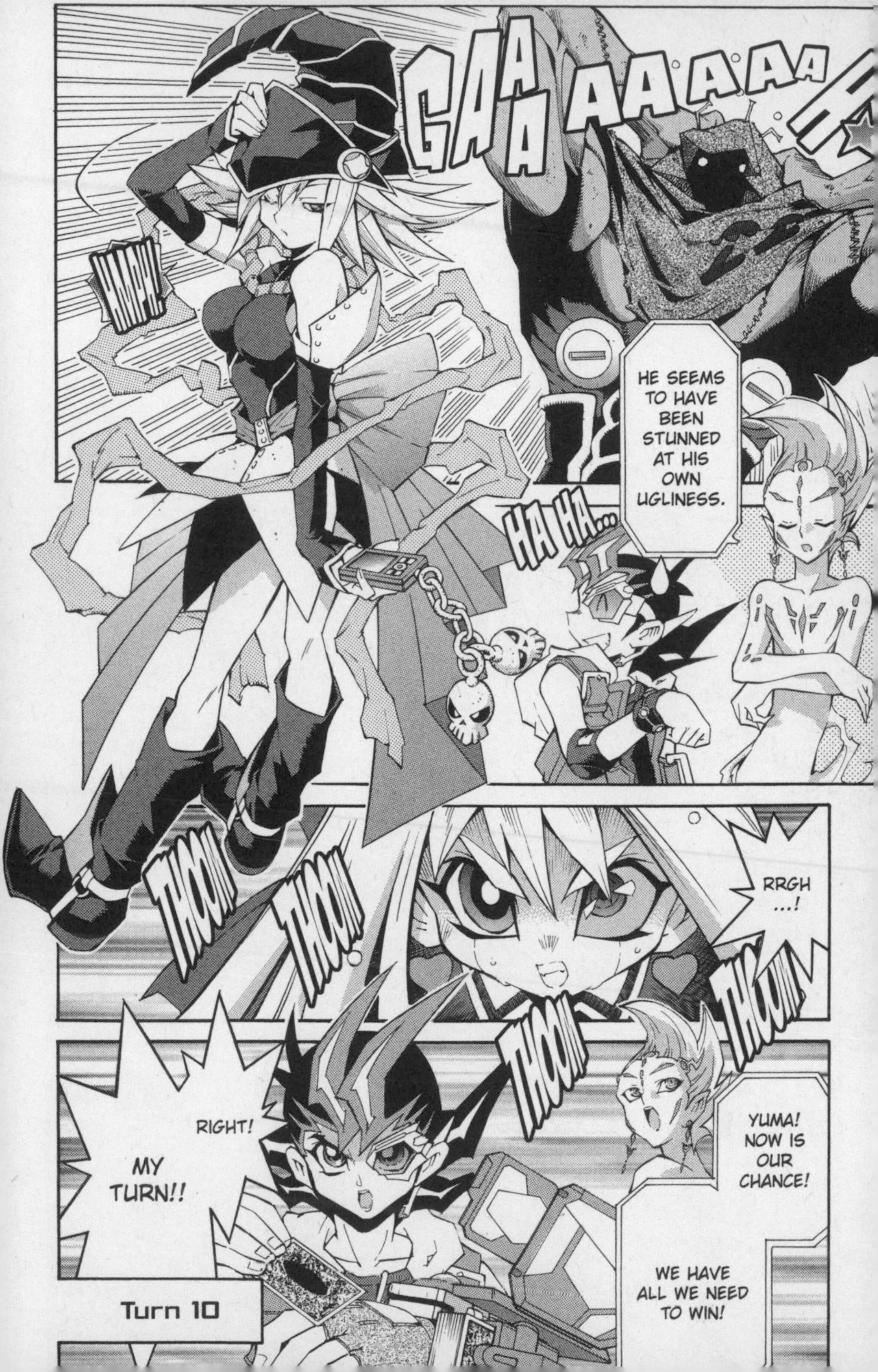
GAAAAAAAH
HMPH!
HE SEEMS TO HAVE BEEN STUNNED AT HIS OWN UGLINESS.
HA HA...
RRGH...!
THOOM
THOOM
THOOM
THOOM
YUMA! NOW IS OUR CHANCE!
WE HAVE ALL WE NEED TO WIN!
RIGHT!
MY TURN!!
Turn 10

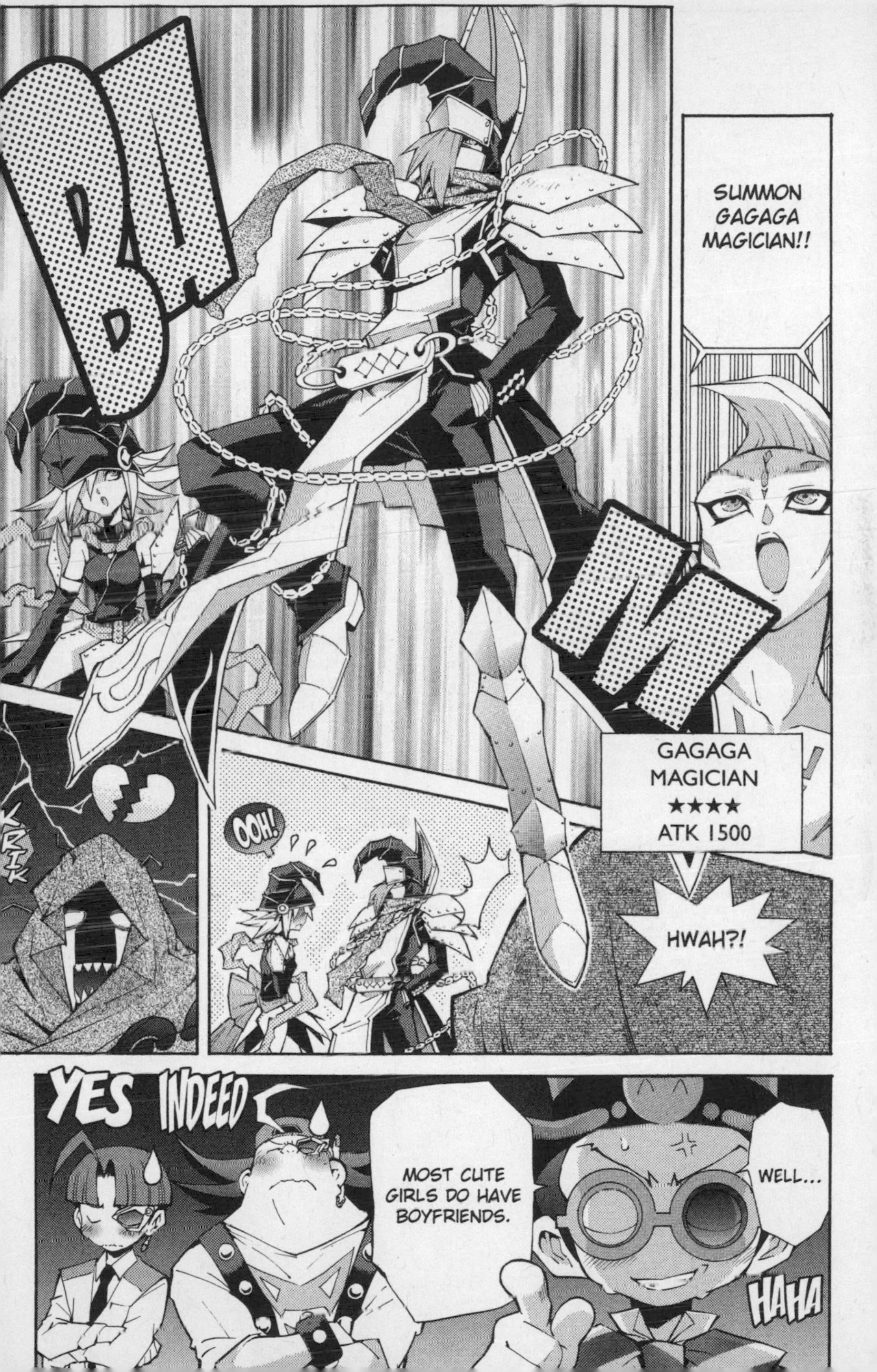
SUMMON GAGAGA MAGICIAN!!
BA!
M
GAGAGA MAGICIAN ★★★★ ATK 1500
HWAH?!
OOH!
KRIK
WELL...
HAHA
MOST CUTE GIRLS DO HAVE BOYFRIENDS.
YES INDEED

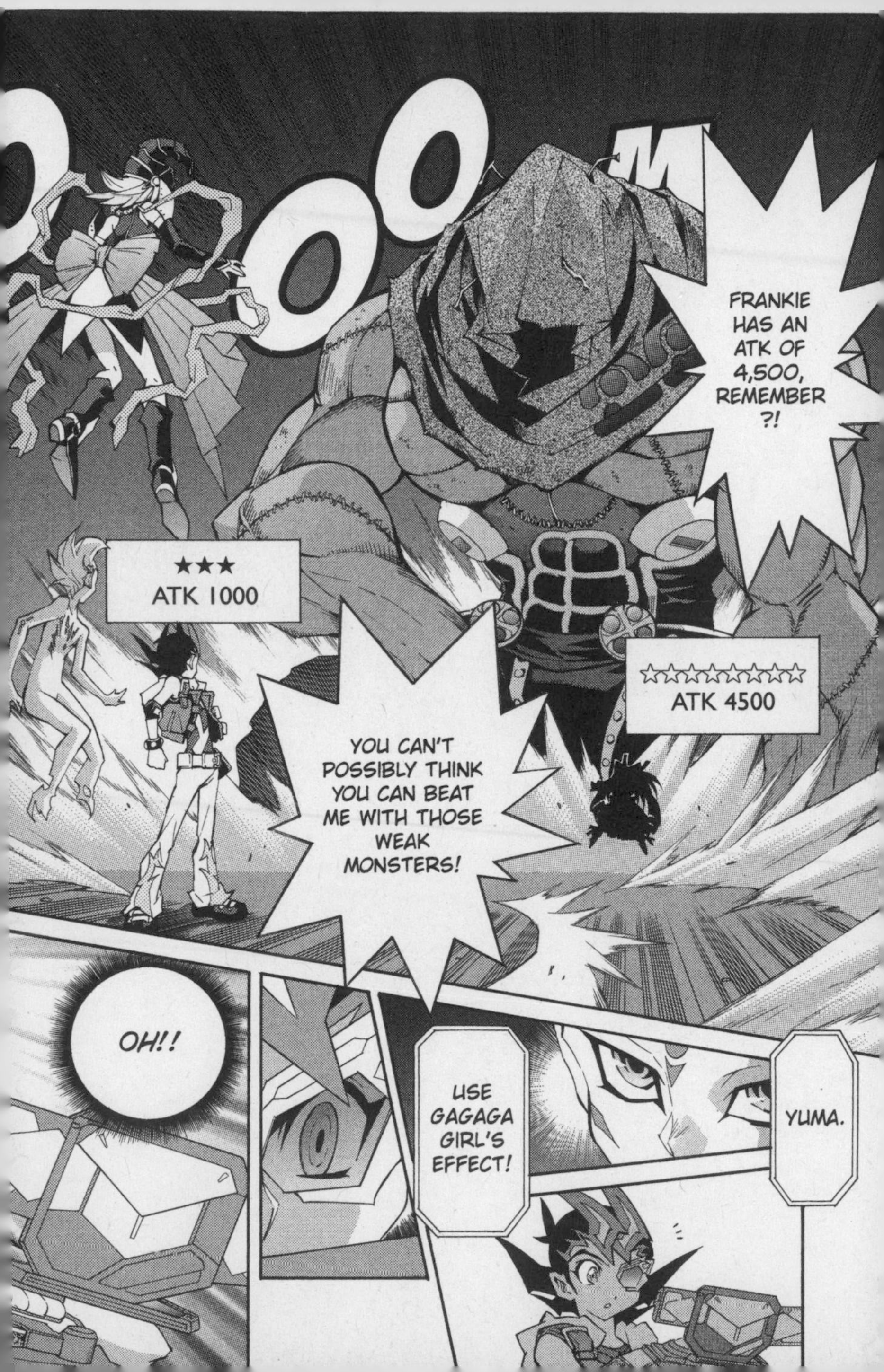
OOOOM
FRANKIE HAS AN ATK OF 4,500, REMEMBER?!
☆☆☆☆☆☆☆☆☆
ATK 4500
★★★
ATK 1000
YOU CAN'T POSSIBLY THINK YOU CAN BEAT ME WITH THOSE WEAK MONSTERS!
YUMA.
USE GAGAGA GIRL'S EFFECT!
OH!!

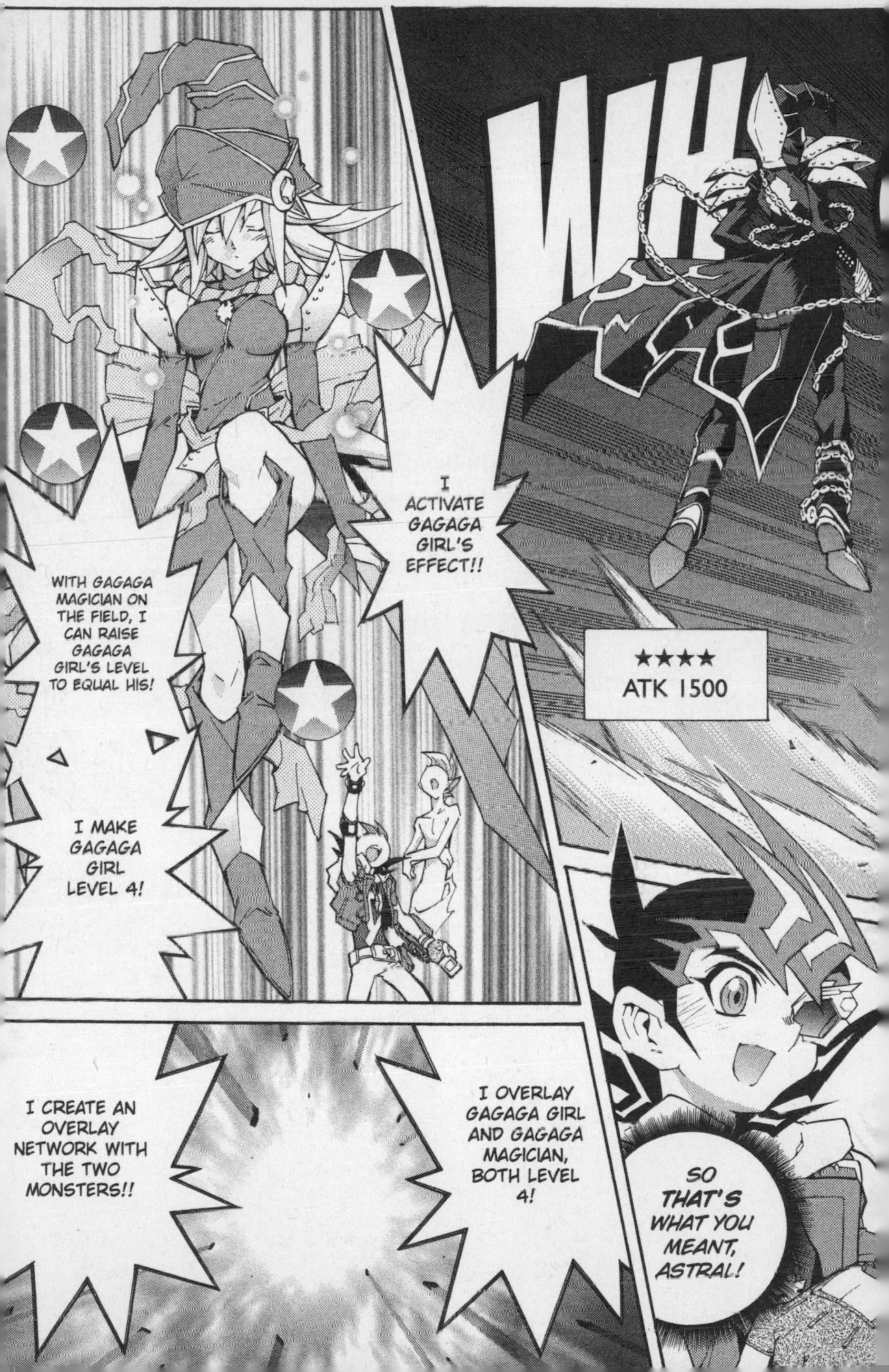

WH
★★★★
ATK 1500
I ACTIVATE GAGAGA GIRL'S EFFECT!!
WITH GAGAGA MAGICIAN ON THE FIELD, I CAN RAISE GAGAGA GIRL'S LEVEL TO EQUAL HIS!
I MAKE GAGAGA GIRL LEVEL 4!
SO THAT'S WHAT YOU MEANT, ASTRAL!
I OVERLAY GAGAGA GIRL AND GAGAGA MAGICIAN, BOTH LEVEL 4!
I CREATE AN OVERLAY NETWORK WITH THE TWO MONSTERS!!

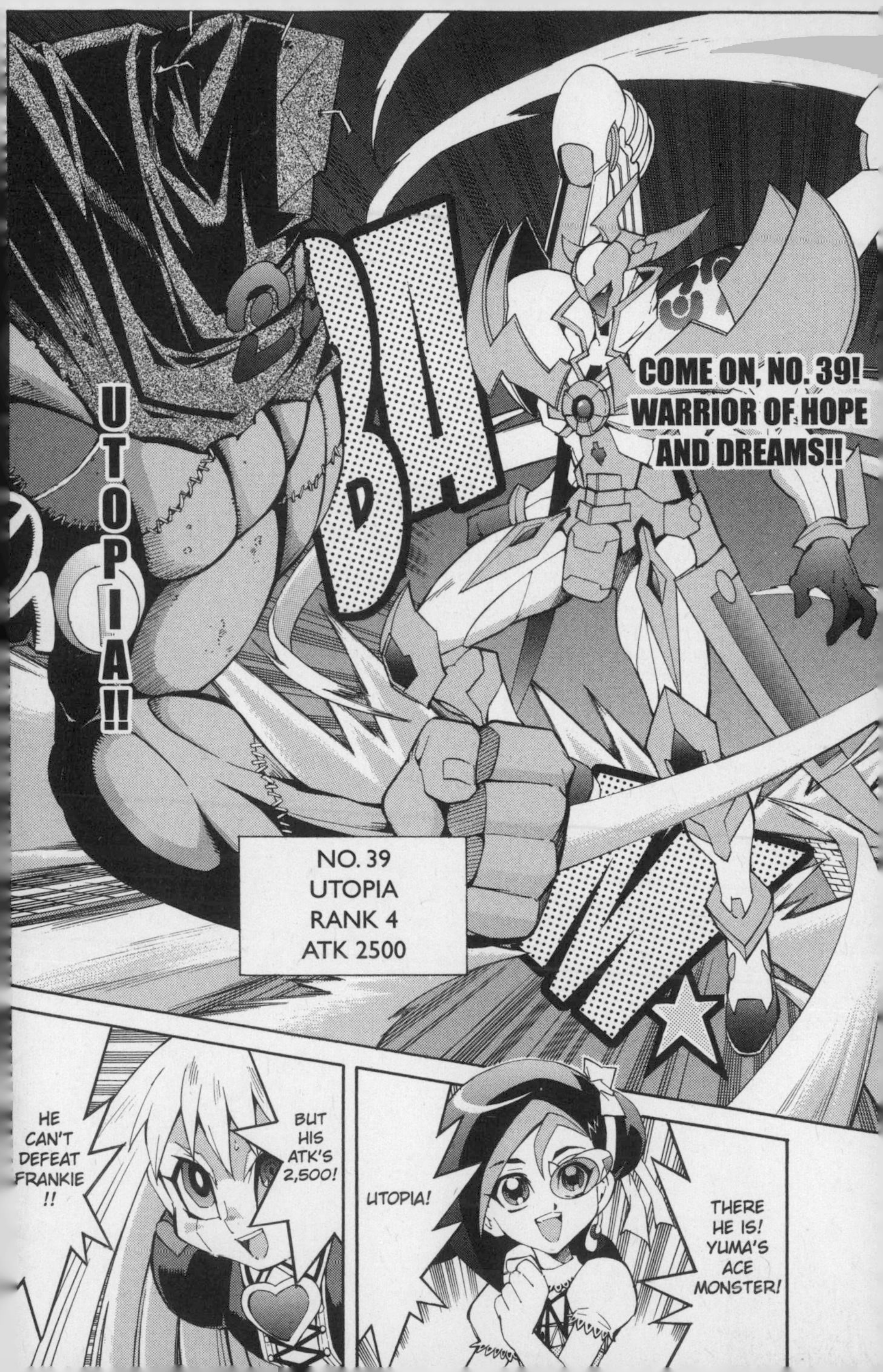
COME ON, NO. 39! WARRIOR OF HOPE AND DREAMS!!
UTOPIA!!
NO. 39 UTOPIA RANK 4 ATK 2500
THERE HE IS! YUMA'S ACE MONSTER!
UTOPIA!
BUT HIS ATK'S 2,500!
HE CAN'T DEFEAT FRANKIE!!

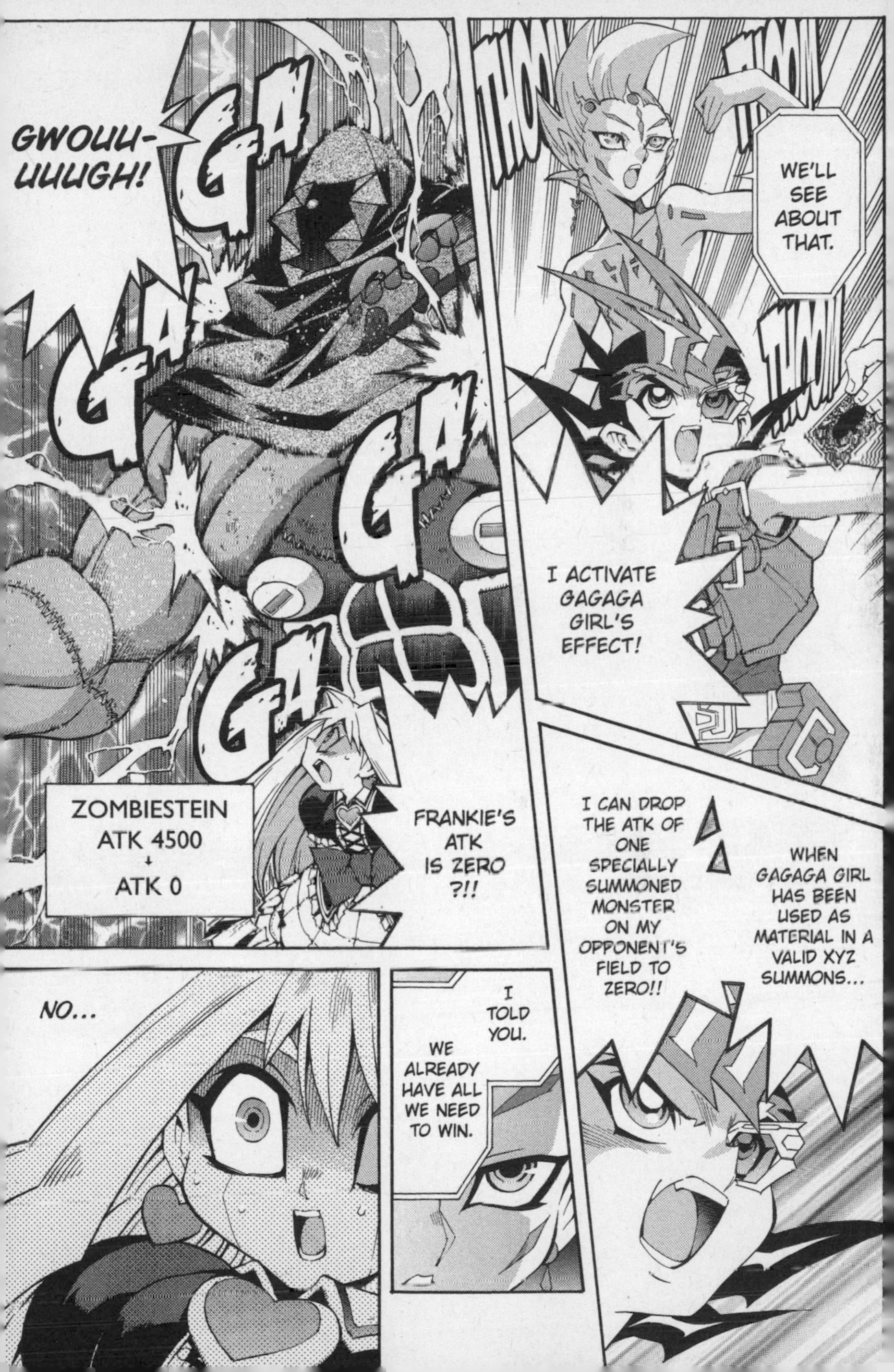
THOO
WE'LL SEE ABOUT THAT.
I ACTIVATE GAGAGA GIRL'S EFFECT!
GWOUU-UUUGH!
GA
GA
GA
GA
ZOMBIESTEIN
ATK 4500
↓
ATK 0
FRANKIE'S ATK IS ZERO ?!!
WHEN GAGAGA GIRL HAS BEEN USED AS MATERIAL IN A VALID XYZ SUMMONS...
I CAN DROP THE ATK OF ONE SPECIALLY SUMMONED MONSTER ON MY OPPONENT'S FIELD TO ZERO!!
I TOLD YOU.
WE ALREADY HAVE ALL WE NEED TO WIN.
NO...

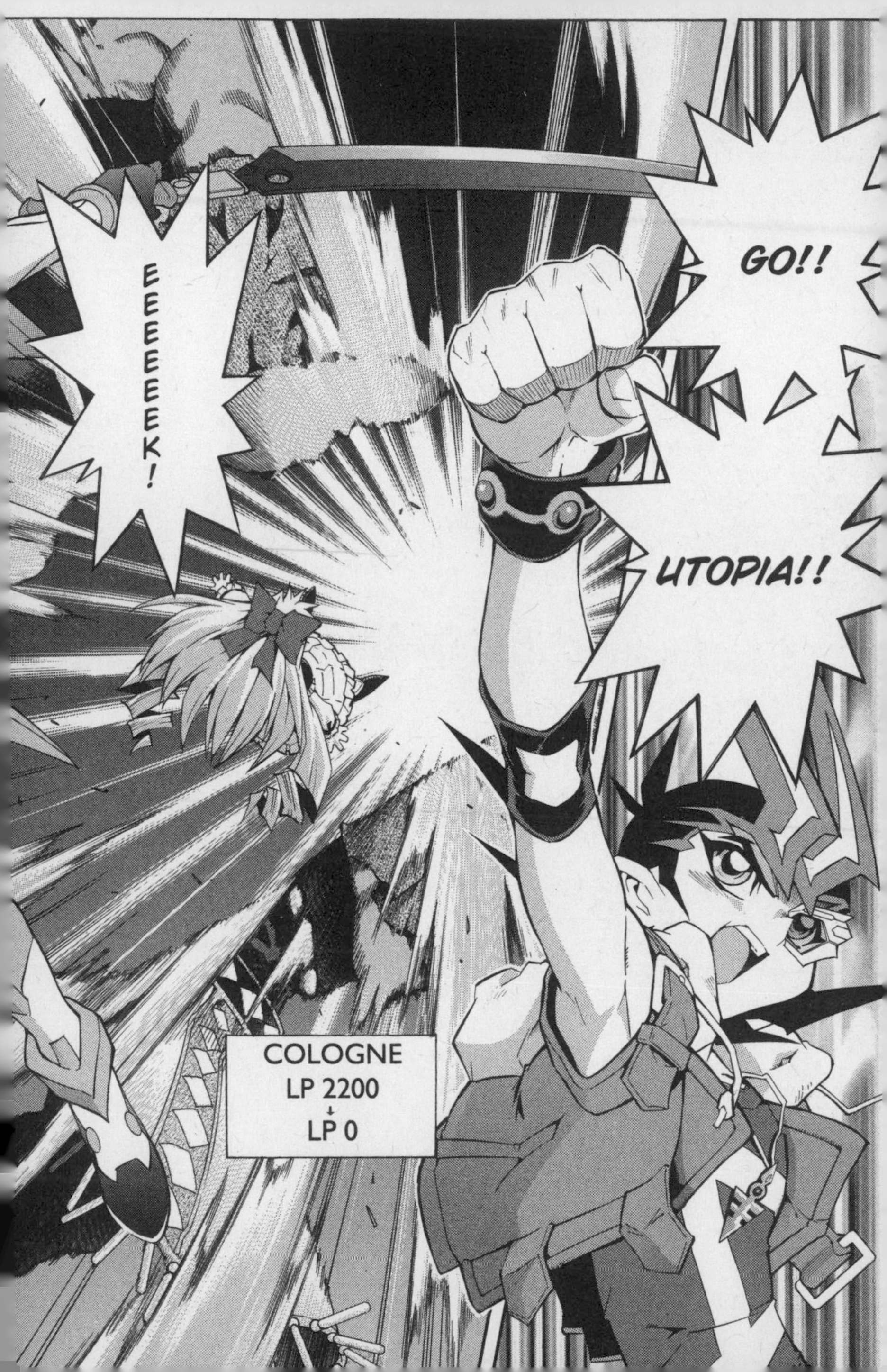
GO!!
UTOPIA!!
EEEEEEK!
COLOGNE
LP 2200
↓
LP 0

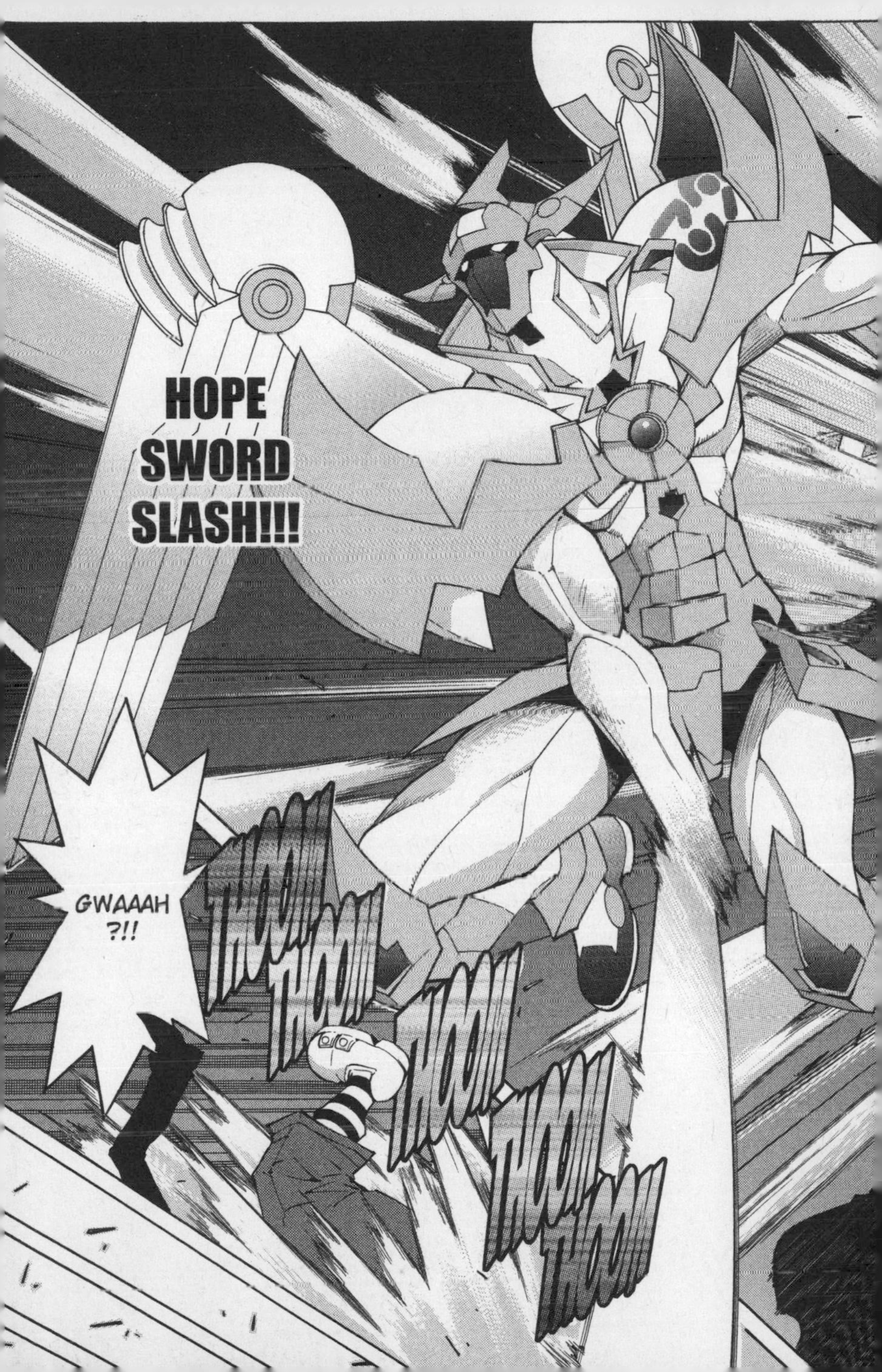
HOPE SWORD SLASH!!!
GWAAAH ?!!
THOOM
THOOM
THOOM
THOOM
THOOM

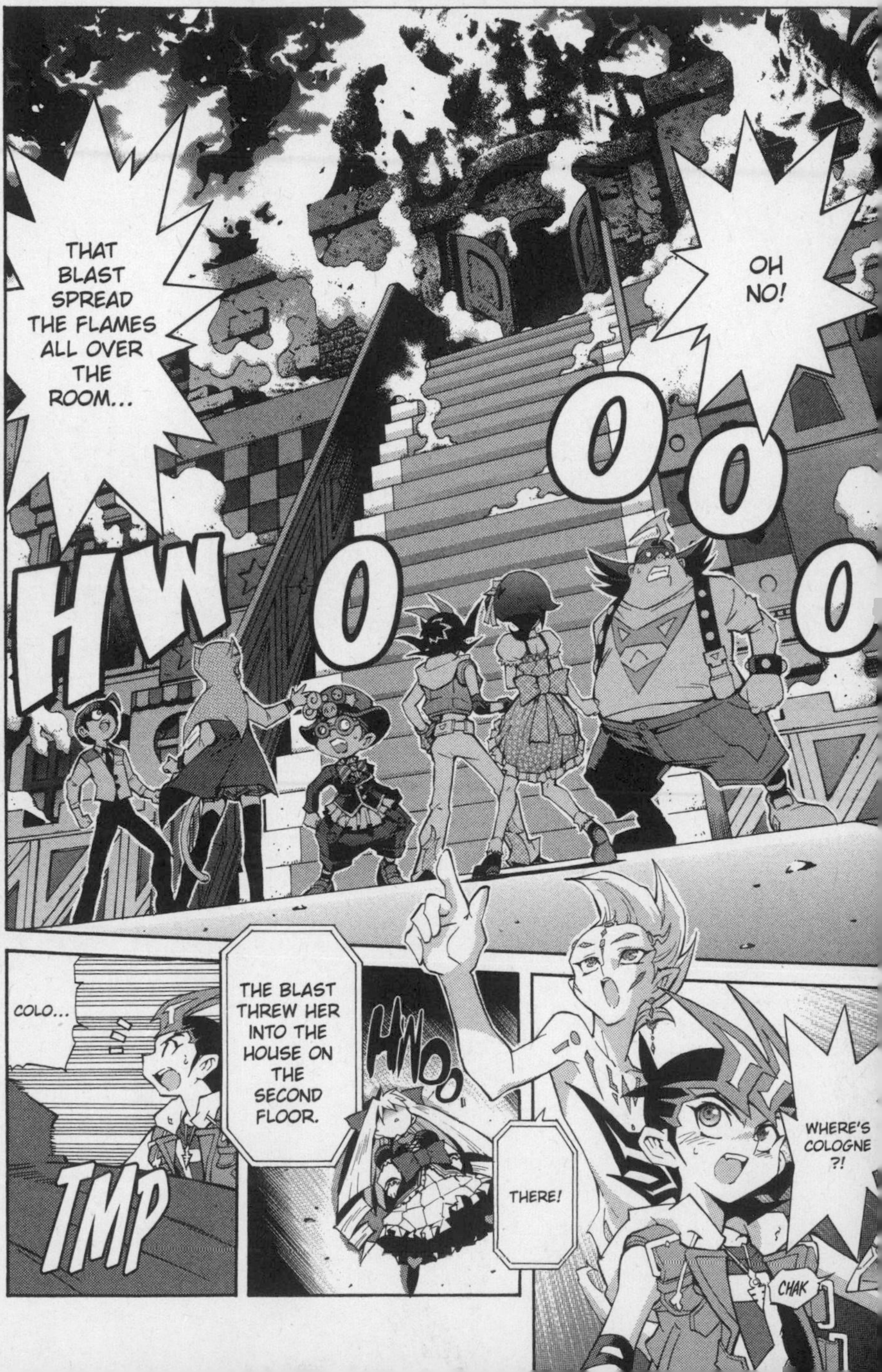
OH NO!
THAT BLAST SPREAD THE FLAMES ALL OVER THE ROOM...
HWOOOOO
WHERE'S COLOGNE ?!
THERE!
CHAK
THE BLAST THREW HER INTO THE HOUSE ON THE SECOND FLOOR.
HWOO
COLO...
TMP

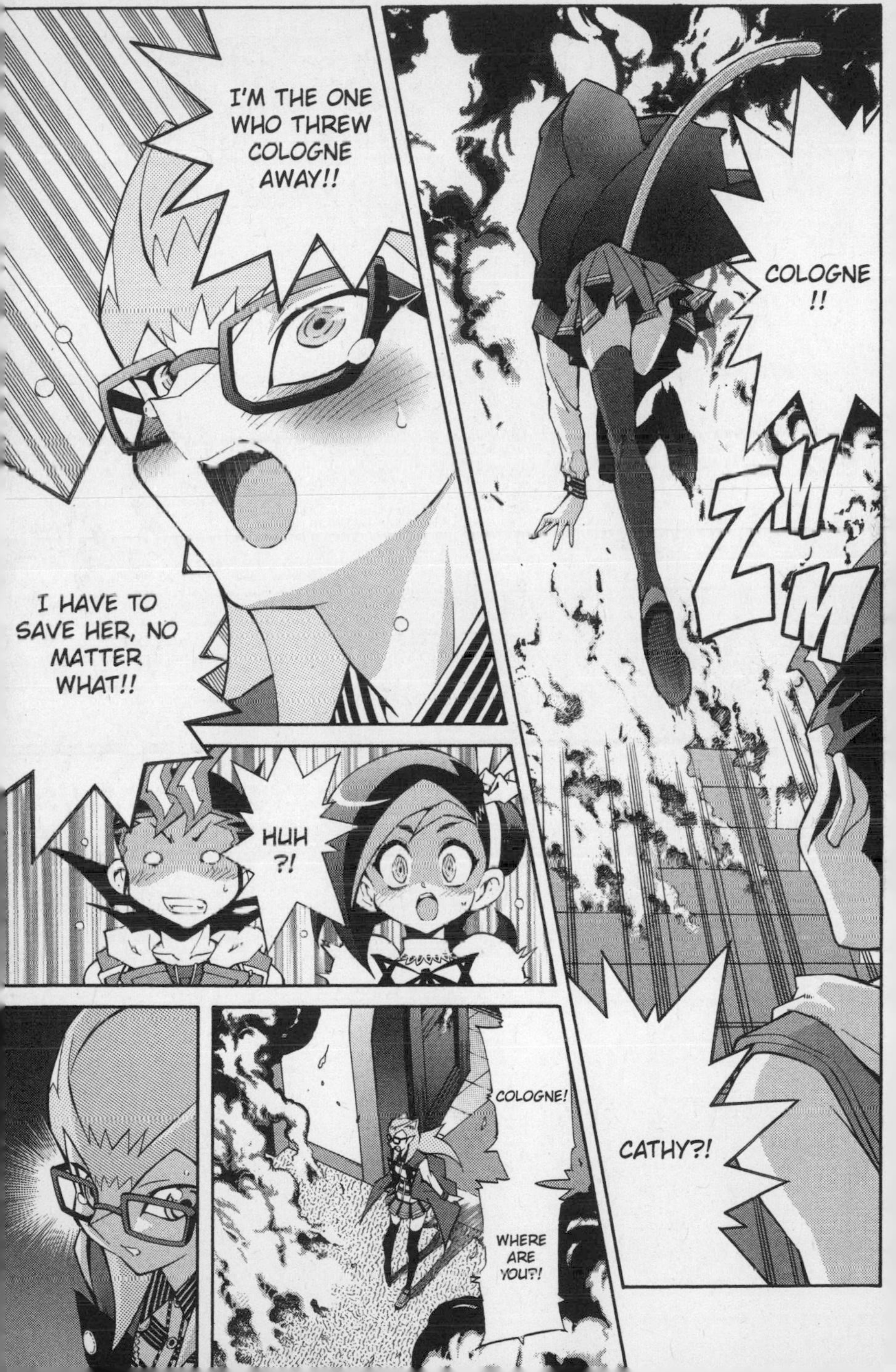
COLOGNE !!
ZM ZM
CATHY?!
I'M THE ONE WHO THREW COLOGNE AWAY!!
I HAVE TO SAVE HER, NO MATTER WHAT!!
HUH ?!
COLOGNE!
WHERE ARE YOU?!

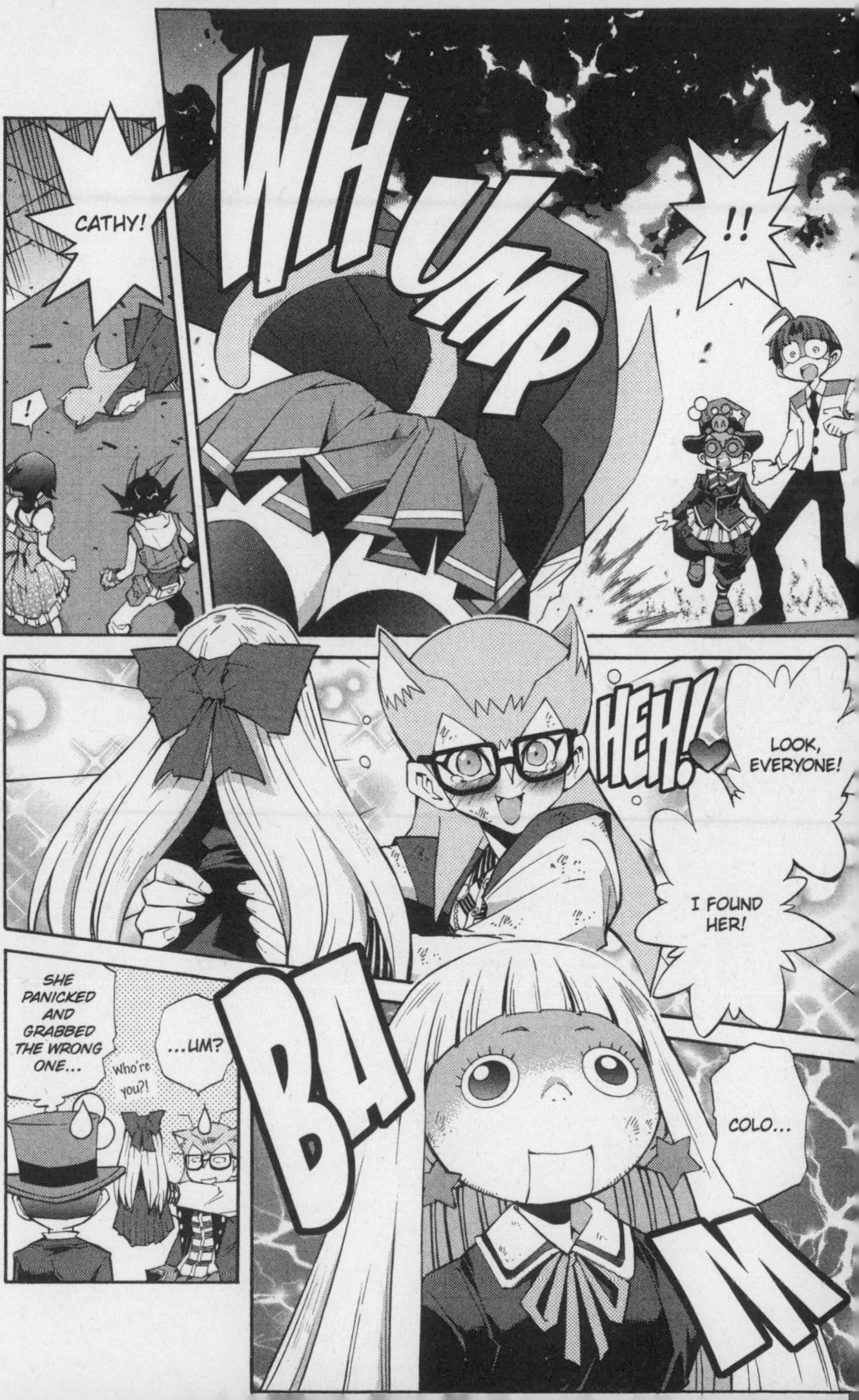
!!
WHUMP
CATHY!
!
LOOK, EVERYONE!
HEH!
I FOUND HER!
COLO...
BAM
...UM?
Who're you?!
SHE PANICKED AND GRABBED THE WRONG ONE...

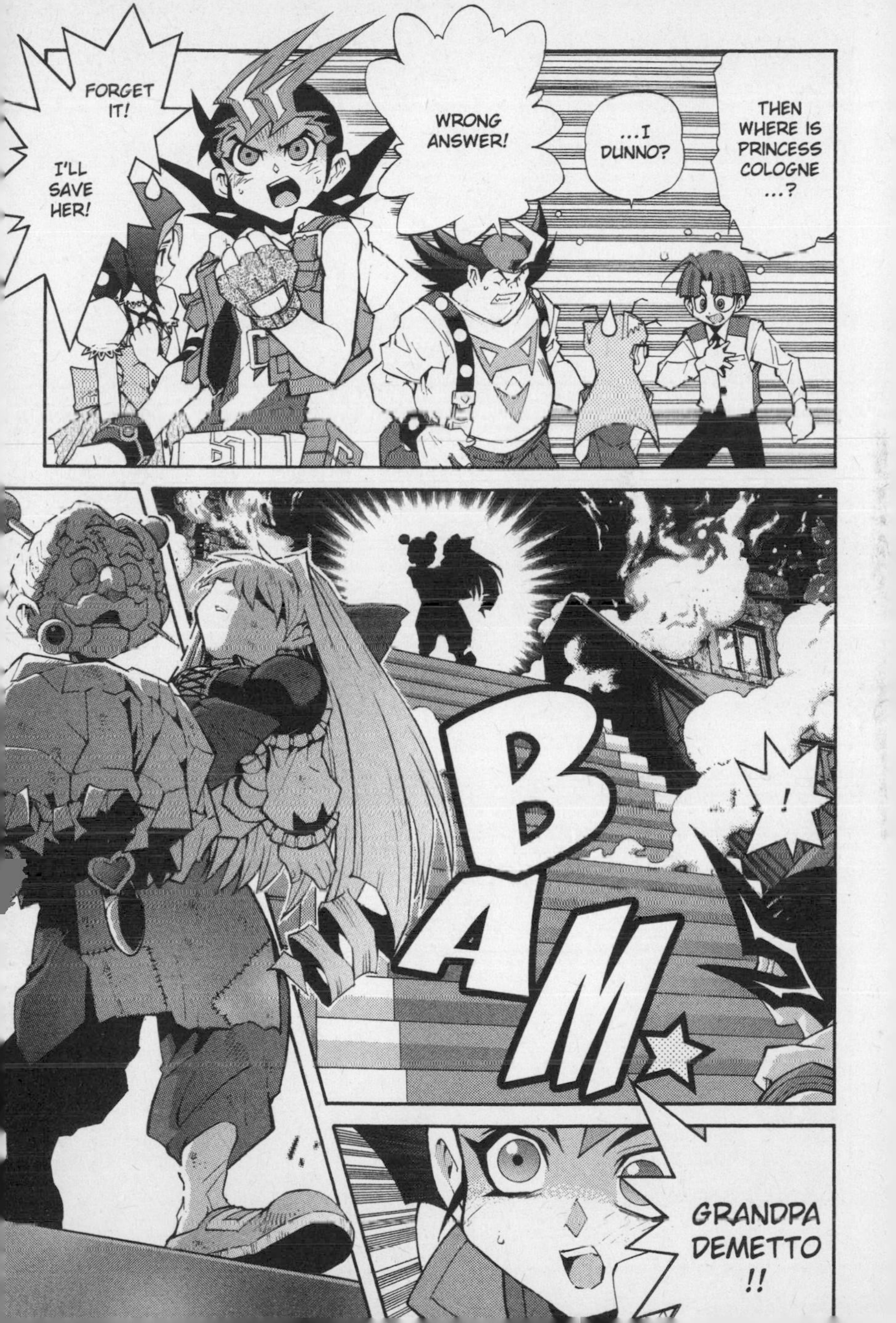
THEN WHERE IS PRINCESS COLOGNE ...?
...I DUNNO?
WRONG ANSWER!
FORGET IT!
I'LL SAVE HER!
BAM
!
GRANDPA DEMETTO !!

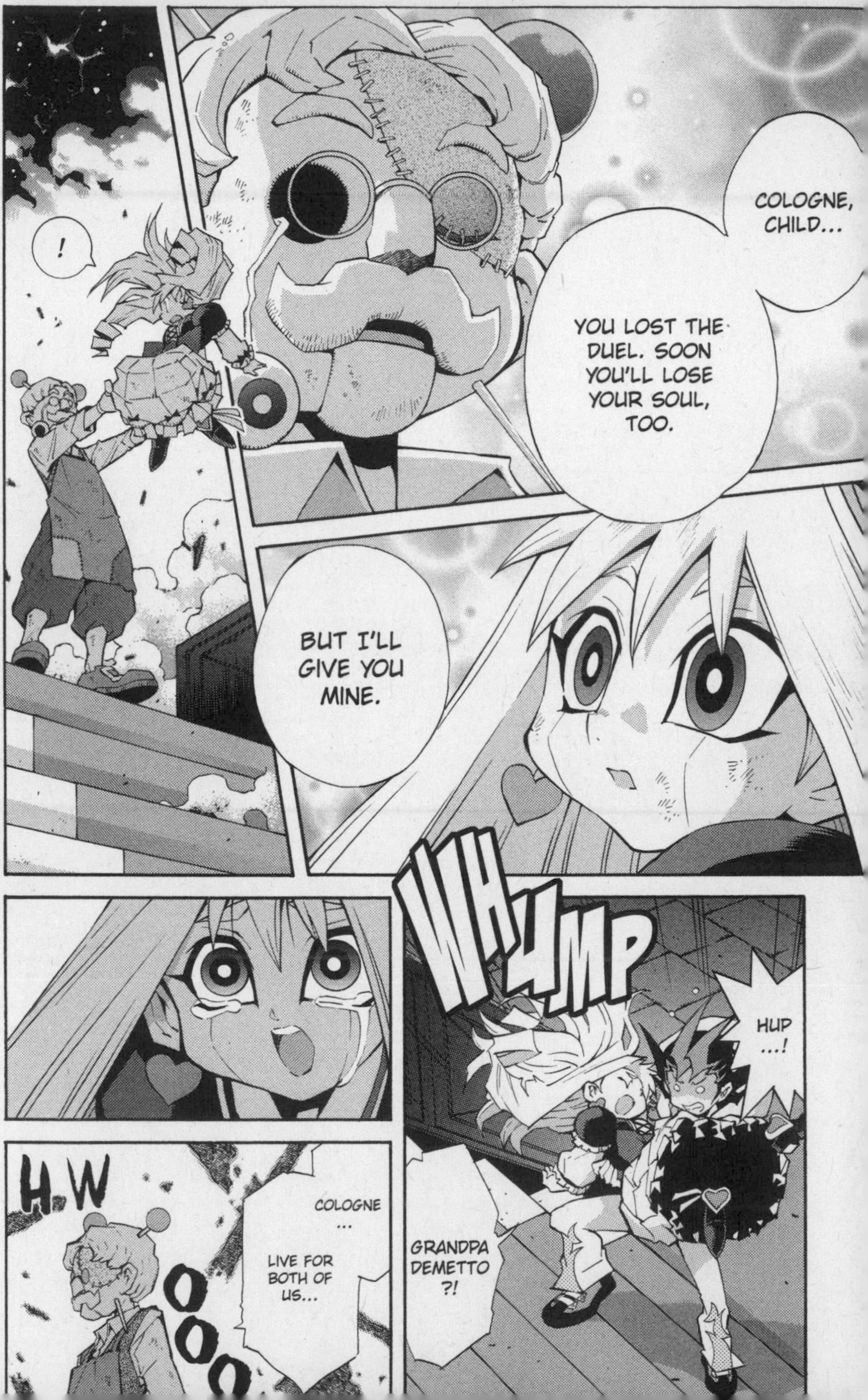

COLOGNE, CHILD...
YOU LOST THE DUEL. SOON YOU'LL LOSE YOUR SOUL, TOO.
BUT I'LL GIVE YOU MINE.
!
WHUMP
HUP ...!
GRANDPA DEMETTO ?!
COLOGNE ...
LIVE FOR BOTH OF US...
HWOOO

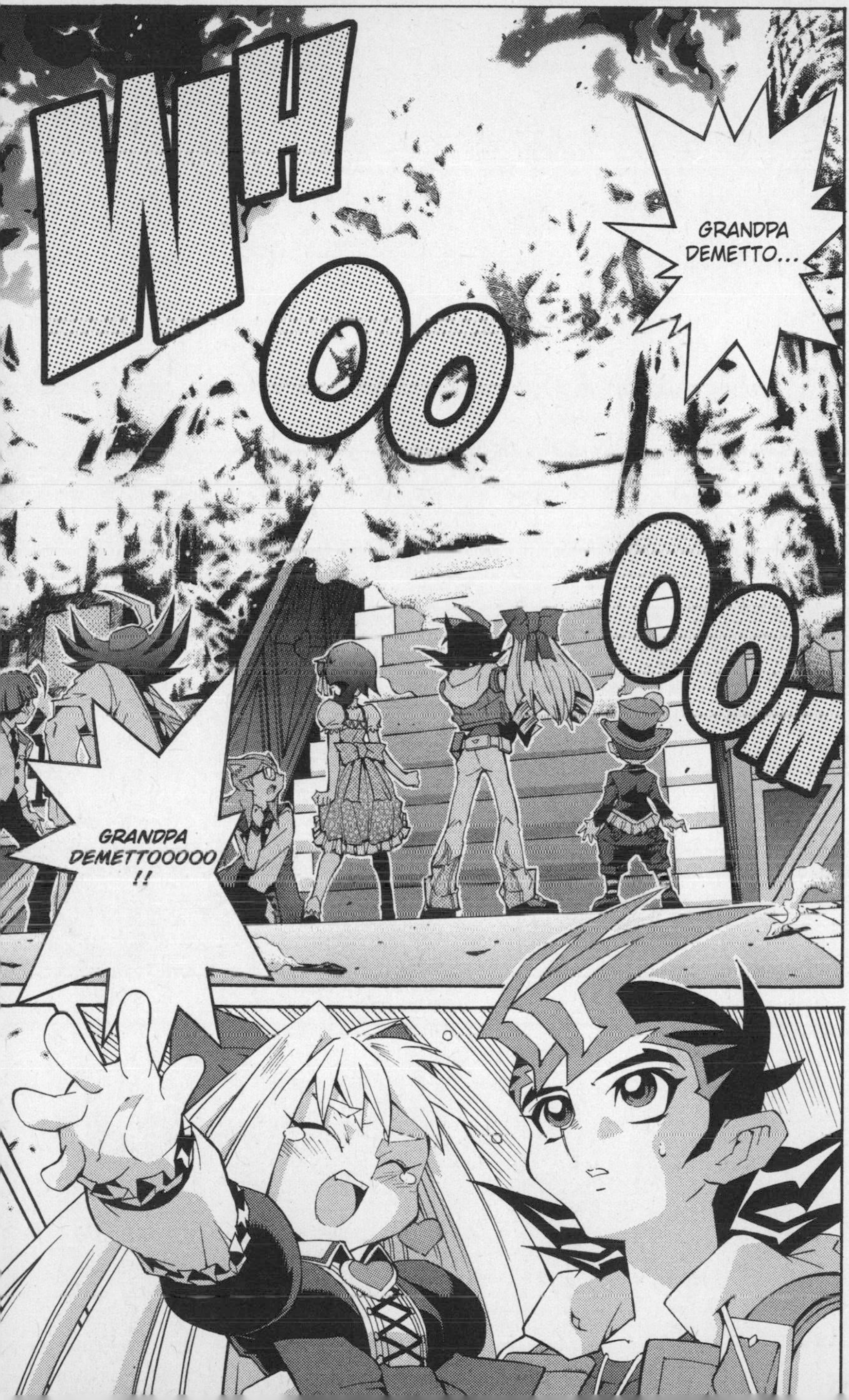
GRANDPA DEMETTO...
WHOOOOOM!
GRANDPA DEMETTOOOOO !!

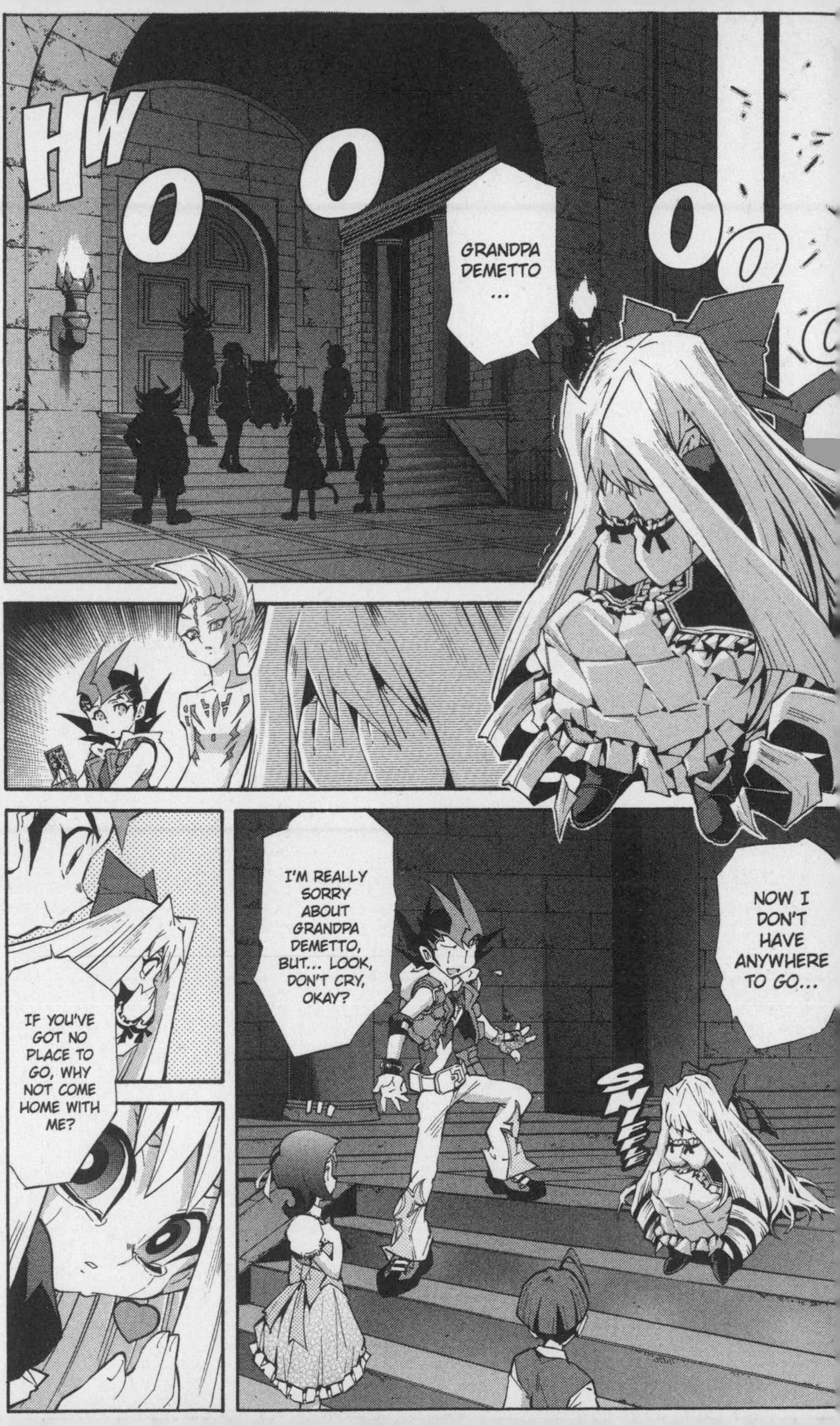
GRANDPA DEMETTO...
HWOOOO
NOW I DON'T HAVE ANYWHERE TO GO...
SNIFF
I'M REALLY SORRY ABOUT GRANDPA DEMETTO, BUT... LOOK, DON'T CRY, OKAY?
IF YOU'VE GOT NO PLACE TO GO, WHY NOT COME HOME WITH ME?

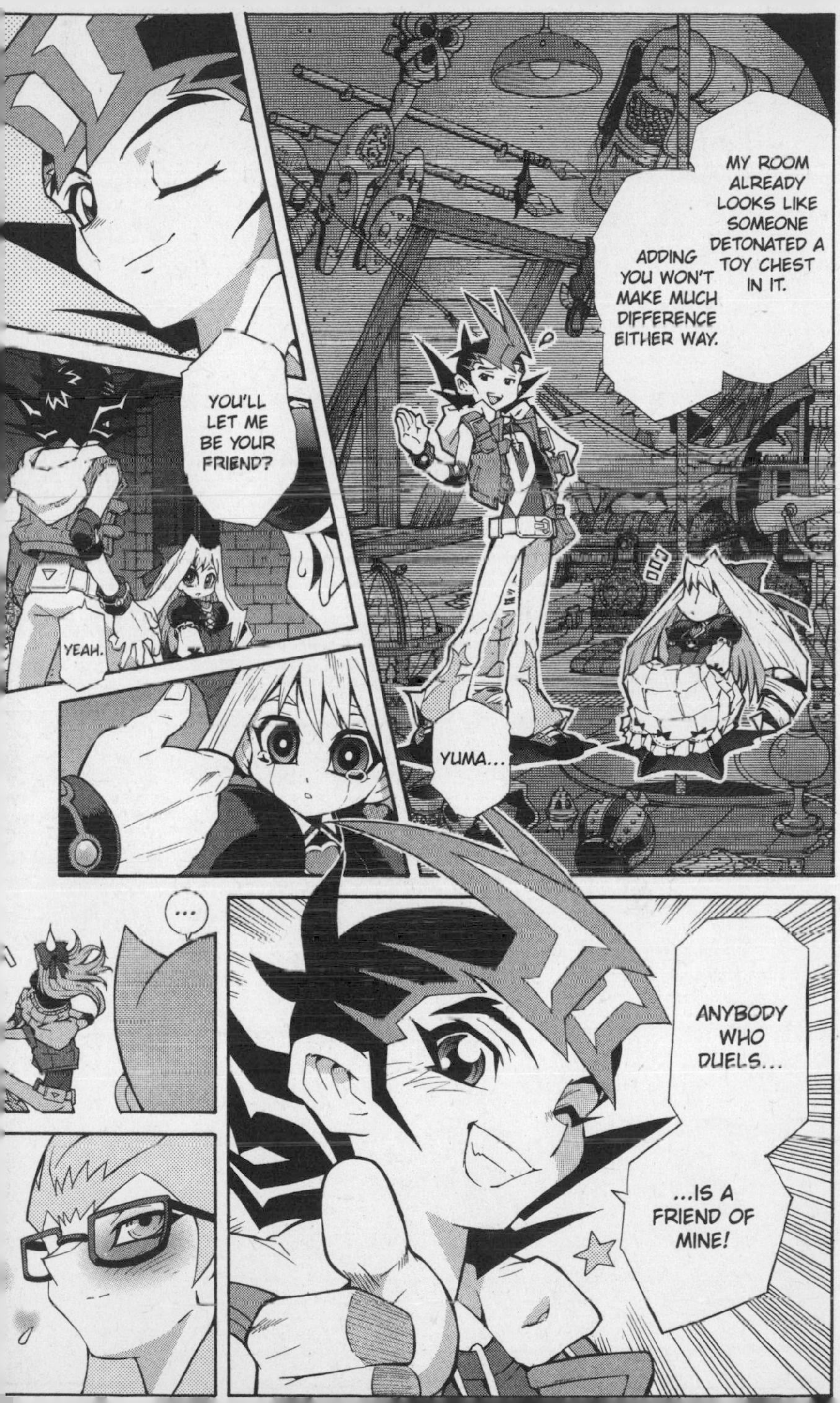
MY ROOM ALREADY LOOKS LIKE SOMEONE DETONATED A TOY CHEST IN IT.
ADDING YOU WON'T MAKE MUCH DIFFERENCE EITHER WAY.
YUMA...
YOU'LL LET ME BE YOUR FRIEND?
YEAH.
ANYBODY WHO DUELS...
...IS A FRIEND OF MINE!
...

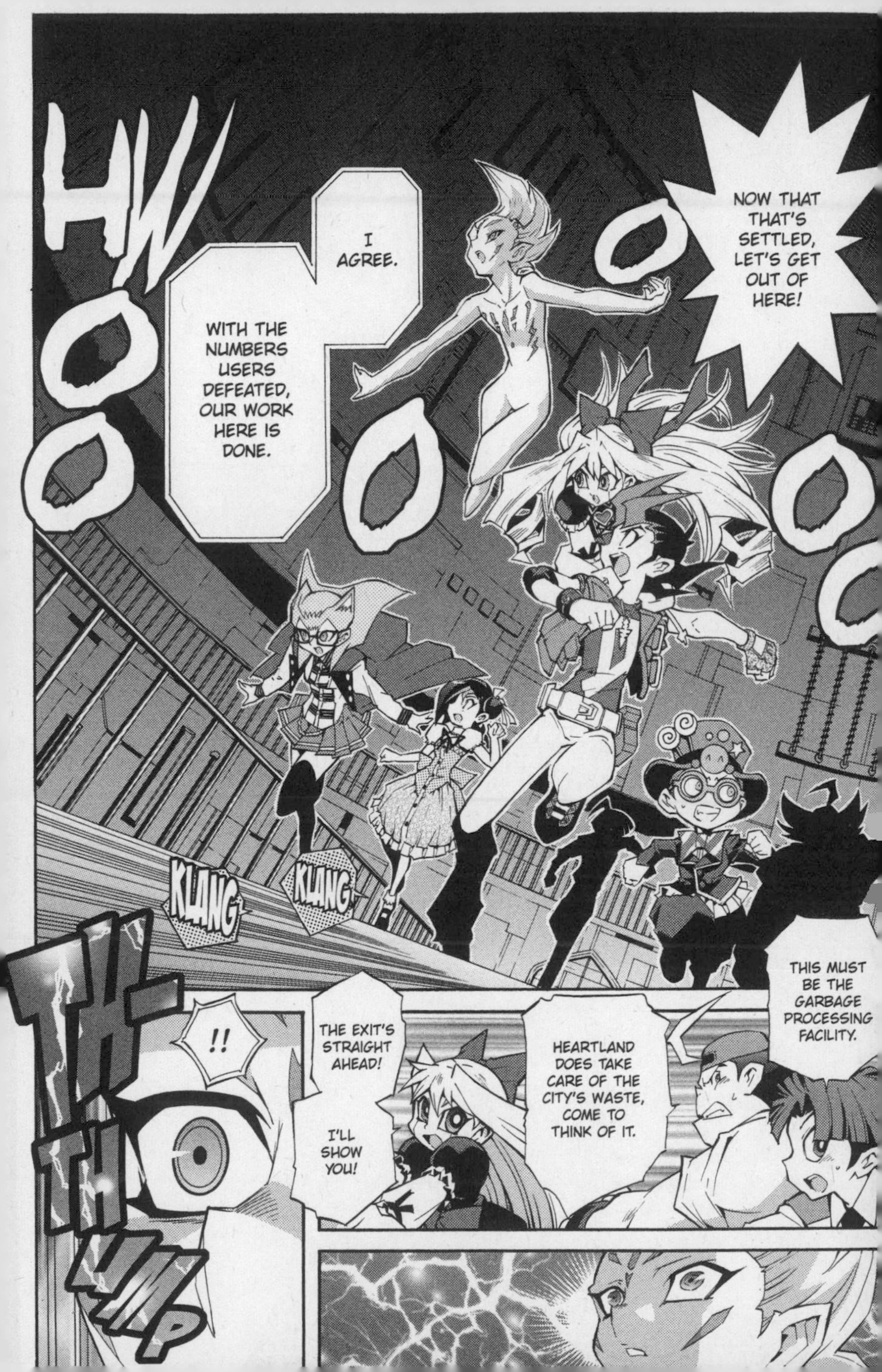
NOW THAT THAT'S SETTLED, LET'S GET OUT OF HERE!
I AGREE.
WITH THE NUMBERS USERS DEFEATED, OUR WORK HERE IS DONE.
HWOOOO
KLANG
KLANG
THIS MUST BE THE GARBAGE PROCESSING FACILITY.
HEARTLAND DOES TAKE CARE OF THE CITY'S WASTE, COME TO THINK OF IT.
THE EXIT'S STRAIGHT AHEAD!
I'LL SHOW YOU!
!!
TH-THUMP

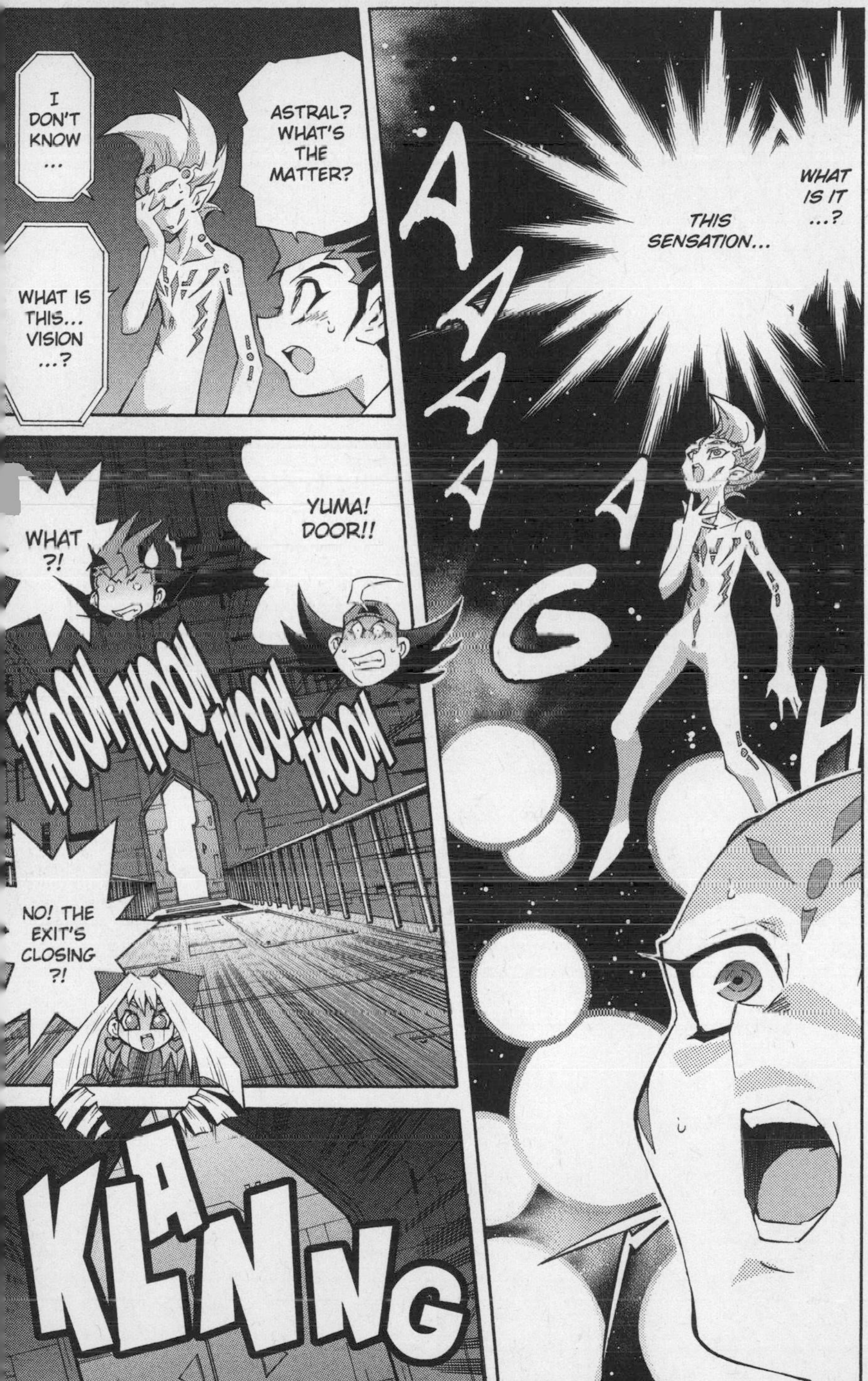
WHAT IS IT ...?
THIS SENSATION...
AAAAAAGH
ASTRAL? WHAT'S THE MATTER?
I DON'T KNOW ...
WHAT IS THIS... VISION ...?
YUMA! DOOR!!
WHAT ?!
THOOM THOOM THOOM THOOM
NO! THE EXIT'S CLOSING ?!
KLANNG

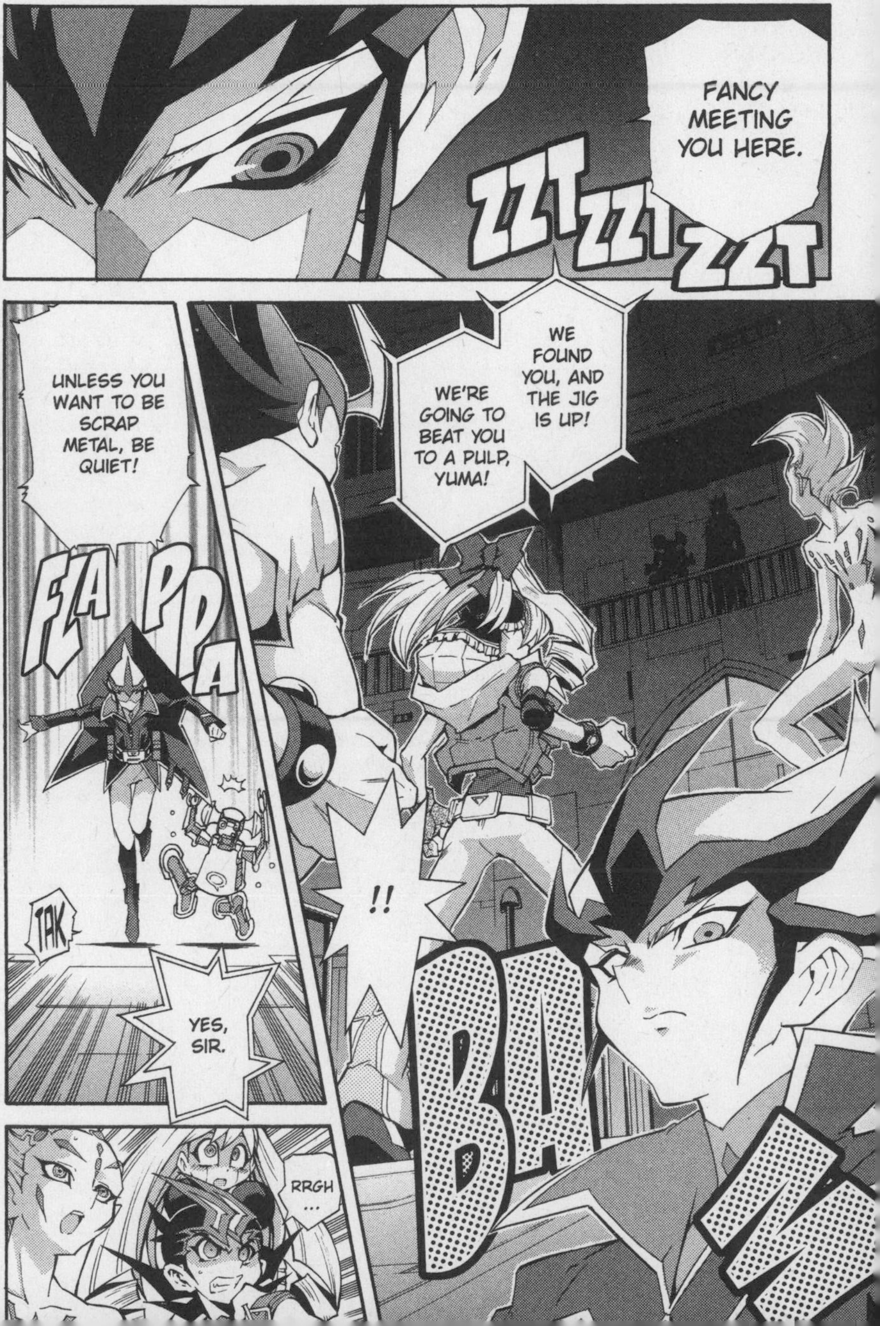
FANCY MEETING YOU HERE.
ZZT ZZT ZZT
WE FOUND YOU, AND THE JIG IS UP!
WE'RE GOING TO BEAT YOU TO A PULP, YUMA!
!!
BA
UNLESS YOU WANT TO BE SCRAP METAL, BE QUIET!
FLAPPA
TAK
YES, SIR.
RRGH...

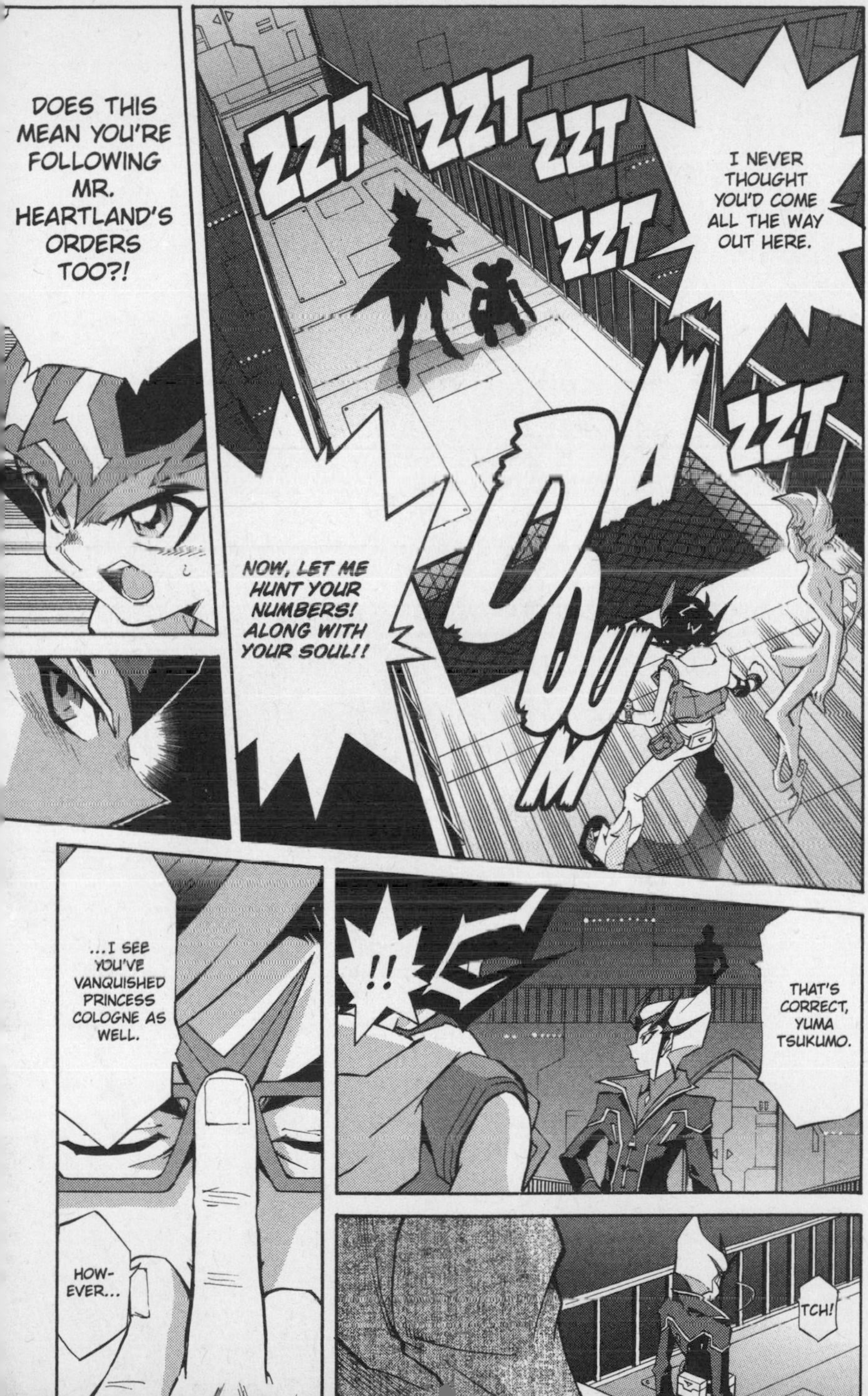
ZZT ZZT ZZT
I NEVER THOUGHT YOU'D COME ALL THE WAY OUT HERE.
ZZT
ZZT
DA
OOUM
NOW, LET ME HUNT YOUR NUMBERS! ALONG WITH YOUR SOUL!!
DOES THIS MEAN YOU'RE FOLLOWING MR. HEARTLAND'S ORDERS TOO?!
THAT'S CORRECT, YUMA TSUKUMO.
!!
TCH!
...I SEE YOU'VE VANQUISHED PRINCESS COLOGNE AS WELL.
HOW-EVER...

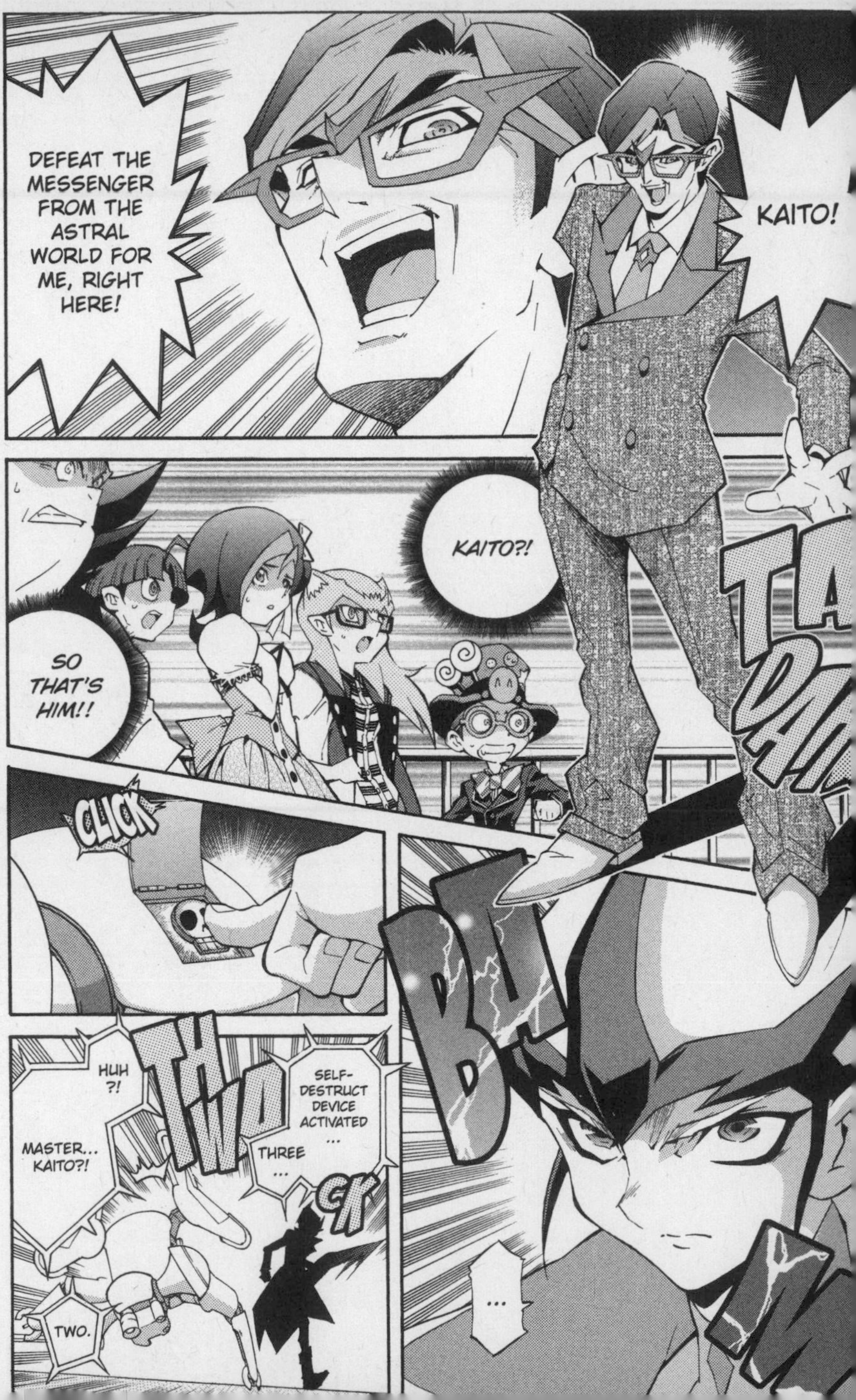
KAITO!
DEFEAT THE MESSENGER FROM THE ASTRAL WORLD FOR ME, RIGHT HERE!
KAITO?!
SO THAT'S HIM!!
CLICK
...
SELF-DESTRUCT DEVICE ACTIVATED ...
THREE ...
HUH ?!
THWO
CK
MASTER... KAITO?!
TWO.

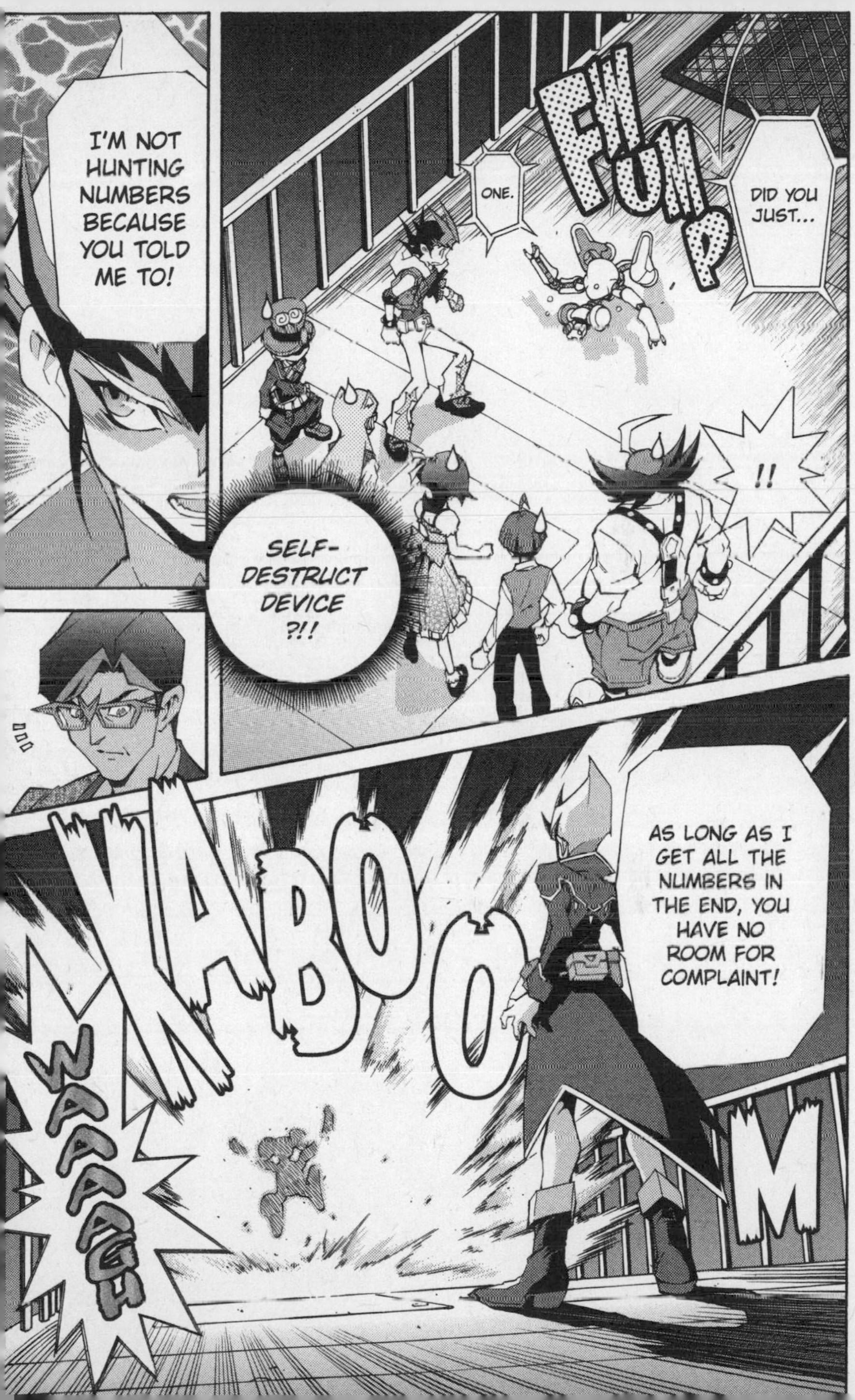
DID YOU JUST...
FWUMP
ONE.
!!
SELF-DESTRUCT DEVICE?!!
I'M NOT HUNTING NUMBERS BECAUSE YOU TOLD ME TO!
AS LONG AS I GET ALL THE NUMBERS IN THE END, YOU HAVE NO ROOM FOR COMPLAINT!
KABOOM
WAAAAGH

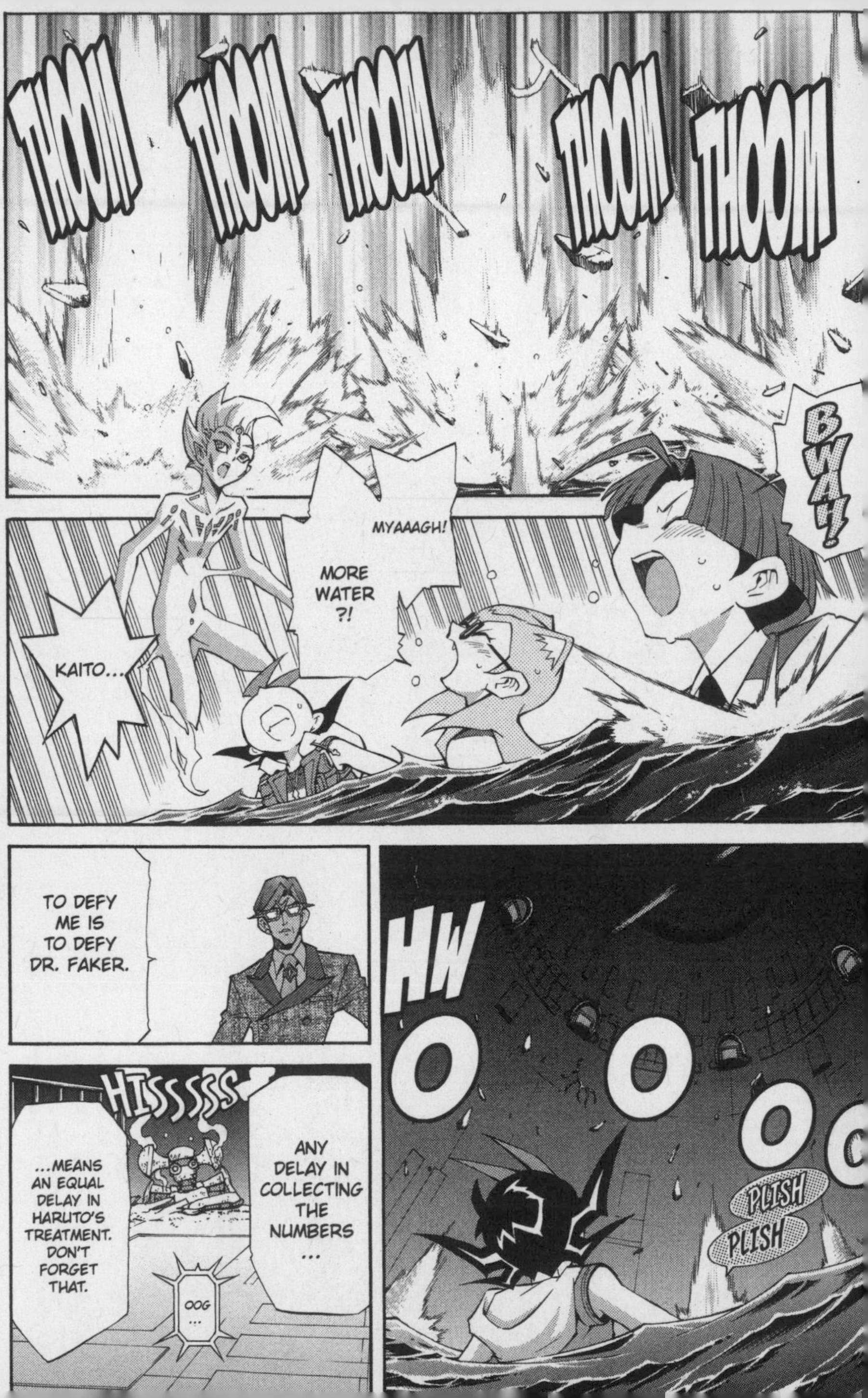
THOOM
THOOM
THOOM
THOOM
THOOM
BWAH!
MYAAAGH!
MORE WATER ?!
KAITO...
HWOOOO
PLISH
PLISH
TO DEFY ME IS TO DEFY DR. FAKER.
HISSSSS
ANY DELAY IN COLLECTING THE NUMBERS ...
...MEANS AN EQUAL DELAY IN HARUTO'S TREATMENT. DON'T FORGET THAT.
OOG ...

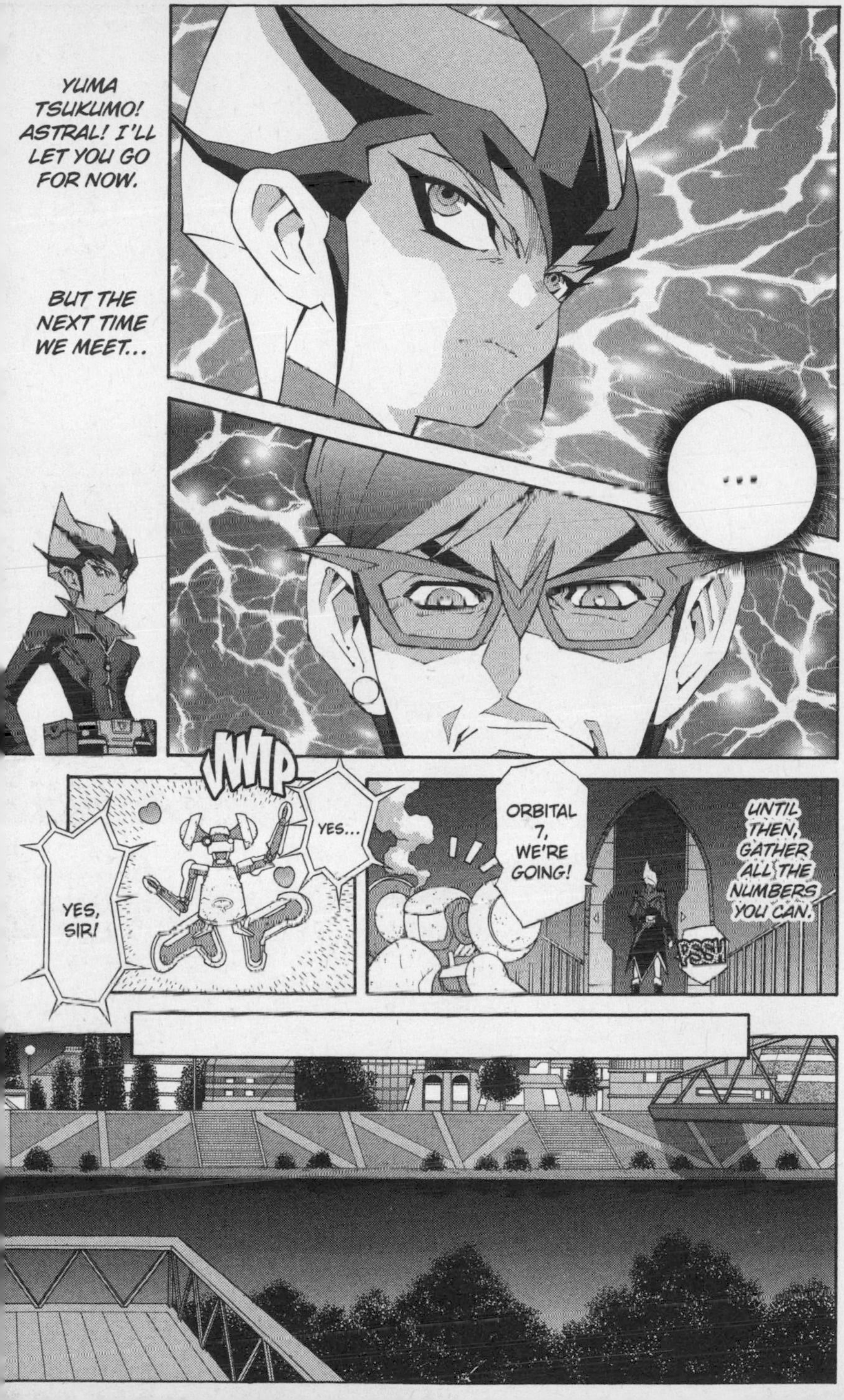
YUMA TSUKUMO! ASTRAL! I'LL LET YOU GO FOR NOW.
BUT THE NEXT TIME WE MEET...
...
UNTIL THEN, GATHER ALL THE NUMBERS YOU CAN.
PSSH
ORBITAL 7, WE'RE GOING!
VWIP
YES...
YES, SIR!

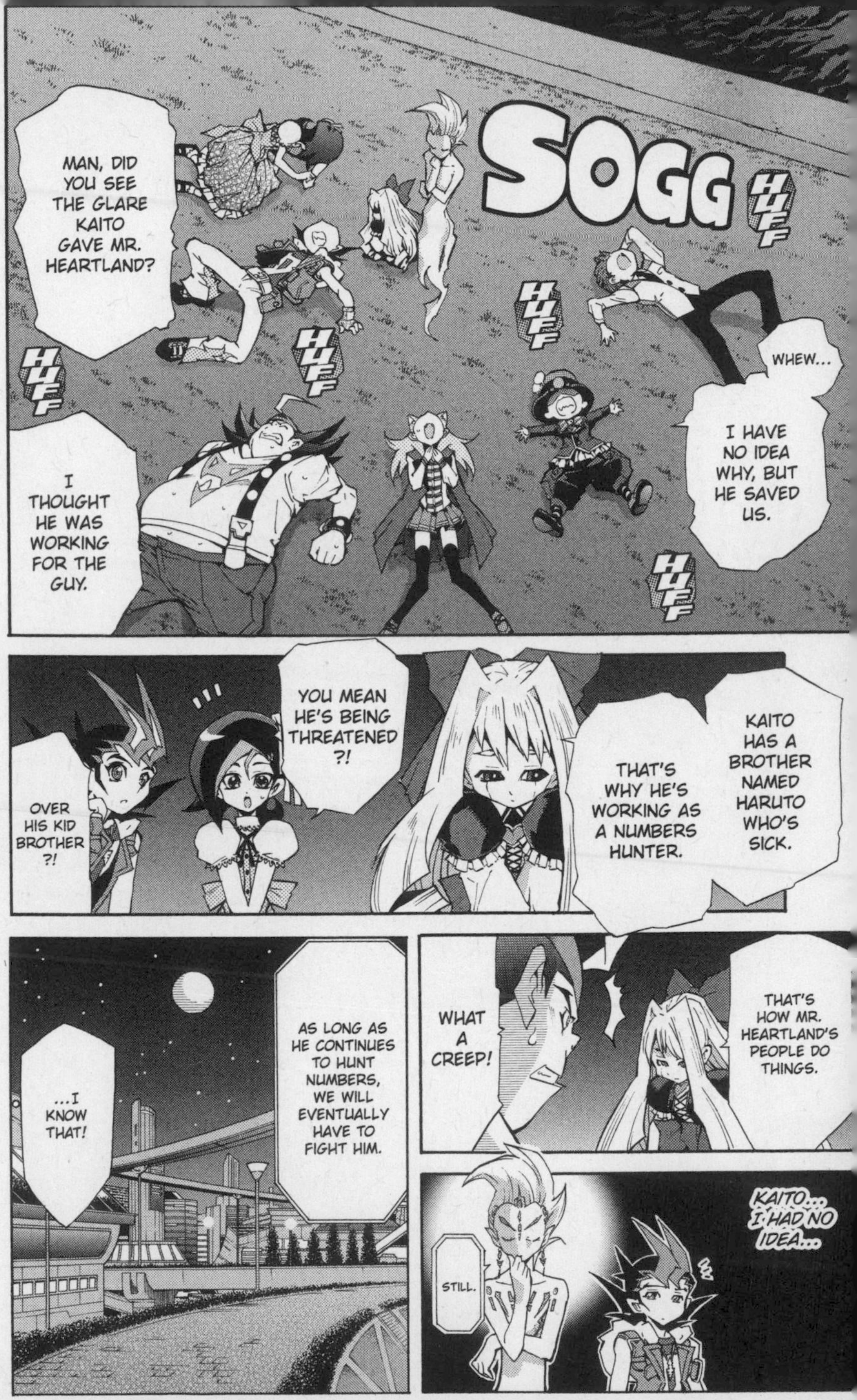
SOGG
HUFF
WHEW...
I HAVE NO IDEA WHY, BUT HE SAVED US.
MAN, DID YOU SEE THE GLARE KAITO GAVE MR. HEARTLAND?
HUFF
HUFF
HUFF
HUFF
I THOUGHT HE WAS WORKING FOR THE GUY.
KAITO HAS A BROTHER NAMED HARUTO WHO'S SICK.
THAT'S WHY HE'S WORKING AS A NUMBERS HUNTER.
YOU MEAN HE'S BEING THREATENED?!
OVER HIS KID BROTHER?!
THAT'S HOW MR. HEARTLAND'S PEOPLE DO THINGS.
WHAT A CREEP!
KAITO... I HAD NO IDEA...
STILL.
AS LONG AS HE CONTINUES TO HUNT NUMBERS, WE WILL EVENTUALLY HAVE TO FIGHT HIM.
...I KNOW THAT!

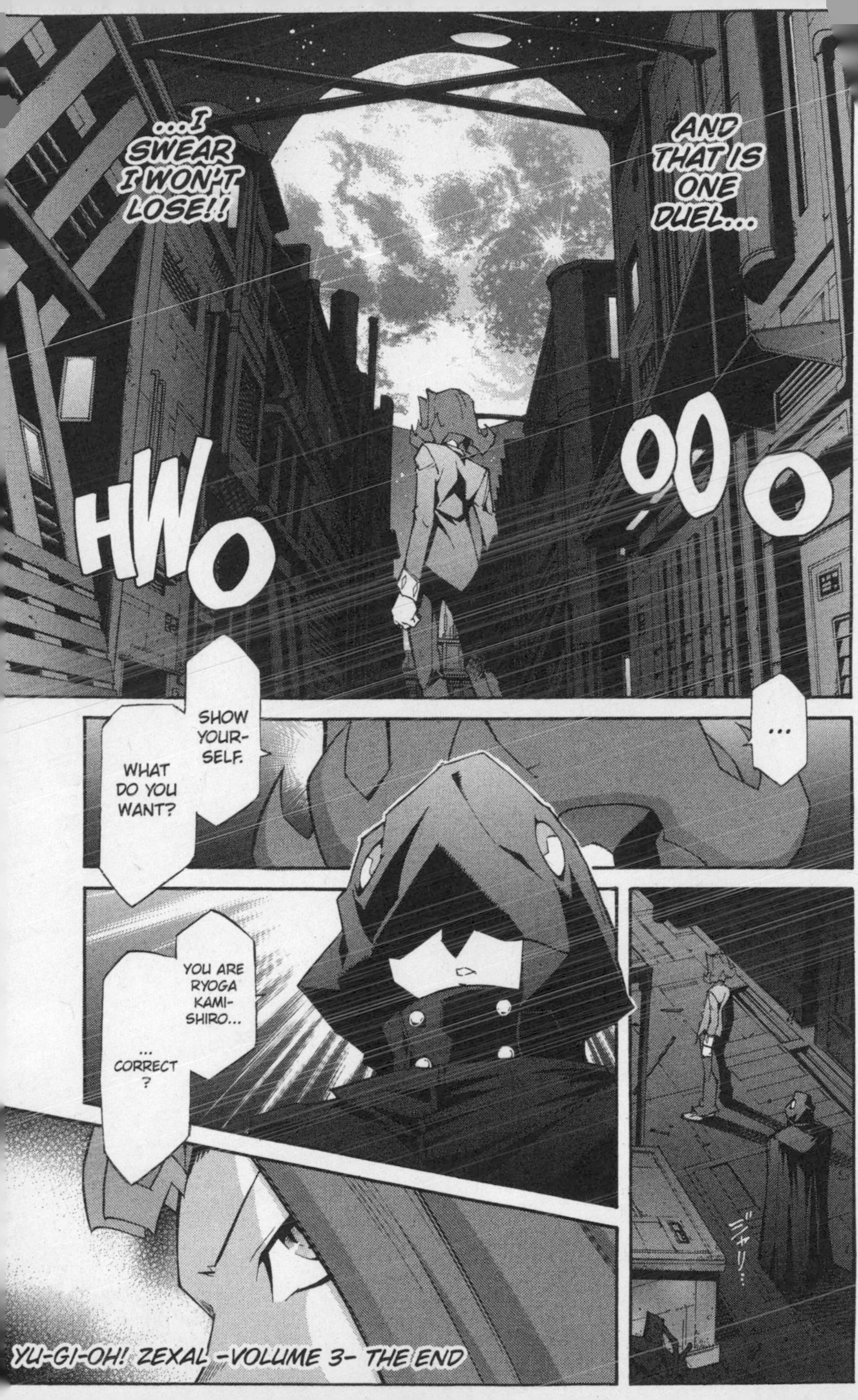
AND THAT IS ONE DUEL...
...I SWEAR I WON'T LOSE!!
HWOOOO
...
SHOW YOURSELF.
WHAT DO YOU WANT?
ジャリ…
YOU ARE RYOGA KAMISHIRO...
...CORRECT?
YU-GI-OH! ZEXAL -VOLUME 3- THE END

Staff

Kazuo Ochiai
Toshiaki Kato
Masahiro Miura
Fumitaka Murayama

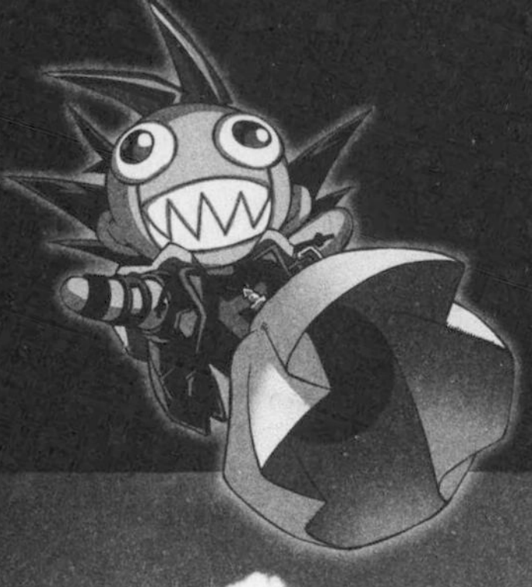

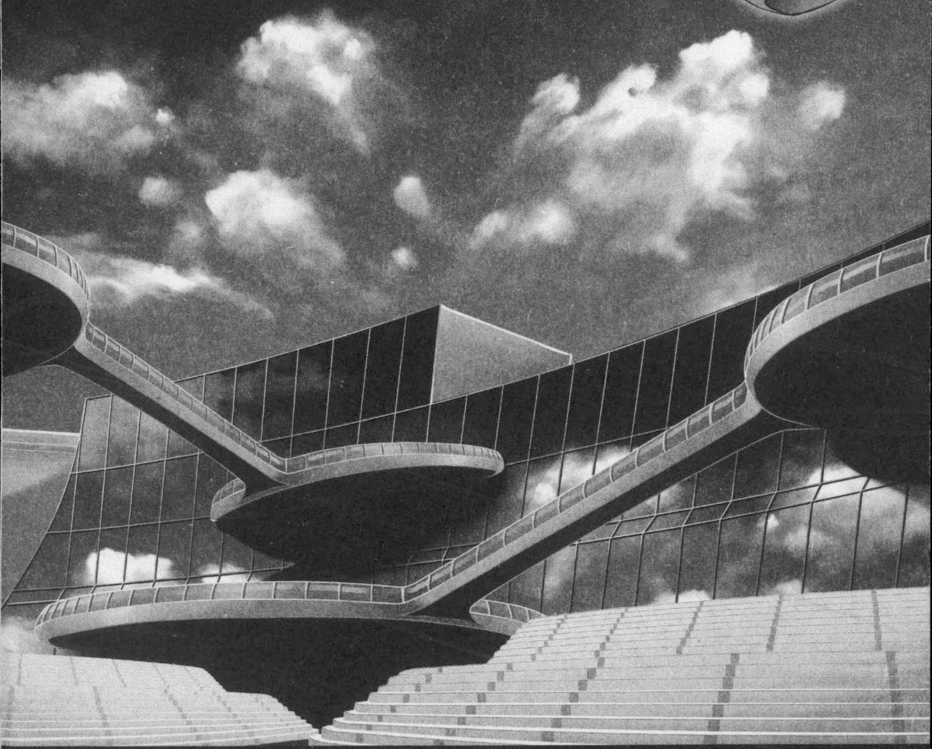

Coloring

Tohru Shimizu
[Cover]
Studio Tac - Takumi Yokooka

Editor

Daisuke Terashi

Support

Gallop

YOU ARE READING
IN THE WRONG DIRECTION!!

**Whoops!
Guess what?**
You're starting at
the wrong end
of the comic!

...It's true! In keeping with the original Japanese format, *Yu-Gi-Oh! ZEXAL* is meant to be read from right to left, starting in the upper-right corner.

Unlike English, which is read from left to right, Japanese is read from right to left, meaning that action, sound effects and word-balloon order are completely reversed... something which can make readers unfamiliar with Japanese feel pretty backwards themselves. For this reason, manga or Japanese comics published in the U.S. in English have sometimes been published "flopped"—that is, printed in exact reverse order, as though seen from the other side of a mirror.

By flopping pages, U.S. publishers can avoid confusing readers, but the compromise is not without its downside. For one thing, a character in a flopped manga series who once wore in the original Japanese version a T-shirt emblazoned with "M A Y" (as in "the merry month of") now wears one which reads "Y A M"! Additionally, many manga creators in Japan are themselves unhappy with the process, as some feel the mirror-imaging of their art alters their original intentions.

We are proud to bring you Shin Yoshida and Naohito Miyoshi's *Yu-Gi-Oh! ZEXAL* in the original unflopped format. For now, though, turn to the other side of the book and let the duel begin...!

–Editor